Democracy and Tradition

NEW FORUM BOOKS   *Robert P. George, Series Editor*

A list of titles in the series
appears at the back of the book

Democracy and Tradition

Jeffrey Stout

PRINCETON UNIVERSITY PRESS

PRINCETON AND OXFORD

IN ASSOCIATION WITH

HEBREW UNION COLLEGE PRESS, CINCINNATI

Library of Congress Cataloging-in-Publication Data
Stout, Jeffrey.
Democracy and tradition / Jeffrey Stout.
p. cm.
Includes bibliographical references and index.
ISBN 0-691-10293-7
1. Religion and politics—United States. 2. Democracy—religious aspects.
3. United States—Religion. 4. Democracy—United States.
5. United States—Politics and government. I. Title.

BL2525.S76 2004
172—dc21   2002039797

British Library Cataloging-in-Publication Data is available

This book has been composed in Janson

Printed on acid-free paper. ∞

www.pupress.princeton.edu

Printed in the United States of America

3 5 7 9 10 8 6 4

BASED IN PART ON

THE GUSTAVE A. AND MAMIE EFROYMSON

MEMORIAL LECTURES

DELIVERED AT THE HEBREW UNION COLLEGE-

JEWISH INSTITUTE OF RELIGION,

IN CINCINNATI, OHIO, APRIL 30–MAY 7, 1997

To the memory of Rob Myslik,
teacher of athletes

———————————————

Democracy is a form of government only because it is a form of moral and spiritual association.
    —John Dewey, "The Ethics of Democracy" (1885)

The heritage [the people] give us is . . . the story of their survival, the sum of adjustments, the struggle, the folk accumulation called sense and the faith we have in that collective experience. . . . It was real, and created our day. Perhaps it encloses us.
    It is the deep from which we emerge.
        —Meridel Le Sueur, *North Star Country* (1945)

CONTENTS

ACKNOWLEDGMENTS

I HAVE KNOWN Stanley Hauerwas, Alasdair MacIntyre, and Dick Rorty for many years. This book grows out of conversations with them that go back to the mid-1970s. I quarrel with them in part 2, and try to build on what I have learned from them in part 3. My debts to them are personal as well as intellectual. Stanley and Alasdair helped get my career started by inviting me to write my first book and publishing it in a series they were editing at Notre Dame. When Dick was still at Princeton and I was a junior member of the faculty, he went out of his way to befriend and encourage me, and his generosity over the years has been a delight. His greatest gift to me early on was a message he conveyed only tacitly, but which Whitman expressed as follows: "You shall not look through my eyes either, nor take things from me, / You shall listen to all sides and filter them from your self."

All three of these men influenced me most strongly some years before they adopted the public personae for which they are now known. Hauerwas was then arguing for the revival of virtue ethics and criticizing pacifists for shortchanging the language of justice. MacIntyre had recently broken with both Marxism and Christianity, and become an independent radical critic. Rorty already admired Hegel and Dewey, but he was mainly writing closely argued articles under the influence of Sellars and Wittgenstein. So perhaps it should not be surprising that I have often found myself speaking on behalf of their earlier selves against their current public images. That I was doing this first struck me at some point in the 1980s while reading Hazlitt's reflections on Wordsworth and Coleridge in "My First Acquaintance with Poets."

But I have also repeatedly found myself uncertain about the extent to which we really disagree. All three have become famous in part by saying things that shock their audiences. As a result, they attract devotees who want to be part of something new and exciting. The price is scorn and ridicule from the establishment. Their critics charge that they go too far in their attempts to debunk what the rest of us hold dear. Their disciples often say that critics take them too literally. It is possible to find passages in which they soften, or even retract, many of the controversial things they have said. But if they are ironical gadflies, not prophets demanding drastic change in how we think about ourselves, one wonders what all the fuss has been about. They can't, in the end, have it both ways. It seems to me that the strategies of rhetorical excess that generated the excitement in the first place have outlived their usefulness. If there is something worth saving in what these men have written, as I believe there is, it will need to be recast in a style that aspires to mean what it says.

This book presents a substantially revised and expanded version of the central argument of my Efroymson Lectures, delivered at Hebrew Union College in Cincinnati during the spring of 1997. It was an honor to give those lectures, and the Efroymson family has my gratitude for making them possible. I found it inspiring and reassuring to spend time in a religious community that is united in sincere concern for justice.

In the original version of the lectures, I spoke mainly about Socrates, Whitman, Emerson, and the "new traditionalists." During the revision process, my discussion of modern sources and contemporary philosophical issues grew considerably. As a result, the material on Socrates no longer fit very well into the overall argument, so I have decided to publish it elsewhere. I have also incorporated material from several articles that have appeared, or are scheduled to appear, elsewhere:

- An earlier version of chapter 2 appeared in *Is It Nation Time?*, ed. Eddie Glaude, Jr. (Chicago: University of Chicago Press, 2002), 234–56. Copyright 2002 by the University of Chicago. All rights reserved. Reprinted with the permission of University of Chicago Press.
- An earlier version of one section of chapter 3 is scheduled to appear in a *Festschrift* in honor of Nicholas Wolterstorff, edited by Terrence Cuneo.
- Fragments of chapters 4 and 5 appeared in "Commitments and Traditions in the Study of Religious Ethics," *Journal of Religious Ethics* 25, no. 3 (25th Anniversary Supplement, 1998): 23–56. Reprinted with the permission of the current editors.
- Another part of chapter 5 appeared in "Homeward Bound: MacIntyre on Liberal Society and the History of Ethics," *Journal of Religion* 69, no. 2 (1989): 220–32. Copyright 1989 by the University of Chicago. All rights reserved. Reprinted with the permission of University of Chicago Press.
- A shorter version of chapter 6 was presented to Societas Ethica in Berlin in August 2001 under the title, "Virtue and the Way of the World: Reflections on Hauerwas," and appeared subsequently in the annual proceedings of that body. Reprinted with the permission of Societas Ethica.
- Chapter 9 includes a few paragraphs from "The Rhetoric of Revolution: Comparative Ethics after Kuhn and Gunnemann," in *Religion and Practical Reason: New Essays in the Comparative Philosophy of Religion*, ed. Frank E. Reynolds and David Tracy (Albany: State University of New York Press, 1994), 329–62.

- Chapter 10 includes material from "Truth, Natural Law, and Ethical Theory," in *Natural Law Theory: Contemporary Essays*, edited by Robert P. George (Oxford: Clarendon Press, 1992), 71–102; and "On Having a Morality in Common," in *Prospects for a Common Morality*, ed. Gene Outka and John P. Reeder (Princeton: Princeton University Press, 1993), 215–32.
- Chapter 11 includes material from "Ism-Mongering," *The Annual of the Society of Christian Ethics* (1990): 55–62. Reprinted with the permission of the current editor.
- Chapter 12 includes material from "Radical Interpretation and Pragmatism: Davidson, Rorty, and Brandom on Truth," in *Radical Interpretation in Religion*, ed. Nancy Frankenberry (Cambridge: Cambridge University Press, 2002). Reprinted with the permission of Cambridge University Press.
- Section 1 of the Conclusion appeared in "Modernity without Essence," *Soundings: An Interdisciplinary Journal* 74 (1991): 525–40. Reprinted with the permission of the current editor.

I am grateful to the various publishers and editors for their cooperation. The second epigraph on page viii is reprinted from *North Star Country* by Meridel Le Sueur, by permission of the University of Nebraska Press. Copyright © 1945 by Meridel Ledueur. The epigraph of chapter 4 is quoted from personal correspondence with the permission of John R. Bowlin. The epigraph of the conclusion is quoted from Bill Holm, *The Music of Failure* (Minneapolis: Prairie Grass Press, 1990). Copyright © 1990 by Bill Holm. Reprinted with permission from Milkweed Editions.

Michael Walzer invited me to write a version of chapter 8 for an Israeli journal that was planning a special issue on the problem of dirty hands. Alas, the troubles in Israel led to cancellation of those plans. Thanks to Michael, though, for getting me to start thinking about the struggle against terrorism before September 11.

I wish to thank Robert P. George, my series editor at Princeton University Press, for inviting me to write this book and Chuck Myers, my acquisition editor, for efficiently shepherding it through the process of editorial review. Scott Davis and Jerry Schneewind served as the official readers of the manuscript for the Press, and gave me extensive, helpful suggestions for revision.

A number of friends have read and commented astutely on at least one version of the entire manuscript: John Bowlin, David Bromwich, Rosemary Carbine, Nina Eliasoph, Tim Jackson, Cleo Kearns, Mike Michalson, Wayne Proudfoot, Jock Reeder, Charles Reynolds, Richard Rorty, Louis Ruprecht, Jim Wetzel, and Phil Ziegler. Several others have given me valuable comments on selected chapters: Beth Eddy, Eddie Glaude, Eric Gregory, Amy Gutmann, the late David Lewis, Steve Macedo, Shaun Marmon, Howard Rhodes, Gene Rogers, Bas van Fraassen, and Nick Wolterstorff. I should single out John Bowlin for calling my attention to the writings of Bill Holm and Meridel Le Sueur, which encouraged me to think that the tradition of Whitman is not dead in Middle America.

Thanks go to present and past members of the Department of Religion at Princeton who have influenced this project by swapping ideas with me: Leora Batnitzky, Beth Eddy, Bob Gibbs, Eddie Glaude, Eric Gregory, Mark Larrimore, the late Victor Preller, Albert Raboteau, and Cornel West. John Gager, Martha Himmelfarb, and Lorraine Fuhrmann have given me much encouragement and support over the years. Thanks are due also to Kerry Smith and Pat Bogdziewicz for their assistance.

Beth Eddy has done more than anyone else to challenge my biases and to push me to make my ethical and political commitments explicit. If it were not for her prodding, this book would not have been written in anything like its current form.

Princeton University supported this project by twice granting me release from my teaching and administrative duties to work on it, but it also brought me into contact with scores of bright students who have influenced the direction and details of my argument. I extend thanks to all of them, as also to my colleagues in the Center for Human Values, the Center for the Study of Religion, and the Department of Philosophy at Princeton. George Kateb warrants mention as the person who did the most to renew my interest in Emerson and Whitman. It was not instruction so much as provocation that I received from him. George is probably too strongly committed to secularism to like this book, but it still owes much to him. When David Bromwich was still in the English Department at Princeton, he and I co-taught a graduate seminar on "Social Criticism" under the auspices of the Humanities Council. What David taught me about Edmund Burke, William Hazlitt, and George Orwell had a major impact on my thinking and reading during the time when the plans for this book were beginning to come together.

What I know about community I have learned mostly from being a part of communities. Except for college and some time traveling, I have spent my whole life in the same county—an unusual experience for intellectuals these days. I didn't plan it out this way; it's just how things worked out. But by now I know where I'm from. My first real connections with a community larger than my own family were forged in a local Civil Rights organization and a campaign to reform the county jail. What democracy means to me is inseparable from these early formative experiences. More recently, I spent a decade coaching, running camps, and administering other programs for young people. Those years delayed the completion of this book while also significantly changing its character. I have learned much about virtue, ethical formation, and the art of tending to arrangements from my many friends in the local soccer community, not least of all from the one to whom this book is dedicated.

It is a pleasure to acknowledge the love and support I have received from my mother, the Brooklyn Stouts, the McKelveys, the Ashtons, the Ewing and Lewisburg Starkeys, the Michalsons, the Levinsons, Noah Scovronick, and his family. My wife, Sally, and my children, Suzannah, Noah, and Livy, will have to be thanked in person. Nothing I could say here would give them their due or strike the right tone. For many of the reasons you might imagine, they are as relieved as I am that this book is finished.

Democracy and Tradition

INTRODUCTION

THE SOLIDARITY of an aggrieved people can be a dangerous thing. No lesson from recent history could be more evident. Any nation united mainly by memories of injustices done to it is likely to behave unjustly in its own defense and to elicit similar responses from its neighbors and enemies. A cycle of self-righteous violence will then ensue. Fear and resentment will escalate all around, placing innocents at home and abroad in further jeopardy. America's newfound solidarity in the age of terrorism therefore warrants suspicion. Many around the world nervously await our next massive use of military power, understandably afraid that we have ceased to be guided by democratic ideals and moral constraints. Solidarity we will surely need in the struggles ahead. But on what basis shall we secure it? We had better have something in common besides resentful fear of our enemies. Yet we have, until recently, been preoccupied with our ethnic, racial, and religious differences. We are not used to discussing what, if anything, links us together.

It is perhaps no accident, under such circumstances, that religious conceptions of national identity immediately come to the fore. Politicians assemble to sing "God Bless America" on the steps of the Capitol or to assure that children acknowledge membership in "one nation under God" at the start of every school day. A prominent Jewish senator declares America an essentially religious nation. Judging from his past pronouncements, he means a Judeo-Christian nation. Others intend something quite a bit narrower or a little broader when they utter the same words. Many Jews and Christians find the civil religion of our day incoherent and alienating—a travesty of true faith. As a student of these traditions, I am inclined to agree. But there is also something self-deceptive, and implicitly threatening, in the appeals to religion as a source of civic unity. Vague references to God from the crepe-lined podium cannot finally disguise the vast array of theistic and nontheistic religions Americans embrace. Need I add that dissenters, free thinkers, atheists, and agnostics are citizens, too?

Some critics charge that the moral and spiritual core of our society is empty. They frequently add that the ethical substance of the predecessor culture has been drained off by liberal secularism. To view the picture in high contrast, consider the Amish, a group that nobody would characterize as either fragmented or secular. It is easy to see both what marks this group as a community and what tradition its members can take for granted when discussing their ethical differences with one another. Any such group is bound together closely by sacred stories, dogmas, and rituals transmitted across generations. Members of such a tradition are united in their beliefs about the world and their codes of conduct, their tables of virtues and vices, their pieties and their aspirations.

In contrast, modern democratic societies appear to lack any such unifying framework. In the eyes of many observers they seem to be inherently at odds with the substantive, comprehensive visions of the religious traditions. The perception of modern democratic societies as morally and spiritually empty is hardly confined to the Amish and similarly isolated sects. It is the common link among the various types of antimodern traditionalism that have appeared in countless times and places throughout the modern era. Edmund Burke, Pope Pius IX, Rabbi Ovadia Yosef, René Guénon, Seyyed Hossein Nasr, Ananda Coomaraswamy, and many others have voiced the same complaint. Since 1980, that complaint has made new gains among religious intellectuals in America, primarily under the influence of Stanley Hauerwas, a Methodist theologian, Alasdair MacIntyre, a Roman Catholic philosopher, and John Milbank, an Anglican theologian. I will call the movement they represent the "new traditionalism." The challenge this movement poses to democratic society is a central topic in what follows.

Liberal philosophers have often reinforced the traditionalist critique of modern democracy in two ways. First, they have endorsed a theory of the modern nation-state as ideally neutral with respect to comprehensive conceptions of the good. Second, they have proposed to establish political deliberation on a common basis of free public reason, independent of reliance on tradition. Not all liberal philosophers have committed themselves to these doctrines, but traditionalists have been quick to take them as definitive of modern democracy—and then to denounce modern democratic societies as embodiments of doctrinal error and secularism. There is no need for me to mount a detailed argument against these liberal ideas here, for other writers have already done the job admirably.[1] My own purpose is more positive. I want to make an affirmative case for seeing modern democracy differently. In the process of making it, I will not, however, be drawing mainly on liberal political philosophy from John Locke to John Rawls. My topic, stated in Rawlsian terms, is the role of free public reason in a political culture that includes conflicting religious conceptions of the good. But I am not trying to construct a theory of the social contract, so I cannot mean by "public reason" what Rawls does. And the object of the "overlapping consensus" I will identify in democratic culture is not what Rawls calls a "free-standing" political conception of justice.[2] We are committed to the legitimacy of constitutional democracy under circumstances like ours and to reasoning with one another about political questions in a way that perfects and honors our democratic norms. You can tell we have these commitments because of how we behave. If we were not committed to the legitimacy of constitutional democracy, we would invest much more energy than we currently do in attempts to alter our basic arrangements. If we were not committed to continuing a discussion that perfects and honors our democratic norms, we would happily accept more restrictive and exclusionary ways of conducting political deliberation.

Yet while our norms have substantive content, we often argue over how to articulate them and what they imply. They clearly commit us to ideals of equal voice and equal consideration for all citizens, to take two examples of normative commitments that distinguish us from our unapologetically hierarchical ancestors. But how to state and apply these ideals has been in dispute since the founding of the republic. It is unlikely that we are going to reach a stable consensus on their philosophical interpretation. The sort of overlapping consensus we are searching for in public discussion is focused on particular policy questions, not on abstract conceptions of justice. Such conceptions have a role to play within the overall discussion, but they tend to be much too controversial and speculative to become the object of our consensus.

Democracy, I shall argue, *is* a tradition. It inculcates certain habits of reasoning, certain attitudes toward deference and authority in political discussion, and love for certain goods and virtues, as well as a disposition to respond to certain types of actions, events, or persons with admiration, pity, or horror. This tradition is anything but empty. Its ethical substance, however, is more a matter of enduring attitudes, concerns, dispositions, and patterns of conduct than it is a matter of agreement on a conception of justice in Rawls's sense. The notion of state neutrality and the reason-tradition dichotomy should not be seen as its defining marks. Rawlsian liberalism should not be seen as its official mouthpiece.

We claim in our official documents to be committed to substantive values. The Preamble of the United States Constitution clearly designates a list of goods that its institutional provisions are meant to serve. It takes the democratic union it formally constitutes to be something the people wish, for good reason, to make "more perfect." The people thereby express their aspiration to "establish justice, insure domestic tranquility, provide for the common defense, promote the general welfare, and secure the blessings of liberty to ourselves and our posterity." Some skeptics say that the Preamble's reference to "the people" is a fiction, designed to disguise the embarrassing fact that the governed have never actually given their consent. But who among us does not hope to receive from government roughly what the Preamble promises? Agreement on the value of such goods and on the value of attempting to secure them in something like the Constitution's way would seem to be a more promising source of solidarity than resentment and fear. A constitutional democracy is in place. We consent to being governed by it insofar as we refrain as a people from pressing for alternatives to it.

Of course, nearly every nation makes grand democratic pronouncements nowadays. Empty rhetoric is hardly an adequate basis for political community. Commitment to democratic values, to be worth anything, must reside in the life of the people, in the way citizens behave. We obviously fall far short of the democratic ideals we espouse, on any reasonable interpretation of their substance. The ideal of equal voice, in particular, is hardly consistent with the dominant role that big money now plays in politics. Yet we continue to demand reasons from one another when deciding on institutional arrangements and political policies. We still make some attempt to hold our leaders responsible to the rest of us. We at least complain that fat cats and bigwigs have the influence they do; and we are pursuing remedies that have some hope of surviving judicial review. It is not on ceremonial occasions alone that we invoke our norms. We use them to call one another to account and in deciding what to do.

In the ancient world, democracy meant rule by a particular class, the commons. For us, its strictly political referent is a form of government in which the adult members of the society being governed all have some share in electing rulers and are free to speak their minds in a wide-ranging discussion that rulers are bound to take seriously.[3] The public deliberation that is essential to this form of government is conducted at various levels. The most prominent of these is that of the people's elected representatives in a congress or parliament. As Oliver O'Donovan has pointed out, it is crucial that the people's representatives play a role in modern democracy distinct from that played in an earlier era by a monarch's council. A council was expected to advise the ruler on how to achieve his or her goals; its term of office could be terminated at the ruler's whim; its representative function was minimal. A congress or parliament, in contrast, serves at the people's pleasure, and is expected to deliberate "not on its own behalf but in response to a wider context of deliberation, open to all, to which it must be attending carefully."[4] This reference to a wider context of deliberation provides the link between democracy in its strictly political form and democracy as a broadly cultural phenomenon in the modern world. By highlighting the significance of public deliberation, democratic political arrangements bring to light their symbiotic relationship to a surrounding culture in which the shared discursive practices of the people are of primary importance.

By engaging in these practices we participate in a common life, a life that both needs to be made "more perfect" and needs to be defended against those who attack it for being morally vacuous or evil. This book concerns a tradition of democratic reasoning, dispositions, and attitudes that the people have in common. My primary aim is to make plain what this adhesive element in our sociality involves. My conception of the civic nation is pragmatic in the sense that it focuses on *activities* held in common as constitutive of the political community. But the activities in question are not to be understood in merely procedural terms. They are activities in which normative commitments are embedded as well as discussed. The commitments are substantive. They guide the discussion, but they are also constantly in dispute, subject to revision, and not fully determinate. They are initially implicit in our reasoning, rather than fully explicit in the form of philosophically articulated propositions. So we must be careful not to reduce them to a determinate system of rules or principles. Because they evolve, we need the historical category of "tradition" to bring them into focus.

In commending this pragmatic conception of democratic sociality, this book addresses readers in their capacity as citizens. It seeks a public, as opposed to a narrowly professional, audience. This is not so much a matter of the size of the audience I expect to reach, a topic on which it is pointless to speculate, as it is a matter of the point of view I am inviting my readers to adopt while reading. The point of view of a citizen is that of someone who accepts some measure of responsibility for the condition of society and, in particular, for the political arrangements it makes for itself. To adopt this point of view is to participate in the living moral tradition of one's people, understood as a civic nation. It is the task of public philosophy, as I understand it, to articulate the ethical inheritance *of* the people *for* the people while subjecting it to critical scrutiny. In inviting readers to adopt the point of view of a citizen, I am also inviting citizens to reflect philosophically on their common life. This is a demanding activity, as is all true philosophizing. It has almost nothing in common with "popular philosophy," a genre that tries to make philosophy accessible by leaving out the arguments—that is, the philosophy.

The people I am addressing, the people whose ethical inheritance I hope to comprehend and assess, are my fellow Americans. Much of what I have to say would apply equally well, however, to other societies animated to some significant extent by democratic attitudes and appeal to democratic norms. When I speak of democratic societies, I do not mean groups that fully live up to such norms, for in that sense there are no democratic societies. But I do mean groups whose members invoke such norms habitually when holding one another responsible for what they say and do and are.

What norms in particular? For example, those expressed in the Bill of Rights, like the freedom to speak one's mind in public, the guarantee of due process, and the prohibition of cruel and unusual punishment. But also norms agreed on only more recently, such as those implicit in the Emancipation Proclamation and the Nineteenth Amendment, in Lincoln's Second Inaugural Address and Sojourner Truth's "Ain't I a Woman?" And also norms still in the process of being hammered out by people who sense that democracy has unrealized implications for families, churches, corporations, and other forms of association.

The continuing social process of holding one another responsible is chiefly what I have in mind when I refer to the ethical life or inheritance of a people. Central to democratic thought as I understand it is the idea of a body of citizens who reason with one another about the ethical issues that divide them, especially when deliberating on the justice or decency of political arrangements. It follows that one thing a democratic people had better have in common is a form of ethical discourse, a way of exchanging reasons about ethical and political topics. The democratic practice of giving and asking for ethical reasons, I argue, is where the life of democracy principally resides. Democracy isn't all talk. Now and then there is also a lot of marching involved, for example. But there is no form of ethical life that generates more talk on the part of more people than does modern democracy. It is in democratic discourse that the claims and reasons of marching protestors get expressed. Protestors rarely just march. They also carry signs that say something. They chant slogans that mean something. They sing songs that convey a message. And they march to or from a place where speeches are given.

The political vision expressed in this book can be summed up in two thoughts from the writings of John Dewey. The first is his twist on a familiar slogan:

> The old saying that the cure for the ills of democracy is more democracy is not apt if it means that the evils may be remedied by introducing more machinery of the same kind as that which already exists, or by refining and perfecting that machinery. But the phrase may also indicate the need of returning to the idea itself, of clarifying and deepening our apprehension of it, and of employing our sense of its meaning to criticize and remake its political manifestations.

Dewey continues by saying that the "prime difficulty . . . is that of discovering the means by which a scattered, mobile and manifold public may so recognize itself as to define and express its interests. This discovery is necessarily precedent to any fundamental change in the machinery."[5] The other thought is that democracy is a "social idea" as well as a system of government. "The idea remains barren save as it is incarnated in human relationships."[6] As feminist theologian Rebecca Chopp has put the point, "democracy is never just a set of laws about equal and fair treatment. Rather it is an ongoing interpretation of itself, an ongoing production of new practices and narratives, of new values and forms of social and personal life that constitute a democracy."[7] By combining these thoughts Dewey hoped to encourage both active identification with democratic practices and an ambitious but realistic program for their improvement. "Only when we start from a community as a fact, grasp the fact in thought so as to clarify and enhance its constituent elements, can we reach an idea of democracy which is not utopian."[8]

Our fellow citizens are going to go on disagreeing with one another about how to rank highly important values no matter what we do. And none of us knows how to bring racial antagonism, poverty, misogyny, and mistrust to an end. We had better work hard, nonetheless, to keep the democratic exchange of reasons going, for that is the best way we have of holding one another responsible. While we should try in various specific ways to raise the quality of our common discourse, we would be foolish to expect it to produce convergence on common conclusions at each point where we now disagree. We should also recognize, however, how disastrous it would be—in an era of global capitalism, corporate corruption, identity politics, religious resentment against secular society, and theocratic terrorism—if most citizens stopped identifying with the people as a whole and gave up on our democratic practices of accountability altogether.

The ethical inheritance of American democracy consists, first of all, in a way of thinking and talking about ethical topics that is implicit in the behavior of ordinary people. Secondly, it also consists in the activity of intellectuals who attempt to make sense of that way of thinking and talking from a reflective, critical point of view. Either of these things, when considered in the dimension of history, may plausibly be termed a "tradition." I believe there is enough continuity between the projects of Dewey and those of various other public intellectuals I admire to warrant speaking of a tradition of democratic thought, but I have to admit that this continuity has sometimes been hard to discern. One set of reasons for this has to do with dubious assumptions about what traditions are, assumptions I will address directly in this work. But another set of reasons has to do with the rhetorical habits of democratic thinkers themselves. Any tradition born in suspicion of deference, and which honors as a cardinal virtue in a thinker what William Hazlitt called mastery of one's own mind and Emerson called self-reliance, may be fated to have a shaky grasp on its own history.

Think of the Zen master who, at the very moment when his pupil is virtually overwhelmed by feelings of piety toward him, insists on being slapped in the face. Acknowledging one's dependence on an exemplar-guide whose help has been a necessary condition of spiritual growth, while also being able to achieve the independence of mind that the exemplary thinker exemplifies, is a high and rare spiritual achievement. Most traditions settle for a more subservient, and therefore more obvious, form of piety in order to have piety at all. This heightens one's sense of belonging to a tradition, but at the expense of a spirit of independence. Many of the great practitioners of democratic criticism have valued independence over the more deferential forms of piety. Their consciousness of their own tradition tends in consequence to be undeveloped. They are too busy slapping one another in the face to dwell for long on what they owe to whom. I am nonetheless persuaded that there are real paths of influence, commentary, and allusion linking later writers to earlier ones within the tradition I have in mind. In any event, my aim at the moment is not to offer a scholarly exposition of a tradition's origins and development, but rather to acknowledge an affiliation, or a bias, that informs my work.

Dewey inherited much from predecessors like Emerson and Whitman. All three stood self-consciously within modernity. They were not appealing to the authority of a premodern tradition, and then imagining themselves to be messengers from a betrayed past. Nor were they identifying themselves with a postmodern future, gesturing vaguely beyond the horizon to something wholly other than the culture in which they lived. They acknowledged that they belonged to the age they were thinking about even in the moments when they found it most despicable and worrisome. They were determined to identify, and identify with, forces within the age that could be bent toward its betterment or made to sustain democratic hope. This critical activity cultivated the ground on which they stood and with which they selectively identified. They did not promise to adhere to the given loyalties or allegiances of a people, but they did actively identify normative sources within their own society that were worthy of their endorsement. Whitman and Dewey belong to the tradition of independent essaying that writers like Hazlitt and Emerson helped create in English-speaking countries. Later writers, like Meridel Le Sueur, James Baldwin, Ralph Ellison, and Bill Holm eventually found a niche in the same tradition. Many of the most important democratic thinkers have found their footing there. Few of them are philosophers.

My predicament is enough like those of the democratic writers I admire to make their precedents instructive. That is as far as I will go; my admiration stops well short of hero-worship. Like Emerson, I call attention to the lapses and limitations in all my favorite authors to keep my pieties within bounds.[9] I claim only that there is moral and intellectual sustenance to be gained from such thinkers, along with much of interest to argue with and reject. Every generation needs to survey the prospects of democracy with its own eyes (and without cant about the past). Whitman exemplifies the expressive vocation of democratic thought most fully when he teaches the necessity of straying from him.

Whitman and Dewey aimed to give expression to the intimations of democracy in their own culture. Their task as intellectuals was to articulate the substance of democratic commitments in a way that would allow such commitments to be held self-consciously and self-critically. The point of doing so was in part to counter the image of democracy as an essentially destructive force with no ethical life or cultural substance of its own. Whitman was writing as a democrat when he posed "the important question of character" to the American people. He called for what amounted to a democratic theory of the virtues—a theory designed "not for a single class alone," a theory compatible with "the perfect equality of women." As I argue in part 1, the question of character is no less important today. Whitman was right to insist that democracy should pose that question to itself, but in its own terms. And Baldwin and Ellison were right to pose it again, a century later, when they spoke of the need to achieve or discover our country.

Our democratic aspirations coexist, however uneasily, with our hatred, cruelty, sloth, envy, greed, and indifference to the suffering of others. The emergence of new elites has combined with various forms of vice, bigotry, arrogance, deference, and fear to deform democratic practices in all societies we loosely label democratic. Justice, as democracy conceives of it, has always and everywhere been a virtue in short supply. But if this judgment applies to us, and not merely to societies that lack free elections and constitutionally protected rights, why continue to trust our fellow citizens and the leaders who represent them? And if one has no good reason to do this, why remain committed to membership in a democratic society at all? These questions arise nowadays in debates over racial injustice, over the separation of church and state, over the moral limits to be observed when defending the people from terrorist attacks, and in many other contexts.

American discussions of character have focused largely on three virtues, all of which are commonly interpreted in religious terms.[10] The first of these, piety, looks toward the past. It concerns proper acknowledgment of the sources of our existence and progress through life. The second, hope, looks toward the future. It concerns our capacity for ethical and political striving when success appears uncertain or unlikely. The third, love or generosity, can be directed to past, future, and distant objects, but it mainly binds us to those with whom we share our time and place. It concerns our capacity to respond appropriately to our fellows, as no less worthy of being cared for and cared about than we are ourselves. The primary aim of part 1 is to take note of what a few influential American thinkers have said about these topics, thus reminding ourselves of a conversation in which we can see our commonalities as well as our differences in play. I give more attention to piety than to hope and generosity because that has generated more controversy throughout our history.

Part 2 takes up a conflict that has emerged over the last several decades between secularist and traditionalist interpretations of our political culture. Here, too, we must come to terms with the implications of deep religious differences among the people. It would be unrealistic to expect membership in religious groups to have no influence on democratic decision making and debate, for one function of religious traditions is to confer order on highly important values and concerns, some of which obviously have political relevance. Yet some prominent political theorists and philosophers are suspicious of individuals who use religious premises when arguing publicly for a political proposal. They ground their suspicion in the notion that reasoning on important political questions must ultimately be based on principles that no reasonable citizen could reasonably reject. I find this notion extremely implausible as an account of what we could conceivably have in common, but here I am less concerned with proving it wrong than with developing an alternative understanding of public reasoning. All democratic citizens should feel free, in my view, to express whatever premises actually serve as reasons for their claims. The respect for others that civility requires is most fully displayed in the kind of exchange where each person's deepest commitments can be recognized for what they are and assessed accordingly. It is simply unrealistic to expect citizens to bracket such commitments when reasoning about fundamental political questions.

Religion is not essentially a conversation-stopper, as secular liberals often assume and Richard Rorty has argued explicitly. Neither, however, is religion the foundation without which democratic discourse is bound to collapse, as traditionalists suppose. The religious dimensions of our political culture are typically discussed at such a high level of abstraction that only two positions become visible: an authoritarian form of traditionalism and an antireligious form of liberalism. Each of these positions thrives mainly by inflating the other's importance. They use each other to lend plausibility to their fears and proposed remedies. Each of them needs a "force of darkness" to oppose if it is going to portray itself as the "force of light."

The result of such posturing is the Manichaean rhetoric of cultural warfare. The pundits would have us believe that we are all embroiled in an essentially two-sided conflict over the culture of democracy. Academics have done remarkably little to correct the resulting forms of paranoid fantasy. The debates, over issues like abortion and same-sex marriage, that do nowadays occasionally erupt into uncivil behavior are more accurately described as marginal skirmishes than as warfare, at least when viewed in historical or cross-cultural perspective. There is some danger, however, that a dualistic picture of our cultural situation, if accepted by enough people, will *become* true. To the extent that believers and nonbelievers accept the caricatures and exclusive choices now on offer, they become more likely to retreat into separate camps that are incapable of reasoning and living peaceably with one another.

It is true that the expression of religious premises sometimes leads to discursive impasse in political debate. But there are many important issues that cannot be resolved solely on the basis of arguments from commonly held principles. So if we are going to address those issues meaningfully, we had better find a way to work around the impasses when they arise. One name for the way I propose is conversation. By this I mean an exchange of views in which the respective parties express their premises in as much detail as they see fit and in whatever idiom they wish, try to make sense of each other's perspectives, and expose their own commitments to the possibility of criticism.

The bulk of part 2 aims to demonstrate the value of carrying on a public conversation of this kind with religious traditionalists. My conversation partners in these chapters are prominent Christians. I have selected them in part because they represent the religious tradition to which most American citizens are committed. It should be obvious that similar forms of traditionalism have proven attractive to some Jews and Muslims. The broader conversation I hope to instigate would include them—and others as well. But one cannot converse seriously with everyone at once, and in this book I have chosen to converse mainly with versions of traditionalism that the Christian majority in the United States has found tempting.

Traditionalists are right, I believe, to argue that ethical and political reasoning are creatures of tradition and crucially depend on the acquisition of such virtues as practical wisdom and justice. They are wrong, however, when they imagine modern democracy as the antithesis of tradition, as an inherently destructive, atomizing social force. I could have made the latter point in a different way by focusing on Christians who are openly fighting to make their tradition more democratic, such as Lisa Cahill, Rebecca Chopp, James Forbes, Peter Gomes, Mark Jordan, Susan Frank Parsons, Rosemary Radford Ruether, Andrew Sullivan, and Garry Wills. This would have had the advantage of diversifying the range of Christian voices under consideration. But a book on those figures would make no impression on readers who are attracted to the new traditionalism. So I have decided to focus my critical attention in chapters 4–7 on the most influential of the new traditionalists: Hauerwas, MacIntyre, and Milbank. My criticisms of them are in some large measure feminist in inspiration, and incorporate points made before by Gloria Albrecht and Susan Moller Okin. I also try to challenge the traditionalists in another way, however, by contrasting their positions with those of theologically conservative but politically progressive thinkers like Calvinist philosopher Nicholas Wolterstorff and Barthian theologian George Hunsinger.

One of my central claims is that modern democracy is not essentially an expression of secularism, as some philosophers have claimed and many theologians have feared. Modern democratic reasoning is secularized, but not in a sense that rules out the expression of religious premises or the entitlement of individuals to accept religious assumptions. Those who lament our failure to agree as a nation on the sanctity of embryonic life and on issues relating to sexual conduct and family life are free to offer their reasons to the rest of us. Some hope ultimately to place a sacred canopy over what Father Richard John Neuhaus calls "the naked public square," thereby rescuing ethical discourse from the perils of secular liberalism. In practice this proposal turns out to be either unacceptable or unrealistic—unacceptable if it employs the coercive power of the state to reverse the secularization of public discourse, unrealistic if it does not. Equally important, it tends to misconceive what the secularization of public discourse involves.

Traditionalists claim that democracy undermines itself by destroying the traditional vehicles needed for transmitting the virtues from one generation to another. Because traditionalists see democracy as an essentially negative, leveling force—as the opposite of a culture—they tend to underestimate the capacity of democratic practices to sustain themselves over time. Because they suspect that moral discourse not grounded in true piety is actually a form of vice, they are tempted to withdraw from democratic discourse with the heathen. Some traditionalists actively foster alienation from the citizenry's public discussion of divisive ethical questions while promoting identification instead with premodern traditions and religious communities. I argue that this move represents an unwarranted form of despair over the current condition of ethical discourse and that it tells a largely false story about the kind of society we live in.

Whether the citizenry can transform itself into a community that more fully warrants the trust essential to democratic practices remains an open question. We had better hope that the answer is yes, because the only alternative is grim. The rhetoric of the new traditionalists and Black Nationalists, to take two examples, implies that they have already given up on democracy. They declare the civic nation or modernity itself innately vicious, and then, having no place else to go, identify strictly with communities distinct from democratic society as a whole. But this message has largely made matters worse. There are practical reasons for resisting it, especially today.

Democratic norms are initially implicit in what we do when we demand reasons for some actions, commitments, and arrangements, while treating others as acceptable by default; or when we treat some reasons as sufficient and others as insufficient; or when we respond unreflectively to something by admiring or deploring it. But norms can also be made explicit in the form of principles and ideals, as they are in our founding documents and in the speeches of eloquent citizens. Our political culture traffics heavily in appeals to explicitly stated norms. This is the most obvious way in which we hold our leaders, as well as our fellow ordinary citizens, accountable to the people. From a pragmatic point of view, the function of moral principles with respect to the ethical life of a people is essentially expressive, a matter of making explicit in the form of a claim a kind of commitment that would otherwise remain implicit and obscure. Public philosophy as I conceive of it is an exercise in expressive rationality.[11] Part 3 attempts to clarify what this conception of public philosophy involves. It argues that a kind of pragmatism can transcend the current standoff between secular liberals and the new traditionalists—and do so by borrowing crucial insights from both sides.

For Whitman, articulating the ethical life of democracy was mainly a poetic task, and he took his understanding of the poet mainly from Emerson.[12] The young Dewey learned from Emerson's essays and from Hegel that the task belonged as much to philosophers as it did to poets. His mature pragmatism was largely an attempt to translate Hegel's philosophical expressivism into the ordinary language of Americans who had no use for the Hegelian logic of identity. One thing he learned from Hegel was that the project of rational self-criticism and the project of bringing the ethical life of a people to self-conscious expression were best understood as two phases or dimensions of a single project. This project is Socratic in its commitment to self-examination and in aiming for self-perfection, but it is carried out simultaneously on an individual and a social scale—as a public philosophy. Dewey's pragmatism sought to explain, in terms a plain-speaking citizen could find intelligible, how one could reasonably aim to make explicit, and then to criticize, the ethical life of one's culture without claiming (dishonestly, self-deceptively) to rise above the perspective of a situated, committed participant in that culture's practices.

Many early champions of modern democracy, influenced by Enlightenment philosophy, had portrayed themselves as the heralds of a complete break from the past; "tradition" was a name for what they opposed; "reason" and "modernity" were names for what they championed. Many of them were revolutionaries who sought to turn the world of pomp and privilege upside down. Their rhetoric implied that they owed nothing to the past. In retrospect, we can see the conceptual continuities that linked them with their predecessors and opponents. There is much to be gained by abandoning the image of democracy as essentially opposed to tradition, as a negative force that tends by its nature to undermine culture and the cultivation of virtue. Democracy is a culture, a tradition, in its own right. It has an ethical life of its own, which philosophers would do well to articulate. Pragmatism is best viewed as an attempt to bring the notions of democratic deliberation and tradition together in a single philosophical vision. To put the point aphoristically and paradoxically, *pragmatism is democratic traditionalism.* Less paradoxically, one could say that pragmatism is the philosophical space in which democratic rebellion against hierarchy combines with traditionalist love of virtue to form a new intellectual tradition that is indebted to both.

Part of the democratic program is to involve strangers and enemies, as well as fellow citizens, in the verbal process of holding one another responsible. This means taking norms that originated in one tradition and applying them across cultural boundaries, in the hope of drawing undemocratic individuals and groups into the exchange of reasons. Philosophers make the task look easier than it is when they claim that all human beings already share a common morality, *the* common morality, simply by virtue of being human. From my point of view, such a claim seems like wishful thinking. It ignores the essential role that traditions play in shaping human thought.

Among the central theses of part 3 are an expressivist conception of norms and the claim that being justified in believing something is a contextual affair. While these two ideas can surely be attributed to Dewey, there are so many points at which I depart from Dewey's specific formulations that it would be tedious for me to spend much time explaining the details. Instead, I draw directly on what I take to be the most important recent developments in pragmatic philosophy. My most obvious departure from Dewey is my claim that truth is not an essentially relative concept. This is a notion that many readers of my previous writings have found hard to square with what I say in praise of Dewey's doctrines on other topics. But I maintain that emphasizing the priority of social practices in the way pragmatism does need not prevent us from thinking of ethical discourse as an objective endeavor in which full-fledged truth-claims play an essential role. A central challenge for pragmatism as a public philosophy is to overcome the suspicion that it cannot adequately distinguish truth from concepts like warranted assertibility and justified belief. Otherwise pragmatism appears to undermine or eliminate essential features of the ethical and political discourse it purports to articulate and defend.

The difficulty this book poses to the nonphilosophical reader rises in chapters 3 and 8–12. These are the places where I spend more time discussing distinctions that have been drawn by philosophers who write mainly for other philosophers. A public philosophy is addressed to the public, and it takes public life as its subject matter, but it is still philosophy. So it ought to hold itself responsible to what philosophers say among themselves. I therefore need to move back and forth, as Dewey did, between explaining ideas honed in academic philosophy and addressing moral, political, and religious concerns that ordinary citizens discuss in public every day. Of course, the professionalization of philosophy since the days of classical pragmatism has widened the gap between the two languages that public philosophy attempts to link together, perhaps to an extent that casts doubt on the bridging I am undertaking here. But I have plunged ahead, in the hope that others have created an audience for the sort of mixed genre to which the present work contributes. In this way, I hope, the ethical heritage of modern democracy can be made more intelligible to at least some of those who have been shaped by it.

I would like to think that a reader who took the time to go through the entire discussion carefully could emerge with an improved understanding of what has been going on recently in the disputed territory where philosophical, political, and religious thought intersect. My argument is addressed to readers—above all young ones—who are struggling to make sense of the social criticism, philosophy, and theology currently in circulation. My objective is to awaken in them a sense of new ethical, political, and intellectual possibilities.

My focus throughout is on democracy in America. I would have written a different book if I had been living elsewhere, hoping to influence some other society. As an act of social criticism, this book is necessarily a somewhat parochial affair. But as a contribution to comparative ethics, it also takes part in a global conversation in which every society with democratic aspirations will need to be heard from on its own terms. If democracy is nowhere fully realized and everywhere in jeopardy, we all have much to learn from particular cases.

PART ONE

The Question of Character

[I]n these States, for both man and woman, we must entirely recast the types of highest personality from what the oriental, feudal, ecclesiastical worlds bequeath us. . . . Of course, the old undying elements remain. The task is, to successfully adjust them to new combinations, our own days.

—Whitman

Chapter 1

CHARACTER AND PIETY FROM EMERSON TO DEWEY

WALT WHITMAN held that "society, in these States, is canker'd, crude, superstitious, and rotten. Political, or law-made society is, and private, or voluntary society, is also." And yet he also held that a vigorously democratic ethos is struggling to be born of the people as they are, and wants midwifery from writers who would be pleased to see it explicit and mature. The "important question of character," as Whitman poses it in *Democratic Vistas*,[1] is what sort of people we can reasonably aspire to be, given the disturbing condition of society as it stands and the influence it has already had on us. It is a question very much with us today, but we have largely forgotten how to pose it in Whitman's democratic way. Indeed, we have largely lost sight of the tradition of reflection that *Democratic Vistas* represents. It is part of my purpose in this chapter to remind America that this tradition exists. I shall be painting in very broad strokes on a large canvas, providing just enough detail—in the form of commentary on quotations from Emerson, Whitman, and Dewey—to challenge received opinion on what the moral and religious landscape of the United States has been like. Think of this as a Ben Shahn mural in prose.

These figures represent only one strand of an American debate over religion, ethics, and political community that has been going on since Emerson's lectures and essays of the late 1830s. Another strand, equally important but much more aware of itself as a tradition, is that of orthodox Christianity from the Puritanism of Plymouth Rock to the denominational soup of our own day. Yet another, to be explored briefly in the next chapter, is a sort of blues spirituality rooted in the practices of African polytheism. In jazz, rock, and film, as well as in novels, essays, and poems, the spirit of the blues and Emersonian striving for perfection have often reinforced one another, creating a combined cultural force that orthodox Christians have found deeply disturbing but have largely misunderstood as an expression of liberal secularism. It is not always easy to distinguish the various strands of American religious thought and practice. Some thinkers, like Cornel West, self-consciously integrate them all. As Harold Bloom has said, many Americans who call themselves Christians are in fact more Emersonian than Augustinian in outlook. Many others care more about the ecstasy of the crossroads than the agony of the cross.

Bloom is being characteristically hyperbolic, however, when he declares Emerson the founding prophet of *the* American religion.[2] The definite article and singular noun reduce something complicated and conflicted to something simple and unitary. American religion is a swirling whirlwind of religious energy and experimentation, accompanied by much open conflict. In this chapter I want to contrast the Emersonian and Augustinian strands of American religiosity without exaggerating their differences. Ever since Emerson's "Divinity School Address" of 1838, he and his followers have been engaged in a tug of war with orthodox Christians over the future of American piety. Christians, ever mindful of Augustine's great work, *The City of God*, have never been reluctant to condemn the Emersonians for underestimating the human spirit's need for settled institutional and communal forms, including a structure of church authority to reign in spiritual excess. The Emersonians, for their part, would rather quit the church than grant that some holder of church office or even a democratically organized congregation has the authority to administer the distinctions between saved and damned, saint and sinner, true and false prophet, scripture and apocrypha. Above all, they have been persuaded from the beginning that the idea of original sin is blight on the human spirit. Orthodox Christians sense in all this the errors of ancient heresies—Montanist and Pelagian, to be precise—and have never tired of prophesying against them.[3]

My focal point in this chapter will be what Emersonians have said about the virtues. I will emphasize one virtue in particular, piety, because this has been central to the broader debate over religion, ethics, and political community. Piety, in this context, is not to be understood primarily as a *feeling*, expressed in acts of devotion, but rather as a *virtue*, a morally excellent aspect of character. It consists in just or appropriate response to the sources of one's existence and progress through life. Family, political community, the natural world, and God are all said to be sources on which we depend, sources to be acknowledged appropriately. Emersonians and Augustinians agree that piety, in this sense, is a crucial virtue, and they share an interest in clarifying the proper relationship between civic and religious piety. But they disagree over how the sources should be conceived and what constitutes appropriate acknowledgment of our dependence on them. It is remarkable, all things considered, that they have remained on speaking terms, for they spend a great deal of time squinting at one another suspiciously and uncomprehendingly. But in fact they have largely agreed on the value of religious freedom, the separation of church and state, and the legitimacy of constitutional democracy in our era. And they have learned much and borrowed much from one another along the way.

One of my aims in this book is to describe the political consensus of Emersonian and Augustinian democrats in a fresh way, without underestimating its fragility. Political philosophers have approached the topics of "overlapping consensus" and "public reason" by developing a theory of the social contract, the central ideas of which derive from the Enlightenment liberalism of John Locke and Immanuel Kant. For reasons that I will elaborate in chapter 3, I find the social-contract model of political community—and especially its conception of public reason—insufficiently historical and sociological. As a student of religion, I am inclined to approach these topics more concretely. That means beginning with the religious visions and perfectionist projects that have actually mattered to most Americans, and only then constructing a philosophical account of the promise and dangers implicit in our political culture.

THE QUESTION OF CHARACTER AND THE DEBATE OVER PIETY

The premise of Whitman's social criticism is that character and society are reciprocally related; each has an effect on the other. We bear responsibility both for society's current condition, which would have been otherwise if we had had different virtues and vices, and for its future condition, which will depend on what we make of ourselves today and tomorrow. If we find society in poor condition, we have reason to fear the effects of that society on us. We may be weakening—may indeed have already ruined—our own capacity as a people to reform. The worse the social circumstances appear, the deeper the suspicion that we may be characters in a tragedy, awaiting only the final compensation for the flaws in our character. The deeper that suspicion goes, the stronger the temptation will be to place one's hope in some temporal power other than, better than, higher than, stronger than, the people.

The question of character is important, in Whitman's view, precisely because we are not self-evidently fit to perform the tasks that our circumstances demand of us if we want to live democratically. "In fact," Whitman writes, "it is to admit and face these dangers I am writing. To him or her within whose thought rages the battle, advancing, retreating, between democracy's convictions, aspirations, and the people's crudeness, vice, caprices, I mainly write this essay" (DV, par. 3). Merely to celebrate our character by joining in chants democratic, instead of looking "our times and lands searchingly in the face, like a physician diagnosing some deep disease" (DV, par. 16), is smugness. It may also involve embracing a form of racial mysticism or chauvinistic idolatry—a despicable piety indeed. That Whitman was himself prone to such crudeness and superstition—for example, in his remarks on the Saxonization of Mexico or on Oregon's exclusion of blacks—shows that the physician of democracy can suffer from the very ills he proposes, in his better moments, to diagnose in the people. A critic who would identify democratically with the people should, in the act of criticizing their self-worshipping cant as so much "hectic glow" and "melodramatic screamings" (DV, par. 16), be conscious of having himself to heal. I will not be praising Whitman for removing hubris and superstition from his identifications.

The question of character gets short shrift, not only from those who worship the people as a race or a nation, thus placing our character beyond question, but also from those who believe that our political and economic systems are structurally immune from whatever faults the people might have. In Whitman's eyes, the latter group is as superstitious as the former. They suffer under "the prevailing delusion that the establishment of free political institutions, and plentiful intellectual smartness, with general good order, physical plenty, industry, &c . . . do, of themselves, determine and yield to our experiment of democracy the fruitage of success" (DV, par. 15). It is simply not the case that our political system can dispense entirely with civic virtue and still survive as a democracy. Our constitutional checks and balances can, to some extent, neutralize the evil effects of self-interest among the people. Our economy does sometimes punish sloth and stupidity with its unseen hand while "uplifting the masses out of their sloughs, in materialistic development, products, and in a certain highly-deceptive superficial popular intellectuality" (DV, par. 16). But there is nothing in either system to guarantee that we will, over time, possess all of the virtues required to sustain the nondeferential conversability of a genuinely democratic politics.

Without help from the people, no constitution can prevent a wealthy and powerful class from rigging the electoral system to favor the wealthy and powerful. If such a class were to gain control of government, it would then be able to use all available constitutional means, including taxation, expenditure, and regulation, to rule plutocratically. It might then succeed in fostering conditions in which gaps between social classes would widen and democratic participation would atrophy. These conditions, in turn, could strengthen a potential oligarchy's hold on power while weakening the people's ability to resist. The result could hardly be termed democratic. It would be more accurately described as a caste system in modern dress— a feudal regime without the grace of chivalry.

Something much like this nightmare of oligarchy was haunting Whitman when he published *Democratic Vistas* in 1871, as the new industrialists and professional elites began to establish themselves in the aftermath of the Civil War. As a Jacksonian democrat, Whitman could not help viewing this development with suspicion:

The depravity of the business classes of our country is not less than has been supposed, but infinitely greater. The official services of America, national, state, and municipal, in all their branches and departments, except the judiciary, are saturated in corruption, bribery, falsehood, mal-administration; and the judiciary is tainted. The great cities reek with respectable as much as non-respectable robbery and scoundrelism. (DV, par. 16)

In retrospect, Whitman's judgment seems prescient, for this was the era in which Wall Street lawyers, northeastern bankers, arms manufacturers, and railroad builders initiated the careers that allowed them to dominate political economy in the Gilded Age.

Another potential oligarchy appears to have arisen today, as a new class of managers and professionals consolidates both political and economic power in the aftermath of the New Deal. The emergent American institutional elite—the upper echelon of officials in government, major corporations, accounting firms, prestigious universities, and foundations throughout the nation—has recently become the object of heated controversy from all sides. Each ideological faction has its own self-serving definition and social analysis of the elite. No one denies, however, that members of the new elite have benefited greatly from the influence they exert on the electoral system, the system of higher education, the professional licensing system, and the economic system. From a democratic point of view, of course, the emergence of any such elite must be viewed with suspicion, as a potential threat to democracy. So much the worse if the elite is dominated by members of the same social class, has already secured its grip on the crucial levers of power, and has significantly widened the gap between itself and everyone else in America.[4] The people retain the right to vote, of course, as well as certain constitutional protections, but their effective political voice appears to be dwindling as rapidly as the average wage earner's share in the common wealth.

Under circumstances like Whitman's and ours, with potentially anti-democratic forces assembling allies and attempting to divide or coopt their foes, the question of character attains utmost importance for friends of democracy. It becomes the question of whether the people can summon the spiritual wherewithal, the moral fiber, to act on behalf of democracy before democracy itself gives way. As stewards of our society, we bear the responsibility for its survival and betterment. As products of our society, however, democratic reformers and critics are themselves bound to be weakened or corrupted by practices and institutions that appear "canker'd, crude, superstitious, and rotten," when surveyed from a democratic point of view. It is hard to see how we, the people, under such circumstances, could possess the virtues required for democratic amelioration of the social conditions that so desperately need our attention. The greater the need for democratically initiated reform, it seems, the smaller the likelihood that the people will be ethically and politically competent to supply it. The question of character acquires highest importance in a democracy at those recurring moments when the viability of democratic reform is itself in question for just this reason. Ours appears to be such a moment.

As I survey the day-to-day lives of my fellow citizens, it seems reasonable to fear that we have largely:

- ignored the plight of the poor everywhere;
- permitted the American state to prop up countless tyrants abroad;
- neither adequately prevented nor mourned the civilian casualties of our militarism;
- failed to hold professional elites responsible to the people;
- acquired a habit of deferring to bosses;
- preferred pecuniary gain and prestige to justice;
- ceased to trust ourselves as competent initiators of action;
- retreated into enclaves defined by ethnicity, race, and lifestyle;
- and otherwise withdrawn from politics into docility, apathy, or despair.

If some or all of these fears are indeed justified, is not our political economy in immediate danger of ceasing in practice to be a democracy in any but a purely formal sense? Would our constitutionally mandated electoral apparatus, checks, balances, and formally recognized rights be enough, by themselves, to give us a government that is of, by, and for the people?

So far, I have simply posed the question of character in something like Whitman's terms—the rhetoric of a committed democrat. I now want to consider antidemocratic versions of the same question, highlighting as I do so the roles that the concept of piety tends to play in them. Whitman was self-consciously rescuing the question from his opponents, showing that it could be made into a question democracy poses to itself. In Whitman's day as in ours, however, the question has most often been posed to America by authors unfriendly to democracy. Whitman refers specifically to Thomas Carlyle's *Shooting Niagara*, confessing that he "was at first roused to much anger and abuse by this essay from Mr. Carlyle, so insulting to the theory of America . . . expressing as it does certain judgments from the highest feudal point of view" (DV, par. 25n). But he was also deeply familiar, as any Romantic poet would be, with Wordsworth's version, which in turn owed much to Edmund Burke. And he was equally familiar with a theological version of the question circulating in American Protestantism.

In part 2, we will see that the question has recently become a pressing concern for major Christian thinkers in America. Hauerwas, MacIntyre, and Milbank pose it in terms borrowed from Aristotle, Augustine, and Aquinas.[5] There are important differences among these traditionalists, but they all tend toward the same negative conclusion with respect to democracy. Democratic individualism, they say, undercuts the structures of tradition and community within which alone it is possible to nurture the virtues that sustain moral education and political life. Democracy is one of the modern forces that level excellence and virtue along with hierarchy, unwittingly clearing ground for a tyranny of the majority to occupy. By eroding premodern social distinctions, it creates a society that is atomistically fragmented yet, paradoxically, also highly prone to conformity. Many similar challenges have been addressed to democracy in recent years, with Leo Strauss and Friedrich Nietzsche perhaps qualifying as the sources most often studied in the universities. But throughout this book, I will have a handful of contemporary Christian writers in mind as representative critics of democracy. Their versions of the question of character deserve a response, and this book is my attempt to supply it. I begin with Whitman largely because he and a host of others inspired by him are so hard to absorb into the story these authors tell about America.

Whitman was severely suspicious of the question-begging terms in which previous generations of traditionalists had cast the question. Why should anyone be surprised, or troubled, if a thinker working with concepts from "feudalism" (DV, par. 4), or from other premodern and Old World sources, were to find the character of the American people wanting? "The purpose of democracy" is that of "supplanting old belief in the necessary absoluteness of establish'd dynastic rulership . . . as furnishing the only security against chaos, crime, and ignorance" (DV, par. 24). It therefore goes without saying that democratic character will, from an antidemocratic point of view, appear to tend toward chaos, crime, and ignorance.

The issue of piety is central to the dispute. Democracy will appear intrinsically impious, and thus vicious, to its foes in part because they see it as an all-out attack on the social structures that have long been taken to be among the sources of our existence and progress through life. Piety, if understood as deference to a hierarchy of powers on which social life depends, seems simply to be washed away in a tidal wave of democratic self-assertion. In deferential respect, common people once bowed down in gratitude and humility to everything higher than themselves in the chain of being. The value of such piety consisted partly in the contribution it made to education in the virtues. The reverence for authority implicit in it fostered docility, which in turn permitted an individual's character to be shaped by tradition and community toward virtue. Democracy, in contrast, trumpets self-reliance and holds docility in contempt. It encourages individuals to stand up, think for themselves, and demand recognition of their rights. Whitman says, "Long enough have the People been listening to poems in which common humanity, deferential, bends low, humiliated, acknowledging superiors. But America listens to no such poems. Erect, inflated, and fully self-esteeming be the chant; and then America will listen with pleased ears" (DV, par. 106).

Lamentation over the fate of piety in the democratic age can be voiced in either a secular or a theological spirit. From Cicero to Machiavelli and down to the present, philosophers and political theorists have often construed religious piety instrumentally. This meant promoting religion not for its own sake, but rather as a convenient means of support for this-worldly virtue. Their real interest was civic piety—piety toward the structures of civil society and the political order itself. If religious piety could be manipulated with an eye toward the well-being of the republic, then, from a Machiavellian perspective, so much the better. Any religious tradition's forms of piety will do as far as the prudent prince is concerned, provided only that its widespread acceptance contributes stability and strength to public order and virtue. In this one respect, Edmund Burke resembled Machiavelli. He displayed little or no interest in the theological question of how God ought to be conceived as the supreme object of our piety. What mattered to him was that the English constitution, by which he meant the entire web of inherited prejudices and practices of English life, in fact included an established religious tradition whose characteristic forms of worship and deference conferred stability and strength upon the whole social fabric. "We know, and, what is better, we feel inwardly," Burke wrote, "that religion is the basis of civil society, and the source of all good, and of all comfort."[6] He refers here to religion, not to God, and his point is quite different from the one that some followers of Augustine would want to make.

All Augustinians hold that the true God should be recognized for what he is and worshipped in the manner that he requires of us, which is the only manner truly appropriate to his nature and fitting as an acknowledgment of our actual dependence upon him. Theological truth is therefore of paramount importance. Not just any form of religious piety will do. To the contrary, only one form could be deemed correct, because only one qualifies as a just response to the ultimate source of our existence and progress through life. Anything less than this, anything other than this, will be vice, not virtue. A way of life that does not have piety toward the true God at its center will be vitiated in some measure, because the most important part of justice will be missing from it. As Augustine put it, "true virtues cannot exist except in those who possess true piety."[7]

There are Augustinians and Augustinians. They all agree that modern democracy is vitiated to some significant degree by its lack of true piety. But some embrace modern democracy, somewhat ambivalently, as a way station in a long journey toward the end of human history. Reinhold Niebuhr and Paul Ramsey defended this position in the twentieth century; Jean Bethke Elshtain defends it today. Niebuhr was fond of quoting Churchill's famous remark that democracy is the worst form of government, except for all of the others; it perfectly expresses his ambivalence. Augustinian traditionalists, however, take modern democracy to be vitiated through and through by its prideful and disastrous secularization of the political sphere. As a result, the Augustinian's characteristic ambivalence toward the political order hardens into a traditionalist rejection of secular society.

It should be clear, then, that those who appeal to traditional piety as part of the fabric of virtue that sustains our society and who vilify democratic individualism as an acid eating away at that fabric do not all have the same vision of piety and virtue in mind. They do tend, however, to employ many of the same rhetorical devices when they describe and denounce democracy. Perhaps the most important of these is a contrast between democracy, understood as a leveling force, and something else—called tradition, culture, civilization, or community—on which the possibility of a virtuous common life is held to depend. Modern democracy is a force that results in fragmentation, not a culture hospitable to its own distinctive virtues and praiseworthy character types. Its characteristic form of moral discourse consists in the assertion and counterassertion of individual rights, not in reflection on and cultivation of the virtues. It is all about self-reliance and self-assertion, not piety. It destroys the character of the citizens who participate in it. So goes the standard traditionalist story.

It was high time, Whitman thought, to recast the question of character in democratic terms. In some passages, he seems to discard ancient and medieval traditions of the virtues altogether, as when he says that "the models of persons, books, manners, &c., appropriate for former conditions and for European lands, are but exiles and exotics here" (DV, par. 66). This move might seem merely to invert the practice of Whitman's opponents, and thus to beg the question from the democratic side. He might well be accused of arbitrarily rejecting all standards that might have any chance of entailing a critical judgment on democratic character, simply on the grounds that they are old or foreign. His celebration of a uniquely American youth and newness is often arbitrary and excessive; it grows from the same root as his mystic euphoria over Anglo-Saxon stock. Yet Whitman was capable of a subtler formulation, which better approximates the pragmatic conceptual strategy I propose to follow when modifying virtue democratically.

He claims in one passage that "the types of highest personality" bequeathed to us by "the oriental, feudal, ecclesiastical worlds" form "a strange anachronism upon the scenes and exigencies around us"—and then adds, crucially: "Of course, the old undying elements remain. The task is, to successfully adjust them to new combinations, our own days" (DV, par. 84). This task is a critical one, and it involves coming to terms with traditional conceptions of the virtues as well as modern, democratic circumstances and persons. To those who would think this task incredible, he offers assurance that it is not. A paragraph later, he speaks of America's need to "cease to recognize a theory of character grown of feudal aristocracies," and to "sternly promulgate her own new standard" (DV, par. 85). He also speaks, charitably and pragmatically, however, of "accepting the old, perennial elements, and combining them into groups, unities, appropriate to the modern, the democratic, and to the practical occasions and needs of our own cities, and of the agricultural regions." He is saying that a critical language will have to be hammered out in which the question of character can be posed fairly and usefully to a democratic society: fairly, so as not to beg the question against democracy; and usefully, so as to make wise critical judgments possible.

When Whitman decides to appropriate the term "culture" for his own democratic project, thus turning the tables rhetorically on those who imagine democracy as the opposite of a culture, he says, remarkably, "We find ourselves abruptly in close quarters with the enemy" (DV, par. 67). He is conscious of the need for "a radical change of category, in the distribution of precedence" (DV, par. 68). His rhetorical challenge will be to say what a *democratic culture* could be, with both terms receiving due emphasis. A culture is an enduring collection of social practices, embedded in institutions of a characteristic kind, reflected in specific habits and intuitions, and capable of giving rise to recognizable forms of human character. He calls for "a programme of culture, drawn out, not for a single class alone, or for the parlors or lecture-rooms, but with an eye to practical life," and he emphasizes the need to take into account both "working-men" and "the perfect equality of women." He then generalizes the point: "I should demand of this programme or theory a scope generous enough to include the widest human area. It must have for its spinal meaning the formation of a typical personality of character . . . *not* restricted by conditions ineligible to the masses" (italics in original).

Whitman is not backing off from his democratic commitment to the language of rights when he embarks on this program of culture and speculates on what the virtues of truly democratic individuals might be. As far as he is concerned, these two strands of democratic discourse are compatible with one another. The existence of *Democratic Vistas* is enough to raise doubts about the kind of story MacIntyre has told, according to which proper thinking and writing about the virtues went into eclipse at about the time Enlightenment philosophers started theorizing about rights (see chapter 5, below). The truth of the matter is that *Democratic Vistas* belongs to a lively modern discourse about the virtues that includes other great champions of democratic tendencies, like Wollstonecraft, Hazlitt, Emerson, Thoreau, and Dewey, as well as representatives of competing traditions. It is true, of course, that academic philosophers paid much less attention to the virtues in the era during which Kant and Mill became canonical figures in the university curriculum, but academic philosophy is only one locus of ethical discourse. In the broader tradition of public discussion, Whitman was hardly unique in seeing rights and virtues as complementary components of democratic culture.

Emerson, of course, is Whitman's immediate precursor within the tradition of democratic virtue theory, just as Dewey is his immediate heir. Whitman's task in *Democratic Vistas* is to extend what Stanley Cavell calls Emersonian perfectionism into the realm of political reflection at a moment of national crisis.[8] "Perfectionism" is a somewhat misleading term in this context, because it appears to imply commitment to "a state, the same for all, at which the self is to arrive, a fixed place at which it is destined to come home to itself" (*Conditions*, 13).[9] No Emersonian posits such a state. Emerson and Whitman are committed to an ethics of virtue or self-cultivation that is *always* in the process of projecting a higher conception of self to be achieved and leaving one's achieved self (but not its accumulated responsibilities) behind. The force of "always" here is to cancel the fixed telos of perfection toward which earlier perfectionisms directed their ethical striving. The Emersonian self is continuously being reshaped by its own aspiration to achieve a higher form of goodness or excellence. Emerson calls this process "*ascension*, or the passage of the soul into higher forms."[10] This is no doctrine of leveling, as far as virtue is concerned. It is democratic in its conviction that each soul has a vocation to ascend, and realistic in its recognition that most persons—perhaps moderns most of all—are content to remain mired in the conformity of the masses. Emersonian perfectionism involves no hesitation to call excellence, mediocrity, and vice by their correct names. Cavell comes closest to expressing the ambition of *Democratic Vistas* when he writes:

> If there is a perfectionism not only compatible with democracy but necessary to it, it lies not in excusing democracy for its inevitable failures, or looking to rise above them, but in teaching how to respond to those failures, and to one's compromise by them, otherwise than by excuse or withdrawal. (*Conditions*, 18)

PIETY RECONCEIVED

We have seen that Whitman happily mixed concepts drawn from Old World theories of the virtues with local conceptual artifacts fashioned by lovers of democracy. He would not have had much left to work with if he had jettisoned all old words with a troubling history. The term "virtue" itself would be problematical to a democratic purist, given its gendered etymology, but Whitman is not deterred. Does his democratic program of culture leave any room for a virtue worth calling "piety"? Is this a word to which the "fossil and unhealthy air" of feudalism clings (DV, par. 53)? Or can we succeed in giving it a fresh, democratic air? It does not matter much whether we retrieve the *word* or not. His fellow democrats, Emerson, Thoreau, and Dewey, were all more attracted to it than was Whitman. It was one of Emerson's favorite words, and he placed it prominently in his table of democratic virtues: "Courage, piety, love, wisdom, can teach; and every man can open his door to these angels, and they shall bring him the gift of tongues."[11] But it was demonstrably part of Whitman's project to ask how the poets of democracy ought to conceive, and respond to, the sources of our existence and progress through life. This constituted much of his literary business. Hence, he had much to say about piety. For piety, in the sense at issue here, is virtuous acknowledgment of dependence on the sources of one's existence and progress through life.

When traditionalists conclude that democracy is antithetical to piety itself, they must be assuming that piety consists essentially in deference toward the hierarchical powers that be. But from a democratic point of view, the only piety worth praising as a virtue is that which concerns itself with *just* or *fitting* acknowledgment of the sources of our existence and progress through life. The philosophical expression of such concern begins in Plato's dialogue, the *Euthyphro*, and extends through such thinkers as Cicero and Aquinas, before reaching the modern period. The Emersonians agree with Plato's Socrates that justice is always at issue in the practices of piety. They hold that justice requires suspicion of power worship in all of its forms. When they denounce piety as a vice, they mean piety as defined in the traditionalist way. When they praise it as a virtue, they are imagining the sources of our existence and progress through life in some other way, while devising their own democratic means of acknowledgment. Imagining or conceiving of those sources and choosing ethically and aesthetically apt expressive means of acknowledging dependence on them are both things for which an Emersonian poet or essayist expects to be held responsible discursively. Whitman can be expected to have his own interpretations of the sources, as well as his own injunctions about how the friends of democracy ought to respond to them.[12] He hardly expects what he says to go without opposition, but he does hope that his readers can, in his words, recognize thoughts they themselves have had but perhaps let slip from their consciousness.

When Whitman says, hyperbolically and prophetically, "There will soon be no more priests," I take him to mean people to whom we should feel bound to defer as custodians of this imaginative work.[13] "Priest" is his poetic name for someone thought to have the authority to proclaim such work already complete. The reason there will soon be no more priests is that self-reliant democratic individuals are in the process of taking the responsibility for such work into their own hands, taking "the rough deific sketches" from the past "for what they are worth and not a cent more."[14] He does not mean that there will soon be no more celebrators of Holy Communion, preachers of divinely inspired words, or spiritual advisors. The remarkable thing is that in America, Whitman's prophecy has largely, astonishingly, come true. There are, for example, men called "priests" in contemporary American Catholicism, and they play important roles in the lives of their communities. But, for the most part, their parishioners no longer defer the imaginative work of piety to them. The "priests" themselves know this; their congregations know it; the Vatican is busily scrambling to find remedies for it. But the proposed remedies will fail. The feudal patterns of deference to ecclesial authority will not soon return. It is a pity that traditionalists are inclined to disparage this achievement as a sin against piety rather than welcoming it as a way of taking responsibility for piety.

Some traditionalists worry that the sort of religious questioning that goes on in many American congregations is tantamount to standing in judgment of the divine source of our being. In *Leaves of Grass*, Whitman taunts them with the intentionally ambiguous phrase, "Taking myself the exact dimensions of Jehovah."[15] Is that not impious? Who are we to decide whether God is worthy of worship? On this point, Socrates, Aquinas, and Whitman are agreed. Any divine being who expects acts of piety, while prohibiting acts of idolatry, had better be prepared to tolerate the thinking—the employment of concepts, the making of judgments, the use of imagination—that is involved on our part in deciding which beings, if any, are worthy of worship. This means that one is, at least implicitly, employing one's own standards of worth. Self-reliant piety seeks to take responsibility for this commitment by making it explicit, poetically or philosophically, in the form of a claim—as something for which reasons can be requested.

Human pride being what it is, it will not be easy to think for oneself, in the pursuit of self-critical but genuine piety, without succumbing to the temptation of denying the very conditions of one's own existence or otherwise masking from oneself the sources on which critical thinking depends. This, I believe, was the vice Dewey had in mind when he condemned "militant atheism" every bit as forcefully as he condemned the equally suspect stance of traditionalist supernaturalism.[16] By *militant* atheism, I take him to have meant an attitude of arrogant disregard for the sources of one's existence and progress through life. Dewey objected to militant atheism, not to atheism as such. He held that it was possible for an atheist to possess "natural piety," that is, "a just sense of nature as the whole of which we are parts." "The essentially unreligious attitude is that which attributes human achievement and purpose to man in isolation from the world of physical nature and his fellows" (CF, 25).

Dewey took traditionalists to be right in maintaining that we ought in some appropriate way to acknowledge the ultimate sources of our existence. But, from his point of view, the traditionalists go wrong in demanding that we must all do so in one, essentially fixed way. He worried that specific religious traditions "now prevent, because of the weight of historic encumbrances, the religious quality of experience from coming to consciousness and finding the expression that is appropriate to present conditions, intellectual and moral" (CF, 9). Behind this worry lay the Emersonian question: "Why should it be assumed that change in conception and action has now come to an end?" (CF, 6). Emerson had complained of the "stationariness of religion" and of our tendency in religious matters to be "idolaters of the old." Referring to ancient founders and kings, Emerson wrote: "Suppose they were virtuous; did they wear out virtue?"[17] Against Emersonian anticlericalism, some Augustinians argue that there can be neither any semblance of virtue, nor any means to participate in a sacramental life of communion with God, outside of a community that recognizes some structure of authority and practice as ordained by God. The choice, as they see it, is not between freedom and arrogance but between anarchy and order.

Dewey sought a spiritual path between the extremes of militant atheism and arrogant traditionalism. Whether he found it is, of course, another question. It seems to me that the version of religious naturalism asserted in *A Common Faith* is itself too militant, too sure of its ability to debunk traditional forms of faith as irrational, to play the role Dewey wanted it to play in his public philosophy. Dewey was right to say that piety owes much to acts of imagination. This is no less true when we defer to the spiritual authority of others than when we work out a self-consciously poetic religious vision. If we are honest, we will admit that the margin of error in religious matters encompasses very nearly the entire subject. In religious pursuits, we all seem to be groping in the dark. Otherwise, how are we to explain the history of religious discord? Hubris, wishful thinking, sadism, and masochism have every opportunity to distort our religious thinking. No doubt, these dark forces help explain why we disagree on religious topics to the extent we do. But if being justified in believing something depends on contextual factors that vary from one person to another, and if the relevant standards of justification are as permissive as pragmatism makes them out to be, then Dewey is not in a position to declare supernaturalism beyond the pale of justified belief. According to pragmatic scruples, this is not something that can be determined in abstraction from the lives of particular human beings. It is therefore unwise to decide the issue between supernaturalism and naturalism on an official basis. Dewey might well be justified in accepting naturalism as his own view. The question is whether his denial of supernaturalism can be an essential component of the *common* faith he proposes for democratic citizens. Why suppose that naturalism can play the role he envisions for it in public culture when most citizens reject it?

In response to this question, Dewey asserts a dubious evolutionary master-narrative that is reminiscent of Auguste Comte:

> History seems to exhibit three stages of growth. In the first stage, human relationships were thought to be so infected with the evils of corrupt human nature as to require redemption from external and supernatural sources. In the next stage, what is significant in these relations is found to be akin to values esteemed distinctively religious. This is the point now reached by liberal theologians. The third stage would realize that in fact the values prized in those religions that have ideal elements are idealizations of things characteristic of natural association, which have been projected into a supernatural realm for safe-keeping and sanction. (CF, 77–78)

Dewey is not the only pragmatist to deploy such a story. (Richard Rorty is another.) But in the absence of a supporting argument, the story seems to be an instance of the same sort of wishful thinking it claims to find at work in supernaturalism. By using the word "would" in the last sentence, Dewey implicitly admits that the final stage of this evolutionary scheme is not working out as a naturalist might wish.[18]

Naturalistic piety presupposes naturalism. It construes the sources of our existence and progress through life in naturalistic terms, and endeavors to acknowledge dependence on those sources in appropriate ways. Naturalists who are not militant atheists will want to express piety toward what Dewey calls the "matrix of human relations" on which we all depend (CF, 70) and toward "the enveloping world that the imagination feels is a universe" (CF, 53). But they will stop short of positing, as an additional object of piety, a supernatural source of that enveloping (natural) world. They might also be inclined to claim that "reference to a supernatural and other-worldly locus has obscured" the "real nature" of the "human abode" and weakened the force of "goods actually experienced in the concrete relations of family, neighborhood, citizenship, [and the] pursuit of art and science" (CF, 71). Supernaturalists, for their part, will see this stopping short as a failure to respond appropriately to the ultimate source of our existence and progress through life. They might also be inclined to explain this failure as an effect of prideful self-assertion, a willful rejection of a human being's actual status as the fallen creature of a perfect Creator.

It would be presumptuous to think that the debate between naturalistic and supernaturalistic piety can be resolved in the foreseeable future. There is no reason to declare either of these types of piety the religious basis of social order. But perhaps it is possible to discern a bit more common ground here than the proponents of naturalism and supernaturalism tend to notice when they get caught up in diagnosing the illusions and sins they impute to one another. If being justified in believing something is a contextual affair, and if differences in upbringing and life experience are relevant contextual factors, then perhaps our religious opponents are justified in believing what they believe. This recognition ought at least to give us pause before we propose an uncharitable diagnosis of our religious differences. The default position will be that our neighbors are justified in believing what they believe. If we are charitable interpreters, we will view those who differ from us religiously, in the absence of clear evidence to the contrary, as people doing their best to offer appropriate acknowledgment of their dependence. Insofar as they do acknowledge that dependence appropriately, given their own conceptions of the sources of our existence and progress through life, they may be said to exhibit an attitude that is worthy of our respect, if not our full endorsement. We can praise this aspect of character as a virtue for the same reason that we can praise the courage, temperance, or wisdom of someone we oppose in battle or debate. We can then leave open whether it satisfies the highest standard of excellence one might want to apply in this area, whether it is a virtue in the strongest sense.

Naturalists and supernaturalists describe the ultimate source of existence differently; accordingly, they acknowledge their dependence on it in different ways. No one knows how to resolve such differences of doctrine and religious practice once and for all by rational means. Of course, on all sides there are people who describe those following a path unlike their own simply as vicious. But this habit displays a lack of generosity that is hard to square with the social virtues in general. In any event, it is not good for democracy.

Once we distinguish Dewey's concept of natural piety from his commitment to naturalist metaphysics, we can see that it belongs to a tradition that goes back to Edmund Burke. This might seem odd, given that Burke was also a source of modern traditionalism. How did it come to pass, then, that followers of Emerson and Whitman like Dewey began thinking of natural piety as a virtue that matters to democracy? The best shortcut I can take through this complicated thicket of intellectual history is to say that Emersonian theorists of virtue sought to democratize a Burkean conception of piety that came to them by way of Wordsworth. Burke, you will recall, was one of those to declare that democracy, in eroding the moral foundations of the received social structure, carries away with it reverence, gratitude, obedience, and loving care for every object of piety on which the common life and virtuousness of the citizenry depend. The objects of piety, for Burke, include God, family, country, place, state, and tradition. Traditional practices of piety constituted for him part of the "moral wardrobe" of the imagination with which society drapes naked human nature and without which we all sink into unmitigated vice. Genuine piety, for Burke, is our natural disposition to acquiesce gratefully in the historically contingent, imaginative constructions that clothe our nakedness in virtuous habits and sentiments. These virtuous habits and sentiments he takes to be our second nature, the cultural covering that distinguishes us from the brutes. It is this acquiescence in our own second nature that democracy threatens to undermine.

In doing so, democracy unintentionally gives rise to an unnatural form of piety that Burke calls "sinister." Here is the passage in which he coins the phrase:

> A species of men to whom a state of order would become a sentence of obscurity, are nourished into a dangerous magnitude by the heat of intestine disturbances; and it is no wonder that, by a sort of sinister piety, they cherish, in their turn, the disorders which are the parents of all their consequence. Superficial observers consider such persons as the cause of the publick [sic] uneasiness, when, in truth, they are nothing more than the effect of it. Good men look upon this distracted scene with sorrow and indignation. Their hands are tied behind them.[19]

This is relatively early Burke, so he is not yet talking about the democratic theorists of rights at the time of the French Revolution, but he has already begun to formulate the contrasting types of piety, genuine and sinister, that he will eventually have in mind when criticizing the Revolution. His later writings describe democracy as a disordering of culture that gives rise to a class of disordered men. Those men do possess a kind of piety, a vicious kind, which expresses itself in gratitude for the disturbances that make their own rise to power and influence possible. They, too, Burke believes, are bound to worship the sources of their progress through life, but we are foolish to praise them for it, because their progress through life comes at the expense of our second nature. Sinister piety is a standing temptation for those "men of talent" who stand to profit personally from democratic disturbance of the received ethical order.

Wordsworth's poetry swerved toward Burkean piety when he abandoned his youthful enthusiasm for the French Revolution. At that turning point in his life, he saw in his own radicalism the sinister piety of a young man of talent. Henceforth he called upon the powers of his Romantic imagination to celebrate poetically what he called, in *The Prelude*, "the discipline of virtue" implicit in the natural lore and folkways of the British countryside. As the Wanderer says:

> Thus, duties rising out of good possessed,
> And prudent caution needful to avert
> Impending evil, equally require
> That whole people should be taught and trained.
> So shall licentiousness and black resolve
> Be rooted out, and virtuous habits take
> Their place; and genuine piety descend,
> Like an inheritance, from age to age.

This is hardly the occasion to undertake an inquiry into everything that Wordsworth meant by "genuine" or "natural" piety. He was clearly using such terms to recommend some form of acquiescence in an essentially traditional way of life attached to a particular place. Yet his poetic practice consisted largely in imaginative redescription of ordinary objects and individuals within the setting of a beautiful and sublime natural world.

This practice made available to Romantic poets who happened to be attached to another particular place, called America, a vocation of imaginative redescription that could be turned to purposes more democratic than Burkean. America, no less than the Lake District of England, puts the beauty and sublimity of the natural world on display. The American poet is no less concerned than his English counterpart with imagining that world well, thereby doing justice to it poetically and acknowledging his dependence on it expressively. His poetry, too, articulates a kind of natural piety. It also, like Wordsworth's, endeavors to describe the moral wardrobe of a people's imagination. But it directs its descriptive powers at the ordinary individuals it finds in its own particular place. In them it sees neither the plush velvet of Burke's imperial monarchy, nor the "glorious habit" of a rural Wanderer, but the loose-fitting clothing of a democratic individuality:

> in youth fresh, ardent, emotional, aspiring, full of adventure; at maturity, brave, perceptive, under control, neither too talkative nor too reticent, neither flippant nor sombre; of the bodily figure, the movements easy, the complexion showing the best blood, somewhat flush'd, breast expanded, an erect attitude, a voice whose sound outvies music, eyes of calm and steady gaze, yet capable also of flashing—and a general presence that holds its own in the company of the highest. (DV, par. 71)

American democracy possesses its own civilizing practices in which "whole people should be taught and trained" and toward which one might reasonably come to feel gratitude, even reverence. "But," as Sabina Lovibond has put it in another context, "*natural* piety must be distinguished from the kind of 'piety' which consists in being 'content to accept' the dominant language-game, regardless of its merits or defects from a critical standpoint, simply because it is there."[20] The language-games involved in the civilizing practices that Emersonians like Whitman and Dewey have in mind are democratic. They are discursive practices *designed* to permit and encourage reflection on their own merits and defects from a critical standpoint. "Thus," writes Emerson, "are we put in training for a love which knows not sex, nor person, nor partiality, but which seeks virtue and wisdom everywhere, to the end of increasing virtue and wisdom."[21]

It is also the case, however, that we would not be the kind of people we are, in our better moments, unless we had been shaped by participating in such practices and unless countless individuals had suffered to create, defend, and perfect them. This is the note struck by Meridel Le Sueur, a twentieth-century heir of Whitman's democratic vocation, in the epigraph from *North Star Country* that I have placed at the beginning of this book.[22] It is significant that Whitman wrote *Democratic Vistas* after visiting and working in the Civil War hospitals, an experience absolutely central to his democratic piety. He deeply admired the ordinary people he witnessed in those hospitals, and he learned much from them and from his own responses to them. "The most moving thing about Whitman after all," writes David Bromwich, "is that he teaches, instead of an absolution of sins, a sort of patience with deformities from which human charity might begin."[23] This patience, when extended by experience and a poet's discipline of observation, itself gives rise to a kind of piety. It is a kind of piety entirely distinct from acquiescence in the dominant practices and institutions or their natural setting simply because they are there. It is a self-conscious identification, undertaken on the part of an individual who, thinking for him– or herself, acknowledges that on which his or her self-reliant judgment depends.[24]

This much is clear for Whitman. Neither working men, nor women, nor the masses of common people are to be deemed virtuous for knowing their place in a hierarchy, or for being disposed to defer to those above them in the chain of being. They will all be encouraged to assume the posture of self-respect. Does it follow from this that democracy is antithetical to piety itself? If piety consists essentially in deference toward the hierarchical powers that be, then democracy and piety are incompatible. Yet it need not be that. If piety is the virtue of fitting or just response to the sources of our existence and progress through life, then nothing in Whitman is opposed to it. The important issues, for him, will then be how the sources of our existence and progress through life should be imagined and how one ought to respond to those sources in attitude and action. Much of Whitman's poetry is devoted to precisely these two questions. It is the bane of doctrinaire religion, from Whitman's Emersonian point of view, to declare the work of religious imagination complete, thereby assuming an essentially deferential posture toward the past in spiritual affairs. Self-reliant piety holds, in contrast, that it is our own responsibility to imagine the sources on which we depend and to fashion lives worthy of our best imaginings. That is why he says, "The priest departs, the divine literatus comes" (DV, par. 6).

Is there room, in the heart of someone assuming this self-reliant posture, for religious gratitude? In the Thanksgiving edition of the *Philadelphia Press* in 1884, Whitman had this to say about one component of democratic piety:

> Gratitude, anyhow, has never been made half enough of by the moralists; it is indispensable to a complete character, man's or woman's—the disposition to be

appreciative, thankful. That is the main matter, the element, inclination—what geologists call the *trend*. Of my own life and writings I estimate the giving thanks part, with what it infers, as essentially the best item. I should say the quality of gratitude rounds the whole emotional nature; I should say love and faith would quite lack vitality without it. There are people—shall I call them even religious people, as things go?—who have no such trend to their disposition.[25]

Gratitude, not loyalty or deference, is, for the tradition of Emersonian perfectionism, the better part of piety.

Dewey is simply carrying this tradition forward when he charges "militant atheism" with a "lack of natural piety."

The ties binding man to nature that poets have always celebrated are passed over lightly. The attitude taken is often that of man living in an indifferent and hostile world and issuing blasts of defiance. A religious attitude, however, needs the sense of a connection of man, in the way of both dependence and support, with the enveloping world that the imagination feels is a universe. (CF, 53)

He concludes, "A humanistic religion, if it excludes our relation to nature, is pale and thin, as it is presumptuous, when it takes humanity as an object of worship" (CF, 54).

Suppose we grant, then, that there is room for gratitude in the self-reliant heart, at the point where self-reliance recognizes its dependence on the natural and social circumstances without which it would be for nothing. Is there a place in such gratitude for recognition of an indebtedness that can never wholly be discharged? The Augustinians suspect that the answer is no. Nietzsche is probably the leading modern critic of piety to press this question in a skeptical direction. What worries him about piety is precisely the implication that we owe more to the sources of our existence and progress through life than we could ever repay. This is, he thinks, a debilitating thought, a seed of resentment that cannot be part of a life that affirms life. But Nietzsche and Whitman both had Emerson as their mentor. And I take it that Whitman, in embracing a kind of pious gratitude that Nietzsche did not, had an Emersonian thought in mind that Nietzsche, who turned against democracy, neglected. This thought is best expressed in the following passage from Emerson's essay "Experience":

When I receive a new gift, I do not macerate my body to make the account square, for, if I should die, I could not make the account square. The benefit overran the merit the first day, and has overran the merit ever since. The merit itself, so-called, I reckon part of the receiving.[26]

Masochistic self-abasement is not a virtue at all by Emersonian lights, even when it goes misleadingly by the name of piety. A host of modern writers since Hume join in its denunciation—Nietzsche among them. But Emerson, the greatest champion of democratic self-reliance, is working hard in this passage to leave room for a spiritually healthy recognition of dependence. I would put the point by saying that it does not belong to the virtue of justice for me to do more than I could possibly do to make the account square. No genuine virtue requires more of a human being than a human being could conceivably do. It is not an expression of justice but a mark of sadomasochistic pathology to demand perfect reciprocation where only imperfect reciprocation is possible.

The genius of the passage from Emerson lies in the grateful but life-affirming spirit in which he was able to receive—and acknowledge dependence on—gifts that could not be fully reciprocated. He knows full well that he is indebted, beyond all capacity to repay, to the sources of his existence and progress through life, but his is a piety cleansed of sadomasochist tendencies by democratic self-respect. He is ready to receive gifts joyously, to acknowledge them justly, without maceration of body or soul. When he says that "the benefit overran the merit the first day, and has overran the merit ever since," he is unafraid to mean *his* merit. He does not take the possibility of merit to be cancelled out by the fact it would not have arisen entirely of its own accord. He is saying that what he really does deserve to be praised for, whether it be his genius or his character, is itself conditioned. His merit does not go all the way down. It is rather part of the receiving, part of the gift. Even so, it is not unmixed with his efforts. Emerson's moral psychology is one in which taking due pride in one's accomplishments, praising others for theirs, and relations of asymmetrical obligation can be recognized under justice—and distinguished from mere hubris.

This does not mean, of course, that hubris represents no danger in a democratic context. It is a standing danger in every person who acquires power, prestige, or wealth. But an Emersonian like Whitman or Dewey will want to balance recognition of the danger it poses with a rhetoric of encouragement and generosity directed especially toward the common people, toward women, toward slaves, and the descendants of slaves. We had better bring all of these people into the scope of democratic individuality before we worry too much about the hubris that might someday arise in their hearts. The relative autonomy of healthy self-reliance is the basis for genuine piety. Dewey was standing within a tradition of self-critical piety indebted to both Emerson and Whitman when he declared that "the reverence shown by a free and self-respecting human being is better than servile obedience rendered to an arbitrary power" (CF, 7).

Now, it would be foolish to expect Augustinians to read such a remark in context and not detect in it a trace of pride, which in their diction names the sin that alienates human beings from their true home in God. What Dewey calls "self-respect" and Emerson calls "self-reliance" is the fruit of a perfectionist spiritual practice that self-consciously refuses to be disciplined by Augustinian warnings or restrained by structures of ecclesial authority. There are profound religious differences here, and they are not to be papered over or taken lightly. But once we bring these differences into focus, we can see why they have not prevented members of either group from identifying with a constitutional order in which church and state are separated.

Augustinian democrats see pride at work in every human heart, including the heart of every Augustinian. So this, by itself, cannot serve for them as a criterion of exclusion from the political community. A political community consisting entirely of prideful sinners still has important business to attend to, things it can do more or less well, more or less justly. Emersonian democrats are more apt to describe the citizenry as asleep or as corrupted than as sinful, but they care as deeply as anyone does about achieving a more perfect union. They count themselves among those with a responsibility to improve on our institutional arrangements, especially by making them properly responsive to the needs and voices of the least well-off. In short, they count themselves as citizens.

Both groups have long been impressed by the limitations of politics. They recognize its historically demonstrated shortcomings, and do not expect it to save anyone's soul. They care too much about piety, as they understand it, to entrust a modern nation-state to define its ultimate object or to mandate practices for expressing and cultivating it.[27] States just aren't good at such things, and have caused a lot of harm when they have overstepped their bounds. Monarchs made a mockery of piety by presuming to have the authority to oversee it. They made war in the name of Christ, coerced their subjects to conform, and caused many to flee their homelands in search of freedom and security. There is no reason to expect democratically elected presidents and legislators to be better vicars of true piety than the kings and queens of centuries past. We are not inclined to put the nature and existence of God to a vote.

A state that imposes religious (or irreligious) conformity on a people prevents dissenters from leading lives that fully reflect their own commitments on matters of great importance. Or worse, it aims to make up their minds for them, thereby robbing selves of the capacity to think their own thoughts. It will come as no surprise that the champions of self-reliance see such bullying as a grave assault on the human spirit. Many Christian communities have learned from their own experience of persecution to call it a violation of conscience. No one supposes that we would be better off if we made our commitments in a vacuum, independently of familial and cultural influence. No freedom that absolute is at issue. In cultivating their own piety, citizens will take sustenance from whatever traditional stories, exemplary lives, communal structures, poetic images, and critical arguments prove valuable. It is up to them to make something of their inheritance and to discard those of its parts that insult the soul. The freedom they exercise is situated in a network of evolving normative constraints. But the state has no business interfering in such matters. Its proper work lies elsewhere.

What is it about a human being that freedom of conscience honors? For that matter, what is it about a human being that the prohibition of murder honors, or the prohibition of cruel and unusual punishment? Christians answer these questions by telling a story about souls created in the image of God. Emerson and Whitman also often talk about souls and about something divine or wondrous that can be discerned in a human being. They are self-consciously waxing poetic at those moments. They think of the Christian story as ossified poetry, and are striving for fresh images of their own. Their intent is not to take dogma and argue with it on its own terms. Their intent is simply to express faithfully something they have experienced and to enliven a similar capacity for awe and love in their readers. Speaking of the poet of democracy in "By Blue Ontario's Shore," Whitman writes:

> He judges not as the judge judges but as the sun falling round a helpless thing,
> As he sees the farthest he has the most faith,
> His thoughts are the hymns of the praise of things,
> In the dispute on God and eternity he is silent,
> He sees eternity less like a play with a prologue and denouement,
> He sees eternity in men and women, he does not see men and women as dreams or dots.[28]

Chapter 2

RACE AND NATION IN BALDWIN
AND ELLISON

THIS CHAPTER considers another American debate concerning piety and peoplehood—that among African-American thinkers over Black Nationalism and its separatist conception of political community. That this form of racial nationalism is a reaction to the racist exclusion of blacks from full participation in the civic nation is a vivid reminder that the virtues most directly linked to the prospects of democracy are justice, friendship, generosity, and hope. For the erosion of these virtues rapidly undermines the trust in others and in the future that is essential to identification with the civic nation as a whole. If the next generation fails to keep democratic hope alive while defending itself against terrorism and responding to other pressing challenges, the most plausible explanation will be that the people were themselves too unjust and hateful to inspire trust in one another. When injustice is bad enough, in particular when large segments of the population have reason to feel humiliated and despised, then the community itself is apt to fall apart into essentially separate communities. One knows this has happened when the respective groups no longer take an interest in giving reasons to one another, in holding one another responsible by discursive means.

Throughout their history white Americans have been uncertain about whether to define their national identity in racial terms. Thinking of the people as a race is a mistake Emerson and Whitman themselves committed more than once, even when they were in the process of defending the abolition of slavery as a condition of securing a more perfect union. Politicians anxious to curry favor with Middle-American whites now repeat the same mistake routinely, if tacitly and with a knowing wink of the eye. White America's racial nationalism has provoked corresponding forms of racial nationalism in the diasporic communities. Black Nationalism is the most important example of this reactive tendency. While it has not achieved any of its original political objectives in the United States, Black Nationalism remains a salient presence in American political culture. There is no denying that its proponents have just cause for desiring separation from a racially conceived American nation. But there is every reason to doubt that the goal of achieving such separation is preferable, all things considered, to the goal of redefining the civic nation in nonracial terms. Structurally speaking, Black Nationalism closely resembles the new religious tradition-alism I will discuss in part 2 of this book. Both of these ideologies are reactions against an exclusionary definition of the democratic community, both involve forms of piety that obscure the relations of mutual depen-dence actually at work in democratic communities, and both have resulted in politically debilitating forms of separatism and cultural alienation. It is advisable to subject them to close scrutiny and to resist the temptations they present, but only after reminding ourselves that they would not have taken root in a society that had inspired trust in the first instance.

A former member of the United States Commission on Civil Rights recently told me over dinner, if I understood him correctly, that racial ha-tred of blacks is essentially a thing of the past in America. I told him that he had been spending too much time with his fellow commissioners and not enough with children from a community several blocks from where we were eating. I then recounted the story of one of those children, a black soccer player named Demont, who played on teams I coached throughout his adolescence. As I write this, he is entering his final year of college. Once, when we were at a tournament in France, a stadium full of Europe-ans cheered his selection as the most valuable player. But on playing fields throughout my own state, I have repeatedly heard Demont denigrated with racist epithets. Parents supporting opposing teams have jeered him, and occasionally encouraged their children to "take him out"—that is, to foul him in such a way that injury would prevent him from continuing. His sin was his hard, fearless play. A friend of mine from another part of the county tells me that a black player on his team received the same treatment. My friend taught his white players to say, "Yeah, we're all niggers on this team."

Many conservative intellectuals now sincerely believe that African-American activists are dreaming up white racism in order to improve their own position in a society corrupted by multiculturalism. They think the only form of racism still thriving among the American people is to be found in the hearts of these activists and the people they succeed in manipulating. But this is not a thought that can survive the test of experience. All one has to do to refute it is spend time, outside the corridors of power and privilege, with ordinary black people. By this I mean African-Americans who are neither leftist activists nor right-wing ideologues. In the university where I work, a handful of African-Americans are in fact treated rather well. But many of them have stories to tell about being harassed by police. And else-where in the same town, there is a largely black and Latino underclass that remains virtually invisible to most of the rest of us. You need not spend much time with those people before you realize that there is still white racism in America.

The American people are both much more deeply marred by their vices and much more capable of transcending those vices than intellectuals typically make them out to be. But how would intellectuals know? Few of them—on either the Right or the Left—today spend much time outside an academic and cultural enclave inhabited entirely by others like themselves.

My focal point here is the critique of Black Nationalism put forward a generation ago by two exemplary defenders of democratic ideals—namely, James Baldwin and Ralph Waldo Ellison. Reexamining these two writers is a good way to restore our grasp on what the democratic tradition of social criticism has stood for (and against) in contexts where hatred and exclusion have given rise to separatist responses. It is a grave mistake to think that we have somehow outgrown the need to hear what they have to say.

The Style of Black Nationalism

To identify a group of people as *blacks* is to substitute one of their features— the color of their skin—for their whole persons. There is nothing intrinsically wrong with the trope being employed, which rhetoricians call "synecdoche." We do not object to the captain who calls out "Twenty sail!" when specifying the number of ships on the horizon or to the presiding officer who "counts noses" when trying to determine whether our assembly has a quorum. The trouble comes when substituting a visible feature for a person is linked with a second substitution—a metonymical reduction—intended to specify something else all members of the group in question essentially share, something that supposedly makes them what they are, qua group members. To make a double-substitution of this kind is to issue an inferential license. The license authorizes an inference from the visible presence of one thing, a feature that members of a group can be seen to share, to the existence of something else that constitutes their shared social identity. The visible feature comes to stand for both the person to whom it belongs and the underlying characteristic that is taken to confer social identity. Where the underlying characteristic is taken to explain or justify superior social status, the visible feature functions as an emblem of that status. Where the underlying characteristic is linked inferentially to inferior social status, the visible feature functions as a social stigma.

Racism, like sexism, relies on inference tickets that transform a person's visible features into stigmata of his or her group's inferior social status by implying explanations and rationalizations of the social identity he or she shares with others. Nationalism, because it cannot always denote social identity by convenient reference to visible features of the human body, such as skin color and genitalia, must often employ cultural artifacts to play the roles of emblems and stigmata. Uniforms and flags, for example, function as emblems of nationality on the battlefield. The Star of David functioned as a stigma during the reign of National Socialism. Once supplied with a suitable set of visible markers, nationalism can, and typically does, disseminate stigmatizing inference tickets of its own. That it often takes over, and thereby reinforces, the markers of race and gender should not be surprising.

Black Nationalism responds to denigration of blackness and glorification of whiteness not by eschewing the visible markers essential to white racism but by changing their valences. The more extravagant forms of Black Nationalism simply reverse the valences. That is to say, they authorize inferences concerning whiteness and blackness that invert those authorized in the social system of white superiority. As Baldwin put it, referring to the outlook of Elijah Muhammad, "the sentiment is old; only the color is new":

> We were offered, as Nation of Islam doctrine, historical and divine proof that all white people are cursed, and are devils, and are about to be brought down. . . . But very little time was spent on theology, for one did not need to prove to a Harlem audience that all white men were devils. They were merely glad to have, at last, divine corroboration of their experience, to hear—and it was a tremendous thing to hear—that they had been lied to all these years and generations, and that their captivity was ending, for God was black.[1]

A more moderate form of Black Nationalism might refrain from mere reversal of the valences of whiteness and blackness in white racism, but it would still have to change them. Black Nationalism need not denigrate whiteness per se, but it does seem always to involve treating blackness as emblematic of something worthy of respect or admiration. That this is one source of its appeal to black people who have been stigmatized by white racism should go without saying, but it does help explain Black Nationalism's survival.

Of course, while all forms of Black Nationalism valorize blackness, they are hardly alone in doing so. Martin Luther King, Jr., is never classified as a Black Nationalist, yet he did use the concept of "negritude" to valorize blackness. He, like Elijah Muhammad, envisioned black Americans as a people. He, too, figured blackness as emblematic of something that black Americans share and in which they should take pride. But it seems likely that King was echoing the rhetoric of Black Nationalists when he made this move. The same can be said for other prominent critics of Black Nationalism, like Baldwin and Ellison, who also owed more than they always cared to admit to the movement they criticized.

Larry Neal was probably inflating such unacknowledged debts when, in an essay originally published in 1970, he termed Ellison a Black Nationalist. While distancing himself from Ellison's famous remark that "style is more important than political ideologies," Neal emphasized "the obvious theme of identity" in *Invisible Man*, the narrator's relentless search for a "usable" African-American past, and Ellison's deep engagement with "the murky world of [African-American] mythology and folklore, both of which are essential elements in the making of a people's history." Speaking more sweepingly, Neal went on to claim that "some form of nationalism is operative throughout all sections of the black community. The dominant political orientations shaping the sensibilities of many contemporary black writers fall roughly into the categories of cultural nationalism and revolutionary nationalism."[2] It is hard to know what to make of such remarks.

Since 1970 or so, debates over Black Nationalism, though often as heated as ever, have seldom been clear. Emotions run strong, but it is hard to say exactly what is at stake. It is common to find a pair of interlocutors locked in fierce disagreement over whether Black Nationalism is a good or a bad thing but unable to agree even on what it is that the one champions and the other abhors. But if the committed Black Nationalist favors one thing while the equally committed antinationalist opposes something else, on what do they really disagree? To what have they committed themselves apart from conflicting attitudes toward a label? Definitions and theories of Black Nationalism abound, yet their very abundance is apt to make one wonder whether there is anything specifiable for all of the sound and fury to signify, something that could retain the interest of disputants even when made clear.

The most instructive way of interpreting Neal's remarks is to suppose that they tell us more about what was happening to Black Nationalism as the sixties came to a close than they tell us about Ellison. If Ellison could now be counted as a Black Nationalist, then Black Nationalism itself had changed. In the process of becoming more inclusive, Black Nationalism had begun trying to absorb into its own canon figures formerly counted as paradigmatic opponents of the movement. Something was happening to the notion of Black Nationalism itself. The rules governing application of the label were changing.

Neal clearly intended his inclusive use of the term "nationalism" as a conciliatory gesture. While moderating his own nationalism, Neal had come to see less of himself in the figure of Ras (*Invisible Man's* unforgettable caricature of a Black Nationalist at the point of complete frustration). Meanwhile, he may have come to discern deeper concern in Ellison's writing for the peoplehood of black people than he had previously suspected. Classifying Ellison as a cultural nationalist implied that, to count as a nationalist, one need not share the revolutionary nationalist's aspiration to achieve some form of political sovereignty for African-Americans. But what would a cultural nationalist favor? Neal did not say. Because the political component of Black Nationalism was becoming fuzzy, the movement was increasingly concerned with promoting attitudes of a certain kind toward black culture.

Ellison saw this development coming in this stunning passage from his marvelous essay from the late 1970s, "The Little Man at Chehaw Station":

The proponents of ethnicity—ill concealing an underlying anxiety, and given a bizarre bebopish stridency by the obviously American vernacular inspiration of the costumes and rituals ragged out to dramatize their claims to ethnic (and genetic) insularity—have helped give our streets and campuses a rowdy, All Fool's Day, carnival atmosphere. In many ways, then, the call for a new social order based upon the glorification of ancestral blood and ethnic background acts as a call to cultural and aesthetic chaos. Yet while this latest farcical phase in the drama of American social hierarchy unfolds, the irrepressible movement of American culture toward integration of its most diverse elements continues, confounding the circumlocutions of its staunchest opponents.[3]

Two decades later, "the irrepressible movement of American culture toward integration of its most diverse elements" has become a far more worrisome thing, played out on a global scale in terms dictated by transnational corporations anxious to cash in on the diasporic identifications of consumers. The culture into which Black Nationalist style is now being absorbed is one in which successful rap artists, novelists, and professors become blips on the screen of an unending infomercial. It is also one in which commodities of all sorts are packaged as emblems of ethnic identities and marketed scientifically to the appropriately susceptible demographic enclaves. The "All Fool's Day, carnival atmosphere" is still here, and growing more chaotic, but now you can purchase its emblematic accoutrements from the local mall and subscribe to representations of diversity from your local cable provider. It is in the interest of the business elite to transform all forms of diasporic consciousness, functionally speaking, into obsession with life-style enclaves by commodifying the symbolic means of identification. People obsessed with buying their way into prestige within an ethnically defined life-style enclave are giving the business elite what they want in two ways: first, through the transfer of cash; second, by remaining oblivious to the widening gap between the managerial-professional class and the underclass in all racial groups.

Today many young people and merchandisers see Black Nationalism as a life-style that one literally buys into through the purchase of clothing reminiscent of Africa, sneakers endorsed by basketball stars, and tickets to the movies of Spike Lee. What teenagers and the business elite agree on tends these days to become social fact. The alternatives to cultural-nationalism-as-life-style are not ideologies, like democratic socialism and libertarian republicanism, but other life-styles made available on the same terms, like the one in which pretend colonialists drive Land Rovers while wearing clothing from Banana Republic. The former enclave is no more likely to provide resistance to the most important oppressive forces at work in this setting than the latter. If the Ellisonian dictum that "style is more important than political ideologies" now applies with a double-irony to

Black Nationalism itself, this hardly means that the movement has gradually come around to accepting an Ellisonian notion of what makes style important. Ellison's dictum expressed his commitment to the ethical-aesthetic ideal of living one's life as if one were creating a work of art, an ideal he seems to have associated with both Emerson and Duke Ellington. The political significance of recalling this commitment today is that it projects the image of a human being too marked by individuality to be content with the life-style options the business elite is merchandising. The social practices Ellison valued were all ones in which individuality, and thus resistance to the commodification of identity, is cultivated. Resistance to the commodification of identity is now the essential starting point for a politics of resistance. Some nationalists may want to canonize Ellison retrospectively, but neither *Invisible Man* nor Ellison's essay collections fit easily within their canon. His style offers a means for resisting the most important features of contemporary culture that is wholly lacking in the contemporary repertoire of Black Nationalism.

Two groups in particular appear to be insistent on defining *Black Nationalism* narrowly. The first is a cadre of radical political separatists intent on retaining the most extreme claims that have entered the movement's rhetorical repertoire during its most militant moments. The second is a set of black conservatives intent on holding everyone to their left equally responsible for those claims. The former group is content to treat Black Nationalism as the badge of their rhetorical extremism. The latter group is really trying to make liberals pay for the breadth of their toleration. Hyperbolic Black Nationalism is just sublime enough, by virtue of the strong intimation of danger it offers, to mesmerize both parties. Their attitudes toward it, pro and con, are both forms of fixation on the sublime.

The question that really divides Neal from Ellison is how much and in what way African-Americans should care about their own peoplehood, given that there are other things (including the broader civic nation) that might be worth caring about. Answering this question well is infinitely more important than deciding which answers to count as nationalist. Beyond a certain point, the term just gets in the way. If nationalists want to redefine their "ism" for the purpose of converting their old opponents into so-called nationalists, and we find this confusing, we can always respond by using the new definition as a standing license to substitute *definiens* for *definiendum*. By thus eliminating the term "nationalism" itself when it seems a distraction, we can easily turn our attention back to the question of how much and in what way one should care about one's ethnic or racial community under circumstances like ours.[4]

Black Nationalism puts the discourse of race and the discourse of nation together. It does so by projecting an imagined national community—a people—for whom blackness serves as an emblem. What is it, then, that black

Americans share, as Black Nationalists imagine them? There have been many answers to this question, but here are some of them:

(a) a common biological or ontological essence;

(b) a common origin in a particular place, namely Africa;

(c) a common history of suffering and humiliation, based on attributions of racial identity linked to denigrated social status;

(d) a common culture, including music, food, folkways, stories, and rites;

(e) a common destiny, given the likelihood that the entire people will endure the same fate from here on out;

(f) a common interest in the achievement of certain ends, such as return to the place of origin, political sovereignty in some newly assigned territory, or economic and cultural self-determination; and

(g) a common interest in employing the means thought necessary to achieve their legitimate ends, such as mass emigration, revolutionary violence, or economic and cultural separatism.

Items (a) through (d) are essentially retrospective and refer to the putative sources of African-American peoplehood. These items may be grouped thematically under the heading of piety. They have all been treated in Black Nationalism as sources on which African-Americans depend for their existence and progress through life and to which African Americans therefore ought to respond with appropriate expressions of gratitude and loyalty. Item (c) is also a focal point for the expression of anger. Items (e) through (g) are essentially prospective and refer to the people's future. They may be grouped thematically under the heading of aspiration. The ends and means of Black Nationalists can themselves of course be broken down into political, economic, and cultural elements, which have received varying interpretations and varying degrees of emphasis at different times.

It should be obvious from the structure of this scheme that it provides for the possibility of countless permutations of the basic themes of Black Nationalism and no criterion for drawing the line, once and for all, between Black Nationalism and its siblings. This is as it should be, for it is unhelpfully ahistorical to assign Black Nationalism an unchanging essence. It would be possible to specify a type of Black Nationalism in relation to this scheme by assigning an appropriate interpretation to each item on the list. The spectrum of interpretations for each item ranges from weak to strong. With respect to most items, the more an interpretation emphasizes separation or difference of African-Americans from other groups, the stronger that interpretation would be. A thinker who assigned weak interpretations to each item would not count as a nationalist at all. A thinker who assigned strong interpretations to each item would count as an extreme nationalist.

But it is also possible to assign strong interpretations to some items while assigning moderate or weak interpretations to others. The type Neal refers to as cultural nationalism, for example, would assign a strong reading to (d) and a strong reading to the cultural component of (f) while assigning weaker readings to some other variables.

The scheme also shows why Neal's distinction between revolutionary and cultural types of Black Nationalism tends to confuse the issue. The notion of revolutionary nationalism focuses on a type of *means* for achieving nationalist aspirations, whereas the contrasting notion of cultural nationalism appears to focus on either a type of nationalist *end*, which may or may not exhaust a particular nationalist's aspirations, or an object of nationalist *piety*. Neal increases the confusion by referring to both of his basic types as "political orientations." He says neither whether they are exhaustive nor whether it is possible, without contradicting oneself, to hold both orientations at once. He does not say what qualifies cultural nationalism as cultural and what qualifies it as political. If the mark of cultural nationalism is that it aspires to achieve cultural objectives (or cultural objectives alone) by political means, whereas revolutionary nationalism aspires to achieve political objectives (as well as cultural ones?) by political means, what about the attempt to achieve political objectives by nonrevolutionary means? Neal's typology and others like it had better be left aside.

Ellison and Baldwin both cared deeply but not exclusively about the peoplehood of American blacks. They embraced a conception of African-American peoplehood emphasizing, from the preceding list, (c) the community's common history of suffering, (d) the value of its cultural heritage, and (e) its common destiny. They rejected (a) the notion of a shared biological or ontological essence. They acknowledged but played down the significance of (b) the notion of a common place of origin, by distinguishing it from (a) and assimilating it to (c) and (d). Africa, for them, was simply a mapmaker's arbitrary name for an expansive, culturally diverse, geographical region in which many distinct peoples have lived. Having ancestors from part of what we now call Gambia would not connect anyone to an African essence equally instantiated in what we now call Egypt or Algeria. Ellison and Baldwin envisioned no such essence. Nor did they imagine that there was once an African golden age. The historical fantasies of today's Afrocentrists would be grist for Ellisonian parody. Baldwin rejected the similar fantasies of an earlier generation when he said that "in order to change a situation one has first to see it for what it is: in the present case, to accept the fact, whatever one does with it thereafter, that the Negro has been formed by this nation [i.e., America], for better or worse, and does not belong to any other—not to Africa, and certainly not to Islam."[5]

Baldwin wished "that the Muslim movement [i.e., the Nation of Islam] had been able to inculcate in the demoralized Negro population a . . . *more individual* sense of its own worth."[6] He meant that the thing shared by the African-American people need not and should not be a sense of fusion, in which individuals experience a loss of separate identity as they merge collectively into an undifferentiated mass. The members of a community do not necessarily experience their bond intensely or agree with one another on a ranking of the highest values. Neither need they imagine themselves to be the vehicles of a common will.[7] The African-American people, like other peoples, have only rarely and fleetingly, if ever, been bound together so tightly as that. This should be considered a good thing, a sign of the individuality that flourishes in free conditions, not something to be overcome by corrective measures.

Baldwin was also a critic of Black Nationalist piety. At their worst, nationalists everywhere have invented and then venerated wholly fabricated pasts, the phoniness of which is palpable to anyone not caught up in collective wishful thinking. Black Nationalists have concocted more than a few of their own. When Baldwin introduced his discussion of the Nation of Islam in "Down at the Cross" by reflecting at length on his early experiences in the Christian church, he simultaneously established ironic distance from both his own former piety and Elijah Muhammad's Muslim variety. This rhetorical move allowed his doubts about the former to undercut the appeal of the latter as well. "Being in the pulpit was like being in the theatre," wrote Baldwin of his days as a youth preacher; "I was behind the scenes and knew how the illusion was worked."[8] The stage has been set for us to see through the illusions at work in Elijah Muhammad's preaching as well:

> This truth is that at the very beginning of time there was not one white face to be found in all the universe. Black men ruled the earth and the black man was perfect. This is the truth concerning the era that white men now refer to as prehistoric. They want black men to believe that they, like white men, once lived in caves and swung from trees and ate their meat raw and did not have the power of speech. But this is not true. Black men were never in such a condition.[9]

The cure for such illusions, as Baldwin put in "Everybody's Protest Novel," consisted of frank acknowledgment that black and white Americans, oppressed and oppressors, "both alike depend on the same reality."[10] The piety of the Nation of Islam simply could not, from Baldwin's point of view, do justice to the realities of mutual dependence among peoples in America.

Ellison's *Invisible Man* can be read, on one level, as a rigorous rethinking of what black Americans owe, culturally speaking, to the traditions of black-American life. It is this pious dimension of the novel that makes Neal want to canonize it. But the kind of piety Ellison expresses toward the traditions of his people, especially toward the tradition of the blues, is a more complicated and subtle thing than any form of Black Nationalism thus far developed in the United States appears able to accommodate. One reason for this is Ellison's way of connecting it to the more general question of what all Americans owe, culturally speaking, to the multiple traditions of American life, black and white. Ellison's detailed acknowledgment of dependence on the various cultural sources of American life is, to my mind, one of the supreme accomplishments of our literature. It is at odds with any form of piety grounded in identification with only one people.[11]

Black Nationalism is not only a vehicle for expressing piety, directed toward the past, but also a vehicle for expressing aspirations, directed toward the future. Ellison and Baldwin charged it with being as unrealistic on the second count as it was on the first. Even relatively curtailed forms of Black Nationalist aspiration seemed to them a tissue of fantasies. Where Black Nationalism in the United States amounts to anything more than vague calls for self-help, self-respect, and recognition—when, for example, it strives for some fairly definite form of separation from American culture, the broader economic system, or the civic nation—it comes up against some hard realities. First, the more ambitious objectives entertained by Black Nationalists, such as political sovereignty for black America, cannot be achieved by any known means. Second, few black Americans would be willing to emigrate to a homeland, either in Africa or somewhere in the United States, even if it somehow became available. Third, the milder forms of separatism, be they economic or cultural, would themselves entail costs that few black Americans would be willing to endure.

The declining significance of political goals within Black Nationalism now manifests itself in nostalgia for the sixties. Many people initially attracted to Black Nationalism have been prepared to admit that the political, economic, and cultural aspirations with which the movement started are unrealistic, but they have been reluctant nonetheless to abandon identification with the movement. Perhaps the reason they do not see themselves as having left the nationalist fold is that they retain the old aspirations of Black Nationalism in the modified form of velleities. Full-fledged aspiration involves intending an end, willing the means necessary for the achievement of that end, and believing that the end can be achieved. A velleity, in contrast, involves what might be called subjunctive or counterfactual willing: if the situation *were* different from the actual one in certain relevant respects, I *would*. . . . The velleities of contemporary Black Nationalism lend it a somewhat wistful tone. This tone expresses a longing for a previous state of affairs in which the original aspirations of the movement at least *seemed* credible.

If Black Nationalism has been weakened in the United States by the apparently unrealistic nature of its original aspirations, one reason for the movement's success in attracting interest and respect in this context has been its capacity to express anger. Some blacks who would admit to finding the pieties of the movement puerile and the political program of the movement unpalatable still turn to Black Nationalist oratory for cathartic release of their outrage against injustice and hatred. They are attracted by its rhetoric of excess—the obviousness of the villains, the clarity of the passions invoked, the *fantasy* of imagined vengeance. They are looking for what Roland Barthes calls "excessive gestures, exploited to the limit of their meaning."[12] Barthes is referring here to professional wrestling, not to the speeches of Louis Farrakhan, but much of what he says would apply to the latter, as well. For blacks who take delight in Farrakhan's rhetoric of excess without ever thinking of converting to his sect, the oratory conjures up a spectacle that functions expressively more or less as a professional wrestling match does. As Barthes argues in reference to wrestling, "What is . . . displayed for the public is the great spectacle of Suffering, Defeat, and Justice. Wrestling presents man's suffering with all the amplification of tragic masks. . . . Suffering which appeared without intelligible cause would not be understood. . . . On the contrary suffering appears as inflicted with emphasis and conviction, for everyone must not only see that the man suffers, but also and above all understand why he suffers" (M, 19f.). "But what wrestling is above all meant to portray," Barthes continues, "is a purely moral concept: that of justice. The idea of 'paying' is essential to wrestling, and the crowd's 'Give it to him' means above all else 'Make him pay' " (M, 21).

The nastiest product of Farrakhan's rhetoric, which has of course received much attention, is the scapegoating of Jews.[13] Cornel West argues:

> In fact, the media will project Farrakhan as attracting black folk because he is anti-Semitic and [imply that] black folk want to hear anti-Semitic rhetoric. There is no doubt in my mind that Farrakhan has deep xenophobic elements in his rhetoric, but that is not why the majority of black people come to listen to him, you see. They come to listen to him because he symbolizes boldness. And they don't join his organization because they don't see the kind of moral integrity they want.[14]

As I see it, Farrakhan's boldness consists in having the courage of his pieties (which provide grounds for the assertion of black pride), his aspirations (which include the "Make them pay" element of fantasized vengeance against the forces of evil as he imagines them), and his anger (which is directed at the perpetrators of injustice as he imagines them). By increasing the audience's sense of danger, an effect he achieves through mythic amplification and personification of the forces of evil, Farrakhan is able to make himself more believable in the audience's eyes as a personification of boldness. But this means that "mythic amplification and personification of the forces of evil" are essential to the performance, even if we take the personification of hyperbolic boldness to be the main attraction for an audience too long made to feel meek and powerless. If I am right about this, two points deserve emphasis. First, scapegoating appears indispensable to the process through which Farrakhan "symbolizes boldness" in his own person. Second, the prospect of being emboldened, of having one's self-image vicariously enlarged and empowered, can be part of what makes scapegoating so attractive psychologically to those who resort to it. For most members of the audience, the scapegoating of Jews may be an affair of the imagination that stops short of licensing actual violence, but this hardly suffices to make the sentiments being expressed ethically acceptable.

Some black intellectuals who distance themselves from anti-Semitism maintain, nonetheless, that only a rhetoric of excess can do expressive justice to the realities of black anger and descriptive justice to the brutalities that have provoked it. Their hope, apparently, is that the scapegoating function of the rhetoric, in which white devils and Jews are made to personify the evils that flow from racial oppression, can be separated from the rhetoric's other devices for expressing the full depth and extent of those evils. They read the early speeches of Malcolm X for the same reason they read Richard Wright's novels, as witnesses responding in the only appropriate way to an excessively bad situation. They suspect that Baldwin and Ellison, who criticized both Black Nationalist rhetoric and Wright's "protest novels" for their excesses, simply failed to respond adequately to the experience of suffering and injustice blacks have endured in this country.

Why need readers feel compelled to choose between Malcolm X's speeches and Wright's novels, on the one hand, and the writings of Baldwin and Ellison, on the other? There are good reasons for keeping all of them on our shelves and syllabi. They do different things for their audiences that need doing. Critics who dismiss Baldwin and Ellison underestimate the resources they offer for coming to terms with outrage and with outrageous circumstances. The point of departure for Ellison's fiction was the realization "that it was not enough" for him simply to be angry, or simply to present horrendous events or ironic events.[15] He transmuted his anger into the literary analogue of a blues sensibility, which hovers at the borderline between tragedy and comedy, borrowing tonalities from each. Anyone who thinks that the anger is not there or is not deep is not reading very carefully. The comic elements are called upon in accordance with the maxim that the "greater the stress within society the stronger the comic antidote required."[16] But they are called upon in such a way that they are never allowed to cancel out the force of the tragic elements to which they respond. The comic elements in Ellison's prose are deliberately compensatory, which is to say that they keep close company with grief and despair but ultimately modify and transcend them.

A Raft of Hope

Ellison's doubts about Wright's success as a novelist aspiring to social realism centered on the incongruity between Wright's depiction of black-American circumstances and Wright's own existence as a writer. There seemed to be nothing in the depiction that could account for the possibility of someone "as intelligent, as creative or as dedicated as [Wright] himself."[17] Ellison concluded that Wright had not adequately accounted for the cultural sources of his own existence and progress through life. Ellison therefore set himself the literary task of reimagining his social circumstances as a black American so that an articulate protagonist—one capable of a blues sensibility, like his own—could be rendered intelligible in them. The narrator-protagonist of *Invisible Man* would be "a blues-toned laugher-at-wounds who included himself in his indictment of the human condition."[18] The prime difficulty Ellison had to face in rendering such a character intelligible was that of describing evils of the kind he had experienced *and* the life of an articulate, spiritually resilient protagonist as products of the *same* situation. (This is Ellison's version of the problem of point of view that we meet again in the new traditionalism.) The ethical and political interest of the task lay in its requirement that he attend simultaneously to the reasons for anger, the temptations to despair, and the grounds for hope in his situation. It is no accident that Ellison's preface refers to the novel as "a raft of hope," or that the novel ends by referring to "the lower frequencies" as the register in which he "speaks for" his reader.[19] What did Ellison mean by a raft of hope? It would seem to be what Kenneth Burke, his friend and interlocutor, meant by a "structure of encouragement" in the following passage:

> Suppose that, gnarled as I am, I did not consider it enough simply to seek payment for my gnarledness, the establishment of communion [between writer and reader] through evils held in common? Suppose I would also erect a structure of encouragement, for all of us? How should I go about it, in the sequence of imagery, not merely to bring us most poignantly *into* hell, but also *out* again?[20]

The best social criticism, it seems to me, takes precisely this form.

There are, I think, two main reasons for the survival of Black Nationalism. The first, which I have already emphasized, is simply the depth of justified anger into which Black Nationalism has so successfully tapped. The second is simply a paucity of political alternatives for addressing the underlying injustices. Both of these reasons ought to be of serious concern to the entire body politic. The rhetorical excess of Black Nationalism reflects the gravity of the wrongs to which it responds. We have allowed ourselves to slip into a cycle of mistrust that makes it hard to persuade

those who have ceased to identify with the civic nation that there is something tangible to be gained by identifying with it. The only fully adequate
response to the anger being expressed is to remove the injustices that have
provoked it. It still needs to be said, however, that Black Nationalism, like
the new traditionalism, reduces the possibility of building large-scale coalitions of the kind needed to achieve large-scale reforms. Without the coalitions, there will be no such reforms. Without the reforms, the underlying
injustices will remain.

"Today blood magic and blood thinking, never really dormant in American society, are rampant among us. . . . And while this goes on," Ellison
remarked some time ago, "the challenge of arriving at an adequate definition of American cultural identity goes unanswered."[21] We have all in the
meantime become complicit in social arrangements that condemn the
wretched of all races and nations to consume, if anything at all, a stream
of images, insignia, and other substances that dull their sensibilities. But
what shall we do? What alternatives do we have?

When accounting for which reformist political movements from the fif-
ties and sixties are surviving in the early years of a new millennium, it is
important to keep in mind the nature of the new environment. Communism has dropped out of the picture altogether, for obvious reasons relating
to global political change and its own history of horrific injustices. Black
Nationalism seems to have adapted in part by allowing its political aspirations to be transformed into a pattern of velleities and life-style ambitions.
In the democratic Left, the velleity aspect is somewhat present, for lack of
consensus about how to make things better. The life-style aspect combines
backpack green, bohemian black, and hard-rock loud. Its representative
voices are a handful of intellectuals, activists, and rock artists whose images
strike the infotainment producers as a salable product. The sound bites
sound radical, but the political effect remains unclear. Perhaps adapting to
the new setting in this way is not necessarily a good thing. As Ellison
taught, there are advantages as well as disadvantages to being invisible.

One can take some consolation from the thought that things have been
this bad, or worse, before. Emerson, Whitman, and Thoreau found a way
to make a difference even when the battle over the meaning of democracy
degenerated into civil war. The tide against which Ellison launched his
"raft of hope" a century later must have seemed nearly as bleak as that—
bleak enough to require strong compensatory measures. In what, then, did
his hope reside? In the style of the raft and the integrity of its maker, in
the place he stood upon when crafting it, in the materials from which he
built it. It also resided in the traditions, African and American and European, from which he drew those materials; and in all the people and practices and institutions, fragile and fallible as they might be, that inspired and
sustained him in the making. These things are all grounds for hope in our

lives today. The same democratic legacy can be our inheritance, should we choose to claim it.

No religious thinker has recently done more to identify and revive the Baldwin-Ellison critique of Black Nationalism than Cornel West. His model of public engagement also offers a self-consciously democratic alternative to the implicitly antidemocratic forms of traditionalism now gaining influence in many religious communities. West and I both identify with a pragmatic intellectual tradition in which Emerson, Whitman, and Dewey—as well as Baldwin and Ellison—figure prominently. But we differ over the grounds of democratic hope in a way that leaves me closer to Ellison and him closer to an Augustinian like Reinhold Niebuhr. West's hope is the fruit of a leap of faith in the face of facts that are not hopeful. It is a hope against hope, always mindful of tragic realities around him. He is a Christian, he says, because otherwise he would go insane.[22] His criticism is cast in the prophetic mode—inspirational in tone, progressive in vision, and admonitory in content. His writings and speeches are often tinged with images of evil and death, two themes he thinks his fellow pragmatists have rarely confronted with sufficient candor. Ours is a "twilight civilization," he says, echoing Eliot's imagery of the wasteland but with a political intent unlike Eliot's.[23]

As responses to evil go, Ellison's comic compensations strike me as preferable to Eliot's elegant moaning.[24] The former seems more profound to my ear than the latter. Ellison's spirituality expresses itself in a blues-influenced recognition that even though things are always quite bad in many respects, it is an artist's business to catalogue the details in a style that leaves room for humor and for hope. The artful trick is to hold the grounds for hope and the catalogue of evils together in the same style, with neither cancelled out by the other. Eliot's wasteland mood is shallow optimism standing on its head. It is a form of alienation that is of a piece with his Anglophilia and traditionalism, both of which look away from his own people to find hope and value in some other place and time. My democratic wager is that the grounds for this-worldly hope and the evils we need to resist are both to be found among the people.

Because he grounds his hope religiously in sources that transcend our social situation, the prophetic social critic might be tempted to dismiss Ellison's effort at finding grounds for hope in that situation as unnecessary and self-deceptive. Prophets of a supernatural God, whether nationalist or universalist, Muslim or Christian, are not merely singing the blues when they lament this-worldly pain, excoriate this-worldly evil, and proclaim hope in a transcendent redeemer. In their eyes, the intimations of goodness in our current social situation, including the prophet's own voice, always have transcendent sources, so the prophet can easily slide into describing the situation itself as essentially rotten without causing a problem of self-referential consistency for the describer. Meanwhile, anger and despair can be given full play in a rhetoric of excess, because the hoped-for compensatory factors are believed to be both wholly other and backed by omnipotent force. The rhetorical exercise of a familiar sort of prophet is to bring oneself (and the audience) as close to despair as possible, in the name of a realistic view of evil. Then, after pausing for breath, the prophet veers heavenward at the last moment, thanking Allah or Jesus for the gift of hope against hope.

The theological antidote for this rhetoric of excess, at least from a mainstream Augustinian perspective, has always been to stress that God not only created this world, but also declared it good, and remains its gracious ruler despite the temporary triumphs of sin. If the world is essentially good, but thrown out of whack by sin, the fitting response to it is not rejection, but an ambivalent mixture of affirmation and condemnation. The affirmative component of this attitude involves a constant search for signs of divine creative energy and redemptive spirit in the workings of the world. At his best, West faithfully expounds this sort of Augustinianism, which he learned from reading Niebuhr's writings from the 1930s. But there are also moments, as in *The Future of the Race*, when he sounds less like Niebuhr and more like Eliot or Wright.

Ellison's blues sensibility, although quite distinct in its religious content, has much in common with Niebuhrian ambivalence at the practical level. He was aware of the style of prophetic excess, and self-consciously avoided it in his own prose. In the Ellisonian blues, good and evil, powers divine and satanic, are all mixed up both in our social situation and in ourselves and are to be dealt with by means of whatever this-worldly social magic and lyrical coping we can muster. Once Ellison embraced this quasi-religious outlook, he had no choice, on pain of despair, but to locate grounds for hope *in* the social situation itself. His hopefulness, which he sometimes misleadingly called "optimism," did not derive from gilding the lily. He took evil and anger as seriously as has any American writer. Coping lyrically with evil is not a way of ignoring it or minimizing it but a way of surviving it, of enduring.

Democratic hope, whether tempered by Augustinian ambivalence or a blues sensibility like Ellison's, is the hope of making a difference for the better by democratic means. The question of hope is whether a difference can be made, not whether progress is being made or whether human beings will work it all out in the end. You are still making a difference when you are engaged in a successful holding action against forces that are conspiring to make things worse than they are. You are even making a difference when your actions simply keep things from worsening to the extent they would have worsened if you had not acted. The failure to achieve progress, though common enough in democratic experience, should not be allowed to sap

democratic aspiration altogether. There is still a beneficial role for democratic efforts even in regressive eras, if only a difference can be made. If
you make hope depend on the thought that things are going to keep getting
better, or on the thought that things will all work out in the end, then you
are bound to be demoralized before long. There is no persuasive evidence
for members of our generation that things are getting better on the whole
or that everything will work out in historical time. If, however, you set your
sights on making a difference, you can give hope a foothold in the life of
the people itself. Hope is not the only ingredient that goes into the work
of justice. Courage, imagination, practical wisdom, generosity, sympathy,
and luck all play their parts. But without hope, the other ingredients count
for nothing. It is therefore no small matter for democratic citizens to find
reasons for hope in the here and now, whatever their religious differences
might be. This is a task that Augustinians can share with the likes of Ellison
and Emerson.

A democratic critic is disposed to condone certain sorts of practices,
traits, and institutions, and to denounce others. Commitment to democracy obliges a critic to discriminate the one from the other. Yet a danger
arises right away, because the act of critical discrimination, if performed
without care and tact as well as suspicion of privilege, threatens to dismem-
ber the people, inviting one faction to exclude another from participation
in the body politic.

For critics inclined to think that good and evil come in large, unalloyed
units, needing only to be weighed on the universal scale and labeled like a
package at the post office, the task appears straightforward. One need only
call every form of evil by its name, identify with its victims, and fight the
good fight. But if good and evil are both here and there, forever alloyed,
in my heart and my party (and perhaps even in the standards I employ), as
well as in those of my plutocratic or racist enemy, then the task is bound
to be delicate and difficult. Democratic criticism begins at home, with
omissions and commissions our allies would sooner ignore. In the act of
finding fault with the people as they are, in holding them largely "canker'd,
crude, superstitious, and rotten," but identifying oneself with that people
all the while, one aims to forge a people capable of democracy. It is remarkable that Whitman and Ellison can say such negative things about the people, and mean them, in the context of essays intended mainly to be generous and encouraging.

Surgeons are not praised for the depth of their rage against disease but
for their contribution to a patient's survival and well-being. We want their
incisions to be wisely chosen and supple in execution, not as deep as can
be. Leaving the patient intact is a minimal criterion of success. Yet we
stupidly prize the wrong kinds of depth in our critics, forgetting that a
democratic critic, who serves the people as a whole, should leave the people

whole at the end of the day. Even the line between the friends and foes of democracy cannot be drawn too violently without defeating its purpose.

An account of the ethical life of democracy, if it wishes to remain democratic in its consequences, must therefore temper its invective against injustice with generosity. Courage and generosity are both cardinal virtues of democratic intellectuals. If a critic's indictment of society is too general, if the debunking becomes too thorough, it is only fair to ask how the critic, as a member of the society in question, proposes to keep the indictment unindicted. An overly general indictment self-destructs like a letter bomb upon delivery. When critics go too far, their opponents rightly charge them with self-contradiction, with an inability to account consistently for the critique itself. The temptation is then to sidestep the charge by claiming a perspective distinct from that of the society under indictment. But this entails that anyone who attains the critic's perspective acquires membership in a morally privileged group, above or apart from the people. It is but a small step from this claim to an antidemocratic politics.

I take for granted that our condition is always bad enough in some respects to disturb anybody with a conscience—bad enough today, surely, to bring a democrat close to despair. Because these respects change somewhat over time, a critic does well to say what they are in precise language free of cant and resentment. I also take for granted, as a postulate of practical faith, that there are grounds for hope and humor if we look hard enough in the right places. This was true for the survivors of the Holocaust and for the victims of chattel slavery, so it must be true for us. There being no virtue in demoralization, a social critic had better keep an eye out for inspiring incidents and comic relief as well as portents of disaster. By mentioning the former along with the latter, Ellison meant to mitigate not outrage but despair. As his namesake, Emerson, wrote, "I do not wish to push my criticism on the state of things around me to that extravagant mark, that shall compel me to suicide, or to an absolute isolation from the advantages of civil society."[25]

PART TWO

Religious Voices in a Secular Society

Who are you indeed who would talk or sing to America?
Have you studied out the land, its idioms and men?...
Have you possess'd yourself of the Federal Constitution?...
Do you see who have left all feudal processes and poems
    behind them, and assumed the poems and processes of
    Democracy?...

What is this you bring my America?...
Have you not imported this or the spirit of it in some ship?
Is it not a mere tale?

—Whitman

Chapter 3

RELIGIOUS REASONS
IN POLITICAL ARGUMENT

RELIGIOUS DIVERSITY, like racial diversity, has been a source of discord throughout American history. Most Americans claim to be religious, but their convictions are hardly cut from the same cloth. Given that some of these convictions are thought to have highly important political implications, we should not be surprised to hear them expressed when citizens are exchanging reasons for their respective political views. Secular liberals find the resulting cacophony deeply disturbing. Some of them have strongly urged people to restrain themselves from bringing their religious commitments with them into the political sphere. Many religious people have grown frustrated at the unwillingness of the liberal elite to hear them out on their own terms, and have recently had much to say against the hypocrisies and biases of secularism. Freedom of religion now strikes some prominent theologians as a secularist ruse designed to reduce religion to insignificance. Part 2 of this book tries to make sense of this controversy.

Freedom of religion consists first of all in the right to make up one's own mind when answering religious questions. These include, but are not limited to, such questions as whether God exists, how God should be conceived, and what responsibilities, if any, human beings have in response to God's actions with regard to them. Freedom of religion also consists in the right to act in ways that seem appropriate, given one's answers to religious questions—provided that one does not cause harm to other people or interfere with their rights. Among the expressive acts obviously protected by this right are rituals and other devotional practices performed in solitude, in the context of one's family, or in association with others similarly disposed. More controversial, however, is a class of acts that express religious commitments in another way, namely, by employing them as reasons when taking a public stand on political issues. What role, if any, should religious premises play in the reasoning citizens engage in when they make and defend political decisions?

The free expression of religious premises is morally underwritten not only by the value we assign to the freedom of religion, but also by the value we assign to free expression, generally. All citizens of a constitutional democracy possess not only the right to make up their minds as they see fit but also the right to express their reasoning freely, whatever that reasoning may be. It is plausible to suppose that the right to free expression of religious commitments is especially weighty in contexts where political issues are being discussed, for this is where rulers and elites might be most inclined to enforce restraint. Any citizen who chooses to express religious reasons for a political conclusion would seem, then, to enjoy the protection of two rights in doing so: freedom of religion and freedom of expression. And these rights not only have the legal status of basic constitutional provisions, but also hold a prominent place in the broader political culture. Otherwise, the framers of the U.S. Constitution would not have had reason to affirm them explicitly in the Bill of Rights.

I have no doubt that the expression of religious reasons should be protected in these ways. Indeed, I would encourage religiously committed citizens to make use of their basic freedoms by expressing their premises in as much depth and detail as they see fit when trading reasons with the rest of us on issues of concern to the body politic. If they are discouraged from speaking up in this way, we will remain ignorant of the real reasons that many of our fellow citizens have for reaching some of the ethical and political conclusions they do. We will also deprive them of the central democratic good of expressing themselves to the rest of us on matters about which they care deeply. If they do not have this opportunity, we will lose the chance to learn from, and to critically examine, what they say. And they will have good reason to doubt that they are being shown the respect that all of us owe to our fellow citizens as the individuals they are.

Of course, having a right does not necessarily mean that one would be justified in exercising it. Clearly, there are circumstances in which it would be imprudent or disrespectful for someone to reason solely from religious premises when defending a political proposal. But some philosophers hold, more controversially, that such circumstances are more the exception than the rule. Richard Rorty, the most important contemporary pragmatist, has claimed that reasoning from religious premises to political conclusions is nowadays either imprudent, improper, or both. The late John Rawls, the most distinguished political philosopher of our time, at first defended a similarly restrictive view. He later made a concession to free expression by qualifying that policy somewhat, but still considered it improper to introduce religious reasons into public discussion of matters of basic justice unless those reasons are redeemed in the long run by reasons of a different kind. In this chapter, turning first to Rawls and then to Rorty, I will explain why their arguments for these positions fail to persuade me. The point is not to refute them, but to provide a rationale for approaching the topic differently.

Religion and Public Reason

In a religiously plural society, it will often be rhetorically ineffective to argue from religious premises to political conclusions. When citizens are deeply divided over the relevant religious questions, arguing in this way is rarely likely to increase support for one's conclusions. Sometimes such reasoning not only fails to win support, but also causes offence. Reasoning from religious premises to political conclusions can imply disrespect for those who do not accept those premises. For example, such reasoning can be calculated to convey the undemocratic message that one must accept a particular set of religious premises to participate in political debate at all. In the United States, such a message is now often reserved for atheists and Muslims, but Jews and Catholics can still occasionally sense it in the air. Therefore, there are moral as well as strategic reasons for self-restraint. Fairness and respectful treatment of others are central moral concerns.

Rawls begins with such concerns, arguing as follows. Political policies, when enacted in law, are backed by the coercive power of the state. To be recognized as a free and equal citizen of such a state is to be treated as someone to whom reasons must be offered, on request, when political policies are under consideration. The reasons that are demanded are not just any reasons. Each citizen may rightfully demand reasons why *he or she* should view the proposed policy as legitimate. It does not suffice in this context to be told why other people, on the basis of their idiosyncratic premises and collateral commitments, have reached this conclusion. It is not enough for a speaker to show that he or she is entitled to consider a proposal legitimate. The question on each concerned citizen's mind will rightly be, "Why should *I* accept this?" Fairness and respect require an honest effort, on the part of any citizen advocating a policy, to justify it to other reasonable citizens who may be approaching the issue from different points of view.

So far, so good. Proper treatment of one's fellow citizens does seem to require an honest justificatory effort of this sort. When proposing a political policy one should do one's best to supply reasons for it that people occupying other points of view could reasonably accept. I wholeheartedly embrace this ideal when it is phrased in this (relatively weak) way. But Rawls goes much further than this.

He argues that citizens should aspire to fulfill a much more demanding ideal of public reason. The unqualified version of this ideal, put forward in the original clothbound edition of *Political Liberalism*, held that our reasoning in the public forum should appeal strictly to ideals and principles that no reasonable person could reasonably reject.[1] By agreeing to abide by such principles and to rely solely on them when reasoning in the public forum, citizens enter a social contract. The contract specifies the fair terms of social cooperation in the form of justice as fairness. According to this conception of justice, the principles of the social contract are those we would select as a basis for social cooperation if we were behind a "veil of ignorance." Behind the veil, we would not know such facts about ourselves as our race, gender, medical condition, intellectual capacities, religious commitments, or comprehensive moral outlook. In ignorance of these facts, but still looking out in a reasonable way for our interests in the resulting system of social cooperation, we would be bound to select fair principles. Political liberalism does not put forward this conception of justice as a component of a comprehensive moral outlook, whether religious or secular. This conception of justice is not premised on a doctrine of what our true good ultimately consists in, on a view of the meaning of life, or even on the full-fledged Kantian liberalism Rawls had defended in *A Theory of Justice*. It is a "free-standing political conception," put forward in the hope that it can become and remain the object of a stable "overlapping consensus" among reasonable persons holding conflicting comprehensive doctrines. As such, it gives priority to the rightness of fair social cooperation, insofar as this might conflict with some idea of the good.

Many of Rawls's religious readers have been prepared to grant that some version of the veil of ignorance would be useful in fleshing out a defensible notion of fairness. A principle designed to regulate economic life, for example, should be chosen from a point of view in which we don't know whether we will end up being among the least well-off. A principle regulating discrimination in hiring should be chosen from a point of view in which we feign ignorance of our gender and racial identities. Fair enough. But Rawls's critics have long expressed doubts about similarly excluding knowledge of one's comprehensive religious and philosophical commitments. Rawls allows those behind the veil of ignorance to have access to a "thin" conception of the good, but his critics hold that in drawing the line between a thin conception and their own comprehensive doctrines, he is begging the question in favor of his own liberal views. For this is the move that underwrites two key components of Rawlsian liberalism: the priority of the right over the good and the conception of public reason with which we are concerned here. The critics protest that neither of these key ideas can meet the high standard Rawls proposes for judging such matters: these are both notions that a reasonable person could reasonably reject.

Public reason, Rawls says, "is public in three ways: as the reason of citizens as such, it is the reason of the public; its subject is the good of the public and matters of fundamental justice; and its nature and content is public, being given by the ideals and principles expressed by society's conception of political justice, and conducted open to view on that basis" (PL,

213). The limits of public reason are meant to apply to deliberation on essential constitutional provisions and matters of basic justice, not to political deliberation on lesser matters (PL, 214). The ideal of circumspection pertains not only to the reasoning of legislators and other officials, but also to the reasons citizens use when arguing for candidates for public office and when deciding how to vote "when constitutional essentials and matters of basic justice are at stake" (PL, 215). These are the sorts of contexts Rawls has in mind when he refers to the public forum. He classifies reasoning expressed in other contexts, such as a university or church colloquium, as private (PL, 220). All of these points are essential from Rawls's point of view. Neglecting any of them makes the ideal of public reason seem much more restrictive than he intends it to be.

Now consider the crucial notion of ideals and principles that no reasonable person could reasonably reject. What is a "reasonable person"? As Rawls sees it, "knowing that people are reasonable where others are concerned, we know that they are willing to govern their conduct by a principle from which they and others can reason in common" (PL, 49 n. 1). What public reason requires of citizens is that they be reasonable in the Rawlsian sense. And this means being willing to accept a common basis for reasoning that others, similarly motivated, could not reasonably reject. In short, to be reasonable is to accept the need for a social contract and to be willing to reason on the basis of it, at least when deliberating in the public forum on basic constitutional and political matters. This definition implicitly imputes *unreasonableness* to everyone who opts out of the contractarian project, regardless of the *reasons* they might have for doing so. "Persons are reasonable in one basic aspect when, among equals say, they are ready to propose principles and standards as fair terms of cooperation and to abide by them willingly, given the assurance that others will likewise do so. Those norms they view *as reasonable for everyone to accept and therefore as justifiable to them*" (PL, 49; emphasis added). "By contrast, people are unreasonable in the same basic aspect when they plan to engage in cooperative schemes but are unwilling to honor, or even to propose . . . any general principles or standards for specifying fair terms of cooperation" (PL, 50). It is clear from the context that the general principles or standards at issue in the last quoted passage are those that meet the requirement I have italicized in the previous one. Notice that someone can count as unreasonable on this definition even if he or she is epistemically entitled, on the basis of sound or compelling reasons, to consider the quest for a *common* justificatory basis morally unnecessary and epistemologically dubious. To count as reasonable, in the sense of "socially cooperative," Rawls assumes that one must find his contractarian quest for a common justificatory basis plausible. My problem is that I don't find this quest plausible. Or more mildly: I am not persuaded that it is going to meet with success. For this reason, I want to explore the possibility that a person can be a reasonable (socially cooperative) citizen without believing in or appealing to a free-standing conception of justice.

Rawls is quick to move from imagining the basis on which citizens "can reason in common" to concluding that *only* by conducting our most important political reasoning on this basis can we redeem the promise of treating our fellow citizens fairly in matters pertaining to the use of coercive power. And this conclusion leads, in turn, to a restrictive view of the role religious reasons can play in the public forum. It is clear that, in our society, religious premises cannot be part of the basis on which citizens can reason in common, because not all citizens share the same religious commitments, and nobody knows how to bring about agreement on such matters by rational means. Religion is a topic on which citizens are epistemically (as well as morally and legally) entitled to disagree. If so, it follows from the considerations just mentioned that using religious premises in our reasoning on basic political issues conflicts with the ideal of public reason as originally stated by Rawls. If the point of the social contract is to establish a basis on which citizens can reason in common, and religious premises are not part of that basis, then introducing such premises in the public forum automatically fails to secure the legitimacy of whatever proposal this basis was meant to support.

This conclusion strikes me as extremely counterintuitive, given that it seems so contrary to the spirit of free expression that breathes life into democratic culture. As Nicholas Wolterstorff says, "given that it is of the very essence of liberal democracy that citizens enjoy equal freedom in law to live out their lives as they see fit, how can it be compatible with liberal democracy for its citizens to be *morally restrained* from deciding and discussing political issues as they see fit?"[2] Rawls seems to be saying that while the right to express our religious commitments freely is guaranteed twice over in the Bill of Rights, this is not a right of which we ought make essential use in the center of the political arena, where the most important questions are decided. Is it always wrong for citizens in the public forum to reason solely on the basis of religious premises, at least when considering matters of basic justice and constitutional essentials?

Rawls implied as much in the first, clothbound edition of *Political Liberalism*, but amended his position in the "Introduction to the Paperback Edition" in 1996 and in his paper, "The Idea of Public Reason Revisited."[3] His amended view is that reasonable comprehensive doctrines, including religious doctrines, "may be introduced in public reason at any time, provided that in due course public reasons, given by a reasonable political conception, are presented sufficient to support whatever the comprehensive doctrines are introduced to support" (PL, li–lii). According to this "proviso," a citizen may offer religious reasons for a political conclusion, but only if he or she eventually supplements those reasons by producing arguments based in the social contract. The amended Rawlsian view is that religious reasons are to IOUs as contractarian reasons are to legal tender. You have not fulfilled your justificatory obligations until you have handed over real cash. I find this version of the position slightly more plausible than the original, simply because it is less restrictive. It makes a bit more room for such instances of exemplary democratic reasoning as the religiously based oratory of the Abolitionists and of Martin Luther King, Jr. But Rawls confesses that he does not know whether these orators "ever fulfilled the proviso" by eventually offering reasons of his officially approved sort (PL, lii n. 27). So, strictly speaking, from a Rawlsian point of view the jury is still out on these cases.

I see it as a strong count against Rawls's current position that these particular speakers will barely squeak by on his criteria, if they manage to do so at all. The alleged need to satisfy the proviso in such cases suggests to me that something remains seriously wrong with the entire approach Rawls is taking. Two main types of reason-giving are to be found in the relevant speeches, but Rawls classifies both of them as private, because they do not appeal to the common justificatory basis. In the first type, which Rawls calls "declaration" (CP, 594), the speakers express their own religious reasons for adopting some political proposal. In the second type, which Rawls calls "conjecture" (CP, 594), the speakers engage in immanent criticism of their opponents' views. As immanent critics, they either try to show that their opponents' religious views are incoherent, or they try to argue positively from their opponents' religious premises to the conclusion that the proposal is acceptable. What they do not do is argue from a purportedly common basis of reasons in Rawls's sense. Rawls does not examine these forms of reason-giving in any detail. He merely classifies them as private and moves on. He does not show why a speaker who combines them when addressing fellow citizens on constitutional essentials, like the right to own slaves and who gets to vote, needs eventually to offer argument of some other kind.

Rawls is similarly ambivalent and therefore unpersuasive on Lincoln's Second Inaugural Address, perhaps the highest ethical achievement of any political speaker in U.S. history. What gets Lincoln barely off the hook is that "what he says has no implications bearing on constitutional essentials or matters of basic justice" (PL, 254). I am not certain that this is true. The speech is about the question of how a nation at war with itself over slavery can remain a union. Lincoln's answer, in effect, is that it can do so only if, at the moment when one side wins the war, the people and the state representing them behave "with malice toward none; with charity for all." This includes behavior intended to "achieve and cherish a just and lasting peace," which in Lincoln's view obviously includes taking the right stand on constitutional essentials and matters of basic justice. In any event, suppose he had addressed such matters directly and at greater length, continuing the theme, introduced earlier in the speech, of two parties that both read the same Bible and pray to the same God, whom they believe to be a just judge of wrongdoers. Suppose he had spelled out his immanent criticisms of the self-righteous religious views, the moralistic dualisms, that both sides were then preparing to enact politically. Would the religious content in Lincoln's speech then have been improper? Would he be engaged in private speech, despite speaking as the president to the people on a very public occasion? Something is deeply wrong here. The speeches of King and Lincoln represent high accomplishments in our public political culture. They are paradigms of discursive excellence. The speeches of the Abolitionists taught their compatriots how to use the terms "slavery" and "justice" as we now use them. It is hard to credit any theory that treats their arguments as placeholders for reasons to be named later.

I do not intend to go very far into the details of the debate between Rawls and his critics.[4] My purpose in this section and the next is rather to determine what it is in his contractarian starting point that leads Rawls and others to say such counterintuitive things. If my diagnosis is correct, then the amended version of his position, while it is less paradoxical than the original, does not overcome the basic difficulties in his approach to the topic. My conclusion will be that we ought to reframe the question of religion's role in political discussion in quite different terms.

The trouble is at least partly a matter of epistemology. I suspect that Rawls has overestimated what can be resolved in terms of the imagined common basis of justifiable principles, and has done so because at this one point in constructing his theory he has drastically underestimated the range of things that socially cooperative individuals can reasonably reject. He has underestimated what a person can reasonably reject, I suspect, because he has underestimated the role of a person's collateral commitments in determining what he or she can reasonably reject when deciding basic political questions. What I can reasonably reject depends in part on what collateral commitments I have and which of these I am entitled to have. But these commitments vary a good deal from person to person, not least of all insofar as they involve answers to religious questions and judgments about the relative importance of highly important values. It is naïve to expect that the full range of political issues that require public deliberation—issues on which we need *some* policy—will turn out to be untouched by such variation. Rawls would grant this. Indeed, it may be part of his reason for viewing "the diversity of reasonable comprehensive religious, philosophical, and moral doctrines found in modern democratic societies" as a central problem for political liberalism to address (PL, 36). The question is why constitutional essentials and matters of basic justice are not also affected, for it is reasonable to suppose, when discussing such elemental issues, that the relative importance of highly important values—a matter on which religious traditions have much to say—is a relevant consideration. Rawls might wish to deny this on the basis of his doctrine of the priority of the right over the good, but this doctrine also strikes me as the sort of thing over which epistemically responsible people have good reason to disagree.

I am tempted to put the point by saying that this doctrine is the sort of thing *reasonable* people would be *entitled* to disagree over. For the moment, let me use the term "reasonable" in a way that departs from Rawls's definition. In this sense, a person is reasonable in accepting or rejecting a commitment if he or she is "epistemically entitled" to do so, and reasonable people are those who comport themselves in accord with their epistemic responsibilities.[5] I do not see how the same epistemology can consistently (a) declare the people holding various comprehensive views to be reasonable in this sense, and (b) declare the people who dissent from the social contract not to be reasonable in the same sense. To make (a) turn out to be correct, one would need to assume a relatively permissive standard of reasonableness. But if one then applies the same permissive standard of reasonableness to those who dissent from the social contract, (b) is going to be very hard to defend. According to my epistemology, the more permissive standard seems to be the right one to apply in both instances. But if we link the term "reasonable" to epistemic entitlement and apply the term in a relatively permissive way, it will be very hard to make those who reject the contractarian project *on epistemological grounds* qualify as unreasonable.

This appears to be why Rawls has a stake in introducing his definition of reasonableness. The point of doing so is to guarantee that a reasonable person will be committed to the contractarian project of trying to find, and abide by, a common basis of principles. But this move only begs the question of why the contractarian project of establishing a common basis is itself something no one can reasonably reject in the sense of epistemic entitlement. We still need an answer to this question. There appear to be sound *epistemological* reasons for rejecting the quest for a common basis, reasons rooted in the permissive notion of epistemic entitlement that lends plausibility to the doctrine of reasonable pluralism in the first place.

Rawls gave an interview to *Commonweal*, a liberal Catholic journal, in 1998 (reprinted in CP, 616–22). In it he asks how we are to avoid religious civil wars like those of the sixteenth century without adopting his position. "See, what I should do is to turn around and say, what's the better suggestion, what's your solution to it? And I can't see any other solution." He continues: "People can make arguments from the Bible if they want to. But I want them to see that they should also give arguments that all reasonable citizens might agree to. Again, what's the alternative?" (CP, 620) Let us see whether we can find one.

Rawls's amended position entails that it would be inherently unfair, when speaking in the public forum on questions of basic justice, to rely solely on religious premises. This would hold, presumably, even in a case where my epistemological suspicions were realized and it proved impracticable to reason on the basis of a principle that all reasonable citizens could reasonably accept. But suppose this did turn out to be impracticable—for the simple reason that some epistemically responsible people who desire social cooperation have reason for rejecting each candidate principle. Must we then not consider the matter at all? Must we remain silent when it comes up for discussion? How could a requirement of silence in such a case be deemed *reasonable*—that is to say, justified?

For that matter, how could it be deemed *fair* in a society committed to freedom of religion and freedom of expression? I do not see how it could be. As Wolterstorff argues:

> It belongs to the *religious convictions* of a good many religious people in our society that *they ought to base* their decisions concerning fundamental issues of justice *on* their religious convictions. They do not view as an option whether or not to do so. It is their conviction that they ought to strive for wholeness, integrity, integration, in their lives: that they ought to allow the Word of God, the teachings of the Torah, the command and example of Jesus, or whatever, to shape their existence as a whole, including, then, their social and political existence. Their religion is not, for them, about *something other* than their social and political existence; it is *also* about their social and political existence. Accordingly, to require of them that they not base their decisions and discussions concerning political issues on their religion is to infringe, inequitably, on the free exercise of their religion.[6]

It might be thought that offering religious reasons, without supplementing them by appeal to the social contract, is inherently disrespectful. But why need this be a sign of disrespect at all? Suppose I tell you honestly why I favor a given policy, citing religious reasons. I then draw you into a Socratic conversation on the matter, take seriously the objections you raise against my premises, and make a concerted attempt to show you how *your* idiosyncratic premises give *you* reason to accept my conclusions. All the while, I take care to be sincere and avoid manipulating you (CP, 594). Now, I do not see why this would qualify as a form of disrespect. Yet it does not involve basing my reasoning on principles that no reasonable citizen could reasonably reject.

The conception of respect assumed in the objection seems flawed. It neglects the ways in which one can show respect for another person in his or her particularity.[7] The reason Rawls neglects these ways is that he focuses exclusively on the sort of respect one shows to another individual by appealing to reasons that *anyone* who is both properly motivated and epistemically responsible would find acceptable. Why would I be failing to show respect for X if I offered reasons to X that X ought to be moved by from X's point of view?[8] Why would it matter that there might be other people, Y and Z, who could reasonably reject those reasons? Suppose Y and Z are also part of my audience. If I am speaking *as* a citizen *to* fellow citizens, unconstrained by expectations of confidentiality, they might well be. This is all I would mean by "speaking in public." Does my immanent criticism of X then show disrespect to Y and Z? No, because I can go on to show respect for them in the same way, by offering *different* reasons to them, reasons relevant *from their point of view*. Socratic questioning is a principal tool of justificatory discourse as well as a way of expressing respect for one's interlocutor as a (potential) lover of justice and sound thinking. But it does not proceed from an already-agreed-on, common basis.

It appears that Rawls is too caught up in theorizing about an idealized form of reasoning to notice how much work candid expression and immanent criticism—declaration and conjecture—perform in real democratic exchange. Immanent criticism is both one of the most widely used forms of reasoning in what I would call public political discourse and one of the most effective ways of showing respect for fellow citizens who hold differing points of view. Any speaker is free to request reasons from any other. If I have access to the right forum, I can tell the entire community what reasons move me to accept a given conclusion, thus showing my fellow citizens respect as requesters of my reasons. But to explain to them why *they* might have reason to agree with me, given their different collateral premises, I might well have to proceed piecemeal, addressing one individual (or one type of perspective) at a time. Real respect for others takes seriously the distinctive point of view *each* other occupies. It is respect for individuality, for difference.

Rawls builds strong assumptions about the nature of discursive sociality into his conception of a "reasonable person." Such a person is by definition someone who is prepared to play by the discursive rules of the imagined common basis on all essential matters. But why not view the person who takes each competing perspective on its own terms, expressing his own views openly and practicing immanent criticism on the views of others, as a reasonable (i.e., socially cooperative, respectful, reason-giving) person? Why limit oneself in the Rawlsian way to the quest for a *common* basis, given the possibility that a common basis will not cover all essential matters? I do not see any convincing answers to these questions in Rawls's writings or in the works of other contractarian theorists. These questions reveal, I think, that the social contract is essentially a substitute for communitarian agreement on a single comprehensive normative vision—a poor man's communitarianism. Contractarianism feels compelled to reify a sort of all-purpose, abstract fairness or respect for others because it cannot imagine ethical or political discourse *dialogically*.[9] Its view of the epistemological and sociological dimensions of discursive practices is essentially blinkered.

Wolterstorff puts the point in a slightly different way:

> So-called "communitarians" regularly accuse proponents of the liberal position of being against community. One can see what they are getting at. Nonetheless, this way of putting it seems to me imperceptive of what, at bottom, is going on. The liberal is not willing to live with a politics of multiple communities. He still wants communitarian politics. He is trying to discover, and to form, the relevant community. He thinks we need a shared political basis; he is trying to discover and nourish that basis. . . . I think that the attempt is hopeless and misguided. We must learn to live with a politics of multiple communities.[10]

My qualm about this way of putting the point I want to make is that it concedes too much to group thinking. We do have multiple communities in the sense that the points of view many citizens occupy fall into recognizable types. And some of these communities work hard, for legitimate reasons, at reaching consensus on topics that matter deeply to them. But the differences that set off one such community from another are not the only differences that make a difference in political debate. There are also differences that set off individuals from the communities in which they were raised or with which at some point they became affiliated. Respect for individuals involves sensitivity to the ways in which they can resist conformity to type. Wolterstorff calls for a "consocial" (114) model of discursive sociality for a democratic society. By envisioning a multitude of discursive communities exchanging reasons both within and across their own boundaries, such a model advances well beyond the social-contract model Rawls employs. But we need another layer of complication to make the picture fully realistic.

On my model, each individual starts off with a cultural inheritance that might well come from many sources. In my case, these sources included the training I received in Bible school, the traditional stories my grandmother told on Sunday afternoons, and the example of a pastor committed passionately to civil rights. But they also included an early exposure to Emerson, Whitman, and Thoreau; the art, novels, and music brought into my home by my bohemian older brother; and countless other bits of free-floating cultural material that are not the property of any group. And they included interactions with hundreds of other people whose racial and religious backgrounds differed from mine. It would simply be inaccurate to describe my point of view as that of my family, my co-religionists, or my race. One would fail to show me respect as an individual if one assimilated my point of view to some form of group thinking. The consocial model still fails to do justice to the kinds of individuality and alienation that modern democracies can promote.

Rawls derives his idea of public reason from conceptions of fairness and respect that are in fact to be found in the political culture of modern democracy. But he develops this idea in a way that brings it into tension with conceptions of free expression and basic rights that also belong to the same culture. It is not clear why this tension should be resolved by adopting a Rawlsian conception of public reason.[11] It seems more reasonable to suppose that one should try to argue from universally justifiable premises, whenever this seems both wise and possible, while feeling free nonetheless to pursue other argumentative strategies when they seem wise. This would be to treat the idea of public reason as a vague ideal, instead of reifying it moralistically into a set of fixed rules for public discussion. The truth in the contractarian argument for restraint is that it would indeed be *ideal* if we could resolve any given political controversy on the basis of reasons that none of us could reasonably reject. But it has not been demonstrated that all important controversies can be resolved on this sort of basis, so it seems unwise to treat the idea of public reason as if it entailed an all-purpose principle of restraint. The irony here is that the contractarian interpretation of the idea of public reason is itself something that many epistemically and morally responsible citizens would be entitled, on the basis of their own collateral beliefs, to reject.

The contractarian position has a descriptive component and a normative component. The descriptive component is an account of what the norms of democratic political culture involve. It distills a rigorist interpretation of the idea of public reason out of various commitments that are found in that culture. The normative component endorses a principle of restraint as a consequence of that interpretation. I worry that religious individuals who accept the descriptive component of contractarianism as a faithful reconstruction of what the norms of democratic political culture involve will, understandably, view this as a reason for withdrawing from that culture. Why should one identify with the democratic process of reason-exchange if the norms implicit in that process are what the contractarians say they are? I believe this thought is in fact one of the main reasons that antiliberal traditionalists like Stanley Hauerwas, Alasdair MacIntyre, and John Milbank have largely displaced Reinhold Niebuhr, Paul Tillich, and the liberation theologians as intellectual authorities in the seminaries, divinity schools, and church-affiliated colleges of the wealthier democracies.

We are about to reap the social consequences of a traditionalist backlash against contractarian liberalism. The more thoroughly Rawlsian our law schools and ethics centers become, the more radically Hauerwasian the theological schools become. Because most of the Rawlsians do not read theology or pay scholarly attention to the religious life of the people, they have no idea what contractarian liberalism has come to mean outside the fields of legal and political theory. (There are a few Rawlsians in religious studies, but they are now on the defensive and vastly outnumbered.) One message being preached nowadays in many of the institutions where future preachers are being trained is that liberal democracy is essentially hypocritical when it purports to value free religious expression. Liberalism, according to Hauerwas, is a secularist ideology that masks a discriminatory program for policing what religious people can say in public. The appropriate response, he sometimes implies, is to condemn freedom and the democratic struggle for justice as "bad ideas" for the church.[12] Over the next several decades this message will be preached in countless sermons throughout the heartland of the nation.

Rawls found it frustrating that Hauerwas and his allies tend to ignore the careful distinctions he draws between liberalism as a comprehensive moral doctrine and the strictly *political* liberalism he had been trying to perfect in his later years. His *Commonweal* interviewer asked whether he denied that he was "making a veiled argument for secularism." He responded by saying, "Yes, I emphatically deny it. Suppose I said that it is not a veiled argument for secularism any more than it is a veiled argument for religion. Consider: there are two kinds of comprehensive doctrines, religious and secular. Those of religious faith will say I give a veiled argument for secularism, and the latter will say I give a veiled argument for religion. I deny both" (CP, 619f.). But nobody is charging Rawls with giving a veiled argument for religion. The charge being made by his secular and religious critics alike is that he is wrong to expect everybody to argue in the same terms, which just happen to be a slightly adjusted version of the same terms dictated by his comprehensive secular liberalism. The critics doubt the need for the kind of decorum the liberal professor wants to impose on the discussion. And they doubt that a reluctance to adopt justice as fairness as a common basis for discussion makes someone unreasonable. These suspicions would not subside, it seems to me, even if Rawls's critics took full measure of all the distinctions and qualifications he has added to his theory. From the vantage of the religious critics, in particular, the complications would still seem both ad hoc and excessively restrictive.[13]

In a later chapter, I will question whether Hauerwas's critique of liberal democracy exemplifies the ideals of Christian charity and Aristotelian friendship that he himself embraces as alternatives to contractarian liberalism. In doing so, I will offer him reasons for embracing the democratic struggle for justice, reasons that ought to carry weight from his point of view, not merely from my own idiosyncratic point of view as an Emersonian perfectionist. They are not reasons that derive from the social contract, however. They do not belong to the common basis. They are reasons rooted in *his* theological commitments, which, needless to say, are not universally shared. I intend the exercise as a demonstration of respectful, sincere, nonmanipulative, immanent criticism.

I have heard that Hauerwas expressed the religious reasons for his criticisms of U.S. militarism in public, before a religiously mixed gathering of citizens in the nation's capital, not long after September 11, 2001. In my view, it was good that he did, regardless of whether he intends to satisfy Rawls's proviso. Hauerwas's audience on this occasion presumably included people who were concerned about such basic questions as whether states have a right to fight wars of self-defense and whether the constitutional provision requiring Congress to declare war continues to apply. These citizens were anxious to hear the arguments of a highly influential pacifist and also to hear those arguments subjected to public criticism from other points of view. Democracy would not have been better served, it seems to me, if these reasons had been circulated only behind the closed doors of churches and religiously affiliated schools, where they would be somewhat less likely to face skeptical objections. Especially given that Hauerwas now enjoys wide influence among American Christians, he ought to be encouraged to speak in public so that the citizenry as a whole can inform itself about the content and strength of his arguments.[14] And if he someday chooses to address a congressional committee or speak on behalf of political candidates, so much the better.

One factor to keep in mind when considering the new traditionalism is that Hauerwas and his allies accept the descriptive component of contractarian liberalism. That is, they take this form of liberalism at face value as an accurate account of what the ethical life of modern democracy involves. It is because they view it as a faithful reflection of our political culture that they are so quick to recommend wholesale rejection of that culture. I hold that the contractarians have distorted what this culture involves by wrongly taking a sensible, widely shared, vague ideal to be a clear, fixed, deontological requirement built into the common basis of our reasoning. If I am right about this, the new traditionalists are wrong to reject that culture as implicitly committed to the contractarian program of restraint—what Hauerwas calls "the democratic policing of Christianity."[15] Rejecting what contractarianism and the new traditionalism have in common will permit us, I hope, to reopen the entire question of the role of religious reasoning in public life.

BETWEEN KANT AND HEGEL

The contemporary contractarian version of the question is, "What moral constraints on the use of religious premises in political reasoning are implied by the common basis of reasoning affirmed in the social contract?"

The sought-for principles might not turn out to be Kant's exactly, but the requirement that they be conceived in terms of a common justificatory basis on the model of a social contract is recognizably Kantian in lineage, self-consciously so in Rawls's formulation. Rawls does depart from Kant in a number of ways, and at some points appears to be conscious of his debts to the expressivism of both Hegel and Dewey. These latter debts are most obvious in his theoretical aspiration to make explicit the central elements of the shared political culture and in his closely related doctrine of reflective equilibrium. On both of these points, Rawls is borrowing ideas from the expressivist tradition in an attempt to transform "Kantian constructivism" into a "political constructivism" tailored to the needs of political liberalism. The theoretical aspiration is a version of Hegel's notion that the task of philosophy is to comprehend its own age in thought. The doctrine of reflective equilibrium articulates a Hegelian conception of dialectical reasonableness. But in his commitment to the metaphor of the social contract and in the definition of the "reasonable person" he uses to explicate that metaphor, Rawls remains a Kantian. From an expressivist point of view, his departures from Kant improve on the work of his distinguished predecessor, but they leave him in an untenable position—in effect, halfway between the coherent alternatives of Kant and Hegel.

Norms, according to an expressivist conception, are creatures of the social process in which members of a community achieve mutual recognition as subjects answerable for their actions and commitments. It is the business of reflective practices to make norms explicit in the form of rules and ideals and to achieve reflective equilibrium between them and our other commitments at all levels of generality. The social process in which norms come to be and come to be made explicit is dialectical. It involves movement back and forth between action and reflection as well as interaction among individuals with differing points of view. Because this process takes place in the dimension of time and history, the beliefs and actions one is entitled to depend in large part on what has already transpired within the dialectical process itself. Hegel considered Kant's preoccupation with universally valid principles epistemologically naïve, and was suspicious of the adequacy of the social contract when construed in expressivist terms as a model of rational commitments implicit in the shared political culture. Rawls briefly discusses Hegel's criticisms of social-contract theories in *Political Liberalism* (285–88), claiming that while these criticisms might be effective against some versions of the social contract, they do not tell against his. I am not persuaded, however, that Rawls takes Hegel's full measure in this response, for he focuses too narrowly on Hegel's explicit commentary on the social contract, without exploring the implications of Hegel's philosophy, taken as a whole. Rawls discusses Hegel at greater length in *Lectures on the History of Moral Philosophy*. But in focusing primarily on Hegel's *Philosophy of Right* and in his understandable attempt to steer clear of Hegel's metaphysical doctrines, he ends up paying too little attention to Hegel's epistemology and his account of concepts, both of which figure heavily in his critique of Kant.[16]

Consider any art, science, or sport you please.[17] It should be clear that the norms of the practice at a given time constrain the behavior of those who participate in it by supplying them with reasons not to do certain things they are physically able to do. Behavior within the social practice is open to criticism in terms of the norms as they have come to be. But conformity to the norms opens up the possibility of novel performances, which have the dialectical potential to transform the practice, thus changing its norms. In the possibility of novel, practice-transforming performances one catches sight of what Brandom calls "the paradigm of a new kind of freedom, *expressive* freedom" ("Freedom," 185; emphasis in original). By foregrounding the dialectical process in which social practices, and the norms implicit in them, evolve over time, Hegel was both borrowing from Kant and moving beyond him. Kant had drawn the crucial contrast between constraint by norms, which he calls freedom, and constraint by causes. Hegel was able to extend the Kantian conception of freedom as constraint by norms by setting it within his dialectical account of norms. For if norms are creatures of social practices, then the sorts of free expression made possible through constraint by norms will vary in accordance with the social practices under consideration and with the dialectic of normative constraint and novel performance unfolding in time.

Once this point is fully understood, it is no longer clear why we need to tether our social and political theory to the search for a common basis of reasoning in principles that all "reasonable" citizens have reason to accept. The principles that one might have reason to reject will depend on one's dialectical location—on the social practices one has been able to participate in and on the actual history of norm-transformation they have undergone so far. Among these practices will be religious practices, which carry with them their own styles of reasoning, their own vocabularies, and their own possibilities of expressive freedom. If the thoroughly dialectical view of epistemic entitlement is correct, why expect all socially cooperative, respectful persons to have reason to accept the same set of explicitly formulated norms, regardless of dialectical location? It is of course possible that they will, and they may indeed do so for a time, but the substance of a common ethical life, according to Hegel, does not reside in the explicitly formulated abstract norms that arise from the dialectical process in which we strive for reflective equilibrium. It resides in the myriad observations, material inferences, actions, and mutually recognitive reactions that constitute the dialectical process itself. This changes at least a bit with every discursive move that is made by every interlocutor. The abstract norms are often misleading or inadequate attempts to make explicit what is implicit in the ethical life of the people. Moreover, they are typically a full step behind the dialectical process—because the Owl of Minerva takes flight at dusk.

We can get at this from another angle by considering the two quite different paradigms of the reasonable person that one finds in the Kantian and expressivist traditions. The Kantian paradigm of the reasonable person is the individual who is prepared to agree to rules that everyone else, acting on the same motivation, would have compelling reason to accept. The Hegelian paradigm is rather the individual who is prepared to engage in discursive exchange with any point of view that he or she can recognize as responsibly held. As the expressivist sees it, the series of exchanges need not operate on a single common basis, tailored to all, but might well involve improvisational expression of one's own point of view and ad hoc immanent criticism of one's interlocutors. The expectation is that different improvisations and different immanent criticisms—indeed, different vocabularies—might well be called for in response to each interlocutor. The one thing upon which a reasonable person can more or less count is the need to transcend whatever set of rules and concepts a distinguished philosopher has described as demanded by our common use of reason.

The point of the contractarian program of restraint was to provide us with security against illegitimate forms of coercive interference on the part of rulers and fellow citizens. This is a matter of *negative* freedom, freedom *from* something. We still have ample reason to concern ourselves with this sort of freedom when assessing the political arrangements that are open to us. But there is also another sort of freedom to nurture and protect, namely, expressive freedom. And this ought to make us hesitant to embark on a Rawlsian program of restraint. Expressive freedom is *positive*, the freedom *to* transform both oneself and one's social practices through a dialectical progression of novel performances and their consequences. To take expressive freedom seriously is to see our capacity to engage in reasoning, including ethical and political reasoning, as something that cannot be captured definitively in the mere application of rules that no reasonable person could reasonably reject. For a reasonable person, in the Hegelian sense, is someone who is always in the process of transforming the inferential significance of the normative concepts at his or her disposal by applying them to new situations and problems.

The social-contract metaphor is too static to serve as an apt model for this process. What contractarianism seems to be looking for is a way of identifying the norms of social cooperation that fixes their inferential significance in advance, so that discursive exchange can be conceptually (and socially) stable. The norms are then taken to be settled and in need only of application in the approved procedures of deliberative discourse. This approach is analogous to what Hegel, in his critique of Kant's theoretical philosophy, calls the faculty of the understanding (*Verstand*), whereas Hegel prefers the more flexible, pragmatic, improvisational faculty of reason (*Vernunft*), which he plausibly associates with the concept of spirit (*Geist*). Brandom develops the contrast between Verstand and Vernunft as follows:

> Understanding concepts in terms of the categories of the Understanding is treating them as fixed and static. It allows progress only in the sorting of *judgments* into true and false, that is, in the *selection* from a repertoire fixed in advance of the correct concepts to apply in a particular instance. But Hegel wants to insist that if one ignores the process by which concepts *develop*—what other concepts they develop out of, and the forces implicit in them, in concert with their fellows, that lead to their alteration (what Hegel calls their "negativity")—then the sort of content they have is bound to remain unintelligible.[18]

I am saying that this idea is also at work in Hegel's worries about Kantian practical and political philosophy. Social-contract theory is an attempt to tame the concepts of ethical and political discourse in the interest of stabilizing the social order. It hopes to settle the basic question of the fair terms of social cooperation so that deliberative discourse can proceed within a stable "contractual" framework. It imagines itself as an alternative to two threats: the communitarian threat to individual autonomy, which achieves stability but in the wrong way, and the anarchic threat of a war of all against all, which does not achieve stability at all. Social stability is to be achieved by fixing the *terms* of social cooperation, the conceptual framework implicit in the notion of the reasonable person. The practical expression of social-contract theory is, unsurprisingly, a program of social control, an attempt to enforce moral *restraint* on discursive exchange by counting only those who want to reason on the basis of a common set of fixed rules as *reasonable*. It is no wonder that the result sits uneasily with the aspirations of expressive freedom. Hegel wants to avoid this outcome by redefining "reasonable" in terms of the dialectic of expressive freedom.

It should now be clear why a democratic expressivist would never be tempted to discount Abolitionist oratory, Lincoln's Second Inaugural Address, and King's sermons as mere IOUs. For such an expressivist sees democratic discourse as an unfolding dialectic in which the paradigmatic instances of "reasonableness" involve either dramatically significant innovations in the application of an entrenched normative vocabulary or especially memorable exemplifications of discursive virtue. They are paradigmatic because they move "reasonableness" forward, thus exercising some (defeasible) authority over future applications of the relevant concepts.[19] For this reason, we cannot tell the story of the unfolding dialectic without giving them a prominent place in it. Any view that makes them appear marginal or something less than paradigmatic instances of "reasonableness," simply because they do not conform to an abstract account of discursive propriety, deserves rejection.

According to Brandom, "Kant tells a *two-phase* story, according to which one sort of activity *institutes* conceptual norms, and then another sort of activity *applies* those concepts. First, a reflective judgment (somehow) makes or finds the determinate rule that articulates [a] concept. Then, and only then, can that concept be applied in the determinate judgements and maxims that are the ultimate subjects of the first two Critiques."[20] It is this two-phase story that Hegel rejects, and he rejects it when it appears in Kant's account of empirical concepts, in his moral philosophy, and in his social-contract theory. Hegel's alternative, dialectical story implies that contractarianism is incorrect in thinking that something like the social contract is *needed* as the basis of social cooperation. Our normative concepts are not instituted at the contractual level and then applied on the basis of the constitutive contract. They are instituted in the process of mutual recognition in which individuals hold one another responsible and implicitly impute to others the authority to keep normative track of one another's attitudes. This process does not *need* the social contract to get going or to get along.[21] The process of exchanging reasons is already a system of social cooperation; it needs no help from the formal structure of the social contract to become one. But if the social contract is unnecessary, if our norms are instituted in a different way, then why define a "reasonable person" as someone who is motivated to forge and live by the principles of the social contract? Why not count anyone as a "reasonable person" who participates responsibly in the process of discursive exchange which has reflective equilibrium as its ever-evolving end? Why not see this process as the way in which democratic citizens strive, at least in their better moments, to become a more perfect union of responsible, socially cooperative selves?

There are at least three commitments that a pragmatist sensitive to these Hegelian concerns would want to bring together in an acceptable self-understanding of democratic practices. Implicit in our way of treating one another is a conception of ourselves as citizens who (a) ought to enjoy *equal standing* in political discourse; (b) deserve respect *as individuals* keeping track of the discussion from their own distinctive points of view; and (c) have a personal and perhaps religious stake in the exercise of *expressive freedom*. Given (a) and (b), we have reason to accept an ideal according to which it would be appropriate, much of the time, to reason from widely justifiable premises in the political arena. But given the emphasis in (b) on the distinctive points of view from which individuals keep track of the discussion, a pragmatist will not be tempted to construe this ideal as an absolute requirement to reason only from a common basis of principles. If we then interpret (c) in terms of the dialectic of normative constraint and novel performance, it seems reasonable to expect that various sorts of hard decisions will have to be made *as the dialectic unfolds*. By applying normative concepts, participants in the process of reason-exchange effectively decide which social and political constraints to accept in the hope of enhancing, among other things, the expressive religious freedom of the citizenry.

Pragmatic expressivists accept the Kantian insight that there need to be constraints if there is to be freedom. But they reject the two-step procedure of social-contract theory—that is, the notion that to have any constraints, we must first *fix* the terms of social cooperation contractually and then simply abide by the agreed upon rules. They also see the central problem to be addressed in social and political deliberation as the question of which forms of expressive freedom we, as individuals and as a group, wish to promote and enjoy. There are infinitely many possible forms of expressive freedom. We opt for some over others not by signing a social contract but rather by promoting some social practices at the expense of others, both through our direct participation in them and the institutional arrangements we make for them. But as Brandom says, the expressivist way of framing the central problem of social and political deliberation does not "even begin to settle questions about the trade-offs between different varieties of negative and positive freedom."[22] For this reason, expressivism has been the preferred idiom of starkly incompatible forms of resistance to contractarian liberalism. On the all-important questions of which social practices to promote and how to promote them, expressivists divide sharply, with Emersonians at one end of the spectrum and traditionalists at the other. Emersonians, who place high value on the possibilities of novel expression, are inclined to use the freedoms afforded by the First Amendment as an institutional framework for promoting nonstandard social practices and the forms of spirited individuality they foster. Traditionalists, however, have argued on expressivist grounds for a much less permissive vision of social life. They have claimed that the higher forms of ethical and religious self-cultivation are possible only within the normative constraints of a relatively strict regimen of established communal practices. Expressivists of this sort have sometimes been willing to impose fairly severe restrictions on the expression of religious dissent in order to reap the rewards of expressive freedom and spiritual excellence they take to be possible only within a religiously unified community.

In the United States, such proposals have not made much headway, but milder versions of them, which involve shrinking the divide between church and state instead of eliminating it entirely, are gaining ground. One thing counting against traditionalist proposals in the American context is that relatively strict church-state separation and ample freedom of religious expression comport well with a political culture that was shaped in large part by immigrants in flight from restrictive religious orthodoxies. Another count against traditionalism is the sheer extent of religious diversity in this society. Members of minority traditions—including those who join me in seeing Emerson, Whitman, and Thoreau as among the greatest spiritual exemplars of expressive freedom yet produced by America—have every reason to oppose restrictions on the public expression of religious dissent against majority views. One can hope that they will do so successfully for the foreseeable future.

My version of pragmatism endorses major themes from Hegel's critique of Kant. It then combines Hegel's dialectical normative expressivism with the Emersonian conviction that the most substantial spiritual benefits of expressive freedom are to be found in a form of social life that celebrates democratic individuality as a positive good. One can see this combination of ideas initially come together, I believe, in Whitman and Dewey.

The Hegelian component of my pragmatism has a number of things in common with the most plausible forms of the new traditionalism. These include an emphasis on the importance of self-cultivation as an exercise of expressive freedom and an understanding of the dialectically social basis of norms. On Hegelian grounds, I sympathize with the traditionalist's distaste for the contractarian liberal's program of restraint. But I do not see resentment of contractarians as a reason for alienating myself from democratic hopes and freedoms. The traditionalist story that a particular religious tradition in fact functions as a community of virtue over against the sinfulness of the surrounding social world strikes me as extremely dubious as well as exceedingly prideful. I do not propose to replace the contractarian program of restraint with its traditionalist counterpart—a different set of restrictions, typically designed to maintain a patriarchal orthodoxy, instead of a liberal professor's idea of discursive decorum.

Finally, I oppose the contractarians and the new traditionalists on the most important point they share. For they both hold, as I do not, that the political culture of our democracy implicitly requires the policing or self-censorship of religious expression in the political arena. If Rawls is right, contractarian theory may require this. But the descriptive component of his contractarianism is only one competing account of what the ethical life of democracy involves. If its picture of our culture is distorted, then we are not already implicitly committed to the social contract featured in that picture. The picture neither supports the contractarian argument for restraint, nor provides a reason for the traditionalist to reject the political culture it depicts. In this one respect, our political culture is a nobler thing than its leading theoretical defenders and detractors make it out to be. Judging by how the members of our society behave, they are more deeply committed to freedom, and to a more substantive, positive kind of freedom, than the theorists suspect. For historically they have not restrained themselves in the way contractarians have proposed. That is why Rawls has trouble corralling his historical examples. The Abolitionists did not restrain themselves in this way. Abraham Lincoln did not. Martin Luther King, Jr., did not. Dorothy Day did not. Rosemary Radford Ruether does not. Wendell Berry does not. Furthermore, many members of our society would resist with considerable fury any traditionalist attempt to establish an orthodox alternative to freewheeling democratic exchange. More power to them.

Let me now sum up how I would want to construe our implicitly recognized norms for employing religious premises in political reasoning. First, I would insist that the ideal of respect for one's fellow citizens does not in every case require us to argue from a common justificatory basis of principles that no one properly motivated could reasonably reject. Second, I would recommend the mixed rhetorical strategy of expressing one's own (perhaps idiosyncratic) reasons for a political policy while also directing fair-minded, nonmanipulative, sincere immanent criticism against one's opponent's reasons. Arguing in this way is not only extremely common, but also easily recognizable as a form of respect.

Third, I would refer, as the new traditionalists do (and as a liberal like Stephen Macedo also does), to the importance of virtues in guiding a citizen through the process of discursive exchange and political decision making. There are people who lack civility, or the ability to listen with an open mind, or the will to pursue justice where it leads, or the temperance to avoid taking and causing offense needlessly, or the practical wisdom to discern the subtleties of a discursive situation. There are also people who lack the courage to speak candidly, or the tact to avoid sanctimonious cant, or the poise to respond to unexpected arguments, or the humility to ask forgiveness from those who have been wronged. Such people are unlikely to express their reasons appropriately, whatever those reasons may be. When it comes to expressing religious reasons, it can take a citizen of considerable virtue to avoid even the most obvious pitfalls. I know of no set of rules for getting such matters right. My advice, therefore, is to cultivate the virtues of democratic speech, love justice, and say what you please.[23]

Is Religion a Conversation-Stopper?

The contractarian program of restraint is a moralistic one. Richard Rorty's argument for restraint in "Religion as Conversation-Stopper" is pragmatic.[24] He claims that the public expression of religious premises is likely to bring a potentially productive democratic conversation grinding to a halt. "The main reason religion needs to be privatized is that, in political discussion with those outside the relevant religious community, it is a conversation-stopper." When someone does introduce a religious premise into a political discussion, Rorty says, "the ensuing silence masks the group's inclination to say, 'So what? We weren't discussing your private life; we were discussing public policy. Don't bother us with matters that are not our concern' (PSH, 171). Assuming that we want to keep the conversation going, we have good reason for excluding the expression of religious premises from public political discussion.

Rorty sounds a bit like a contractarian when he endorses what he calls the "Jeffersonian compromise that the Enlightenment reached with the religious" (PSH, 169) and an epistemology he associates not only with Dewey and C. S. Peirce, but also with Rawls and Habermas (PSH, 173). The content of the Jeffersonian compromise, he says, is that we should limit conversation to premises held in common, thereby excluding the expression of religious premises. But he does not go on to theorize about universally valid principles, about which he has expressed doubts on other occasions. So the Jeffersonian compromise implies the same program of restraint that the social contract does without having the same purported epistemic status and without being expressed in the same moralistic tone. Why Rawls and Habermas emerge as model epistemologists in this context remains unclear. Rorty does not say that employing religious premises in public conversation violates a universally justifiable principle of respect; he says that doing so is in "bad taste" (PSH, 169).

This argument is hardly Rorty's most rigorously developed contribution to public life, but it is, I think, a more accurate reflection of our political culture than is the Rawlsian argument. There are in fact many situations in which the introduction of religious premises into a political argument seems a sign of bad taste or imprudence on the part of a speaker. This is what I was getting at near the end of the previous section when I referred to the need for practical wisdom and tact. The reason that relying on religious premises is often imprudent when debating matters of public policy is not, however, that it violates a compromise supposedly reached between "the Enlightenment" and "the religious." It is rather that, in a setting as religiously divided as ours is, one is unlikely to win support for one's political proposals on most issues simply by appealing to religious considerations.

Is it true that religion is essentially a conversation-stopper? I would have thought that the pragmatic line should be that religion is not *essentially* anything, that the conversational utility of employing religious premises in political arguments depends on the situation. There is one sort of religious premise that does have the tendency to stop a conversation, at least momentarily—namely, faith-claims. We can understand why faith-claims have this tendency if we describe them in the way Brandom does. A faith-claim, according to Brandom, avows a cognitive commitment without claiming entitlement to that commitment.[25] In the context of discursive exchange, if I make a faith-claim, I am authorizing others to attribute the commitment to me and perhaps giving them a better understanding of why I have undertaken certain other cognitive or practical commitments. I am also making the claim available to others as a premise they might wish to employ in their reasoning. But I am not accepting the responsibility of demonstrating my entitlement to it. If pressed for such a demonstration, I might say simply that it is a matter of faith. In other words, "Don't ask me for reasons. I don't have any."

It should be clear how this common sort of discursive move tends to put a crimp in the exchange of reasons. If, at a crucial point in an argument, one avows a cognitive commitment without claiming entitlement to that commitment, and then refuses to give additional reasons for accepting the claim in question, then the exchange of reasons has indeed come grinding to a halt. But there are two things to keep in mind here. First, a claim can be religious without being a faith-claim. It is possible to assert a premise that is religious in content and stand ready to demonstrate one's entitlement to it. Many people are prepared to argue at great length in support of their religious claims. So we need to distinguish between discursive problems that arise because religious premises are not widely shared and those that arise because the people who avow such premises are not prepared to argue for them.

Second, as Brandom points out, faith is not "by any means the exclusive province of religion" (AR, 105). Everyone holds some beliefs on nonreligious topics without claiming to know that they are true. To express such a belief in the form of a reason is to make what I have been calling a faith-claim. One would expect such claims to be fairly common in discussions of especially intractable political questions. When questions of this kind get discussed there are typically hard-liners on both sides who not only propose answers, but also claim to know that their answers are right. Yet there is typically a group of people in the middle who are prepared to take a stand, if need be, but would never claim they knew that they were right. The abortion debate is like this, and so is the debate over the problem of dirty hands in the fight against terrorism. In fact, the phenomenon of nonreligious faith-claims is quite common in political discourse, because policy making often requires us to take some stand when we cannot honestly claim to know that our stand is correct. That is just the way politics is.

It is important in this context to recall the distinction between being entitled to a belief and being able to justify that belief to someone else. Even in cases where individuals do plausibly claim to be epistemically entitled to religious premises, they might still be unable to produce an argument that would give their interlocutors reason to accept those premises. To assert such a premise would not qualify as a faith-claim in the strict sense that I have just defined, but it would create a potential impasse in conversation. Yet here again, the same sort of difficulty arises for all of us, not only for religious believers, when we are asked to defend our most deeply engrained commitments, especially those that we acquired through acculturation instead of through reasoning. We are normally entitled to hold onto commitments of this kind unless they prove problematical in some way—for example, by turning out to be either internally incoherent or too hard to square with newly acquired commitments that strike us as highly credible. If the reason for excluding the expression of religious commitments is that they create this type of discursive impasse, then the only fair way to proceed is to exclude the expression of many nonreligious commitments, as well. But if we go in this direction, Rorty's view will require silence on many of the most important issues on the political agenda.

As Rorty grants, many citizens in fact affirm political conclusions that are influenced in some way by their religious commitments. Such commitments typically have a bearing on how one ranks highly important moral concerns. When President Truman was deciding what strategy to pursue in bringing World War II to an end, for example, he had to come to terms with two conflicting moral concerns. One of these had to do with his hope to minimize the number of deaths resulting from his strategy. The other had to do with his qualms about dropping atomic weapons and firebombs on civilian targets. When the question arises of how we should instruct our future leaders to act when they face a similar conflict, citizens are free to speak their minds. If a group of citizens deems the latter concern more important than the former, or vice versa, they should feel free to say so. But when they do, they are likely to be pressed for reasons. Suppose their actual motivating reasons are religious ones not widely shared among their fellow citizens, and it is clear that some citizens, employing their own reasonably held collateral commitments as premises, would be entitled to reject them. In that case, there appear to be three options: (1) to remain silent; (2) to give justifying arguments based strictly on principles already commonly accepted; and (3) to express their actual (religious) reasons for supporting the policy they favor while also engaging in immanent criticism of their opponents' views.

I see nothing in principle wrong with option (3), especially in circumstances that tend to rule out option (2). It could be, for example, that option (2) is difficult or impossible to pursue because the principles that supposedly belong to the Jeffersonian compromise, when conjoined with factual information accessible to the citizenry as a whole, do not entail a resolution of the issue. It is plausible to suppose that the problem of dirty hands has been hard to resolve precisely because some reasonable citizens are justified in rejecting one solution of the problem, while other reasonable citizens are justified in rejecting the opposite solution. But even if this is not granted, it is clear that there are other issues that cannot be resolved solely on the basis of commonly accepted principles. Kent Greenawalt argues persuasively that the debates over welfare assistance, punishment, military policy, abortion, euthanasia, and environmental policy all fall into this category.[26]

It appears, then, to be a consequence of Rorty's argument for restraint that we should leave a long list of important political issues both unresolved and, even more implausibly, unaddressed.

In *Contingency, Irony, and Solidarity*, Rorty has this to say:

> All human beings carry about a set of words which they employ to justify their actions, their beliefs, and their lives. These are the words in which we formulate praise of our friends and contempt for our enemies, our long-term projects, our deepest self-doubts and our highest hopes. They are the words in which we tell, sometimes prospectively and sometimes retrospectively, the story of our lives. I shall call these words a person's "final vocabulary."[27]

Rorty then explains this term as follows: "It is 'final' in the sense that if doubt is cast on the worth of these words, their user has no noncircular argumentative recourse. Those words are as far as he can go with language; beyond them there is only helpless passivity or a resort to force." What Rorty is describing here is the sort of discursive commitment one can be entitled to even though one would not know how to defend it. I can imagine no way of banning the use of final vocabularies, in this sense, from political discussion, even if it were a desirable thing to do, which it plainly is not. What makes some people religious is that the vocabularies in which they tell the stories of their lives—including their stories of our common political life—have religious content. Like Rorty, they tend to be speechless when pressed for linear reasons for adopting their final vocabularies. But unless those vocabularies become severely problematical, what reason would they have for abandoning them?

Rorty grants that there is "hypocrisy involved in saying that believers somehow have no right to base their political views on their religious faith, whereas we atheists have every right to base ours on Enlightenment philosophy. The claim that in doing so we are appealing to reason, whereas the religious are being irrational, is hokum." He is also realistic enough to admit that "religious beliefs, or the lack of them, will influence political convictions. Of course they will" (PSH, 172). So his point in endorsing the Jeffersonian compromise appears to be simply that it is always wise, pragmatically speaking, to confine the premises of our political arguments to commitments held in common. Religious premises are to be excluded not because they involve faith-claims and not because they involve vocabularies that cannot be defended without circularity, but rather because they are not held in common. He seems to mean *actually held in common*; he is not referring, as the contractarians do, to what all *reasonable* persons *would* accept. But the problem remains the same. Reasons actually held in common do not get us far enough toward answers to enough of our political questions. The proposed policy of restraint, if adopted, would cause too much silence at precisely the points where more discussion is most badly needed. The policy would itself be a conversation-stopper.

Suppose you are debating an issue of the type Greenawalt highlights, and you are still trying to argue your case solely by reference to commonly accepted principles and generally accessible information. Imagine that one of your interlocutors, sensing that you are not fully disclosing your own premises, says, "But what's your actual reason? What really moves you to accept this conclusion?" Now you must either dissemble or choose between options (1) and (3). But why not choose (3)? There are many circumstances in which candor requires full articulation of one's actual reasons. Even if it does lead to a momentary impasse, there is no reason to view this result as fatal to the discussion. One can always back up a few paces, and begin again, now with a broader conversational objective. It is precisely when we find ourselves in an impasse of this kind that it becomes most advisable for citizens representing various points of view to express their actual reasons in greater detail. For this is the only way we can pursue the objectives of understanding one another's perspectives, learning from one another through open-minded listening, and subjecting each other's premises to fair-minded immanent criticism.

Like the contractarians, when Rorty discusses the role of religion in politics, he completely neglects the potential benefits of ad hoc immanent criticism in overcoming momentary impasses. But he does, in other contexts, recognize the value of carrying on a discussion at this level. His name for such discourse in *Philosophy and the Mirror of Nature* was "conversation."[28] There Rorty suggested that "*conversation* [be seen] as the ultimate context within which knowledge is to be understood" (389; emphasis in original). What he meant by conversation was a kind of discursive exchange in which "Our focus shifts . . . to the relation between alternative standards of justification, and from there to the actual changes in those standards which make up intellectual history" (389f.) The role of edifying philosophy, as Rorty presented it in that book, is to keep discursive exchange going at those very points where "normal" discourse—that is, discourse on the basis of commonly accepted standards—cannot straightforwardly adjudicate between competing claims. Conversation is a good name for what is needed at those points where people employing different final vocabularies reach a momentary impasse. But if we do use the term "conversation" in this way, we shall have to conclude that conversation is the very thing that is not stopped when religious premises are introduced in a political argument. It is only the normal discourse of straightforward argument on the basis of commonly held premises that is stopped. The political discourse of a pluralistic democracy, as it turns out, needs to be a mixture of normal discourse and conversational improvisation.[29] In the discussion of some issues, straightforward argument on the basis of commonly held standards carries us only so far. Beyond that, we must be either silent or conversational. But we can be conversational, in the spirit of Rorty's most edifying philosophical work, only by rejecting the policy of restraint he endorses.

I came of age ethically, politically, and spiritually in the Civil Rights movement, where I acquired my democratic commitments from prophetic ministers. In college, when I moved rapidly down the path that leads from Schleiermacher to Feuerbach, Emerson, and beyond, I found myself collaborating mainly with dissenting Protestants, secular Jews, and members of the radical Catholic underground in the struggle against U.S. involvement in the Vietnam War. I have known since then that it is possible to build democratic coalitions including people who differ religiously and to explore those differences deeply and respectfully without losing one's integrity as a critical intellect. This book is offered in the hope that similarly diverse coalitions and equally full expression of differences remain possible in democratic culture today, if we can only summon the will to form them.

Chapter 4

SECULARIZATION AND RESENTMENT

Resentment is easy. Theology is hard.
—John Bowlin

IN THE 1960s Christian theologians made news by extolling the virtues of the secular city. Nowadays, however, they often denounce secularized political culture in vehement terms. John Milbank and his fellow proponents of "radical orthodoxy" hold that "for several centuries now, secularism has been defining and constructing the world. It is a world in which the theological is either discredited or turned into a harmless leisure-time activity of private commitment." The only appropriate response, they conclude, is a theology that "refuses the secular." This means rejecting both "secular reason" and the "secular state" as spheres of discourse not essentially "framed by a theological perspective."[1] While Richard John Neuhaus is more favorably disposed toward modern democracy than Milbank is, he nonetheless bemoans "a religious evacuation of the public square." He declares that "secular humanism has had a pervasive and debilitating effect upon our public life," and warns that "the notion of the secular state can become the prelude to totalitarianism."[2]

Theological resentment of the secular deserves attention from theorists of democracy not only because it gives voice to an animus felt by many religiously oriented citizens, but also because it reinforces that animus and encourages its spread. Radical orthodoxy is currently the hottest topic being debated in seminaries and divinity schools in the United States, and thus a significant part of the subculture within which future pastors are being educated. Neuhaus's journal, *First Things*, takes the case against secularized political culture to an audience that reaches well beyond the seminaries.

In chapter 3, I discussed two forms of liberalism that unwittingly fuel the resentment of the secular expressed in the writings of Milbank and Neuhaus. Rawls's political liberalism holds that religious premises may be used in democratic deliberation and debate of essential matters, but only if they are eventually supplemented by reasoning that appeals to a freestanding conception of justice. Rorty's pragmatic liberalism holds that introducing religious premises into political argument is more or less guaranteed to break off the discussion and therefore best avoided. Milbank and Neuhaus would reject both of these positions as secularist. That liberalism is secularist in this sense may be a reason for religious believers to reject it as an ideology or political theory. But is this also a reason for them to reject the political culture of which liberals propose to give a theoretical account? Only, I suggested, if that theoretical account is *descriptively* adequate, which it is not.

In this chapter, I want to focus on ambiguities surrounding the notion of secularization and their implications for theological and religious expression. There is a sense in which the ethical discourse of most modern democracies is *secularized*, for such discourse is not "framed by a theological perspective" taken for granted by all those who participate in it. But secularization in this sense is not a reflection of commitment to *secularism*. It entails neither the denial of theological assumptions nor the expulsion of theological expression from the public sphere. And it leaves believers free to view both the state and democratic political culture as domains standing ultimately under divine judgment and authority. That believers view the political sphere in this way does not entail that others will, of course. But this just means that the age of theocracy is over, not that the anti-Christ has taken control of the political sphere.

How Ethical Discourse Became Secularized and What This Means

Many religious traditions inculcate habitual deference to the expert interpreters of scriptural texts on questions of moral, religious, and political practice. The experts' claim to authority on these questions consists in their ability to interpret and apply the relevant texts. In Judaism, for example, each rabbi establishes his authority to interpret the texts by learning Hebrew, studying Scripture and the commentaries for many years, and debating the fine points of interpretation with others who have spent a significant portion of their lives engaging in these activities. In Catholicism and Islam, priests and imams enjoy a comparable sort of authority. But all of this assumes, first, that particular texts, if properly interpreted, include authoritative answers to the sorts of questions being addressed. Second, it assumes that some interpreters are in a better position to interpret those texts than others are.

Now consider the early-modern debates among Christians of various types over moral and political questions. Here we have numerous groups, all of which were committed to treating the Christian Bible as an authoritative source of normative insight into how such questions should be answered. Yet they did not differ only on what this text says and implies. They also differed on who is entitled to interpret it, on whether it is the sole authoritative source of normative insight into such matters, and on who is entitled to resolve apparent conflicts between it and other putative sources of normative insight. Because they differed on all of these points, they eventually found themselves avoiding appeals to biblical authority when trying to resolve their ethical and political differences. The reason was simple; the appeals did not work. So the differing parties increasingly tried to resolve their differences on other grounds. In this respect, their ethical discourse with one another became secularized.

A case study can illustrate how and why this sort of secularization took place. In his study of appeals to the Bible in seventeenth-century English politics, the distinguished historian Christopher Hill asserts that the Bible passed from a position of considerable authority in political debate, cited by virtually all parties, to a position of diminished authority and centrality as the century unfolded. By the end of the 1650s, the Bible had essentially been "dethroned."[3] Among many other signs of this decline, Hill reports that in 1657 members of Parliament laughed at one M.P. for repeatedly citing Scripture in support of his conclusions. Why did the other members find him ridiculous? It could have been for any number of reasons. It is unlikely, however, that each jeering M.P. had ceased to ascribe infallible authority to the Bible in forming his own commitments and no longer respected anyone who did. As Hill puts it, "Twenty years of frenzied discussion had shown that text-swapping and text-distortion solved nothing: agreement was not to be reached even among the godly on what exactly the Bible said and meant" (EB, 421). The change seems to have had less to do with each individual's process of commitment-formation than with what they were able to take for granted in their public discourse with one another.

Imagine that you ascribe infallible authority to the Bible and consult it regularly in forming your own opinions. Suppose further that all members of your society are similarly committed to conforming their opinions to what the Bible says, and you know this. It does not follow that it will make sense for you to appeal to the Bible in settling disputed questions in a public forum. Why? Perhaps you know that members of your society do not have compatible views of what the Bible says on political and economic matters. You notice that when members of the group use reasoned discussion to forge consensus on questions of biblical interpretation, they almost always fail. You therefore conclude that it will be unwise for any of you to appeal to the Bible as an infallible authority even though each of you believes that it is. Any such appeal, in this sort of setting, is going to be useless, and anyone who makes it is going to appear foolish.

So we have two things that might be meant by the Bible's authority. The first is a matter of how individuals form their commitments. If a given person is prepared to defer to whatever the Bible says on a moral or political question, call this the Bible's authority over an individual's conscience. The second is a matter of what individuals can reasonably appeal to as an arbiter in disputes with other groups. Call this "public discursive authority." Now that I have drawn this distinction, I want to recommend putting more weight on the second than on the first in telling the story of secularization in general and the story of the Bible in seventeenth-century English politics in particular. Only a few of Hill's examples give clear evidence that the Bible's authority over individual consciences declined. They do not settle the question of how widespread that decline was. But even if the decline of the Bible's authority over conscience was limited to relatively small segments of the English population, as I suspect it was, it still seems plausible to conclude that the Bible's public discursive authority had virtually disappeared by the end of the century.

On the assumption that only a few intellectuals and radical groups abandoned the Bible as an infallible authority in forming their individual consciences on various matters, why did the Bible's role as public discursive authority decline so rapidly and thoroughly? The answer to this question should already be clear. It is that the members of English society were unable to find means of reaching rational agreement on questions of biblical interpretation, and in the absence of such means, the Bible could not play the public role of arbiter it had played earlier in the century. But this answer begets another question. Why was it so hard for these particular people to reach rational agreement on the interpretation of this document?

Hill's examples give hints about how to answer this question. English Protestants ascribed authority to the Bible because they took it to be a book authored by God. It was the word of God, and it could be trusted as an infallible authority because God is both morally perfect and omniscient. Many of them had downgraded church tradition to the status of fallible authority or nonauthority on the ground that it had obviously been corrupted, so they were unable to settle issues of interpretation by appeal to tradition. This left them appealing for interpretive guidance to what Milton called the "supreme authority . . . of the Spirit, which is internal and the individual possession of each man." But while this sort of appeal might leave each individual convinced that he or she had been guided by the Spirit toward infallibly correct conclusions, it did not provide a public means for resolving differences between one person's conclusions and another's. Moreover, the explanation one would be inclined to give for such differences was that anyone disagreeing with one's own conclusions must have been guided by some force other than the Spirit, most likely a demonic one. That sort of explanation of disagreement tends to undermine the rationale for trying to resolve differences by exchanging reasons. It encourages the thought that one's opponents need to be fought rather than offered reasons.

Another consequence of viewing the Bible as an infallibly authoritative book authored by God is a requirement of consistency. Internally, each biblical passage will need to be read in such a way that its sense can be reconciled logically with the sense of all other biblical passages. Apparent inconsistency within the book as a whole—for example, with respect to the birthplace of Jesus—will need to be explained away. Yet there can also be a requirement of external consistency. Each biblical passage will need to be read in such a way that its sense can be reconciled with whatever one is firmly committed to regarding as true. The idea that what the Bible says *must* be true exerts pressure on the interpreter to read the Bible in such a way that it does not conflict with his or her strongest commitments. The strongest proponents of biblical authority therefore often have the strongest reasons, from their own point of view, for being what we might call "strong" readers of the biblical text. They proclaim the primacy of the Bible at one moment and then a moment later push the text hard in the direction of truths with which it must in the end prove compatible, given that God is no author of falsehoods.

The need for external consistency acquired new force in the sixteenth and seventeenth centuries, as the idea of the "Book of Nature" became central to the projects of astrologers, alchemists, and champions of the new science. For here was another book authored by God, and therefore equally certain to disclose only truths to those who interpret it correctly. It followed that a correct interpretation had to make everything in both books add up to a set of consistent propositions, no matter how much the interpreter was required to go beyond or against the so-called plain sense of Scripture. Even those not captivated by the idea of a second divinely authored book often found themselves giving readings apparently at odds with the plain sense of the biblical text in trying to address the problems of internal and external consistency. They then either had to abandon the Protestant commitment to the priority of the Bible's literal sense or they had to engage in special pleading while stretching the plain sense beyond recognition.

Different individuals responded to this set of problems in different ways, as Hill's examples make clear. A few, like Samuel Fisher, abandoned the idea of the Bible as a divinely authored book and formed their own opinions without relying on it essentially. Others, like the radical woman known as M. M., continued to rely on it while drawing a distinction between the essential truths revealed in the text and the merely human vessels into which the divine wine had been poured. The truths were divinely authored, then, but not the book itself, at least as we have it.[4] Both of these moves were meant to dissolve, rather than solve, the problems caused by the quest for internal and external consistency. And both moves relieved the pressure to supply typological and allegorical readings that can be made congruent with the plain sense.

It is not at all clear that most people made these moves. Many people just went on trying to solve the problems that Fisher and M. M. tried to dissolve. The important point, however, is that the plain sense was no longer the sort of thing *anybody*, even a die-hard, Bible-thumping literalist, could appeal to in settling a public dispute over what the Bible meant. The reason for this was not that most people agreed with M. M. or Fisher. Two other reasons appear to have been involved. The first was that the appeal to inner persuasion was not publicly persuasive. The second was that the plain sense had already been stretched beyond the breaking point by the quest for consistency. Readings supposedly grounded in the plain sense of Scripture had multiplied so rapidly that the plain sense could no longer function as a publicly effective constraint on interpretation. And once this had happened, the Bible's public role as arbiter was gone.

My account of secularization concerns what can be taken for granted when exchanging reasons in public settings. A setting is public in the relevant sense if it involves no expectation of confidentiality and if it is one in which citizens address one another qua citizens. What makes a form of discourse secularized, according to my account, is not the tendency of the people participating in it to relinquish their religious beliefs or to refrain from employing them as reasons. The mark of secularization, as I use the term, is rather the fact that participants in a given discursive practice are not in a position to take for granted that their interlocutors are making the same religious assumptions they are. This is the sense in which public discourse in modern democracies tends to be secularized.

Notice that secularization in this sense does not reflect a commitment to secularism, secular liberalism, or any other ideology. It is true that modern democratic discourse tends not to be "framed by a theological perspective," but this does not prevent any of the individuals participating in it from adopting a theological perspective. They are free to frame their contributions to it in whatever vocabulary they please. What they cannot reasonably do is expect a single theological perspective to be shared by all of their interlocutors. But this is not because the discourse in which they and their interlocutors are engaged commits everyone involved to relying solely on "secular reason" when thinking and conversing on political questions. Nor does it involve endorsement of the "secular state" as a realm entirely insulated from the effects of religious convictions, let alone removed from God's ultimate authority. It is simply a matter of what can be presupposed in a discussion with other people who happen to have different theological commitments and interpretive dispositions.

In my previous work, I have referred to the secularization of public discourse as an effect of the "kinematics of presupposition."[5] To avoid misunderstanding of this point, however, it is necessary to draw a distinction between two senses of the term "presupposition." Suppose Martin Luther King, Jr., asserts that God is love. In making this assertion, King presupposes, but does not explicitly say, that God exists. So it makes sense to say that commitment to the existence of God is one of King's presuppositions. Presuppositions in this first sense are either assumptions that individuals self-consciously make when saying certain things or assumptions that must be true if what they are saying is to make sense.

Now suppose that a Unitarian addresses an argument about same-sex marriage to someone she knows to be a Catholic bishop. Obviously neither the Unitarian nor her interlocutor can in this case take for granted the details of a common theology. They cannot argue with one another on the basis of that as a given. We can put this by saying that the discursive exchange going on *between* these two parties does not presuppose a theology. The exchange no doubt has some presuppositions, which might include the proposition that God exists, but they do not include agreement, for example, on God's triune nature or on the interpretation of his commandments. If an atheist, a Muslim, and an orthodox Jew were now to join the discussion, the overlap in theological assumptions would diminish further, and the discussion would be able to presuppose still less. Here we are talking about "presuppositions" in a second sense of the term. Saying that the Unitarian is now participating in a discursive exchange that lacks theological presuppositions does not entail anything about what theological commitments she herself has made, how important they are to her in her personal deliberations, whether she is justified in accepting them, or whether she is free to express them.

My account of secularized discourses employs the second sense of "presupposition." Secularized discourses, as I am defining them, do not necessarily involve or produce participants who lack religious commitments. Most U.S. citizens profess some sort of belief in God, but their public ethical discourse is secularized in the sense I am trying to specify. This is a major advantage of my account over accounts of secularization that focus on an alleged loss of religious belief or on "disenchantment" of the world. The theory I offer is an account of what transpires between people engaging in public discourse, not an account of what they believe, assume, or presuppose as individuals. It has nothing to do with their experience of the world as a disenchanted universe, emptied of divine intentions and spiritual meaning.

Public ethical discourse in modern democratic societies tends not to presuppose agreement on the nature, existence, and will of God. Nor does it presuppose agreement on how the Bible or other sources of religious insight should be interpreted. As a result, theological claims do not have the status of being "justified by default"—of being something all participants in the discursive practice are effectively obliged to defer to as authoritative or justified. And this consequence of theological plurality has an enormous impact on what our ethical discourse is like. It means, for example, that in most contexts it will simply be imprudent, rhetorically speaking, to introduce explicitly theological premises into an argument intended to persuade a religiously diverse public audience. If one cannot expect such premises to be accepted or interpreted in a uniform way, it will not necessarily advance one's rhetorical purposes to assert them. And if theological premises therefore receive little discursive attention for this perfectly understandable reason, why would anyone have just cause for resentment of the resulting type of secularized discourse? When people want to exchange reasons with others who differ from them theologically, this type of discourse is likely to increase drastically in significance. Resentment of this fact is indistinguishable from resentment of religious diversity.

It is useful in this context to keep in mind the distinction between saying that a person is justified in believing a claim and saying that a claim is justified. A *person* is justified in believing a claim if he or she is entitled to be committed to it, given his or her discursive context and cognitive conduct. A *claim* is justified in some discursive context if *everyone* in that context is justified in believing it (either because they have no relevant reasons for doubting it or because it has already been successfully defended against all relevant reasons for doubting it). In modern democracies, theological claims tend not to have the default status of being justified in the latter sense when uttered in public settings—for the simple reason that these settings tend to be religiously plural. It is also the case, however, that most modern democracies are liberal in the innocuous sense of treating individuals as (defeasibly) entitled by default to make whatever theological commitments they see fit to make and free to express those commitments in speech or in action.[6]

Ethical discourse in religiously plural modern democracies is secularized, according to my account, only in the sense that it does not take for granted a set of agreed-upon assumptions about the nature and existence of God. This claim pertains to presuppositions in the second sense. It means that no one can take for granted, when addressing a religiously plural audience, that religious commitments have default authority in this context. It does not entail any limitation on what an individual can presuppose in the first sense. To the contrary, the discursive practice in question is secularized, according to my theory, precisely because many of the individuals participating in it do have religious commitments that function as presuppositions in some of their own deliberations and pronouncements. It is because these commitments vary from one citizen to another that they cannot qualify as presuppositions in the second sense. But this leaves open the possibility that citizens who hold one or another set of religious commitments could be rationally entitled to those commitments.

Some theologians hold that the citizenry's common discourse on ethical and political topics suffers from incoherence in the absence of commonly held theological assumptions. They conclude that we should all therefore accept a common stock of theological assumptions in order to restore our shared discourse to coherence. But whose assumptions shall we adopt? And by what means shall we secure agreement on them? The crux of the issue is that nobody currently knows how to bring about by acceptable means what the theological opponents of secularized discourse are suggesting. Their proposals are unrealistic if pursued without resort to coercion and morally harmful if pursued coercively. Some of my critics say that I overestimate the dangers, but the only dangers I am referring to here are the dangers that *would* obtain *if* an antisecularization strategy were pursued by coercive means. These are the same dangers that did obtain during the state-forming wars of early-modern Europe and today still plague nations where civic trust, tolerance of religious differences, and constitutional democracy have yet to establish themselves. Since my critics are not proposing coercion, my issue with them has more to do with the fact that their program is unrealistic than with any dangers that might be involved. I am not saying that it is dangerous nowadays in the United States to employ religious premises in political reasoning. That is a different issue completely.[7] Neither am I saying that theologians, as individuals, should abandon their theological commitments. That, too, is a different issue, which involves a different sense of secularization.[8]

Our society is religiously plural, and has remained so for several centuries despite constant efforts on the part of its religious members to appeal to their fellow citizens with reasons for converting to a single theology. So when people discuss political issues with one another publicly—say, by addressing a school board meeting or participating in a debate of presidential candidates, as opposed to taking part in a colloquy of co-religionists—the religious differences among them will make it impossible for them to take theological propositions for granted. In such a setting you could of course make a theological assertion, and in making it implicitly commit yourself to a theological presupposition in the first sense. But you could not rightly assume that theological presuppositions in the second sense are already in place, tacitly agreed upon as the framework within which discussion proceeds. What shall we do, then, to achieve the coherence that some theologians believe we lack? I fail to see how the sea change these theologians are calling for is going to happen. There is no point in trying to wish the social reality of religious diversity away, or in resenting this diversity as long as it lasts. Until it does go away, our public discourse will be secularized, in the sense I have specified, whether we want it to be or not.

RADICAL ORTHODOXY'S REFUSAL OF THE SECULAR

Because theologians like Milbank see the secularization of political culture as a reflection of secularism—an ideology—they have a story to tell about its emergence that differs significantly from the one I have been telling.

My story focuses on what can reasonably be taken for granted by ordinary speakers under conditions of religious diversity, whereas their story focuses on the social and discursive consequences of an intellectual error. As William T. Cavanaugh tells the story in *Radical Orthodoxy*, the secularist error involves both "the progressive stripping away of the sacred from some profane remainder" and "the substitution of one *mythos* of salvation for another."[9] It "proceeds logically from the anthropology of individual *dominium* on which the liberal state is based" (RO, 193). The secular state, in this view, is essentially dedicated to replacing the Christian account of salvation with a secularist one. Secularized discourse under the auspices of such a state is therefore *secularist* discourse, a violent disruption of what was once a single scheme of participation in the divine and an attempt to usurp the soteriological function that the church has always claimed for itself. Yet, says Cavanaugh, "the state has failed to save us" (RO, 192), and necessarily so, for a secular state is ill-equipped to save us from anything, least of all the violence implicit in the social contract itself.

Cavanaugh clearly strives to put the "secular state" in the worst possible light. He achieves this objective in part by unfairly omitting mention of the fact that most liberal theorists have taken pains to deny that the state is appropriately seen as a vehicle of salvation. But the story being told here is also flawed in the sort of historical significance it attributes to liberal theory. From what source does the "secular state" derive? From a deeply mistaken "mythos." And this mythos, according to radical orthodoxy, can itself be traced back to a mistaken conception of the secular instituted in late-medieval thought when theological voluntarists got the upper hand and a genuinely participatory outlook went into eclipse. The problem is, at root, a theological error and is to be corrected by theological means— specifically, by a *radical* recovery of Platonic-Augustinian *orthodoxy*.

I find the intellectualism in this account of secularization extremely implausible. Intellectual errors do sometimes have significant social and political consequences, but history rarely works in the theory-driven way that philosophers and theologians imagine. One reason for doubting that the mythos or ideology of secularism is what caused the secularization of public discourse is that its proponents have never had the numbers or the clout to change the world as dramatically as Cavanaugh's story supposes. The irony here is that radical orthodoxy appears to be taking over the basic elements of what was originally a secularist theory of secularization. According to this theory, modernity is a progressively secularizing force in the sense that it tends to produce increasing levels of disbelief and disenchantment. The trouble is that this theory now lies in shambles, having had nearly all of its predictions falsified over the last four decades.[10] If there is no sociological reason to suppose that secularization, in a sense that involves increasingly widespread acceptance of secularist ideas, has been occurring at all, there is also no reason to accept an intellectualist account of how the process of secularization works and what set it in motion. The story that radical orthodoxy tells about secularization is about as credible as the story that Heidegger tells about the origins of the age of technology in the onto-theological tradition. I have been trying to tell a story of a more down-to-earth sort.

According to my account, secularization was not primarily brought about by the triumph of a secularist ideology, "first constructed," as Milbank puts it, "in the discourses of liberalism" (TST, 4). Nor did it result from a thoroughgoing disenchantment or desacralization of the world. What drove the secularization of political discourse forward was the increasing need to cope with religious plurality discursively on a daily basis under circumstances where improved transportation and communication were changing the political and economic landscape. Secularization of the kind I have described did, however, give rise to desacralization of the political sphere and to secularist ideology as an attempt to explain and justify it. It is not that these latter things are mere fantasies, lacking a substantial effect on the social order. They are present, to be sure, even if they do not have the causal significance that a now discredited sociological tradition and radical orthodoxy have assigned to them.

Medieval political theology was in a position to take for granted that its own Christian vocabulary was the one required for explaining what it meant for the ruler of a Christian political body to be Christ's vicar.[11] Political theology essentially made explicit the norms according to which a kingdom or principality in Christendom stood under God's authority. That these norms obviously needed to be made explicit in theological terms made it natural for all concerned to view the political community as sacralized. But under circumstances in which a theological vocabulary proves an obstacle to the rational resolution of political differences, and most political agents begin relying largely on nontheological vocabularies when making their political arguments, the political community itself can appear to have been removed from its former sacralized status. Political theology will in that event inevitably come to seem somewhat less essential to the task of making explicit the norms to which appeal is being made. Intellectuals will then attempt to make those norms explicit in some nontheological way. This is the context in which liberal secularism can arise as an ideological explanation and justification of the new form of political order.

As we saw in the previous chapter, however, it is a mistake to assume without argument that ideologies accurately reflect the social formations they are intended to serve. Secularized political discourse has given rise to various competing philosophical accounts of itself. Among the least plausible of these, descriptively, is liberal secularism. So we must at least entertain the possibility that secularized political discourse in modern democratic societies can to some large extent be disentangled from the antireligious animus of some of its ideological defenders.

It remains the case, nonetheless, that secularization has deposed political theology from the social role it became accustomed to performing in Christendom. There is thus a sense in which the political community appears to have been desacralized in modern democratic societies. For rather than being thought to possess authority directly from God as vicars of Christ, rulers are now thought to possess authority directly from the people. The consent of the governed, respect for the rights of the people, and proper concern for the common good are all recognized as conditions for the possession of such authority in modern democracies, but none of them is explicitly theological. Where, if at all, does God's authority over all of creation figure into this picture? This is a central question for political theology in societies where political discussion has been secularized.

Radical orthodoxy answers it, as we have seen, by taking secularism's account of modern democracy at face value and then refusing the secular as essentially antitheological. To restore a proper sense of God's authority over the political community, political theology must renounce the form of political community whose essence it is to deny God's authority over it. This is one possible answer. But its descriptive premise is, to say the least, questionable. If secularization of the kind I have described can occur even in a community whose members agree that God has the *ultimate* authority to judge all creation, including all political orders, then it is not clear that rejection of a secularized political community is theologically necessary. Every Christian is free to affirm God's ultimate authority over every political community, including his or her own, whether or not others agree. Indeed, Christians who make this affirmation are bound to infer that Christ is now ruling democratic political communities providentially, no matter who acknowledges or fails to acknowledge his authority. The central task of contemporary Christian political theology is to discern how Christ's rulership of such communities manifests itself. Radical orthodoxy's refusal of the secular seems to imply a simple answer to this question—namely, that Christ in his capacity as judge declares such communities utterly vitiated by their lack of true piety and their refusal to participate in the gracious outpouring of divine love in the church.

In giving this answer, Milbank claims fidelity to Augustine's *City of God*. But in making good on it, he finds himself struggling against Augustine's evident ambivalence toward pagan "virtue."[12] The question of how the relevant passages in Augustine should be interpreted will receive much attention from Christian ethicists and historical theologians in the next decade. For our purposes, however, we can bracket the issue of fidelity to Augustine and highlight three properly theological questions that Milbank's refusal of the secular tends to suppress:

- is it not possible to discern the workings of the Holy Spirit, and thus some reflection of God's redemptive activity, in modern democratic aspirations?
- is there nothing in the political life of modern democracies, or in the lives of those who are struggling for just and decent arrangements within them, that a loving God would bless?
- if the plentitude of God's triune inner life shines forth in all of creation, cannot theology discern some such light in democratic political community?

These questions must be high on the agenda of any Christian political theology that hopes to acknowledge the sovereignty of God while transcending both resentment of, and absorption into, the secular. It is unfortunate that Milbank tends to respond to them only indirectly, when issuing his summary verdicts on the political theologians of the modern period. The hero of his critique of recent Catholic political theology (TST, chap. 8) is Maurice Blondel, whose work is said to represent "a new philosophy which goes beyond both positivism and dialectics so as to anticipate a postmodern 'discourse about difference' " (TST, 209). Much of the account is devoted to tracing the ill effects of Karl Rahner's theology among the Latin American liberationists and such Germans as Johann Baptist Metz and Helmut Peukert. Milbank holds Rahner responsible for a conciliation with Enlightenment philosophy that spoils whatever it touches. The entire discussion is carried out at such an abstract level, however, that the three questions I have identified are never addressed directly.

Milbank grants that the liberationists were right to see "the whole concrete life of humanity [as] imbued with grace" and to infer from this that "it is surely not possible to separate political and social concerns from the 'spiritual' concerns of salvation" (TST, 206–7). But they ended up committed to "another effort to reinterpret Christianity in terms of a dominant secular discourse of our day" (TST, 208). Milbank expresses support for genuinely Christian socialism, and distances himself from "reactionaries in the Vatican." His point is that theology should itself determine what Christian socialism means. If Milbank means by this only that Christian political theology must take pains to be true to its belief in divine sovereignty when interpreting what the ideal form of socialist practice would be, let us grant the point for the purposes of argument. The methodological implication he wishes to draw follows straightforwardly—namely, that theology, when fulfilling its own tasks, must not allow some form of secular thought to dictate an understanding of the political sphere. "Mediating theology," as exemplified in Rahner's work, is too eager to defer to secular philosophy and social theory, and must therefore be rejected if Christian orthodoxy is to be maintained.

But suppose we descend from the methodological level and inquire into the implications of Milbank's admission that "the whole concrete life of humanity is imbued with grace." Does this not include the political life of humanity in modern democracies? And if Christian socialists, understanding themselves in terms drawn from Blondel's "supernaturalizing of the natural," join forces with socialists of other kinds to ameliorate the condition of workers and the unemployed, what is political theology to say about the non-Christians in the coalition? If Milbank is prepared to declare them unwitting collaborators in God's gracious rulership of the world, while granting them the freedom to interpret the shared socialist project in their own terms, then one wonders why the resulting political theology should advertise itself as a "refusal of the secular." For the secular would then be understood not as a domain outside of the realm of divine sovereignty and grace but simply as a domain of political action and discourse that is secularized in the sense I have specified. On the other hand, if Milbank wishes to take a less charitable line on non-Christian socialists, he needs to explain what his theological reasons for doing so might be.

It is at this level that political theology makes a difference. The practical issue is whether Christians, for their own theological reasons, may join hands with others in the struggle for justice—and do so without holding their noses in the presence of their comrades. If Milbank thinks they may, then he is implicitly granting the legitimacy of what I am calling a secularized political sphere, and his conclusions are much less radical than they are made to seem. If he thinks they mustn't, then he has little to offer besides nostalgia, utopian fantasy, and withdrawal into a strongly bounded enclave. In that event, he would owe his readers reasons for avoiding the conclusion that his theology has restricted divine sovereignty and inhibited charity toward the non-Christian other. In the absence of a persuasive argument, readers will probably conclude that Rahner was right about "anonymous Christians" after all.

Now consider Milbank's summary verdicts on modern social theorists. Take, for example, the case of John Ruskin.[13] Milbank portrays Ruskin as the supreme social theorist of the nineteenth century, and presents him as a worthy rival of both liberal and Marxist forms of secularism. But he goes out of his way to quarantine him from the fallen secularity of modernity by declaring him "a relatively isolated prophet" (TST, 200). Milbank makes clear that Ruskin's critique of capitalism is centered in his understanding of the virtues, and briefly considers his version of medievalism in order to distinguish it from the more vulgar varieties. He does not mention Ruskin's influential precursor, William Cobbett, or, a more proximate influence on Ruskin, Thomas Carlyle. He mentions William Morris only in passing (TST, 188), though Morris was surely among those most strongly influenced by Ruskin. By omission of these examples, Ruskin can be made to seem relatively isolated. But in fact he was nothing less than a major representative of a major tradition of social criticism in the modern period—a tradition centrally concerned with character and the virtues in relation to politics, the economy, and architecture. By the turn of the century, his influence was considerable, not least of all in the labor movement, in which Christian and non-Christian socialists collaborated actively. Again, what does radical orthodoxy imply about such collaborative efforts and about the agnostics and atheists who participate in them? Milbank doesn't say.

Neither does he look closely at the details of Ruskin's normative thinking. Certain strands of Ruskin's work may deserve retrieval, but the task of disentangling those strands from attitudes that deserve rejection would be a delicate operation. On a general level, the issue to be confronted is essentially this. Marxist and liberal forms of secularism are currently under attack, for good reason. What, then, shall we make of earlier religious and romantic forms of social criticism, which seem necessary in saying what bothers us about the inhumanity of the capitalist global economy, but which also often seem implicated in noxious attitudes concerning race, gender, and hierarchy? Philosophers and theologians have not yet done well with this question. But to pose it honestly, one needs to acknowledge the democratic commitments that make it hard for most of us to swallow certain features of Ruskin's thinking. Presumably, Milbank would revert here to Blondel's theology as a framework for making sense of his own democratic commitments. But how did it come to pass that a theologian like Blondel, writing at the end of the nineteenth century, came to abandon the hierarchical thinking he inherited from Catholic theology? Where did the democratic tendency in his thought come from historically? Milbank's massive treatise on theology's relation to social theory in the modern period leaves democracy almost entirely out of the picture. Blondel's abandonment of hierarchy appears as if by miracle out of thin air.

Now consider the case of Samuel Taylor Coleridge. Milbank (TST, 4) places Coleridge in a tradition that amounts to "a kind of counter-modernity," which "continues to shadow actual, secular modernity." None of the writers in this tradition is allowed to count as a counterexample to the proposed theory of modern secularity, however. They are instead redefined in advance as essentially not belonging to their own setting. Milbank does not portray them as comprising a modern tradition of thought and practice that has been able to have an influential voice in a secularized political community, but rather as a countertradition criticizing "the secular" from a perspective wholly at odds with it. By framing his story in this dichotomous way and then proceeding through his narrative at breakneck speed, Milbank allows himself to evade all sorts of important complications and ambiguities.

He tells us nothing, for example, about Coleridge's complicity in the injustices of a regressive monarchical regime in the years after turning his back on the revolutionary hopes of his youth. We hear nothing of Coleridge's greatest critic, William Hazlitt, who sought to reconnect Romanticism with the democratic sympathies he inherited from his father's dissenting Protestantism. Nor does Milbank's story make reference to self-consciously religious figures on the other side of the Atlantic, like Emerson, Whitman, and Thoreau, who sought in their own ways to democratize the Burkean Romanticism of Coleridge and Wordsworth. If one tugs a little on Milbank's references to Ruskin and Coleridge, the whole tale begins to unravel. The democratic vitality of the modern period has been eclipsed by "the secular" writ large.

BEYOND RESENTMENT

If Milbank hopes to overcome the "false humility" of modern theology by reasserting its claim to stand in judgment of other discourses, Neuhaus is engaged in a more mundane endeavor. He is a lieutenant in the culture wars, with a zeal for fighting it out in the ideological trenches. If he is nostalgic, it is not for medieval theocracy, but for a relatively recent past, when American leaders and intellectuals were nearly unanimous in affirming the need for Christian faith as a source of virtue and solidarity in democratic political community. In the 1960s Neuhaus was a Lutheran pastor heavily involved in the Civil Rights movement and a leader of the religious Left's opposition to U.S. military involvement in Vietnam. But in the 1970s he became a neoconservative and eventually converted to Roman Catholicism.

Neuhaus holds that what Pope John Paul II calls "the culture of death" may also aptly be called the culture of secular liberalism. Disrespect for living persons, he argues, grows from the twin root of a secularist denial of the necessity of religious foundations for moral and political order and a liberal elevation of individual freedom above all other human values. America remains a religious country at the grass-roots level, but has been ruled by secular liberals for half a century. The result is that many religious Americans have been conned into acceptance of secularist practices. Political speech has been hollowed out. Neither sin nor the common good receive mention. The public square has been stripped of all symbols that once directed attention to a transcendent source of divine judgment and moral order. The sacred canopy that used to hang over the public square has been torn down.

A thinker like Wolterstorff would applaud Neuhaus's critique of secularism, while remaining suspicious of the conservative political implications he draws from it. Many to Neuhaus's left worry that he is not so much hoisting a traditional sacred canopy over the public square as he is wrapping it around the shoulders of the politicians who have made life worse for poor people at home and the victims of U.S. militarism abroad. George Hunsinger, to my mind the most interesting of Neuhaus's critics, argues the case as follows:

> The litmus test . . . of just what Neuhaus wants to legitimate is whether he can countenance a systematic critique of America's role in the name of democratic ideals. The fact is that he cannot. Anyone with serious doubts about America's current influence for good is accused not of poor judgment but of disloyalty. Neuhaus implies that such persons are guilty of betraying their country. Denial of the overall benevolence of American influence is taken as though it were a betrayal of democracy itself. By resorting to rhetoric of disloyalty and betrayal at the crucial point, Neuhaus displays a striking incapacity to differentiate between the American system and democratic ideals, thereby indicating how thoroughly he equates them. In any case, whether the object is America or democracy or both, religion appears here strictly for purposes of legitimation.[14]

These are strong words, but they carry theological authority in part because Hunsinger is equally disturbed by similarly ideological uses of Christian theology on the Left. He proposes as his alternative to Neuhaus's 1981 antisecularist manifesto, "Christianity and Democracy," the "Barmen Declaration" of 1934, written primarily by the great Swiss theologian, Karl Barth, and approved courageously and unanimously by a synod consisting of delegates from Lutheran, Reformed, and United churches.

In the Barmen Declaration, according to Hunsinger, we have a clear example of what it means for the confessing church to maintain the integrity of its theological commitments without defaulting on its urgent obligation to join with others in the struggle for justice and peace. The Declaration says in no uncertain terms that theological commitments must determine the church's political stance in the world, that nothing stands outside the Lordship of Christ, and that theology may not be subordinated to secular programs or ideals. Barth's language is no less compromising than Milbank's. But while the Declaration, in Barth's retrospective view, was somewhat lacking in specificity, its "No!" to Nazism was clear enough to set the confessing church on a "collision course" with the state in Germany. Barth was not content with mere refusal of the secular. He committed himself to a definite program of progressive politics consistent with orthodox Christian doctrine. Hunsinger argues that a similarly bold progressive politics is required of Christians today if they wish to avoid the idolatry of American power he believes to be at work in Neuhaus's writings.

Hunsinger's critique of Neuhaus might seem to be little more than another contribution to the culture wars, but it is not. I find it encouraging not only because the politics being proposed is to my liking, but also because it is serious about political theology in a way that Milbank appears not to be. Radical orthodoxy has benefited from the widespread impression that its refusal of the secular is the only theologically acceptable alternative to Neuhaus's neoconservatism, on the one hand, and to liberalism and liberation theology, on the other. Hunsinger's appeal to Barth and to the politics of resistance that flowed from the Barmen Declaration illuminates another alternative. It is no less orthodox than radical orthodoxy, but much more concrete in its political implications and much more direct in addressing the theological questions I have charged Milbank with neglecting. The result is a theologically rich account of what it means for Christians to be involved in modern, secularized political communities.

As we have seen, Barthian political theology resembles radical orthodoxy's refusal of the secular insofar as it emphasizes both Christ's actual rulership over the domain of secularized politics and the necessity, for Christians, of acknowledging the authority of "the authentic, scriptural voice of Jesus Christ" over their political decisions. But after affirming these principles, Hunsinger immediately goes on to say that they do "not imply that nothing good, beautiful, true, or worth noticing exists outside of Scripture or the church."[15] The secular world is not to be feared or merely refused by anyone committed to charity and justice in dealing with others. It is rather an arena in which a Christian can hope to proclaim God's word and observe the transfiguring effects of God's love on the lives of his creatures. The spirit of Hunsinger's political theology is most concisely expressed in Barth's dictum that "God may speak to us through Russian Communism, a flute concerto, a blossoming shrub, or a dead dog."[16] If God may speak through godless Communism, why not, then, through the words both Christians and non-Christians speak when holding one another responsible democratically for the justice and decency of their institutional arrangements?

Hunsinger pursues this theme in the epilogue of his book, *How to Read Karl Barth*, which explicates the relevant passages in volume 4, part 3 of *Church Dogmatics*.[17] This is where Barth provides orthodox Christian theology's most fully developed response to the questions about the secular world that radical orthodoxy evades. The boldface thesis with which Barth begins his discussion comes from the Barmen Declaration (IV/3, 3, 86). Barth once again affirms that Jesus Christ is *the* Truth and *the* Light and that all else stands under his authority.

To those who complain that the "arrogance" of such an affirmation "makes quite impossible the discussion and interchange between those who champion it and those who cannot or will not accept it, that it leads to the breakdown of communication and even in the last resort of fellowship between Christians and non-Christians," Barth says calmly that Christians "have no option in this matter" (IV/3, 89–90). A Christian is one who accepts Jesus Christ as *the* Truth and *the* Light. To say less than this is to affirm something other than Christian doctrine. To view this affirmation as intrinsically capricious or intolerant is thus to eliminate the possibility of a discussion that includes Christian affirmation from the outset. But Christians, in affirming Christ as *the* Truth, are not properly claiming to possess Christ. To the contrary, if Christ is *the* Truth, then a Christian who affirms him is not *the* truth. Rightly understood, the affirmation enjoins humility. "The only necessary concern of the community and Christians is that they do not make [the affirmation] in any other way but in the submission and humility enjoined upon them, too, by what it says" (IV/3, 91).

Christians who openly affirm Christ as *the* Truth speak truly, according to Barth. They utter *a* truth. The difference between the definite and indefinite articles matters greatly in this context. The church is one place where truths are spoken. It is also, however, a place where many falsehoods are spoken. And it is not the only place where truths are spoken. It does not follow from affirmation of Christ as the one Word of God "that every word spoken outside the circle of the Bible and the Church is a word of false prophecy and therefore valueless, empty and corrupt" (IV/3, 97). What follows is that "the Word spoken in the existence of Jesus Christ" is distinct "from all others." "When we think of these others, we do well to include even the human words spoken in the existence and witness of the men of the Bible and the Church. *In distinction from all these*, Jesus Christ is the one Word of God" (IV/3, 99; emphasis added).

Thus, when Christians are considering the question of where truths—in the plural—are to be found, they must be prepared to look both inside the church and outside of it. Wherever they look, they must be suspicious and critical, as well as open to the possibility of needing to change their minds. Wherever they find important truths being spoken by other human beings, they must take themselves to have been addressed by Christ himself, by *the* Truth, *the* Light, *the* Word. Barth refers to true words spoken (or true lives lived) outside the church as secular "parables of the kingdom" (IV/3, 114). As in the case of the New Testament parables, Jesus Christ is their ultimate source as well as the criterion a Christian must use to appraise them.

> Does Jesus Christ speak through the medium of such words? The answer is that the community which lives by the one Word of the one Prophet Jesus Christ, and is commissioned and empowered to proclaim this Word of His in the world, not only may but must accept the fact that there are such words and that it must hear them too, notwithstanding its life by this one Word and its commission to preach it. . . . Can it be content to hear it only from Holy Scripture and then from its own lips and in its own tongue? Should it not be

grateful to receive it also from without, in very different human words, in a secular parable, even though it is grounded in and ruled by the biblical, pro-phetico-apostolic witness to this one Word? . . . Has it any good reason to refuse this kind of stimulation and direction, whatever its origin or form? . . . Does it not necessarily lead to ossification if the community rejects in advance the existence and word of these alien witnesses to the truth? (IV/3, 115)

Barth concludes that Christians "can and must be prepared to encounter 'parables of the kingdom' in the full biblical sense, not merely in the witness of the Bible and the various arrangements, works and words of the Christian Church, but also in the secular sphere" (IV/3, 117). There must not, then, be any simple refusal of the secular, for this would be tantamount to denying Christ's freedom to fashion secular parables as he sees fit; it would involve turning one's back on a sphere in which God's Word is being spoken through the words of human beings. "For we must not forget that, while man may deny God, according to the Word of reconciliation God does not deny man. Man may be hostile to the Gospel of God, but this Gospel is not hostile to him. . . . How can it be any less probable, or even impossible, that it should actually be exercised and demonstrated in relation to him too?" (IV/3, 119)

Why is all of this a matter of life and death, from Barth's point of view? First of all, because the affirmation of Christ as the truth concerns the one who rules over life and death. But also because mere refusal of the secular shuns the Christian's obligation to discern the difference between true and false words being lived and spoken outside the church, and in doing so places the lives and hopes of innocent human beings at risk. It is to remind his readers of this that Barth begins his discussion by quoting from the Barmen Declaration. Mere refusal of the secular in Germany in 1934 and in most other contexts amounts to complicity in falsehood and evil. Christians must always be prepared to enter a broader discussion in which various words will be spoken. Their utterances in that domain should display the courage of their convictions. They must speak the truth as they see it, which means affirming Jesus Christ as the truth, and be ready to pay the price for saying what they believe. They should resist any form of pluralism or relativism that would be incompatible with the practice of making truth-claims or with their own commitment to this particular truth-claim. All parties involved in the discussion will have their own affirmations to offer. Without truth-claims, there would be no communication, no exchange of reasons. No one can make declarative statements without implying that those who deny the propositional content of those statements are committed to falsehoods. This, by itself, is not arrogant. But as Hunsinger says, the "truth is where one finds it."[18] It would therefore be arrogant to assume that one knows in advance which human voices are speaking truly. This is what secularists assume when they rig the rules of discussion to exclude religious voices. And it is also what Christians assume when they treat the church as the only source of truths.

THEOLOGY, THE PUBLIC SQUARE, AND THE ENCLAVE SOCIETY

In chapter 3, I argued that we would all benefit from fuller expression of whatever ethically relevant commitments our religious and nonreligious neighbors harbor. In a religiously plural society such as ours, it is even more important than in other circumstances to bring into reflective expression commitments that would otherwise remain implicit in the lives of the religious communities. Members of a religious communion can benefit from such expression by learning about themselves and putting themselves in a position to reflect critically on their commitments. Outsiders can benefit from listening in, so as to gain a better grasp on the premises that our fellow citizens rarely have an opportunity to articulate in full. This is one of the ways in which we can overcome the caricatures of religious believers that dominate the rhetoric of the culture wars. The vocation of theologians, as Hans Frei once said, is akin to the calling of Geertzian ethnographers. Their main expressive task, of course, is to make explicit the commitments implicit in a community's practices as an aid to reflective self-understanding.[19] But their contribution to discourse outside of the church consists in a kind of thick description that allows fellow citizens to correct prejudice and misunderstanding concerning what believers think and care about.

Clearly, no theology in our setting can expect to bring into expressive equilibrium the commitments and practices shared by all members of a modern democratic society. But this is not a limitation that theologians alone have to accept. All defenders of what Rawls calls comprehensive doctrines are in the same position, because a religiously plural democratic culture no more shares atheistic commitments than it shares theological ones. When it comes to religious questions, intellectuals in our setting can bring their own commitments, as individuals, into expressive and critical equilibrium. They can perform a similar service for a particular group to which they belong—their fellow Catholics, Muslims, Conservative Jews, fans of Wordsworthian natural piety, village atheists, or whatever. But when they do this, there is no point in pretending that they are articulating the implicit commitments and practices of their fellow citizens as a whole. This implies no limitation, however, on whom they may address or who might wish to listen in.

The recent debate over "public theology" is beset by confusion over what this phrase means. There is clearly little hope for public theology if this means the attempt to bring into expressive equilibrium the theological commitments all members of our society share, for there are no such shared commitments. A theologian can give up this ambition as unrealistic, however, without giving up the hope of addressing a public audience—an audience that includes citizens who are outside of the church. Needless to say, some intellectuals are simply uninterested in theology, while others express hostility toward it or are inclined to ridicule it. There are also theologians who describe atheists as despicable fools who have willfully, half-knowingly, and selfishly turned their backs on religious truth. But why let these people keep the rest of us from achieving some mutual understanding?

Part of the problem derives from thinking of the public sphere as a place, as in Neuhaus's image of the public square. It is not a place. One is addressing the public whenever one addresses people as citizens. In a modern democracy, this is not something one does in one place or all at once. Wherever two or three citizens are gathered whom one might address as citizens, as persons jointly responsible for the common good, one is in a potentially public setting. Suppose you address a few members of the civic nation in their capacity as potential political actors, and do so in the full expectation that your claims might someday enter into their ethical reasoning or be circulated by them to other members of the body politic. Then you are, in the only relevant sense, speaking publicly. A private communication, in contrast, would either not pertain to matters of concern to the people as whole, or involve an expectation of confidentiality. If you express theological commitments in a reflective and sustained way, while addressing fellow citizens as citizens, you are "doing theology" publicly—and in that sense doing public theology. The theologian who realizes that it would be foolish to try to systematize the religious convictions of all citizens in a single "public theology" need not, for that reason, retreat altogether, qua theologian, from public discourse.

I have suggested that democracy would profit if more citizens engaged in the "lengthy, even leisurely unfolding" of their commitments. Our ethical discourse has become rather thinned out—for understandable reasons, which my account of secularized discourses sets out to explain. We often find ourselves wanting to persuade various others unlike ourselves to agree with our conclusions, so we adopt a thinned-out vocabulary that nearly everyone can use, regardless of their religious differences. This tends not to be a theologically inflected vocabulary, because any such vocabulary will tend to embody assumptions that some of our fellow citizens will have religious reasons to reject. And so we reason publicly from premises likely to have the greatest appeal to the greatest number. But even if we win the day, this kind of reasoning sometimes does little to make explicit the language and premises we used when first reaching the conclusion for which we wish to argue.

The reasons we offer to others unlike ourselves, when trying to persuade them to accept a conclusion we care about, are not necessarily the same reasons that led us to reach the conclusion in the first place. The more that public giving of reasons thins out in this way, the less fellow citizens tend to understand one another's languages of personal deliberation. Public discussions can then easily degenerate into a series of attempts to manipulate the populace for unstated reasons. When this happens, cynicism about political speech can spread rapidly, and individuals may prefer to withdraw into smaller, more uniform communities, where a language of personal deliberation is shared. But discussions confined to members of the subgroup can easily degenerate in these circumstances, as suspicion deepens concerning the unspoken motives of other subgroups. The wider society's pluralism will then come to seem inherently vicious. Once cynicism and suspicion begin to take hold in this way, they can be extremely difficult to overcome, because the mutual withdrawal of citizens into the various enclaves available to them tends to block access to the kind of evidence that might restore trust and mutual respect.

Such trends are currently being exacerbated by changes in the technology and economics of information-exchange. Talk radio, cable television, and the Internet have significantly increased the proportion of information that the average individual receives from sources entirely within his or her particular enclave.[20] It is therefore increasingly difficult for claims and arguments circulating within one enclave to get an undistorted hearing in another. For it is typically in the interest of the ideologues and corporations in control of a given information outlet to keep the enclave for which they serve as providers of news and opinion both sharply differentiated and intact. Indeed, it is in their interest to undermine, insofar as possible, the respectability and economic viability of outlets meant to provide news and a sampling of political discourse to the public as a whole. It should hardly be surprising, then, that much of the ideological content of some infotainment providers is intended to portray such outlets as the *New York Times*, National Public Radio, and public broadcasting as tools of a biased establishment. If trust in these institutions can be destroyed, the enclave-oriented providers will benefit financially, as more and more individuals withdraw into enclaves and various forms of marketing and persuasion are devised to manipulate and satisfy their desires and opinions. But there is also a political benefit, because the individuals thus gathered generally constitute a discrete voting block in which candidates for public office are likely to take an interest.

So there are reasons to be alarmed about the current condition of public discourse. But if I am right about the historical causes of secularization and the material conditions of contemporary fragmentation, the school of resentment in theology is actually making things worse. Theologies designed to articulate, defend, and reinforce resentment of the secular are symptoms of the disease they are meant to cure. They are the ideological expression of the enclave society. Their social function is to legitimate identification with the enclave as the primary social unit. The main means they employ to generate solidarity within the small group is the bashing of liberals, practiced as a form of ritual sacrifice.[21] The ritual comes in two types, depending on whether the scapegoats are selected from inside or outside the enclave. The former type makes a negative example of believers, especially theologians, who have identified with movements of democratic reform in the broader society. The latter type holds up nonbelievers as symbolic representatives of the secularism that supposedly defines the broader society. In both cases, the effect of the exercise is to define the enclave boundary and discourage others from crossing it.

Of course, radical orthodoxy does not officially prefer the enclave as a social form. It sometimes speaks—ever so briefly and abstractly—about the possibility of a Christian socialism. Otherwise, it wavers between nostalgia for Christendom's theocratic vision and a utopian dream of "eucharistic anarchism" that promises government without states.[22] Milbank says that the church has "misunderstood itself" when it draws boundaries around "the same' " and excludes "the other."[23] But radical orthodoxy's critique of the secular tends, under current circumstances, to reinforce the sort of boundary-drawing it officially opposes. It rejects the existing public sphere for failing to recognize the need for evangelical obedience to the rulership of Christ—that is, for failing to be the sort of political community that ceased to be possible when Christendom gave way to secularization. But both nostalgia for Christendom and the utopia of eucharistic anarchism, if not supplemented by a political theology more like Hunsinger's, threaten to condemn the world outside of the church to utter darkness. From within radical orthodoxy's refuge of aggressive like-mindedness, prophetic denunciation of the secular "other" and the unmasking of liberal theological error ritually reinforce the enclave boundary, rather than healing the world.

Thinkers committed to exercising the vocation of theology in a democratic context often experience a tension between the virtue of open-minded charity in listening well to others and their calling as expounders of the commitments of their ecclesial community. Their ecclesial office may demand charitable habits of listening, but it also imposes an obligation not to abandon what makes the community's commitments distinctive. Many are the academic theologians who have felt this tension acutely when, in dialogue with others, they have felt the force of reasons at odds with their confession of faith. Van Harvey coined a term for those who resolve the tension in one way when he spoke of the "alienated theologian." Alienated theologians remain preoccupied with God-talk but abandon some or all of the basic commitments of their faith communities. As a result, their communities have trouble treating them as spokespersons. In extreme cases, they speak for themselves only, and become theologians in a different sense. The obligations of an ecclesial office then cease to apply. An alienated theologian's role in the culture is no different from that of anyone else who develops a distinctive set of answers to important questions. This involves expressing one's own commitments, not making explicit commitments that are shared by a group.

Alienated theologians should be welcomed into the democratic conversation along with all citizens of good will. Their intellectual honesty and independence can contribute much. Theologically, most of them are moving in the direction of heresies that I embrace, so I welcome their company. But democracy will suffer greatly, I fear, if orthodox Christians are unable to find a way to maintain their own convictions while also taking up their responsibilities as citizens. Theologians who are not alienated from their faith communities therefore have a crucial role to play in responding to our current crisis.

Hunsinger is hardly an alienated theologian. He is someone wholeheartedly committed to his ecclesial office as an expounder of a religious tradition's "final vocabulary." Like the rest of us, he is not in a position to argue for that vocabulary in a noncircular way. Admitting this is part of the point of using Anselm's phrase, "faith in search of understanding," as a Barthian theological motto. It means that he is arguing from premises he does not know how to argue for in a straightforward, linear way. But he does take full responsibility for explaining and defending the inferential and practical commitments implicit in his final vocabulary. He explicates and tests his premises in a self-critical spirit. And he puts himself in a position to converse with, and learn from, Christians and non-Christians who see things differently.[24]

It is a good thing that Hunsinger is speaking his mind, in a distinctively theological idiom, about issues that matter to people both inside of and outside of the church. Persuaded by Barth's claim that the "boundary between the Church and the secular world can still take at any time a different course from that which we think we discern," he is pleased to gain a hearing on both sides of that boundary.[25] It would of course be pointless to demand that a conversation across such a boundary have Christian theological presuppositions (in the second sense I have defined). But this does nothing to diminish the integrity of the message Hunsinger articulates (which obviously has theological presuppositions in the first sense). He neither anxiously imitates some form of thought outside his own tradition, nor resents the existence of the secular world. No aspect of the created world, in his eyes, has ever been outside the reach of God's grace or ever will be. That includes the secularized practices of a modern democratic society. His arguments imply that mere refusal of those practices, from a genuinely ortho-dox point of view, must be deemed an offense to the sovereignty of God.

Does Hunsinger see any grounds for hope among Christians in the United States? He does indeed—above all, in "the vitality of the black church," which has always done much "to keep the rest of us honest." In contrast, he believes the white church has split "into an unfortunate, self-perpetuating, and ugly division between fundamentalism without justice and liberals without doctrine." But there are other positive signs, including "spiritually grounded civil disobedience" of various kinds:

> Forces of spiritual renewal—among Roman Catholics, groups like Pax Christi; among Protestants, groups like World Peacemakers—bear fruit in actions of resistance. Good Friday vigils through the streets of Manhattan ending in civil disobedience at nuclear-weapons research institutes; Peace Pentecosts in which Christians singing gospel songs and praying for peace are dragged in arrest from the rotunda of the Capitol building while within earshot Congress debates funding for the *MX* missile program—these could be seeds of a confessing church tomorrow.[26]

Democracy and orthodoxy will both be well served if this message gains as much attention from Christians in the next decade as the school of resentment has received in the last.

Chapter 5

THE NEW TRADITIONALISM

ALASDAIR MacINTYRE and Stanley Hauerwas have already entered these pages a number of times as representative critics of the political culture of modern democracy. As I have already suggested, their influence is especially strong in the seminaries, where the term "liberal" is nowadays as unlikely to be used in praise of someone as it is in the arena of presidential politics. Their writings are clearly one source of the animus against secularism discussed in the previous chapter.[1] I want now to look closely at the form of traditionalism MacIntyre and Hauerwas espouse. Its most troublesome feature, from the perspective of this inquiry, is its tendency to undermine identification with liberal democracy. In MacIntyre's account of modernity, the term "democracy" scarcely appears. But all things liberal come in for much abuse in his writings, and he obviously has liberal democracy as well as totalitarianism in mind when he dismisses "modern politics itself" as something anyone "who owes allegiance to the tradition of the virtues" must reject. As MacIntyre sees it, modern democracy is merely "civil war carried on by other means."[2] And on each of these points, Hauerwas not only pronounces MacIntyre correct; he ups the ante, outbidding MacIntyre in a rhetoric of excess.

Friends of democracy therefore have reason to be concerned about the influence these writers enjoy, especially in quarters where the fine print is likely to be ignored. But there is also a serious intellectual challenge here that democratic thinkers need to address. For MacIntyre and Hauerwas have done more than any other recent writers to confront us with a crucial question. Do we have reason to be happy with the kind of people we have become under the influence of modern ideas, practices, and institutions? The traditionalist answer to this question, of course, is no. We are exactly what the market and the liberal state have made us—namely, self-interested individualists, out to get what we want. As the traditionalist prefers to put it, we simply lack the virtues required to sustain an admirable way of life. Because we are not bound together by commitment to a single shared tradition we cannot take very much for granted when conversing with one another. As a result, our public ethical discourse is a cacophony of disparate claims. The function of such discourse is merely to express how we feel, so we should not be surprised that nothing gets resolved.

There must be something to these charges; otherwise, the new traditionalism would have trouble garnering attention, let alone followers. Its picture of modern ethical discourse is sufficiently disturbing, and perhaps sufficiently plausible at first blush, to require a seriously considered response. It seems to me, however, that many of those who have been attracted to MacIntyre and Hauerwas have some lingering democratic sentiments that are either discounted or neglected in the new traditionalism. For example, these readers would not in fact be willing to join a traditional community in which women lacked the rights that men enjoy or in which a king denied his subjects the freedom to speak openly on political questions. They would find premodern forms of trial and punishment deeply revolting. And they would rebel against the prospect of a marriage arranged for them by their parents. Such people are therefore acting in bad faith, or with a divided heart, whenever they use traditionalist categories to express their misgivings about our society while leaving their democratic sentiments unvoiced and unexplained.

The categories that most obviously require scrutiny in this context are the matched pair, *tradition* and *modernity*. Traditionalism needs to define these concepts dichotomously; otherwise, it cannot impose the sharp and simple partition it uses to justify rejection of "modern politics itself." The half-conscious thought at work in this dichotomy is that genuine modernity, being in essence antitraditional, does not have traditions. Modernity—specifically, modern democracy—is something that brings about the demise of tradition, and leaves us *after* virtue. We will see that MacIntyre and Hauerwas sometimes trade on this thought in a way that consigns much of modern ethical discourse to invisibility. Among the varieties thus rendered invisible, I would argue, are both the strand of Romantic traditionalism to which the new traditionalists owe their basic tropes and the strand of Emersonian thinking carried forward in the work of Whitman and Dewey. As I tried to show in chapter 1, the latter is a form of self-consciously modern thinking that is no less concerned with the virtues than the traditionalists are. One thing that makes it different from traditionalism, however, is its interest in reconceiving the virtues in democratic terms. The upshot of my analysis will be that the new traditionalism tells a largely false story about modern ethical discourse. I will begin, in this chapter, by examining several different versions of the story as MacIntyre has told it, and then turn, in the following two chapters, to Hauerwas's variations on the same themes.

THE PROBLEM OF POINT OF VIEW

MacIntyre published *A Short History of Ethics* more than three decades ago.[3] He has been rewriting it ever since: resolving problems in the structure of his narrative, making explicit various assumptions on which his account of our predicament depends, defining and redefining his allegiances, changing his mind about some details, filling in many others, but never deviating from profound discontent with liberal society. Already in 1966, MacIntyre was saying that "the acids of individualism have for four centuries eaten into our moral structures" and that "we live with the inheritance of not only one, but of a number of well-integrated moralities" (SH, 266). The book was more ambitious than the introductory textbook it might have seemed, for it set out to explain both how modern moral philosophy had reached an impasse through neglect of its own history and how moral discourse itself had been fragmented in the course of the same history.

"Conceptual conflict," he wrote, "is endemic in our situation, because of the depth of our moral conflicts" (SH, 268). He now often puts it the other way around, with conceptual conflict explaining the depth of moral conflict. But the resulting choices are equally pressing either way: "Each of us therefore has to choose both with whom we wish to be morally bound and by what ends, rules, and virtues we wish to be guided. These two choices are inextricably linked" (SH, 268). How is the choice of a vocabulary to be made? This depends on whether one stands within a coherent community, already committed to its outlook, its practices, and its modes of reasoning. "Speaking from within my own moral vocabulary, I shall find myself bound by the criteria embodied in it. These criteria will be shared with those who speak the same moral language" (SH, 268). But if I do not already stand within a coherent community, committed to its standards of judgment, how can my choice of a vocabulary be more than an expression of arbitrary preference or will?

MacIntyre's first book, *Marxism*, appeared in 1953, when he "aspired to be both a Christian and a Marxist." By the mid-1960s, however, he had grown "skeptical of both" outlooks and accordingly revised the book under the new title *Marxism and Christianity*.[4] Neither Christian nor Marxist any longer, he had not moved closer in the meantime to liberalism. What, then, was he? He seems to have found himself outside of the moral traditions he had once tried to integrate, still alienated from the broader society in which he found himself, yet unable to affiliate himself in good conscience with another identifiable community or tradition. These words from *A Short History of Ethics* thus take on a certain poignancy: "And I must adopt some moral vocabulary if I am to have any social relationships. For without rules, without the cultivation of virtues, I cannot share ends with anybody else. I am doomed to social solipsism. Yet I must choose for myself with whom I am to be morally bound. I must choose between alternative forms of social and moral practice" (SH, 268).

Poignant these words may be on a personal level, but they also raised a problem of theoretical consistency for *A Short History of Ethics*, as MacIntyre later acknowledged. I have called this the problem of point of view. A narrative that explains in moral terms how morality has disintegrated, and pronounces this outcome disastrous, leaves one wondering from what point of view the verdict could have been reached and how that point of view is itself to escape the implied condemnation. If MacIntyre did not already occupy an identifiable and defensible normative point of view, the tragic tone of his historical narrative and the various evaluations expressed in it would be groundless. Yet in this period he was prepared to take his stand only *against* the self-images of the age.[5] The ground on which he had taken that stand remained invisible.

MacIntyre therefore set himself the task of elucidating the point of view from which he had been writing his history and expressing his discontents. This task involved making previously unacknowledged assumptions explicit, correcting and extending them through systematic reflection, and locating them within a suitably revised narrative of the history of ethics. *After Virtue*, the most influential theoretical expression of the new traditionalism, merely begins the task of elucidation. The reasoning that led to the writing of *After Virtue* seems to have gone more or less as follows.

If MacIntyre hoped to justify a sweepingly negative verdict on the moral discourse of the age, he would have to articulate a point of view that belongs to the age he condemns but does not share the incoherence he ascribes to it. In his scathingly critical 1970 book on Herbert Marcuse in the Modern Masters series—the main thesis of which seems to have been that Marcuse did not deserve inclusion among the modern masters—MacIntyre pronounced Marcuse's most famous book deficient on precisely these grounds: "The central oddity of *One-Dimensional Man* is perhaps that it should have been written at all. For if its thesis were true, then we should have to ask how the book came to have been written and we would certainly have to inquire whether it would find any readers. Or rather, to the extent that the book does find readers, to that extent Marcuse's thesis does not hold."[6] The same criticism can be raised against *A Short History of Ethics*. MacIntyre could sidestep the criticism, while maintaining his condemnation of the age, only by locating himself in a marginal position, taking a point of view in the age but not of it.

What point of view might that be? It should, first of all, be consistent with rejection of liberal individualism. It should also, however, disown various forms of modern radicalism, including Marxism, which MacIntyre views as symptoms of the diseases they aim to cure. It should, furthermore, be sufficiently coherent and complex to provide defensible criteria of rational choice—criteria that would justify MacIntyre's criticisms of the age. Otherwise, the moral critic will be condemned to mere assertion. Finally, it should, if possible, allow the critic to share ends with at least some of his contemporaries, thereby avoiding social solipsism and political impotence.

The Rhetoric of *After Virtue*

If we assume that MacIntyre was reasoning in roughly this way, we can see why he felt a need to affiliate himself openly with a particular "well-integrated" moral tradition. One way to discover such a tradition would be to leaf back through the chapters of his moral history and locate the point at which premodern moral tradition begins to be displaced by liberal modernity. And this is what MacIntyre did in *After Virtue*. His name for the tradition that suffered rejection at the outset of our era was "the tradition of the virtues." He intended to show, above all, that this tradition, although largely rejected and isolated in our age, now deserves to be revived and, in light of its misfortunes, reformulated. Writing as an advocate of this tradition, he believed he had finally resolved the problem of point of view, but he now had to recast his history of ethics accordingly. For the narrative had acquired not only a self-conscious point of view, but a new protagonist. The villain of course remained the same.

I do not think that any critic has done full justice to *After Virtue's* imaginative power. I have in mind, first of all, the striking imagery with which the book begins. We are asked to imagine "that the natural sciences were to suffer the effects of a catastrophe," with the consequence that the current practitioners of science "have largely forgotten what it was," while possessing only "fragments" of a once-coherent empirical practice and theoretical discourse. This imagery of catastrophe belongs to the collection of tropes used since Longinus as indicators of sublimity. MacIntyre uses his imaginary tale about science to introduce his main thesis, which is that ethical discourse now lies in ruins analogous to the condition of scientific discourse in his tale. The image of ruin strives to reveal the energies of mind and heart that were, on his interpretation, concentrated in the practices of a previous epoch, and MacIntyre measures the height of that epoch's achievement by the sharpness of the break.[7] In the bolt of light cast by the opening paragraphs of *After Virtue*, our familiar patterns of discourse take on the uncanny appearance of fragmentary ruins—in Hazlitt's phrase, "stupendous . . . structures, which have been suffered to moulder into decay."[8] In introducing his major thesis in this strongly figurative way, before his reasons have been offered, he somehow manages not to call attention to the artifice of the rhetoric. The uncanniness of those paragraphs consists in the sense that we have learned something we already knew but have kept hidden.

It is with the stage thus set that MacIntyre introduces, in chapter 2, his account of "The Nature of Moral Disagreement Today and the Claims of Emotivism." Here he attempts the boldest of figurative reductions. We are meant to see the essence of our contemporary culture as condensed in—of all things—the emotivist moral philosophy of C. L. Stevenson. This vision startles ethical theorists, in part because they know that no more than a few contemporary philosophers believe that Stevenson's moral philosophy is true. This audacious synecdoche is accomplished primarily through the use of three examples of modern ethical debates. These examples are meant to license an inference to the conclusion that modern ethical discourse itself lies in virtually complete fragmentation. That is a lot to show on the basis of three examples sketched in a total of only two pages: the debates over war, abortion, and economic justice. MacIntyre counts on his readers to know these debates by heart. They are the very stuff of every newspaper's editorial page and of the "moral problems" courses currently being taught in our colleges. MacIntyre says that "it is their typicality that makes them important examples here" (AV, 8). What they typify, he adds, is the interminability of moral debates in our culture. This, he argues, is to be explained by appeal to the incommensurability of the premises from which the participants in modern ethical discourse argue their cases. Once we see this, he concludes, we will realize that the arguments, although cast in the form of impersonal appeals to reason, actually function only to vent and manipulate emotions. That is why we live in the age of Stevenson, for it was his emotivism that explained how our ethical discourse really functions, despite pretenses to the contrary on the part of those of us who engage in the debates.

Well, these are ethical debates, and it is true that they have yet to end. This shows neither that they are interminable nor that the interminability they allegedly exemplify is characteristic of our ethical discourse as such. Any ethical debate now going on is a debate that has not yet ended. This goes without saying. Are there no examples of ethical debates in our culture that have come to an end? MacIntyre does not ask this question. Suppose we go back to mid-nineteenth-century America. What is the most impassioned ethical debate of the day? Clearly, it is the debate over the abolition of slavery. This is not, I am happy to add, an unfinished debate. It would be foolish to pretend that it was settled solely by reasoning, but it would also be foolish to think that the reasoning it involved can be explained away as nothing more than Stevensonian hot air. In the meantime, we have had great debates over whether women should be permitted to vote, whether alcoholic beverages should be banned in a society that cares about the virtue of temperance, and whether blacks should be allowed to sit in the front of the bus. Each of these more recent debates, so far as I can tell, is now over. They were settled, moreover, without massive bloodshed. Incommensurable premises did not prevent our fellow citizens from reaching a high level of consensus on them by exchanging questions and reasons with one another. No doubt, each of these debates seemed interminable at the height of public controversy on the issue in question. Each of them produced great examples of ethical discourse, both religious and secular in inspiration, that deserve to be preserved in historical memory. Yet they are entirely missing from MacIntyre's account.

After Virtue takes many twists and turns before it reaches its memorable conclusion, in which MacIntyre assembles his readers once again among the sublime ruins to initiate a quest for forms of "community in which civility and the intellectual and moral life can be sustained through the new dark ages which are already upon us" (AV, 263). The book exerts its persuasive power through an intricate interweaving of argumentation and historical narrative unlike anything else in twentieth-century moral philosophy. It is hard to imagine a book less like Rawls's *Theory of Justice* in form or content than this one.

Beyond *After Virtue*

MacIntyre stressed that his history of ethics was "a work still in progress" (AV, 278) and immediatedly promised a sequel, which appeared in 1988 under the title *Whose Justice? Which Rationality?*[9] Nobody would think of calling *Whose Justice* a short history of ethics. Perhaps it needed to be a long and intricate book, given the problems remaining to be solved in Mac-Intyre's position. The most obvious of these was that *After Virtue* had not expounded or defended its pivotal assumptions about the dependence of rationality upon tradition. If those assumptions cannot withstand scrutiny, the necessity of affiliating with a single "well-integrated" tradition of thought and practice is called into question. I shall return to this problem later. It will suffice for the moment to note that his recognition of this lacuna in his previous work explains MacIntyre's preoccupation with the theme of practical rationality and the concept of tradition in *Whose Justice?*

Another relatively obvious problem was that *After Virtue's* historical narrative had achieved its dramatic effect by focusing our attention on sharp contrasts and major transitions. This meant deferring the detailed discussion of specific figures and of scholarly counterargument that would, in the end, be required to sustain the narrative's central claims. The sequel, in contrast, offers finely drawn portraits of a wide range of figures from ancient Greece, medieval Christendom, and eighteenth-century Scotland. It concentrates not on the shifting fortunes of "the virtues," but rather on those of two virtues in particular, justice and practical wisdom, and this requires MacIntyre to enter more deeply into the writings of the figures he discusses. The book also works much harder than its predecessors did at vindicating its interpretations over against alternative views in the scholarly literature. If the interest of most readers is bound to flag ten pages into an account of Sir James Dalrymple of Stair or ten paragraphs into a dialogue with John Cooper's reading of Aristotle on the practical syllogism, those of us who lament the dearth of good ethical historiography are bound to feel deeply in MacIntyre's debt. As a work of historical scholarship, *Whose Justice?* has hardly silenced expert critics, but it is easily MacIntyre's most impressive accomplishment to date.

Since I have argued on previous occasions that *After Virtue*'s historical narrative is inadequate, I want to take this opportunity to point out several respects in which *Whose Justice?* does better.[10] The first of these has to do with my charge that "the tradition of the virtues" championed in *After Virtue* is too amorphous to play the role assigned to it. Upon close inspection, it becomes clear that this tradition, although presented in such a way that Aristotle can be its principal spokesperson, was meant to include anyone who gives sufficient prominence to "the virtues" and "the good" in ethics. Because it was arrived at initially in a quest for an all-purpose "Other" in comparison to which liberal modernity could be seen as hopelessly divided and incoherent, it gathers together people with vastly different tables of virtues and conceptions of the good. These include many people who would want to dissociate themselves from a tradition in which Aristotle could be cast as the central figure. Any tradition so diverse could not supply the wanted contrast with liberal modernity, nor could it satisfactorily resolve the problem of point of view. To do those things, MacIntyre would have to commit himself to a particular conception of the good life and a correlative table of the virtues.

Whose Justice? speaks of four distinct traditions: Aristotelianism, Augustinianism, the Scottish Enlightenment, and liberalism. And MacIntyre brings his spiritual autobiography if not full circle, at least homeward bound, by identifying himself openly with the Thomistic strand of Augustinian Christianity. This confession does indeed clarify the position MacIntyre intends to occupy while criticizing liberal society and reworking his account of Western culture's allegedly downward slide. It helps us see, furthermore, which of the "local forms of community" vaguely alluded to in the concluding pages of *After Virtue* MacIntyre wants us to inhabit while the "new dark ages" are upon us. It also, of course, underlines the significance of the role religious traditions have played and continue to play in our moral history.

A second criticism I had made of *After Virtue*—one I had made on another occasion when discussing *A Short History of Ethics*—was that its neglect of the religious traditions seriously vitiated its historical reconstruction of our past.[11] In the postscript to the second edition of *After Virtue*, MacIntyre acknowledged the validity of this charge and promised to do better in the sequel. The ample space given in *Whose Justice?* to Augustinian tradition and to the influence of Calvinism on eighteenth-century Scottish culture redeems that promise. What, then, is gained from such additions, aside from mere comprehensiveness?

One benefit emerges clearly in the new account of Aquinas, which is not only much longer than the corresponding section of *After Virtue*, but also vastly more adequate. I had complained that *After Virtue* read Aquinas through the eyes of his later scholastic interpreters, thereby overestimating the place of natural law in his thought and underestimating the place of Aristotelian practical wisdom. The result, I claimed, was a highly misleading picture of Aquinas as a rigid system-builder partly responsible for the lamentable demise of Aristotelian practical wisdom in Western culture. The picture was also designed to highlight what MacIntyre then took to be Aquinas's inability to account for moral tragedy, and here I suggested that MacIntyre's case was at best radically incomplete.[12] The interpretation of Aquinas in *Whose Justice?*, however, includes none of these deficiencies. The assertion that Aquinas is unable to account for moral tragedy has been withdrawn. MacIntyre has converted. More to the point, he has broken free from scholastic Thomism's reading of Aquinas and given not only a more detailed but a more accurate reading of the relation between Aristotelian, Stoic, and Augustinian elements in the *Summa Theologiae*. Where he had expressed suspicion of Aquinas's attempt to produce a total system, he now emphasizes, rightly, that the system is self-consciously unfinished in form and that its mode of inquiry is dialectical in nature.[13]

Upgrading his assessment of Aquinas in these ways does, however, have its costs. *After Virtue* had explained the misfortunes of Aristotelian tradition after Aquinas in part by declaring its view of moral tragedy deficient and its metaphysical commitments excessive. Now that MacIntyre has changed his mind on these matters, the explanation will have to take a different shape. It also will need to show why metaphysical commitments once thought excessive, and thus a source of weakness for the Aristotelian tradition as it entered the modern age, are now essential.

Augustinian liberals, recognizing that these commitments are not generally shared by the citizenry as a whole, are content to factor them into their own moral thinking without expecting fellow citizens in the earthly city to do likewise. MacIntyre shows no signs of becoming that kind of Augustinian, but he has thus far done little to clarify the role he envisions for theological assumptions in public life. His position appears to be that ethical discourse cannot be sustained as a coherent rational process without taking some such assumptions for granted. Another of my criticisms of *After Virtue* bears directly on this issue. I had said that by neglecting the role of religious traditions, and thus of religious conflict, in moral history, MacIntyre had simultaneously neglected one of the reasons that public discourse in many modern settings has become secularized, in the sense defined in the previous chapter. When high levels of agreement on metaphysics or on a complete theory of the good life could not be achieved through rational argument, some parties used coercion (often in the form of armed force or torture) to compel acceptance of theological presuppositions. Others, however, tried to hammer out a way of thinking and talking about ethical issues that did not presuppose theological agreement. Both alternatives were tried repeatedly in early modern Europe. The bloodshed, unrest, and spiritual misery caused by the former made the latter increasingly attractive.

Whose Justice? uses a similar hypothesis, albeit somewhat tentatively, to repair MacIntyre's explanation of the rejection of Aristotelianism:

> That [the] coexistence of Aristotelianism in the moral sphere with a variety of Augustinian theologies and with increasingly anti-Aristotelian modes of theorizing in the sciences should have proved fragile is scarcely surprising. But what most profoundly finally moved the largest part of Europe's educated classes to reject Aristotelianism as a framework for understanding their shared moral and social life was perhaps the gradual discovery during and after the savage and persistent conflicts of the age that no appeal to any agreed conception of *the* good for human beings, either at the level of practice or of theory, was now possible. (WJ, 209; emphasis in original)

Needless to say, from my point of view this change promises to improve the account considerably. Yet MacIntyre neither integrates this hypothesis into the narrative as a whole nor allows it to influence his appraisal of liberal society. So despite his admission that the facts of pluralism may have been the most important factor in the rejection of Aristotle, the rest of the book shows no traces of this thought. In particular, MacIntyre does not grapple with the apparent implication that the educated classes of early-modern Europe may have had good reason to tailor their institutions and vocabularies to accommodate diverse reasonable perspectives on theology and the good.

How Not to Discuss Liberalism

This failure of integration becomes especially problematic in a chapter called "Liberalism Transformed into a Tradition." Of the four traditions treated in *Whose Justice?*, only liberalism is dispensed with in a single chapter. The beginning of the chapter concludes the discussion of Scotland begun more than a hundred pages earlier, leaving only barely more than a dozen pages on liberalism as such, at the end of which MacIntyre acknowledges the need to do much more. Why didn't he do more here? Perhaps he feared the book was getting too long as it was, but he also knew that because he was still writing *against* liberalism, he could not do without some account, however cursory, of its salient features. The result is utterly unsympathetic caricature at the very point where the narrative most urgently requires detailed and fair-minded exposition if it means to test its author's preconceptions with any rigor at all.

MacIntyre once criticized Marcuse for "his way of lumping together very different thinkers under a common label for purposes of either castigation or commendation" (HM, 84). Yet castigation-by-lumping is the main function performed by the label "liberalism" in both *After Virtue* and *Whose Justice?* So the plentiful proper names that filled out the chapters on Greece or Scotland give way here to such oversimplifying abstractions as "the liberal system of evaluation" and "the liberal self," as well as heavy reliance on the passive voice. Readers will be hard-pressed to discover just who is being discussed. After asking why it matters that Marcuse's version of the history of philosophy is highly selective, MacIntyre said this in 1970: "The answer is that by omitting so much and by giving a one-sided interpretation of those authors whom he does invoke, Marcuse is enabled to exaggerate, and in some instances to exaggerate grossly, the homogeneity of the philosophical thought of a given age" (HM, 15). Similarly, MacIntyre complained about Marcuse's "willingness to rely upon abstractions" instead of talking about particular people (HM, 18), of his tendency "too much to read the history of culture through the lenses provided by his own version of the history of philosophy" (HM, 15–16), and of his contentment with "incidental illustrations of his theses" where he should have offered "evidence in a systematic way" (HM, 14). All these criticisms apply to MacIntyre's chapter on liberalism in *Whose Justice?*

My point is not that MacIntyre had higher and better standards back when he had not yet gone traditionalist. The standards he applied to Marcuse are built into his current theory of rationality, which requires members of traditions in crisis to meet challenges from their opponents by learning alien languages and engaging in reasoned debate with competing traditions, while leaving open the possibility of refutation. The same standards are reflected in his praise of Aquinas's attempt to overcome the conflict between Augustinian and Aristotelian traditions. Such conflicts, MacIntyre says, achieve resolution only when they move through at least two stages: one in which each tradition describes and judges its rivals only in its own terms, and a second in which it becomes possible to understand one's rivals in their own terms and thus to find new reasons for changing one's mind. Moving from the first stage to the second "requires a rare gift of empathy as well as of intellectual insight" (WJ, 167), a gift Aquinas's writings exemplify. MacIntyre shows great empathy for ancient Greeks and for the religious tradition from which he was once alienated but none whatsoever for liberal modernity. After three major books and half a dozen minor ones, his dialogue with liberalism has yet to reach the second stage.[14]

The chapter on liberalism does include a promising, if grudging, concession. The section in which the concession is made begins with a familiar and unpromising claim "that the project of founding a form of social order in which individuals could emancipate themselves from the contingency and particularity of tradition by appealing to genuinely universal, tradition-independent norms was and is not only, and not principally a project of philosophers. It was and is the project of modern liberal, individualist society" (WJ, 335). Here MacIntyre identifies liberalism with an antitraditionalist quest, one that seeks to rise above all tradition to the vantage point of universal reason and that is expressed in both liberal thought and liberal practice. It is *the* project of liberal society as such. But MacIntyre immediately goes on to say that the history of this project, and in particular the interminability of its debates over supposedly universal principles, demonstrates that liberalism is in fact one tradition among others. Liberalism, then, is a tradition, but one whose necessarily frustrated project is to cease being what it is.

This line of reasoning has often been used, by Hauerwas as well as MacIntyre, to dispense with liberal society as the embodiment of an obviously incoherent project. In *Whose Justice?*, MacIntyre stops just short of that conclusion. He clearly intends to make the idea of "liberalism transformed into a tradition" strike the reader as paradoxical, and he thinks liberals have reason to feel embarrassed by this transformation, but he also makes a concession when he adds that:

> increasingly there have been liberal thinkers who, for one reason or another, have acknowledged that their theory and practice are after all that of one more contingently grounded and founded tradition . . . unable to escape from the condition of a tradition. *Even this, however, can be recognized without any inconsistency* and has gradually been recognized by liberal writers such as Rawls, Rorty, and Stout. (WJ, 346; emphasis added)

It can indeed be recognized without any inconsistency, and even without a slight air of paradox or embarrassment, but only if we reject MacIntyre's definition of the liberal project. The idea of "liberalism transformed into a tradition" remains a paradox or an oxymoron only if liberalism is initially defined as MacIntyre has defined it. What should we do if we reject MacIntyre's definition? Let me consider two options.

The first is to replace his definition of the liberal project by another one. MacIntyre's new account of the rejection of Aristotle in early-modern Europe suggests a candidate at once. We can say that the liberal project was simply to tailor the political institutions and moral discourse of modern societies to the facts of pluralism. Saying this would supply an answer to the question MacIntyre poses in *Whose Justice?*: "What kind of principles can require and secure allegiance in and to a form of social order in which individuals who are pursuing diverse and often incompatible conceptions of the good can live together without the disruptions of rebellion and internal war?" (210). Speaking in this way allows us to view the quest for a standpoint above all tradition and the attempt to abstract entirely from consideration of the common good as two, but only two, possible expressions of the liberal project. We are free to declare them completely discredited without abandoning that project in the least. Notice that one can, on this view, remain a liberal while abhoring virtually everything MacIntyre identifies with liberalism in *Whose Justice?*, including not least of all "the liberal self" and "the liberal system of evaluation."

The second option is to drop the notion that there is something worth calling *the* liberal project. We might then use the phrase "liberal society," if at all, simply as a name for the configuration of social practices and institutions we in the United States and certain other countries happen to be living with right now. We might add that any such configuration is too complicated to be explained as the expression of a single project. We might insist, with this in mind, that social criticism is not well served by sweeping pronouncements either for or against liberal society, but rather by balanced and detailed commentary on its various features and prudent counsel on how one or another of them should be changed. We might even come to think of "liberalism" as the name for a particular kind of obsolete ideology whose critics and defenders thought there was something worth calling *the* liberal project and who therefore engaged in fruitless debates over whether it was a good or a bad thing.

Both options have advantages. I advocate the second, and in this book have steered clear of the term "liberalism" whenever possible. (That is why I feel slightly uncomfortable when MacIntyre refers to me as a liberal writer.) Reading his chapter on "liberalism" reconfirms my suspicion that the very term may at this point be blocking the path of inquiry. He may respond, however, by charging that my use of the phrase "liberal society" implicitly concedes the central contention of *After Virtue*, that our society is too fragmented and incoherent to sustain rational moral discourse. *Whose Justice?* defends this contention by describing the metaphysically austere "internationalized languages of modernity" as the result of attempts to abstract discourse from "all substantive criteria and standards of truth and rationality" (WJ, 384). The intended implication seems to be that the languages in fact being used in liberal society make rational moral discourse impossible. Users of such languages, like the social solipsist mentioned at the end of *A Short History of Ethics*, can make choices but not rational ones, for they lack any framework of criteria and standards within which reasons for action might be found.

I say that this *seems* to be the implication MacIntyre intends, but at the end of the chapter in which he gives his account of the "internationalized languages of modernity," he adds a qualification:

the condition which I have described as that characteristic of the late twentieth-century language of internationalized modernity is perhaps best understood as an ideal type, a condition to which the actual languages of the metropolitan centers of modernity approximate in varying and increasing degrees, especially among the more affluent. And the social and cultural condition of those who speak that kind of language, a certain type of rootless cosmopolitanism, . . . is also ideal-typical. (WJ, 388)

MacIntyre's ideal-types are caricatures by another name. Caricatures have legitimate uses. They can draw attention, by means of exaggeration and abstraction of actual traits, to significant truths. They do not take the place of realistic portraiture. What we need to know if we are to judge the rationality of our moral discourse by MacIntyre's theory, and what he has not yet shown, is the precise degree to which the "languages-in-use" in our society approximate the extreme that his dystopian ideal describes.

In the final chapter of *Whose Justice?*, MacIntyre grants that few of us are social solipsists, "alien to every tradition of enquiry" we encounter and utterly deprived of the resources of rational traditions (WJ, 395–96).

Most of our contemporaries do not live at or even near that point of extremity. . . . Instead they tend to live betwixt and between, accepting usually unquestioningly the assumptions of the dominant liberal individualist forms of public life, but drawing in different areas of their lives upon a variety of tradition-generated resources of thought and action, transmitted from a variety of familial, religious, educational, and other social and cultural sources. (WJ, 397)

Here the term "liberal" is applied only to those features of our society that MacIntyre finds contemptible. The "tradition-generated resources of thought and action" are admitted to be present in our society, but they are made out to be residues of something nonliberal or preliberal.

This way of speaking, like his use of ideal-types, allows MacIntyre to depict anything he approves of in our society as inessential to it. He is then free to discount apparent counterevidence to his claims about "liberal society" as beside the point. The counterevidence merely shows that there are forces and tendencies not yet crushed under the foot of the liberal project. We are not meant to be thankful to liberal democracy for allowing "tradition-generated resources" of *various* kinds to survive the early-modern war of all against all. I refer once more to MacIntyre's critique of Marcuse's *One-Dimensional Man*:

He holds that there are forces and tendencies in society which run counter to the tendency that his book describes. He asserts that *One-Dimensional Man* is concerned with these counterforces and tendencies also; but they do not, except for one or two paragraphs, appear in his book until the penultimate page, and then no great hope is attached to their prospects. Marcuse's pessimism . . . is only very loosely supported by an appeal to evidence. (HM, 70)

MacIntyre's pessimism about "liberal society" analogously depends upon rhetorical devices in which, first, that society is identified with an essentially antitraditionalist project and, second, any counterforces within it are dissociated from the vacuous and rootless condition toward which it aspires.

It therefore comes as no surprise when MacIntyre condemns not only the few social solipsists in his midst, but also the majority of his contemporaries, who live "betwixt and between": "This type of self which has too many half-convictions and too few settled coherent convictions . . . brings to its encounters with the claims of rival traditions a fundamental incoherence which is too disturbing to be admitted to self-conscious awareness except on the rarest of occasions" (WJ, 397). But this harsh judgment against both his contemporaries and the somewhat younger man who wrote *A Short History of Ethics, Marxism and Christianity,* and *Herbert Marcuse: An Exposition and a Polemic* has not been established. To establish it MacIntyre would have to do two things he has not yet done. He would have to show, first of all, the precise point at which eclectic diversity of "tradition-generated resources of thought and action" becomes mere fragmentation, thereby condemning most members of a society to "fundamental incoherence." And he would also have to show that our society has already passed that point. The theory of rationality defended in *Whose Justice?* fails to perform the first task. His caricature of liberal society could hardly perform the second.

MacIntyre deploys these same devices in a slightly different way in his 1990 book, *Three Rival Versions of Moral Enquiry.*[15] Here he sets out to debunk two major modern alternatives to his own Thomism. One position, which he labels "genealogy," is exemplified in the writings of Friedrich Nietzsche, Paul de Man, Gilles Deleuze, and Michel Foucault. The other, which is meant to suggest what became of Enlightenment liberalism in the course of its nineteenth-century decline, is exemplified in the Ninth Edition of the *Encyclopedia Britannica. Three Rival Versions* does have the virtue of associating liberalism with the writings of particular people. MacIntyre mentions a number of proper names: J. G. Frazer, Henry Sidgwick, and Edward Burnett Tylor, among others. He offers an analysis of the ethos that the contributors to the Ninth Edition shared. The analysis is much more detailed and substantive than anything in the corresponding chapter of *Whose Justice?* But suppose we grant that MacIntyre has adequately characterized the men who put together the Ninth Edition. Grant, further, that MacIntyre is right to declare the encyclopedists the losers in the debate he has arranged for them with the representatives of genealogy and tradition. Assume, in other words, that the form of liberalism they represent really does lie in shambles by book's end. What does this dialectical exercise teach us about modern people who neither collaborated on the Ninth Edition, nor subscribed to the ethical and philosophical premises of those who did?

MacIntyre clearly intends the encyclopedists to represent something larger than themselves. But why let Sidgwick and his fellow encyclopedists stand for Whitman or Dewey or, for that matter, T. H. Green? There is an undefended principle of selection at work here—one that serves only to reinforce the sharp dichotomy between tradition and modernity. MacIntyre has interesting and effective criticism to offer of the works he discusses, but he does nothing to vindicate his selection of opponents. Why suppose that Sidgwick, Nietzsche, and Pope Leo XIII represent an adequate sampling of late nineteenth-century ethical inquiry? In *After Virtue*, the choice presented to the reader was given in the title of chapter 9, "Nietzsche or Aristotle?" This assumed, of course, that the "Enlightenment project" had already been dismantled in earlier chapters, after having been exposed to Nietzsche's relentless criticism. In *Three Rival Versions*, the encyclopedists stand in for the likes of Hume and Kant. Nietzsche retains his previous role. And the Thomism of Pope Leo XIII represents Aristotelian ethics in its latter-day, Augustinian form. So the choice we are being offered remains essentially the same.[16] But, as before, MacIntyre has given us no reason to suppose that modern ethical discourse can be reduced so easily to a small handful of theoretical options.

At one point in *After Virtue* (243), MacIntyre describes William Cobbett, along with Jane Austen and the Jacobins, as one of the last great representatives of the tradition of virtue ethics. This is a bold and provocative claim, for which MacIntyre gives no support. Is it true? Only, I think, if we define "virtue ethics" very narrowly, so that only a form of ethical discourse conforming closely to an Aristotelian or Thomistic framework qualifies. Loosen up the definition a bit and look in the right places, and you will find discourse on the virtues permeating the ethos of modern democratic culture. Cobbett himself was a towering, ethically ambiguous, transitional figure, with one foot in medievalist nostalgia and the other in modern democracy. His writings are almost as important as Thomas Paine's and Mary Wollstonecraft's for anyone who wants to understand the relations among religion, critical thought, and the emergence of democratic culture in Britain and America. As E. P. Thompson has shown, Cobbett's journalism played a major role in creating a mass audience for social criticism in Britain in the decades after the French Revolution.[17] Another historian, Christopher Lasch, assigned him an equally important role in the development of modern populist thought.[18] Cobbett's debunking *History of the Protestant Reformation* is a major modern source of antiprogressivist nostalgia for medieval times.[19] He also set in motion those forms of modern radicalism that take their inspiration from an image of premodern communities and virtues. *Rural Rides* inaugurates the kind of observational (eye-witness) social criticism that twentieth-century readers might associate with works like Orwell's *Road to Wigan Pier* or Agee's *Let Us Now Praise Famous Men*.[20]

Cobbett's *Thirteen Sermons* and the countless issues of the weekly magazine, the *Political Register*, which he not only edited but wrote almost single-handedly for years, were among the most widely read texts of the period.[21] In short, Cobbett is far more important than MacIntyre implies, and mainly for a reason that MacIntyre's history cannot easily make room for, which is that so many strands of modern ethical discourse can be traced directly to his influence. Once it dawns on us that the heirs of Cobbett's observational social criticism include Orwell and Agee, among many others, we ought also to begin suspecting that MacIntyre's examples of ethical discourse after Cobbett are either arbitrarily or self-servingly chosen. If Cobbett is, as MacIntyre suggests, an exemplary social critic, and if other exemplary social critics were in fact inspired by his example, then modern ethical discourse begins to seem somewhat less bankrupt, even by MacIntyre's own standards.

Wendell Berry may be the best contemporary example to use in making this point. Berry, who works by day as a farmer in Kentucky, is a gifted practioner of observational social criticism. Much of his work has the rural flavor and antimetropolitan animus of *Rural Rides*. The themes of tradition, community, and the virtues (in the plural) are also much in evidence in his writing. His work is not properly described, then, as antitraditional or "after virtue." It is, however, very much a product of democratic culture. Hazlitt, Thoreau, Emerson, and Whitman all appear in his quotations, and one can sense their influence on his prose style as well as his normative commitments. Berry's work, not MacIntyre's, is the closest thing to Cobbett's that we have from a living writer. It is, by my lights, a more honest and rigorously conceived body of work than MacIntyre's. And it has three sizeable advantages over MacIntyre's: first, by virtue of expressing in a quite beautiful style a profoundly spiritual sensibility; second, by doing so, for the most part, without resorting to cant or posturing; third, because it includes both *The Unsettling of America* and *The Hidden Wound*, respectively the most important book on environmental ethics ever written and the best book on race that I know of by a white writer.[22] The point to draw attention to here, however, is that Berry's work, with its open embrace of both traditionalist and democratic elements, exists at all, or rather that it exists *in democratic modernity*.

But then so does MacIntyre's. Because MacIntyre's traditionalism itself belongs to modern ethical discourse, and could not have sprung out of nowhere, it is bound to have trouble accounting for itself without abandoning its contention that Cobbett and Austen were without modern heirs. In *Three Rival Versions*, MacIntyre does acknowledge indebtedness to the Thomists among his modern predecessors, but the rhetorical patterns we have already identified in *After Virtue* cannot be accounted for by this acknowledgement alone. For one thing, writing *After Virtue* was part of the path that led MacIntyre to rediscover his Thomist forebears. The Thomistic destination, which appears not to have been foreseen in advance, cannot be used to explain his movement down the path. For another thing, the connection to Thomism would not fully explain the rhetorical use of the sublime to which I have already drawn attention. In point of fact, the book belongs to a prominent strand of Romantic ethical discourse that has never been far to find in the modern period and has always relied, in just the way MacIntyre does, on the rhetoric of ruin and fragmentation. It is a very modern form of ethical discourse, but also a form that has a stake in not being able to recognize itself as belonging to the setting against which its criticism is directed.

TRADITION AND RATIONALITY

I will take the liberty of referring to both traditionalism, from Burke and Coleridge to MacIntyre and Hauerwas, and modern democratic thinking, from Emerson and Whitman to Nancy Fraser and Cornel West, as traditions. By speaking in this way, I am able to locate Berry in an area where two traditions interact. All I mean by the term "tradition" in this context is a discursive practice considered in the dimension of history. No general criterion for individuating traditions is assumed in this way of speaking, and so I shall offer none. I am content to let pragmatic considerations settle the question of individuation on a case-by-case basis. On another day, with a different purpose in view, one might have reason to refer to the likes of Coleridge and the likes of Emerson as embraced by a single, larger, looser tradition. MacIntyre sometimes uses the term in roughly the way I use it, but he also uses it in a narrower, normatively charged way. Susan Moller Okin, in her incisive feminist critique of MacIntyre, rightly observes that he equivocates between two senses:

> In spite of MacIntyre's persistent use of gender-neutral language, it is clear that most women, as well as men who have any kind of feminist consciousness, will not find in any of his traditions a rational basis for moral and political action. Where, then, do we stand? Are we outside all traditions and therefore, in MacIntyre's view at least, "in a state of moral and intellectual destitution"? Can one be anything *but* an outsider to a tradition that excludes one, and some of the things one values most, from what it regards as the best human life? . . . [H]e gives conflicting accounts of what a tradition *is*. At times he describes it as a defining context, stressing the authoritative nature of its "texts"; at times he talks of a tradition as "living," as a "not-yet-completed narrative," as an argument about the goods that constitute the tradition.[23]

Okin goes on to point out that feminism, though not a tradition in the sense of being defined by deference toward authoritative texts, is a tradition in the second sense. I am proposing that the second sense be explicated in terms of the concept of a discursive social practice viewed diachronically.

MacIntyre uses the second of Okin's two senses of tradition to gain credibility for the notion that rationality as such depends on tradition, which it surely does, if all we mean by a "tradition" is an enduring discursive practice. He uses the first, narrower sense to create the impression that unless we identify with a discursive practice of a very particular kind, we necessarily place ourselves outside the bounds of rational discourse itself. The kind of discursive practice he takes to be essential to the exercise of rationality involves deferential submission to authoritative texts and authoritative interpreters of texts, though this requirement does not, he assures us, preclude the ability to make large-scale revisions of inherited commitments when faced with epistemological crises. Equally essential to the rationality of a practice, according to MacIntyre's account, is its embodiment in institutions that are capable of securing agreement on a doctrine of the human good (presumably, by means of catechism directed at newcomers and a combination of magisterial suasion, discipline, and excommunication directed at dissenters).[24] Once tradition is identified with *traditionalist* practice (and the hierarchical institutional structure that goes along with it), it becomes possible to argue that modern democracy, because its ethical discourse is obviously not governed by a tradition *in this sense*, is nothing more than a scene of conceptual fragmentation. Yet once the ambiguity of the term "tradition" is made plain, it becomes obvious that the debate over the new traditionalism is best construed not as a debate between traditional and modern varieties of ethical discourse, but rather as a debate involving at least two traditions or strands of modern ethical discourse: a tradition dedicated to a very narrow conception of how traditions ought ideally to operate and a tradition dedicated to the project of loosening up that conception democratically and dialogically. It is also possible, of course, to identify a third tradition involved in this debate— namely, the Cartesian one I once described as the tradition that would rather not be a tradition at all.

Earlier in this chapter, I tried to show what mischief MacIntyre causes by defining liberal modernity reductively as the social expression of the Enlightenment project's antitraditionalism. Here I simply want to call attention to the existence of multiple strands of ethical discourse in modern societies and to point out the dangers of confining our attention to ethical traditions in the narrow sense. MacIntyre has not demonstrated that traditions of the kind he favors are uniquely capable of fostering rational discourse, so he has not shown that such traditions are the only ones *worthy* of study or allegiance. Furthermore, if we study only the rigid kind of tradition that Coleridge stood for when he called for the creation of a virtuous clerisy as an antidote to modern fragmentation, we will not be able to hear both sides of the debate in which Coleridge was himself participating. Indeed, we will not be able to do justice to the complexities of the modern debate over traditionalism at all. This debate has been going on now for two centuries. The relatively loose kind of tradition represented by the patterns of influence that lead from Wollstonecraft, Hazlitt, and Emerson to their contemporary heirs is essential to understanding what modern ethical discourse has been like outside of the institutional settings in which clerisies exercise power. It should not be surprising to find that some writers, anxious to avoid being dominated by such a clerisy, have sought to distance themselves from it by denouncing "tradition" itself. What such rhetorical moves imply, in context, is often hard to make out, but the same writers have often had the agility to elude hyperbole on other occasions and acknowledge indebtedness to a discursive practice that evolves from one generation of discoursers to the next. Emerson and Whitman are perhaps the best examples of this. MacIntyre's prose is not the only place where the term "tradition" slips back and forth between two senses.

Of the thinkers who first reflected on the opposition between the Enlightenment and traditionalism, it was Hegel who understood most fully the importance of overcoming the assumption that moderns must choose between reason and tradition if they wish to escape the rule of arbitrary will. MacIntyre flatly rejects the likes of Thomas Paine under the heading of the "Enlightenment project." He denounces the traditionalist Edmund Burke as a shoddy theorist, a turncoat, and an "agent of positive harm."[25] Burke's most important theoretical error, according to MacIntyre, was his failure to overcome the Enlightenment opposition between reason and tradition, a failure that required him to embrace an irrationalist type of traditionalism if he wanted to resist the intellectual and political consequences of antitraditional reason. This is a sound criticism. It was, however, not only fully appreciated by both Wollstonecraft and Hazlitt, but articulated at the highest level of philosophical theory by Hegel. In books like *Marxism and Christianity* and *Against the Self-Images of the Age*, one can sense MacIntyre's continuity with, and dependence on, Hegel's overcoming of this dualism. Consciousness of this continuity may be part of what kept him on course, in those days, as a radical social critic sensitive to the sources of his own thinking. His writings of the 1960s already embodied an exercise of critical reasoning that was conscious of its own dependence on an unfolding dialectic.

In one of the best critical discussions of *After Virtue*, Richard Bernstein concludes that "there is very little in MacIntyre's critique of the Enlightenment project that was not stated or anticipated in Hegel." Bernstein laments, however, that after a brief reference to what "Hegel called philosophical history" (AV, 3), MacIntyre proceeds to discuss modern society and ethical theory as if Hegel never existed. "This is a curious omission considering the array of thinkers MacIntyre does discuss, the sensitive un-

derstanding of Hegel exhibited in MacIntyre's earlier writings, and especially because of the relevance of Hegel to MacIntyre's central concerns."
MacIntyre seems to have lost all awareness of how much he "himself appropriates from this tradition in his critical reconstruction of the virtues."[26] It
would not take much to bring MacIntyre's theoretical reflections on tradition and rationality into line with the commitments of a Hegelian pragmatist like Bernstein or me. One need only eliminate the arguments that depend on equivocating between Okin's two senses of "tradition" and then
eliminate all traces of the unwittingly Burkean assumption that all traditions worthy of the name are traditionalist. But larger corrective measures
are required to set straight his history of modern thought and society. For
at the time he wrote *After Virtue*, his long-standing hatred for all things
liberal combined with his loss of faith in Marxism in a way that seems to
have occluded his historical memory. The *modern* intellectual traditions
to which he owes the most receive no acknowledgment whatsoever. This
peculiar form of amnesia has everything to do with his grim conclusion
that the exhaustion of Marxism "is shared by every other political tradition
within our culture" (AV, 262).

MacIntyre was not a less rational man at mid-career than he is today. He
could by now write the modern analogue of Augustine's *Confessions*. The
story of his reasoned movement betwixt and between the various traditions
with which he has affiliated himself is itself strong evidence against a theory
according to which rationality can be exercised at its best only within highly
coherent and "well-integrated" traditions. MacIntyre has for many years
been one of our most interesting and thought-provoking social critics. Even
his mistaken arguments often instruct; even his caricatures often advance
the debate. But he has performed a valuable service to his culture precisely
by being the sort of person his current theory of rationality frowns upon.

What kind is that? It is the kind who, from time to time, finds it necessary
to abandon a morality so well integrated that it suffocates thought, who
has the courage to take a stand for which there is not yet a convenient label
or easily defined lineage, and who has the practical wisdom to fashion a
critical language for himself out of materials borrowed from many sources.
All of this can be done without engaging in *the* liberal project, aspiring to
be a citizen of nowhere, or ceasing to be one of us. One of the things I
most like about our society, despite its many horrors and injustices, is that
it breeds such people and occasionally rewards them, justly, by buying their
books, debating their ideas, and sometimes even offering them distinguished professorships. When MacIntyre complains that one of the "most
striking facts" about our society is its lack of "institutionalized forums
within which . . . fundamental disagreements can be systematically ex-

plored and charted" (WJ, 2), I have trouble squaring his complaint with the facts of his career or the existence of the various journals and presses he and I have used to express our disagreements with each other. By the same token, when I consider his traditionalist theory of rationality and the story he wants to tell about modernity, I cannot help suspecting that he may himself be the best case against his own central claims.

Chapter 6

VIRTUE AND THE WAY
OF THE WORLD

STANLEY HAUERWAS is surely the most prolific and influential theologian now working in the United States. He has also done more than anyone else to spread the new traditionalism among Christians in the English-speaking world. But in the introduction to his recent book, *A Better Hope*, he confesses that he has "grown tired of arguments about the alleged virtues or vices of liberalism."[1] This is understandable, because he has argued against the vices of liberalism countless times, often while invoking MacIntyre's authority, in the many books he has written since the latter's *After Virtue* appeared in 1981. The index to *A Better Hope* contains more than twenty listings under the term "liberalism." The book begins by arguing against the temptations of Rawlsian political liberalism (BH, 26–27, 30), and eventually gets around to claiming, more generally, "that if the gospel is true, the politics of liberalism must be false" (BH, 124).

If *A Better Hope* offers little evidence that Hauerwas has tired of such arguments and claims, perhaps it does show signs that he is growing uneasy with the posture in which they have left him. He warns his readers—and reminds himself—that "Christians cannot afford" to let themselves be defined by what they are against. He describes the book as his "attempt to make the 'for' more determinative than the 'against' " (BH, 9). His "problem has never been with political liberals," he says, "but rather with the widespread assumption shared by many Christians that political liberalism ought to shape the agenda, if not the very life, of the church" (BH, 9). He wants to make those who read him as a sectarian "think twice" (BH, 10). It must be said, however, that he has stated the "against" in his message much more forcibly than the "for."

Over the last two decades the principal targets of his criticism have been twentieth-century theologians who have dedicated themselves to social justice and sought to make the church safe for democratic aspirations. If Hauerwas has his way, such people will no longer hold a place of honor in the memory of American Christians, for, despite their noble intentions, they were caught up in the way of the world, not the work of Christian virtue. He has other figures to propose as models of virtue. There is no doubt that the main effect of his antiliberal rhetoric, aside from significantly widening his audience, is to undercut Christian identification with democracy. No theologian has done more to inflame Christian resentment of secular political culture.

How Hauerwas Became a
Traditionalist

To understand what attracted him to MacIntyre's ideas in the first place, one needs to keep in mind, first of all, that Hauerwas is a Methodist. After teaching briefly at Augustana College, he joined the Department of Theology at the University of Notre Dame, a Catholic institution, and accepted a position in the Methodist divinity school at Duke University in 1984. But one constant in his thinking from the beginning has been his own tradition's emphasis on the power of the Holy Spirit to transform the life of the believer. John Wesley, the founder of Methodism, taught that once God had "justified" the believer through the gift of faith, thus setting straight his or her personal relation to God, it remained for the believer to be made holy through the achievement of Christian perfection. This process of transformation, which is called "sanctification," depends on divine grace but also requires a serious and sustained effort of self-cultivation on the part of the justified sinner.

Hauerwas's commitment to the Methodist doctrine of sanctification led him to become dissatisfied with the leading forms of Protestant ethics he studied while pursuing his doctorate at Yale. He began rethinking a teaching that had been central to the Protestant Reformation—the doctrine of *sola fides*. According to this doctrine, the sinner is justified, or set straight, solely by divine grace through the gift of faith. This means that one cannot achieve a proper relationship with God by behaving morally or by striving virtuously but can do so only by receiving the gift of faith from God. There is much truth in this doctrine, from Hauerwas's point of view, but many Protestants had gone seriously wrong by using it, in effect, to undermine the equally important doctrine of sanctification, which obliges the justified sinner to cultivate the virtues of Christian perfection. Lutheran theology, in particular, is partly responsible for dislodging the virtues from their formerly central place in Christian ethical reflection. Hauerwas set out to give virtue its due. In ethics this meant shifting the balance between the right and the good. In theology it meant playing down the image of God as one who issues commands while playing up the image of God as one who both personifies goodness in the figure of Christ and graciously reshapes the character of those called to follow him.[2]

In his doctoral dissertation, Hauerwas not only explicated the Wesleyan and Calvinist conceptions of sanctification, but also connected this doctrine with an older tradition of thinking about the virtues that goes back to Aquinas and, through him, to Aristotle.[3] One can see what led Notre Dame to hire him as a teacher of theological ethics in what Hauerwas then called "an ecumenical department of theology in a Catholic university."[4] For here was a bright, young Protestant theologian, articulating doubts about the very doctrine that inspired the Protestant Reformation and arguing for a retrieval of themes from *the* moral theologian of Catholicism. But what interested Hauerwas about Aquinas from the start was his account of the virtues, not the natural-law account of moral principles attributed to him by scholastic Thomists. Catholics had not done much better at giving virtue its due in moral theology than had the Lutherans. For the Methodist Hauerwas, Christian ethics is perfectionist. It is mainly about what kind of people Christians are called to be, not about what one ought to do, and he has always read Aquinas mainly with this thought in mind.

Hauerwas's writings of the 1970s had an enormous impact on theology in the United States, for he was largely successful in persuading theologians representing a wide spectrum of denominations to reconsider the role of virtue in Christian ethics.[5] These writings drew upon and consolidated the work of thinkers like Elizabeth Anscombe, Iris Murdoch, Stuart Hampshire, and Edmund Pincoffs, who had already been raising doubts about similar imbalances in philosophical ethics. His most influential essay from this period is probably a piece entitled, "From System to Story: An Alternative Pattern for Rationality in Ethics" (TT, 15–39), which was coauthored by one of his Catholic colleagues at Notre Dame, David Burrell. This essay's nickname for modern ethical theory is "quandary ethics," an expression Pincoffs had introduced in a paper originally published in *Mind* in 1971. What quandary ethics tends to focus on, as Pincoffs first put it, is "a quandary which arises because I fall into a certain situation. The situation is such that it can be described in perfectly general terms, without any reference to me as an individual, including my personal conceptions of what are and are not worthy deeds and attitudes and feelings: worthy of me."[6] A quandary, then, is an example capable of causing moral perplexity, a problematical case in search of a moral principle under which to be subsumed. Quandary ethics is the variety of ethical discourse in which one performs the legalistic task of formulating moral principles and subsuming cases under them. It is a variety of discourse, according to Hauerwas, in which character is effectively eliminated from ethical consideration.

A quandary is essentially a case, and a case is essentially a narrative rendering of a situation that has been stripped of all but a few details that are necessary for displaying its potential for falling under conflicting generalities. To qualify as a case, an example must first pass through a filter, so that it becomes thinly narrated and, from the perspective of someone applying rules to it, clear. Hauerwas and Burrell argued that the resulting narratives are too thin and abstract to retain the actual moral significance of the problems we face in real life. Focusing mainly on examples of this kind tends, therefore, to distort the situations that do call for ethical reflection. It also tends, over time, to distort our understanding of the moral life as a whole. Quandary ethics gives rise to a view of the moral life as nothing more than a succession of problems calling for decisions and thus to a view of the self as little more than a principled will. Wherever quandary ethics is the dominant variety of ethical discourse, ethical theory is bound to become preoccupied with the formulation of principles designed to systematize and rationalize our intuitions about quandaries. Modern ethical theory "represents an attempt to make the moral life take on the characteristics of a system" (TT, 23).

The alternative Hauerwas and Burrell propose is an ethics of character. In place of the quandarist's cases, ethics must attend to narratives that are rich enough to display the significance of virtuous and vicious traits of character in particular human lives. Narrative, as defined here, is "the connected description of action and of suffering which moves to a point. The point need not be detachable from the narrative itself; in fact, we think a story better that does not issue in a determinate *moral*" (TT, 28; emphasis in original). The stories that someone cares about determine the substance of his or her ethical life. Quandary ethics, with its thinned-out cases, is too abstract to have much substance. Religious faith essentially involves "accepting a certain set of stories as canonical" (TT, 38), but they tend to be stories quite unlike the cases of the modern ethical theorist. They are rather stories like the Gospels or Augustine's *Confessions*, which present "an exemplary instance" of divinity, holiness, or virtue (TT, 31).

His critique of quandary ethics was one of the most influential arguments Hauerwas put forward during the 1970s. It quickly became associated with the topic of narrative theology that was then attracting much attention in the divinity schools. Meanwhile, however, Hauerwas had been learning much from the other Protestant then teaching theological ethics at Notre Dame, John Howard Yoder. Yoder represented the Mennonites, a pacifist church that originated in the radical wing of the Protestant Reformation under the leadership of the renegade Dutch priest, Menno Simons. In a powerfully argued 1974 essay, "The Nonresistant Church" (VV, 197–221), Hauerwas offered a detailed analysis of Yoder's views. He claimed that Yoder's pacifism, conceived in vocational terms as a form of discipleship to Christ, was left essentially untouched by the standard arguments against pacifism. And he endorsed Yoder's claim that the church's task is not to transform the sociopolitical order through direct engagement with it, but rather to establish its own community of discipleship—*in* the world, but not *of* it. The essay stopped just short of committing its author to a pacifist stance. What prevented him from taking the final step appears to be his worry that "the nature of evil is broader than the questions of violence in itself. We constantly confront and perpetrate on others subtle forms of aggression and injustice that are all the more fatal for their nonviolent forms. What form would nonresistance take in the face of this kind of problem in our lives?" (VV, 221) At this point in his development, Hauerwas worried that pacifism fails to acknowledge the difficulty of extricating oneself from complicity in the evils of the world. Refraining from killing can, of course, have unintended but foreseeable violent consequences. And violence is not the only bad thing there is to avoid.

The final section of the essay raised several other serious questions for Yoder's position. One of these, which "concerns Yoder's interpretation of the nature of the dualism between faith and unbelief," is "whether some forms of justice based on the possibilities open to unbelief do not have a more positive relation to the life of faith" than Yoder was prepared to grant (VV, 217).[7] Hauerwas then asked whether "Yoder's theological predisposition has not prevented him from considering a more positive understanding of the nature of political community. Yoder's assertion that violence is the essence of the state fails to appreciate that the state as a form of community cannot be explained or reduced to a Hobbesian mutual protection society" (VV, 218). Hauerwas complained that "Yoder seems to assume that the language of justice is completely determined by sin and thus from the perspective of faith can only be negatively understood. . . . Thus the language of faith can have no positive relation to the language of justice." But Hauerwas wondered whether "any discriminating social judgments by the Christian can be made without buying in at some point to the language of justice" (VV, 219). The underlying difficulty is that Yoder seems to assume "an exact parallel between faith and the new aeon [of God's kingdom], unbelief and the old aeon." "There would be no difficulty in this," Hauerwas concludes, "if Yoder's understanding of the relationship between the two aeons were more dynamic" (VV, 220).

Hauerwas continued to develop his accounts of narrative and virtue while wrestling with Yoder's influence throughout the 1970s. But by the early 1980s he had taken on two important commitments that changed the tenor of his writing significantly. First, he had resolved his doubts about Yoder's position and declared himself a pacifist. Henceforth, he will argue that the church is essentially a community of *peaceable* virtue. The purpose of this community is to follow Christ's nonviolent example, thus exemplifying in its own conduct God's way of dealing with evil in the world. Second, when MacIntyre's *After Virtue* appeared in 1981, he immediately embraced him as the paradigmatic philosophical critic of our time. Henceforth, he will use MacIntyre's traditionalist framework to say much of what he wants to say about virtue and narrative. For here is a philosopher who not only agrees with him that these concepts are of central importance, but also provides an impressive historical explanation of how quandary ethics had come to dominate the scene. According to this story, much of what is wrong about modern society and modern thought can be explained by neglect of the very concepts that Hauerwas had been emphasizing. The change in Hauerwas's thinking can first be seen in his 1981 essay collection, *A Community of Character*, and emerges more fully in his 1983 book, *The*

Peaceable Kingdom, which remains the most unified statement of his mature theological and ethical outlook.[8]

Both of these books describe the church as a community of virtue in a "divided" or "fragmented" world (CC, 89–110; PK, 1–16). The latter (PK, 4–5) quotes a full page from the sublime opening of *After Virtue* to set the tone for the volume as a whole, and then adds:

> If MacIntyre is correct we live in a precarious situation. Life in a world of moral fragments is always on the edge of violence, since there are no means to ensure that moral argument itself can resolve our moral conflicts. No wonder we hunger for absolutes in such a world, for we rightly desire peace in ourselves and in our relations with one another. Granted the world has always been violent, but when our own civilization seems to lack the means to secure peace within itself we seem hopelessly lost. (PK, 5–6)

Hauerwas agrees with MacIntyre that the citizens of a liberal democracy are essentially rootless individuals, not members of a community united by their commitment to the same "canonical stories" and "exemplary instances." As individuals, they have their own private conceptions of the good, and they strive to satisfy their own desires. In order to do this, they may adopt roles and enter into associations with other people as they wish. But they lack the sort of narrative framework they will need if they want to make sense of their lives, cultivate the virtues, and sustain meaningful discourse with one another on ethical and political questions. Ethical theorists, like the rest of us, start out with a collection of inherited moral rules that have been uprooted from the traditional contexts in which they originally made sense. They then try in the midst of all of the fragmentation to supply some source of stability by searching for principles that every rational person would have reason to accept. It is precisely the fragmentation caused by the disintegration of a traditional way of life that makes people want to cling to such principles. But because the theoretical project merely reflects the underlying fragmentation, it is doomed to fail.

In the modern period, according to this story, ethics ceases to be a matter of cultivating the virtues and instead becomes a quest for universally acceptable principles. Because neither ordinary people nor ethical theorists have been able to reach agreement on what the correct principles are, it is hard to see why anyone should think that there really are principles of the kind being sought. Each ethical theory offers evidence that its competitors are mistaken, yet each claims to have found *universally acceptable* principles. The Catholic natural-law theorists appear to be in the same business as the modern moral philosophers. But too many people disagree with Catholic claims about the basic principles of the natural law for it to be plausible to think that these principles are written upon our conscience by God. If such principles are there, they generate too much controversy among apparently rational people to do us much good.

Another problem with natural-law theory, says Hauerwas, is the impression it leaves that distinctively Christian beliefs do not make much difference to ethics. The task of Christian ethics should be to say what difference Christian commitments and practices make to ethics. If Christian beliefs do make a difference to ethics, it should not be surprising that people who are brought up outside the church reach ethical conclusions that put them at odds with Christians. The primary way for a Christian to persuade such people, as Hauerwas sees it, is to preach the gospel and to conduct oneself in a way consistent with the gospel, so that people can see what the Christian way of life looks like. They may still reject it. When God ordains that they convert to Christianity, they will. The Christian task is to preach and live out the gospel, not to find the philosophical basis on which anybody, Christian or non-Christian, can stand. The project of trying to find reasons that would be compelling for any rational person, regardless of upbringing and circumstance, is not only destined to fall short of its goal, but also deflects the church's efforts from the task to which it has been called, which is simply *to be the church*. Being the church, according to the view Hauerwas now takes over completely from Yoder, is a matter of maintaining a pacifist community of virtue in the midst of a violent world, thus providing a foretaste of the peaceable kingdom in which God reigns absolutely and eternally.

Rather than striving for universally acceptable moral principles, Hauerwas is concerned to figure out to what Christians, as members of a particular community, are committed. At the center of Christian practice over the centuries are the retelling of certain stories and the cultivation of certain habits and dispositions. He begins, in other words, not with foundational principles discovered by pure reason, but simply with the liturgical and ethical practices that he and his fellow believers engage in as members of the church. Christian ethics, he concludes, is essentially in need of the qualifier, "Christian" (PK, 1–2, 17–34). For him, every form of ethics requires some kind of qualifier—an adjective that specifies connection to some particular tradition or community. Even natural lawyers, who try to do ethics from a universal standpoint, are really expressing the beliefs and commitments of a particular historical tradition of thought and practice. Like everybody else, the Christian starts somewhere. But not everybody starts in the same place, and where you start is bound to shape how and what you think and how and why you act. Future experience and dialogue with others may convince you to change your mind. Being reasonable requires openness to that possibility. There are no guarantees in this life. We can only begin where we are and do our best to deal reasonably with what we inherit from our tradition, changing our minds when we have good reason, from our own point of view, for doing so.

When he argues against the quest for universally valid principles and grants that everyone has some sort of traditional inheritance for which to take responsibility, one can see how much Hauerwas has in common with Emerson's perfectionism, Whitman's emphasis on character, and Dewey's pragmatism. He might seem, then, to be preparing the way for a pluralistic conversation among people representing varying reasonable points of view—a conversation at least partly about the demands of justice both inside and outside of the church. For these were the demands he had charged Yoder with neglecting. Hauerwas appears to have been actively exploring this way forward in the essay collections he published in the 1970s. But in *The Peaceable Kingdom*, he implicitly forecloses this possibility by envisioning the political culture surrounding the church in terms that combine MacIntyre's antiliberalism with Yoder's "dualistic" conception of the relation between faith and unbelief. And in his subsequent books, he makes the foreclosure explicit by rejecting the surrounding political culture in increasingly strident terms. "Liberal society," "the secular," and "democracy" become his names for what the world has become in an age of fragmentation after the demise of virtue and tradition.[9] His previous doubts about Yoder's "dualism" suddenly and thoroughly recede from view.

CHURCH AND WORLD

Hauerwas does not like being called a "sectarian." In the introduction to *Christian Existence Today*, he protests that the Mennonite conception of the church he takes over from Yoder does not entail withdrawal from the world.[10] Christians, as he rightly points out, are not faced with a simple choice between "*complete* involvement in culture or *complete* withdrawal" (CET, 11; emphasis in original). They must decide on their own terms which forms of involvement are compatible with Christian commitments and which are not. This is something that must be decided contextually. "It is certainly true," he adds, that he has "been critical of liberal social and political presuppositions, particularly as these are played out in American society. . . . The ahistorical character of liberal social and political theory strikes me as particularly pernicious, as in the name of freedom manipulative social relations are legitimated" (CET, 12). But Hauerwas reminds his critics that he has "written about why and how Christians should support as well as serve the medical and legal professions, Christian relations with Judaism, how we might think about justice, as well as an analysis of the moral debate concerning nuclear war" (CET, 7). So it should have been clear that he is not recommending complete withdrawal even from liberal political orders.

Furthermore, Hauerwas explicitly denies "that the only community in which Christians can or should live is the church." "Christians rightly find themselves members of many communities. Thus I am not only a Christian but a university teacher, a Texan, a United States citizen, and a devoted fan of the Durham Bulls" (CET, 15). The point of this remark, I take it, is to acknowledge that, as a citizen of the United States, he can acquire certain obligations to his fellow citizens. But Christian integrity, he insists, requires careful scrutiny of putative obligations arising from any social bond other than the church. "What is required for Christians is not withdrawal but a sense of selective service and the ability to set priorities." In particular, "Christians must withdraw their support" from any social or political order that "resorts to violence in order to maintain internal order and external security" (CET, 15).

Hauerwas has repeatedly argued that Yoder's conception of the church, when properly stated, does not entail an unacceptably rigid form of church-world dualism. He charges his critics with a failure to appreciate Yoder's position on its own terms. Their bias, he says, derives from the severely skewed distinction between "church" and "sect" drawn by Ernst Troeltsch (CET, 7). I do not propose to challenge Hauerwas on the question of how Yoder and Troeltsch should be interpreted. Indeed, I suspect that if Hauerwas and his critics could agree to write and speak for a full decade without using the epithets "sectarianism" and "liberalism," we would quickly find out how much they really have to say. Both of these terms are loaded in ways that skew the debate. The term "sectarianism" can all too easily be used to imply, misleadingly, that Christians "may always, as a matter of their own decision, be respectable—as though martyrdom were a temperamental disposition or an ecclesiastical policy."[11] People with a conscience can always be faced with a social and political order that must simply be rejected in the name of their basic commitments. The question is always open whether ours is such a moment. It is true that Hauerwas sometimes writes as if no such total rejection of American society is necessary just now. But he underestimates the extent to which his heavy-handed use of the term "liberalism" as an all-purpose critical instrument continually reinforces the impression that total rejection is in fact required. This, I believe, is what keeps the charge of sectarianism alive.

The real issue, then, is what happens when Hauerwas combines Yoder's church-world distinction with MacIntyre's antiliberalism. In responding to the charge of sectarianism, Hauerwas has said almost nothing about the significance of his debts to MacIntyre. That this is the issue should have been clear from the start. If Yoder's outlook, taken separately, were the real issue, then the critics would have been writing mainly about him, and Hauerwas would be viewed as a relatively minor figure—a herald preparing the way for the master. But in fact it is Hauerwas's amalgam of themes from Yoder and MacIntyre that generates the controversy. It is therefore crucial to determine what MacIntyre adds to the mix.

As we have seen in the previous chapter, MacIntyre's traditionalist rhetoric depends on a traditional-modern dualism, the intended effect of which is to eliminate ambivalence in one's response to modernity. "Modernity" and "liberalism" become almost interchangeable categories, two names for a scene dominated by vicious individualism in the epoch after virtue ceases to matter. When this rhetoric is conjoined with Yoder's conception of the church, the result, regardless of Hauerwas's intentions, is an especially rigid form of church-world dualism. This, I take it, is at the root of what Hauerwas's critics are complaining about. *One cannot stand in a church conceived in Yoder's terms, while describing the world surrounding it in the way MacIntyre describes liberal society, without implicitly adopting a stance that is rigidly dualistic in the same respects that rightly worried Hauerwas in 1974.* A defense of this stance that focuses solely on Yoder's conception of the church begs the question.

There is, however, another reason that the controversy over sectarianism soon escalated rather than subsiding. Not long after publishing *Christian Existence Today*, Hauerwas seemed to be turning away from his previous interest in questions of justice. By the time he published *After Christendom* in 1991, his rhetorical posture appeared to divorce the "language of faith" from the "language of justice" in the same way he had formerly criticized Yoder for doing.[12] Chapter 2 purports to explain "Why Justice Is a Bad Idea for Christians." Hauerwas likes to shock first and qualify later, and in this case the fine print is slightly less worrisome than the bold. The chapter begins by contending that "the current emphasis on justice and rights as the primary norms guiding the social witness of Christians is in fact a mistake" (AC, 46). Hauerwas does not support this contention by appealing to Yoder; indeed, he would have trouble doing so, for I see no evidence that Yoder argues in this way. Instead, Hauerwas appeals to arguments from MacIntyre as warrant for criticisms of Rawls (AC, 47–50, 60–62) and suggests that liberation theology may have "underwritten a sense of liberation [that is] at odds with the gospel" (AC, 53). On the final page of the chapter, however, he indicates cryptically that it is not his intention to imply that Christians "must give up working for justice in the societies of modernity." Is the point, then, that *the liberal conception of justice* is a bad idea, whereas *working for justice* for sound biblical reasons is a good idea? Hauerwas does not say. Neither does he take it upon himself, in any work that I know of, to explain what those biblical reasons might be.[13] What seems clear, however, is that the "language of justice" has now dropped almost completely out of Hauerwas's thinking.

To see the effects of this, consider the contrast between the way Hauerwas discusses the social processes in which selves are shaped and the way democratic feminists do. According to Hauerwas, most of our actions, beliefs, and character traits are not what they are as a result of decisions we make on the basis of reasoning. They result rather from our having been raised in a certain way and from our daily participation in the practices and institutions of our society. The process begins in infancy. We learn to play one set of games rather than another. We hear stories and learn to recognize and assess the kinds of characters they involve. Imitating our elders, we participate in the rituals of daily life. In one society this might mean bowing and scraping in the presence of certain people. In another it might mean shaking hands firmly and looking people squarely in the eye when you meet them. The possible variations are endless, but it matters greatly to which ones we happen to be exposed, because that determines what kinds of people it is possible for us to be. Hauerwas thinks that Christian ethics needs to be constantly aware of the ways in which social practices shape selves. He thinks that the basic question to ask of any society is what kinds of people it produces. If the basic character types made possible by a society are bad or vicious, he thinks, then you know the most important thing about the society in question.

Gloria Albrecht, who has written an interesting feminist critique of Hauerwas, agrees that societies shape selves through games, storytelling, and other practices.[14] She also agrees that an important question to ask of any society is what kinds of people it produces. She even agrees that critical reasoning can operate only within some delimited social location or other and that ethics therefore always needs a qualifier, just as Hauerwas says it does. But she thinks that Hauerwas does not come entirely clean about his own social location. I would say that one reason for this is that he does not employ the language of justice when discussing the ways in which he and his audience have been shaped into particular sorts of people. He therefore ends up proposing an ethics that tends, by default, to reinforce unjust arrangements.

Albrecht and Hauerwas obviously differ over what kinds of people would count as genuinely virtuous. She thinks that democracy in general and feminism in particular have taught Christians important lessons about what the virtues are. I take Albrecht to be reminding us that justice is one of the virtues, just as Aquinas said it was. But justice, as the virtue that gives each person his or her due, cannot take for granted in our setting that a patriarchal authority structure—whether it be found in church, family, business, or the state—adequately reflects what men and women actually deserve. We do need to look at how societies create the kinds of people that inhabit them. But if we do that in a way that shows genuine concern for all of the kinds of people involved, we will see, according to Albrecht, that Hauerwas is insensitive to a range of vices that his form of traditionalism fosters.

When some feminists refer to their goal as the liberation of women, they seem to imply that their project involves taking away the social constraints that are now in place so that the real essence of women will be able to shine forth for the first time. Albrecht recognizes, however, that there will always be some social constraints or other. You cannot just take away social constraints altogether. The question is what the social constraints are going to be, not whether there are going to be any. Whichever practices and institutions replace the current ones will in turn create the kinds of men and women there can be in that social setting. Hauerwas makes a similar point in some of his writings against liberation theology (e.g., AC, 50–58). If you get carried away with the ideal of liberation, he says, you end up thinking that the ultimate goal is to be freed from all social constraints. But a self that was freed from all social constraints would not be free to do much of anything. To be free to do most things that are worthwhile, one needs to acquire skills and habits by participating in practices and institutions. One becomes free to excel in soccer, jazz, essay writing, or cathedral building by participating in activities that place constraints on one's behavior, where not just anything one does counts as acceptable, where people of superior experience and accomplishment can serve as role models and offer criticism. The ideal of perfect freedom or complete liberation does not help us here. Hauerwas is right about all of this—if not always fair in characterizing the views of the "liberals" and "liberationists" he is criticizing.

His positive purpose in making this argument is to show that the categories of virtue, tradition, and narrative are crucial to ethics. He prefers these categories to the concept of liberation because he thinks they help him get at the question of what kinds of people our society is producing and the even more basic question of to what social practices and institutions we should be committed. Albrecht would grant that it is incoherent to strive for a society in which we would be completely free of constraining influences. If a young woman is going to become an excellent jazz musician, she will have to deal with standards of competence and excellence and strive to constrain her musical performances accordingly. She will be well served by apprenticing herself to someone more experienced and accomplished than herself and, up to a certain point in her development, by imitating models of excellence. But a prerequisite for becoming free to play jazz well is the freedom to play at all. Another is access to competent teachers who care about helping her get better and offer her encouragement. If the institutions currently in place deprive her of that opportunity because she is a woman, the constraints being placed on her will be constraints from which she needs to be freed. In other words, she will need to be liberated from the kinds of social constraints that either exclude women from social practices or inhibit their performance once they are allowed to engage in them. You can strive to be liberated from constraints of those kinds without thinking it is possible or desirable to do away with constraints altogether.

One thing women need to be liberated to participate in, I would argue, is the democratic practice in which we try to take responsibility, as a people, for the activities and institutions that constitute our common life together. The institutions in question include the family, the firm, the market, the university, and the church. The practices include nurturing the young, the production and distribution of goods, the pursuit of learning, and worship. Hauerwas seems not to imagine this democratic, critical activity as a practice that involves the cultivation of virtues or the construction and telling of narratives.

He thinks of democratic questioning not as a valuable social practice, like jazz or baseball, but as one of the acids of individualism eating away at tradition. In his vision—and here it is MacIntyre's influence that matters—liberal democracy and tradition appear as opposites, necessarily opposed to each other. Because he thinks of them in this way, he slides into thinking that the only way to shape virtuous people is to favor the particular kind of premodern, authoritarian tradition he has in mind. In this book, I have been defending the notion that democratic questioning and reason-giving are a sort of practice, one that involves and inculcates virtues, including justice, and that becomes a tradition, like any social practice, when it manages to sustain itself across generations. I reject as incoherent the quest for a social situation completely free of constraints.[15] Freedom, in my view, is a kind of constraint by norms. The question before us, as I see it, is to what norms we are entitled to commit ourselves, given everything else we know. If, as I will argue in part 3, norms are creatures of social practices, then the question boils down to which practices and institutional arrangements we ought to foster. The choice is not between an incoherent quest for unconstrained existence, on the one hand, and authoritarian practices and hierarchical institutions, on the other. Nor, for that matter, is the choice between an ethics of conduct and an ethics of character, between deontic and aretaic considerations. Rules are important because they make explicit the normative constraints on conduct that arise in social practices and institutions. These normative constraints make possible specific kinds of expressive freedom, different roles and aspirations, and therefore different kinds of people. Reference to the virtues is important because it allows us to make explicit our ideals for judging the kind of people we have become, which in turn allows us to double back and ask whether changes are called for in social practices and institutions.

Commitment to democracy does not entail the rejection of tradition. It requires *jointly* taking responsibility for the criticism and renewal of tradition and for the justice of our social and political arrangements. As Hauerwas originally put the point when criticizing Yoder, it is doubtful that "any discriminating social judgments by the Christian can be made without buying in at some point to the language of justice" (VV, 219). The responsibility we share for the justice of our political arrangements inside of and outside of our religious communities not only concerns who gets to play what roles; it also concerns what the basic roles and character types are going to be. Albrecht is saying that, in our day, taking responsibility for the social roles and character types in our social system raises the question of how we might adjust all of our practices and institutions so as to give shape to selves who are capable of treating women justly. This question was already on the minds of Mary Wollstonescraft, Harriet Martineau, and Virginia Woolf, none of whom aspired to a society absolutely free of constraint.[16]

Hauerwas, however, shows little interest in feminist complaints about what kinds of people our society produces and the roles it makes available to them. The role he is most interested in—and understandably so—is that of disciple. Discipleship, he might say, is open to all Christians. The trouble is that the normative constraints it involves are bound to be neglected unless the church can keep its mind on its own proper vocation. Even in the Middle Ages, according to Yoder, the mainstream church had already succumbed to the temptation of taking an essentially non-Christian interest in justice. The trouble started when the Emperor Constantine converted to Christianity. Suddenly, Christians were being asked to advise emperors on how to run an empire. When Catholic Christianity became the official religion of that empire, Yoder says, it lost connection with its true calling as a community of peace and hospitality intended to serve as a foretaste of God's kingdom. The Catholic attempt during the medieval period to run a world civilization on Christian principles of justice in fact made Christianity too much a thing *of* the world. Christian moralists found themselves addressing the odd question of how to rule empires and fight wars lovingly. According to Hauerwas, this tied them into all sorts of intellectual knots, including the talk of double-effect that lies at the core of just-war thinking. They became very adept at telling Christians where and when and how to coerce or kill somebody in the name of Christ.

All of this happened, Hauerwas claims, because Christians stopped caring enough about the implications of their own master narrative, which is a story about God's way of dealing with evil. What God does in response to the evils of the age is to suffer nonviolently on the cross in perfect virtue. This is the way of life (and sacrifice) to which Christians are called. Christians abandoned the ethos of the early church precisely when they started trying to rule society lovingly. All they were really doing when they did that was to place a veneer of love-talk over the realities of imperial violence. Christians who concern themselves nowadays mainly with the struggle for justice are simply the democratic descendants of Constantine. They are busy basting the rotten carcass of governmental violence with holy water, but succeed in changing neither the taste nor the smell of the thing.

It is not clear how Hauerwas proposes to combine this anti-Constantinian narrative with the antimodern narrative he takes over from MacIntyre. One difficulty in combining them, of course, is that they locate the crucial dramatic reversal—the fall, if you will—in different places. Yoder locates it around the time of Constantine's conversion, whereas MacIntyre locates it around the time of Luther and Machiavelli. Perhaps Hauerwas wants to claim that the broader social world within which Christians find themselves has always had the disadvantage of being outside the City of God, but that its spiritual and ethical condition only worsened, horribly, in the modern period. Yoder, then, explains how the church became confused over its vocation. MacIntyre, on the other hand, explains how things got worse, morally and spiritually, for everyone outside of the church when liberals proposed to dispense with the kind of overall narrative framework that would allow them to make sense of their lives ethically. Pagans in the ancient world could at best exhibit splendid vices, given that they did not worship the true God, but at least they were trying to live virtuously in terms of a shared narrative framework. Their modern successors, having lost their grip on the concept of virtue and being content to live in a society that treats commitment to large-scale narratives as a private affair, are simply vicious.

By combining the two stories in something like this way, Hauerwas leaves the world outside the modern church in a doubly darkened condition. It is a world not only outside of the church, but also after virtue. As such, its vices are not splendid but especially ugly. It is this way of describing these vices that leads many of his readers to assume that he sees the world of liberal democracy as wholly lacking in grace. Notice, however, that Yoder intended his historical narrative as a criticism of the church, not as a criticism of the world. It was therefore possible, in principle, for Hauerwas to develop Yoder's conception of the church in a nondualistic direction, as seems to have been his intention in 1974. All he needed to do was to emphasize that the world, like the church, is a realm ordained and ruled by God—an arena in which those with the eyes to see can perceive the workings of God's gracious providence. He could reinforce this emphasis by adopting the Barthian view, discussed in chapter 4, above, that "the boundary between Church and the profane still and repeatedly takes a course quite different from that which we hitherto thought we saw." The main effect that MacIntyre's traditionalism has had on Hauerwas's thinking is to hinder the possibility of taking Yoder's "politics of Jesus" where he had once wanted to take it. For he seems no longer to be moving in the direction of a world-engaging conversation about the biblical injunction to build communities—ecclesial, familial, and national—in which justice and peace visibly embrace. One reason for this is that justice has largely dropped out of the picture. Another is that what Barth saw as an ever-shifting boundary between church and world appears to have hardened in Hauerwas's rhetoric into a rigid and static line between Christian virtue and liberal vice. It is clear that he does not intend to allow the boundary to harden in this way at the level of doctrine. But his antiliberal rhetoric can easily give the impression that the boundary has hardened in practice. In practical terms, Barth was engaged in a project quite unlike Hauerwas's. He wanted both to utter an absolutely unequivocal "No!" to Nazism and to counteract the tendency of the confessing church to believe that it could have the gospel without progressive politics.[17] Hauerwas utters his "No!" to liberalism, but there is little in his work that resembles Barth's active commitment to democracy and socialist reform.

A detailed doctrinal comparison of Hauerwas and Barth on the nature of the church would take us too far afield. In *The Peaceable Kingdom* (166–67 n. 5), Hauerwas quotes favorably from two passages in *Church Dogmatics*, IV/2. The first addresses the need for a humble conception of the church as "itself only a human society moving like all others to [Christ's] manifestation." The second asserts that "if the community were to imagine that the reach of the sanctification of humanity accomplished in Jesus Christ were restricted to itself and the ingathering of believers, that it did not have corresponding effects *extra muros ecclesiae*, it would be in flat contradiction to its own confession of its Lord." Hauerwas goes on to claim that a suitably humble conception of the church as "a natural institution in no way lessens the demands the church puts on any society in which it finds itself—not the least of which is the demand for the free preaching of the gospel." Barth, of course, as the principal author of the Barmen Declaration, would agree. More recently, however, Hauerwas has criticized Barth for denying the necessity of the church as a medium of faith and failing to account for the role its social practices play in the sanctification of believers.[18]

There is an important theological controversy developing here. From Barth's point of view, the issue is whether the church maintains a proper recognition of the distance between the human social practices it embodies and God's freedom to act graciously wherever and however he sees fit. From Hauerwas's point of view, the issue is whether the church can be given its due as a herald and foretaste of the kingdom of God. A Barthian critic might want to argue that Hauerwas's one-sidedly negative polemic against liberal society—his failure to distinguish what he calls liberalism from democracy—is the fruit of a theological error. But it seems to me that one could resist Barth's especially austere view of the church without endorsing Hauerwas's description of "the world" in its current form as an expression of "particularly pernicious" liberal ideas. His debt to MacIntyre's antiliberalism remains the key issue.

Many of Hauerwas's theologically orthodox critics welcome his call for increased emphasis on the visibility of the church, insofar as he offers a corrective to liberal and liberationist theological programs that tend to *reduce* the church to a movement for social democracy. They also welcome his bold criticisms of secularist liberalism as an ideology intent on excluding the voice of theology from public discussion. Their worry is that Hauerwas habitually expresses these valuable points in a way that threatens to vitiate his message. Several temptations are at issue: (1) an uncharitable attitude toward the world, especially in its democratic forms; (2) a failure to distinguish adequately between disappearing into the world and pursuing justice as a responsible member of one's national community; and (3) excessive pride in the visible church as a virtuous community. The first and third temptations combine to form another: (4) excessive certainty that one possesses the virtue of discernment, the capacity to tell the difference between the way of the world and the stirrings of the Spirit. The critics would not say that Hauerwas always succumbs to these temptations. The question is whether he is prepared, on the whole, to take sufficient care in guarding against them, especially in works designed to reach the broadest possible audience.

Recently Hauerwas remarked that people who think he writes too much should tell him which parts to leave out. The quip comes in the introduction to *In Good Company*, and it leads into a series of reflections that merit quotation.[19] Hauerwas says that there "are two standard criticisms against those who write a great deal: (1) we are repetitious, or (2) we are not careful" (IGC, 12). He adds:

> I do not believe, however, that my work is "careless" though I know what I am trying is risky and the risk is increased by my "contrarian" or polemical style. The risks I take are of the academic sort and, therefore, not all that "risky." I know that I recklessly cross academic lines, which makes me vulnerable to those who know "more," but given the task before theology I cannot conceive of any alternative. Such risks are minor given the challenges before the church. (IGC, 13)

This passage casts Hauerwas in the role of a taker of risks on behalf of a noble cause. It says that he is the one made vulnerable by his risky business, as if there were no danger here of misrepresenting his interlocutors or the society he is discussing. The risk he runs, he implies, is the merely "academic" one of feeling embarrassed when charged with wrongdoing by the academic border police.[20]

In a note connected to the same passage Hauerwas names his principal targets: "my 'contrarian' style is necessitated by my polemic against theological and political liberalism. The liberal, of both kinds, is committed to 'englobing' all positions into liberalism" (IGC, 224 n. 32). What Hauerwas does not face with sufficient candor is the fact that his desire to reduce all opponents to a single figure, "the liberal," gives him an interest in ignoring the details of what the targets of his critique actually say and do. Once they have been reduced in this way, the same arguments can be used on all of them. Reduction and repetition are both rhetorically intrinsic to the procedure. The issue of interpretive charity, then, is whether he takes appropriate care to get his opponents right, to listen to what they are saying and observe what they are doing, before bagging them as argumentative quarry. And the opponents are not merely fellow intellectuals like Rawls, Niebuhr, and Albrecht, but his fellow citizens, who, by accepting his portrayal of them, may come to view the social world outside of the church as *merely* "pernicious" and forget how to trust and identify with one another. For an author of his prominence and style, the risks are not merely academic.

How would this be described in the Aristotelian language he often appropriates? It would be called "unfriendliness." The careless misrepresentation of others would be called "negligence," and repeated instances of the same behavior would be called a bad habit, a "vice." Yet he now has an audience larger than that of any other theological ethicist in the English-speaking world. Only a small percentage of his readers read the books he criticizes, so they can only applaud the amusing professor who defends virtue against the heathen. If Hauerwas were to leave out the passages in which he offends against the vocation of charitable interpretation, he would have to leave out a great deal. But the remaining parts would be both voluminous and valuable. I think especially of his extensive writings on care for the disabled and retarded, which express the sort of patience with deformity that I have praised in Whitman,[21] as well as his reflections on medicine and suffering and his many insightful contributions to virtue theory.[22] When he does not succumb to the temptation of repeating his diatribes against liberal society, he is often an imaginative and generous thinker.

Recall that one of the questions Hauerwas posed to Yoder in 1974 was how the pacifist church proposed to disentangle itself from complicity in the evils of the world so as to exemplify genuine virtue, given that killing is only the most obvious form of impropriety at issue. Here, too, the early Hauerwas is his own best critic, for he has done little to clarify how Christians are supposed to go about disentangling themselves from the liberal society and militarist state he denounces. A similar message of fidelity to the ethos of early Christianity would come across differently if spoken by a Dorothy Day, a Tolstoy, or even by an actual Mennonite. For, in those cases, the living example of the messenger constitutes the ethical substance of the message while also demonstrating exactly what must be sacrificed for the disentangling to count as authentic. In Hauerwas's case, it is hard to see that any nonverbal disentangling has been attempted at all.

A cynic might say that the secret of Hauerwas's vast influence in the church in the 1980s and 1990s lay in the imprecision of the sacrifice he appeared to be demanding of his followers. Surely he was not proposing that the strength of one's sentimental identification with the church could by itself secure noncomplicity with the evils of the world. His favorite patristic text appears to be Origen's *Exhortation to Martyrdom*.[23] But in the absence of a clear statement of the price Christians must be willing to pay, his audience was able to indulge itself in fantasies of martyrdom without experiencing actual poverty or persecution at all. Many of Hauerwas's readers probably liked being told that they should care more about being the church than about doing justice to the underclass. At some level they knew perfectly well how much it would cost them to do justice. So they hardly minded hearing that justice is a bad idea for Christians. It was tempting to infer, half-consciously, that following Jesus involves little more than hating the liberal secularists who supposedly run the country, pitying poor people from a distance, and donating a portion of one's income to the church. Hauerwas has not done much to guard his readers against this temptation.

Votes cast by Christians influence the rate of taxation, the condition of the environment, the fate of the underclass, and the nature of foreign policy. Far from making this point effectively, Hauerwas relentlessly criticizes theologians who draw attention to it. They are guilty of diluting the wine of the gospel with the water of liberalism. The alternative, from his point of view, is to let the church be the church. The slogan is succinct, and it has caught on among those who find the "social gospel" of Christian liberalism thin. But there is no wisdom in replacing one reductive interpretation of the gospel by another. Reducing the gospel to democracy and reducing it to ecclesiology are hardly the only alternatives. Christians have every reason to concern themselves with the integrity of the church and with the question of what way of life it is meant to exemplify. Yet they are also, as Hauerwas once pointed out, members of families, unions, professions, colleges, ethnic groups, and nations. They are all active consumers, and many hold positions of influence in corporate and governmental bureaucracies. Christian ethics has traditionally taken all of these roles as falling within its scope, and made it its business to evaluate existing social arrangements in light of stringent standards of justice and love. In doing so, it has entered into conversations and alliances with groups outside of the church. In the modern era, the conversations have often been about democracy; the alliances have involved such aims as the abolition of slavery, the equal recognition of women, and the avoidance of cruelty. In his polemical writings, the ones that have made him famous, Hauerwas seems to see in all of this little more than a corruption of the gospel—the spoiled fruit of a misguided Constantinianism. His critics are struggling to articulate a more balanced view that would be more charitable both to the tradition of Christian ethics from Augustine to Barth and to the history of Christian political involvement from the Putney debates to the March on Selma.

The core of Hauerwas's anti-Constantinian teaching is absolute pacifism, justified on biblical grounds as a vocation of discipleship to Christ. Most of his readers have found this commitment hard to swallow, but they have often been prepared to treat it as a side-issue, while focusing instead on his critique of liberalism. Hauerwas, to his credit, has long insisted on the centrality of pacifism to his outlook. He has not, however, made clear what his pacifism demands, practically speaking. Given that military conscription is no longer the law of the land, his followers face no governmental pressure to serve in the armed forces. He does not, as Hunsinger does, hold up Pax Christi, World Peacemakers, and the sanctuary movement as exemplary concrete practices. To my knowledge, he has advocated neither the withholding of taxes that finance the military, nor participation in costly acts of civil disobedience, nor refusal of communion to soldiers and their commanders. For this reason, Hauerwas's pacifism has often come across more as a quixotic gesture than as the demanding doctrine he intended it to be. If nothing much follows from it, what is there to worry about?

The social significance of his position appears to be changing, however, in the months since September 11, 2001. In the new political situation, pacifism as such is a controversial matter. To advocate it at a time when cells of terrorists are actively plotting the murder of one's fellow citizens is to place those citizens at risk. With the implications of his pacifism suddenly in clear focus, it is dawning on Hauerwas's audience that he is saying something they don't necessarily want to hear. Saying "Amen" to his jeremiad now requires more courage. Meanwhile, a rapidly widening rift has become visible between the quite different forms of traditionalism represented by Hauerwas and Neuhaus. With the latter lamenting the passing of Christendom, adding his blessings to militarism, and proclaiming America's providential role in global politics, it is becoming much harder for the new traditionalists to present a united front in opposing a society supposedly dominated by secular liberalism. What, in the end, do Hauerwas and Neuhaus agree on, aside from calling themselves Christians? The very thing that links them, ironically, to Islamic radicals—namely, the proposition that secular liberalism needs to be opposed because it destroys the tradition that inculcates true virtue. But it is now plain to all concerned that very different traditions are being proposed as remedies for secular liberalism's alleged deficiencies, even by those who speak for Christianity.[24] It would not be a bad time to question whether traditionalism provides an adequate critical vocabulary for diagnosing what has gone wrong with our society and for prescribing remedies, whether by peaceable or other means.

Hauerwas's theological ethics can succeed on its own terms only if it faithfully espouses the life and teachings of Jesus in their entirety. With the pacifism in his position receiving the emphasis he has always intended it to have, his main challenge will now be to explain more clearly than before why some apparently strict teachings from the New Testament warrant a rigorist emphasis while others do not. He has taken a clear stand against abortion, which is not mentioned in the New Testament but strikes him as obviously incompatible with a commitment to nonviolence. Perhaps he has somewhere drawn morally rigorous conclusions on topics concerning which the New Testament would seem to be a costly teaching for many of the people in his audience—remarriage after divorce, for example, or the chances of a rich man to enter the kingdom of God. If so, the pronouncements have escaped my notice.[25] It is hard, at this point, to escape the conclusion that his ethics rests on an extremely selective reading of the Bible.[26]

The language of justice, which Hauerwas once prized as a way of being faithful to the biblical call to righteousness, is currently of paramount importance in the struggle against terrorism. It is the language one needs when explaining why we have just cause to bear arms against terrorists, why our armed forces should not be firing at civilians, and why we should not be supporting regimes that depend on us to thwart the democratic aspirations of their own people. And there are many other worthy purposes in social ethics for which this language seems essential—such as the critique of global capitalism, the reform of tax law, and the restructuring of familial roles. If Hauerwas were to stop thrashing his liberal straw man, rediscover the language of justice, and put that language to use in prophetic works of social criticism, his reviewers would surely stop charging him with sectarianism. And much good would ensue. He is as well positioned as any intellectual to pose the challenge of the twenty-first century to American Christians.[27]

Hauerwas wants to articulate the situated ethos of a living tradition, not a utopian ideal or categorical imperative based on pure reason. We have seen that the new traditionalism rejects the formalism of modern ethical theory. The reasons it offers resemble the ones Hegel invoked against Kant two centuries ago. Like Hegel, it seeks a *sittlich* alternative to formalism. It aims to make explicit the ethical life of a community. In this sense, it is expressivist. But what community is at issue here? The new traditionalism does not harbor the hope Hegel and Whitman had of articulating the self-consciousness of a nation. It finds modern society *"generally perverted"* by the "activity of individuality," and therefore aims to articulate the claims of "virtue" over against "the way of the world."[28] In doing so, as we have seen in the previous chapter, it must, however, resolve the problem of point of view. It must find a place *in* the modern world, but not *of* it. Otherwise it will lack an intelligible standpoint for its critique of that world. It does not want to adopt the posture of mere nostalgia. It therefore claims to make explicit the ethical substance of a *living* community of *premodern* virtue. For MacIntyre, the relevant community is a form of Thomistic Catholicism, and he can readily point to the parishes that embody this outlook. Hauerwas claims, with equal self-assurance, to be speaking for the actual church of communion, homilies, Bible study, and potluck dinners. But where are we to find the community of nonviolent discipleship he has in mind? He is a Methodist, not a Mennonite, and has strong ties to Catholicism. So one wonders where he locates the visible legacy of the martyrs of the early church. Hauerwas is usually much less concrete than Hunsinger, who takes inspiration from the Barmen Declaration and holds up contemporary American examples of resistance and civil disobedience to clarify what it means to identify with the confessing church today. Hauerwas concludes his Gifford Lectures, *With the Grain of the Universe*, with a chapter entitled "The Necessity of Witness," in which he offers John Howard Yoder, John Paul II, and Dorothy Day as representatives of the church as he understands it. His reference to Day appears to have been an afterthought. It consists of only a single, brief paragraph (230) that does not even begin to come to terms with the politics of the *Catholic Worker*, whereas both Yoder and John Paul II are treated at some length. Nonetheless, it gives me hope that Hauerwas may be heading in a more promising direction.

In its Hauerwasian form, virtue's rejection of the way of the world leads to an unpleasant dilemma. On the one hand, the stronger its claim to represent virtue as distinct from the way of the world, the more quickly it degenerates into a form of "conceit" that cannot honestly be sustained. The actual church does not look very much like a community of virtue, when judged by pacifist standards. A large percentage of those who call themselves Christians favor capital punishment, the possession of nuclear weapons, and using force to defend their nation against terrorists. On the other hand, admitting that the community of virtue itself exhibits the vices it accuses the world of exhibiting causes the substance of virtue to evaporate into mere ideality, leaving it "a virtue in name only, which lacks substantial content." Either way, it is in danger of collapsing into something it purports to criticize. This is why Hauerwas has difficulty in articulating the "for" of his position as clearly as he articulates the "against." An extended, sensitive treatment of Dorothy Day and her politics would make the "for" both clearer and more concrete. It would also give Hauerwas an opportunity to retrieve his earlier commitment to the language of justice. So long as he shows little interest in persuading Christian citizens of their obligations to the least well-off, "the knight of virtue's own part in the fighting [will remain], strictly speaking, a sham-fight." Mere pacifism—in which the memory of distant martyrs and the vision of the peaceable kingdom are divorced from a visible practice of social justice—is "like the combatant who, in the conflict, is only concerned with keeping his sword bright."

Chapter 7

BETWEEN EXAMPLE AND DOCTRINE

THE PREVIOUS CHAPTER invited Hauerwas to put an end to the controversy over his alleged sectarianism by giving up his antiliberal polemic and recasting his social criticism in somewhat different terms. I am not encouraging him to be less vehement or less theological in denouncing evil and vice. He is surely right in saying that American society has a lot to answer for given its conduct over the last several decades. And if he spoke less theologically, he wouldn't be Hauerwas. My hope is that he will do much in the future to clarify the wrongs we have committed and the flaws in our character as a people. But there seems little chance of achieving this promise if he continues to lean as heavily on MacIntyre's traditionalism as he has done over the last two decades. In the first two sections of the present chapter, I want to consider what has become of his early contrast between an ethics concerned with systematizing our intuitions about moral quandaries and an ethics of character centered in narratives about exemplary lives. In the final section, I will bring the argument of part 2 full circle by discussing the relationship between Hauerwas's views and those of political theorist Seyla Benhabib.

THE ETHICS OF EXAMPLE

Hauerwas's complaints about quandary ethics attempt to make room within ethical discourse for consideration of a person not as a locus of dignity or as a bearer of rights but as this particular human being, in all of his or her individuality. When ethical judgment is conceived simply as an attempt to subsume cases under principles, human beings can appear in ethical discourse only in relatively abstract and generalized terms. The project of subsumption requires thin description of selves and cases. In *The Peaceable Kingdom*, Hauerwas argues that an ethics of character need not do away with casuistry altogether, but that it does need to concern itself with better, richer examples than those upon which quandary ethics has focused. The narratives we reflect on critically need to be detailed enough in their description of situations and of the people involved in them to allow concrete traits of character, life histories, projects, and needs to come into view.

On this much Hauerwas and I are agreed. But when Hauerwas connects this thesis with MacIntyre's story about modern ethical discourse, something goes seriously wrong. Like MacIntyre, Hauerwas thinks that the secular philosophical quest for rationally justified, highly general moral principles—the kind under which any rational agent could subsume examples—has failed. He also accepts the conclusion that MacIntyre infers from this premise, that modern ethical discourse as such is indefensible. This inference assumes, however, that the theoretical defenses of modern ethical discourse put forward by the ethical theorist are at least *expressively* accurate, that the ethical theorists adequately reflect the ethical discourse of the age. I want to suggest another possibility—that the ethical theorists have drastically oversimplified what modern ethical discourse has been like.

Consider that many ordinary people find the austere and often technical language of ethical theory ridiculous, pretentious, or unintelligible. They often take offense at having their thoughts recast in theoretical terms as "deontological" or "consequentialist." Most people show no interest in having the benefits of ethical theory conferred upon them. They find many of the imaginary cases discussed by theorists to be absurd. More people seek their moral edification from poems, novels, essays, plays, and sermons than from moral treatises or philosophical articles. I take it that these facts are not really in dispute. Every college professor who teaches a "moral problems" course in the standard way is familiar with them. The temptation of the ethical theorist is to dismiss these responses to quandary ethics as signs of antiphilosophical, or anti-intellectual, prejudice. Prejudicial they may sometimes be, but they also show that ethicists are often moving against the grain of the attitudes and language they purport to analyze. I think they should give an ethical theorist pause. If it is the business of ethical theory to reflect critically on ethical discourse, and resistance to systematic theorizing is a recurring theme in modern ethical discourse, as it surely is, then ethical theory needs to take such resistance seriously.

When we turn to the written evidence, it becomes clear that there are patterns of reasoned suspicion here, not merely unthinking reactions. Some modern writers explicitly criticize ethical theory. There are parodies and satires of it, as well as straightforward arguments for avoiding it. There are also immanent critiques, which stand within theoretical constructions in order to undermine them. More numerous, perhaps, are the writers who, though familiar with ethical theory, self-consciously eschew it. Sometimes they leave their reasons for doing so unstated, but sometimes the reasons are stated as clearly as can be. There are at least three standard complaints that have been brought against systematic ethics repeatedly in the modern period. The first is that it represents a dangerously disruptive operation of power, in which intellectuals as a class assert privileged claims for themselves, as arbiters of universal reason, against the traditions and customs essential to the order and well-being of an established community. The second is that it is a misguided flight from the practical demands of the struggle against evil and injustice. The third is that it represents a temptation to engage in presumptuously dogmatic and excessively abstract thought.

In fact, all three of these complaints can often be paired with a specific discursive alternative to the theoretical style of quandary ethics. Edmund Burke, who directed the first complaint against the philosophers of the French Revolution, favored traditionalist narratives of declension, nostalgic appeals to hierarchical order, and sudden flashes of sublime poetic imagery. Gerrard Winstanley, who directed the second against contemplative university ministers, adopted a prophetic stance, claimed the divine inspiration of a "power within," and employed the iconoclastic invective of the Puritan jeremiad to move his Digger readers to action. Michel de Montaigne, who directed the third against every variety of moral philosophy and theology known to him, invented the modern essay, with its conversational diction, its preference for particulars, and its questioning, independent, author.

These examples are suggestive because each of them stands at the head of a modern tradition in which distinctive ways of thinking, talking, and writing about ethical topics have been kept alive for many generations. Not everyone who contributes to these traditions repeats or endorses the original complaint about ethical theory. For example, some latter-day Burkeans try to combine a formalist ethical theory centered on the concept of natural law with other elements of Burke's rhetoric. But each of these traditions continues to breed doubts about ethical theory by keeping old complaints in circulation and occasionally updating them or adding to them. More to the point, each of these traditions inculcates and exhibits patterns of ethical reasoning that differ significantly from those usually studied within ethical theory.

Let us reflect for a moment on the tradition of Montaigne. His descendants in Britain include essayists like William Hazlitt, George Orwell, and Virginia Woolf. His American heirs include Ralph Waldo Emerson, Walt Whitman, James Baldwin, Ralph Ellison, and Adrienne Rich. Together, these writers have done much to define for their respective political cultures what it means to have a moral imagination. Most of them have their prophetic moments, writing as if they were addressing the wayward people in ecstatic furor, but they usually prefer to address their readers as Montaigne addressed his—namely, as individuals. They model their essays on conversation and eschew all claims to privileged standing. They are not addressing a congregation from a pulpit. Nor are they theorizing systematically about ethical topics in the sense that Kant and Sidgwick are. They may take pride in being principled, like Hazlitt and Orwell, but they are not trying to arrange principles and intuitions into a set order. Neither are they endeavoring to give a complete account of the meaning, justification, or truth of their principles. They are not interested in closure. They are simply thinking something through, in light of experience and in the expectation that someone will answer back. They write in a style that invites the respondent to respond. All of them favor the essay over the treatise or the academic article. Some experiment with historiography, the novel, and iconoclastic invective. The essay is not the only mode in which they choose to discourse on ethical topics. But it is surely one of them, and its resources for resisting quandary ethics and the discourse of ethical theorists are ample.

Essays in this tradition aspire neither to system nor to story, though they often assess systems and tell stories in the course of their work. The essay inserts itself discretely between story and system, between the particular event and the general idea—in Robert Musil's words, "between example and doctrine."[1] For the systematic philosopher, as we have seen, the example becomes a case, something to be subsumed under a general law. Montaigne, however, often begins with examples, without being sure what they exemplify, and then invites readers into a movement of critical thought. He traces and retraces paths between abstract ideas and anecdotal details without seeking either doctrinal or narrative closure. The outcome of an essay, again in Musil's words, is neither a system nor a story but "rather the unique and unalterable form assumed by [an individual's] inner life in a decisive thought" (MWQ, 273). In contrast, here is what Musil has to say about the habits of mind displayed in the systematic style of philosophical theory: "Philosophers are despots who have no armies to command, so they subject the world to their tyranny by locking it up in a system of thought" (MWQ, 272). Musil counts it a good sign of the times that "epochs of progressive civilization and democracy fail to bring forth a convincing philosophy." I take him to mean that the ethical life of democracy is too fluid and dialogical to be locked up in a formalistic system.

Montaigne was no democrat. Nor were most of the writers in Hume's generation who held up Montaigne and Seneca as models for emulation. But it did not take long before essayists, in the aftermath of the French Revolution, began to write for, and expand, the public that came into existence to read Tom Paine's prophetic tracts and William Cobbett's *Political Register*. In the meantime, the essayistic discipline of thinking for oneself "between example and doctrine," and of addressing readers of all classes as individuals capable of thinking for themselves and of answering back, has, I believe, contributed much to the development of democratic spiritual and ethical aspirations. Hazlitt and Orwell claimed that the conversational style of the familiar essay is the form of writing best suited to democratic thinking and the one most likely to create and sustain an audience disposed to democracy and suspicious of violence and privilege. Reading any good collection of modern essays should suffice to dispel the impression that traditional ethical topics, like character and the virtues, have been entirely eclipsed by talk of rights and utility in the modern period. There is a massive modern democratic literature on character and the virtues awaiting exploration outside of the philosophical canon. The essayists write character sketches, character typology in the style of Theophrastus, and advisory epistles to the young. They meditate on how to characterize groups in relation to supposedly representative traits or individuals. Each of these subgenres has its distinctive ways of relating abstractions to narratives and descriptive details.

Hauerwas has written many essays; nearly all of his books are anthologies of them. But he uses the genre to propose that Christian ethics should give pride of place to the genre that Peter Brown, the classical historian, has termed *the classic life*. Brown writes as follows:

> The Greco-Roman world, in which the saints later appeared, was a civilization of *paideia* in the same way as our own is a civilization of advanced technology. It invariably tended to opt for the necessary self-delusion that all its major problems could be both articulated and resolved in terms of its one major resource—in this case, by the paradigmatic behavior of elites groomed by a *paideia* in which the role of ancient exemplars was overwhelming. The tendency to see exemplary *persons* as classics was reinforced by the intensely personal manner in which the culture of *paideia* was passed on from generation to generation. Intensive male bonding lay at the heart of the "Civilization of Paideia."[2]

The goal of the education was to mold oneself into the form of true excellence. The medium of the education was direct exposure to an exemplar, the teacher, who would also place before you ancient and accepted models of eloquent speech, straight thinking, and virtuous living. Judaism and Christianity introduced their own distinctive emphases into this mode of moral education, not the least of which was the latter tradition's conviction that the canonical Gospels reveal the character of the living God. For Christians, Jesus Christ, the exemplum par excellence, not only exemplifies virtue perfectly for his disciples, but also personifies divinity.

In *The Peaceable Kingdom*, Hauerwas prescribes exactly the kind of moral education that Brown associates with the culture of ethical aristocracy surrounding the cult of the saints. What Christians require, to be a faithful people, are "examples of people whose lives have been formed" by the memory of their community. "The authority of Scripture is mediated through the lives of the saints identified by our community as most nearly representing what we are about. Put more strongly, to know what Scripture means, finally, we must look to those who have most nearly learned to exemplify its demands through their lives." By what criterion do we know them? It is not, Hauerwas says, "so much like a principle as it is like a story that the saints' lives exhibit. Through the lives of the saints we begin to understand how the images of Scripture are best balanced so that we might tell and live the ongoing story of God's unceasing purpose to bring the world to the peace of the Kingdom" (PK, 70–71).

More recently, in *Resident Aliens*, Hauerwas and his coauthor William Willimon introduce the concept of sainthood by saying that "a primary way of learning to be disciples is by being in contact with others who are disciples. So an essential role of the church is to put us in contact with those ethical aristocrats who are good at living the Christian faith." Christian ethics takes the "antidemocratic," Aristotelian view that there are "ethical aristocrats" and that the only way to become virtuous is to follow their example by becoming, as it were, their "apprentices." Saints are the "significant examples," the "ethical aristocrats," of Christian faith. "Epistemologically, there is no substitute for 'saints'—palpable, personal examples of the Christian faith—because . . . we cannot know the Kingdom unless our eyes are opened to see it."[3]

I agree with Hauerwas's claim that an ethical aristocracy is essential to the maintenance of a virtuous community, assuming that "aristocracy" is here being used metaphorically. But in that case, the claim is hardly antidemocratic—not, at any rate, if Emerson, Whitman, and Thoreau qualify as paradigmatic democratic thinkers. Democracy, in their view, is not an attempt to level qualitative distinctions in the various domains of human life. They all believed that the excellence of "representative" individuals raises them above the mediocre mean, and confers on them a high vocation of awakening others to virtue.

Say, if you like, that these exemplars constitute an aristocracy. But surely Hauerwas does not suppose that they are to be found in a particular social class or that their spiritual gifts can be correlated with the titles, ranks, or offices of some existing institution, ecclesial or secular. The Bible says that such gifts might be found in any human being among us—old or young, male or female, free or enslaved (Joel 2:27–28, Acts 2:17–18). No idea is more central to modern democracy—or to "liberalism" in the best sense of the term—than this one. It is because Emerson, Whitman, and Thoreau were suspicious of institutional arrangements that might prevent inspirited speech or true prophecy from being heard that they affirmed the democratic ideal of equal voice. In doing so, they were carrying forward a substantive *spiritual* concern that informed both the conciliar movement of fourteenth-century Catholicism and the Protestant radicalism of the English Civil War.[4] The ideal justifies equal access to public discussion. Its motivating premise is that society must take care not to block the expression of thoughts that might prove to be inspired. It is therefore at odds with the silly notion that all speech will be equal in value. If there were no significant qualitative distinctions among the contributions that people make to public life, there would be no need to hear from or examine more

than a few. Everyone knows that free speech increases the volume of mediocre ethical discourse—in both senses of "volume." But this is the price we
pay for democracy, not the reason we pay it.

If Hauerwas wishes to prosecute the case against modern democratic
thinkers on theological grounds, the most plausible charge would be that
of the Montanist heresy. Full-fledged Emersonians (like myself) resemble
the Montanists theologically because we question the authority of the established church to decide the difference between truly inspired speech
and false prophecy. This does mark a crucial departure from theological
orthodoxy—while nonetheless putting me in remarkably close proximity
to Barth. But anti-Montanist Christians can still consistently embrace the
proposed rationale for insisting that public discussion be open to all voices,
for this rationale is the common link between Emersonian dissent and the
varieties of Christian orthodoxy that shaped the outlook of the framers of
the Constitution. The rationale pertains to who gets to speak, not to who
has the ultimate authority to judge some speech truly inspired. Freedom
of speech, like freedom of religion, rests on a crucial point of spiritual
concord between the forms of Protestantism that influenced Madison and
the unchurched forms of Emersonian heterodoxy that emerged several decades later. Subsequently, most American Jews embraced this consensus.
John Courtney Murray drew many Catholics into the consensus in the
1950s, and the Second Vatican Council ratified his theological reasoning a
few years later. Some Muslims are now in the process of joining in, for
theological reasons of their own. Hauerwas is the most important theologian to challenge this expanding democratic consensus in many years. I am
questioning whether he has a clear notion of what he is opposing when he
inveighs against "democracy."

SIGNIFICANT EXAMPLES IN MODERN LIFE

The Gospels and lives of the saints are the primary genres of Christian
ethical discourse, as Hauerwas would have us conceive it. They both traffic
in "significant examples"—examples *of* divinity, holiness, love, faith, forgiveness, nonviolence, examples *for* a disciple to follow. When Hauerwas
defends an ethos of exemplary lives, he is offering it explicitly as an alternative to modern ethical discourse, which he declares bankrupt. But when he
refers elsewhere to the novel as another narrative genre we should treasure
as "a school of virtue," he shows no awareness that he is praising a feature
of modern culture.[5] He reads modern novels and mines their ethical significance, yet they do not appear in his account of modernity. He writes
essays and cultivates an authorial persona reminiscent of Cobbett and
Chesterton, yet the tradition of modern essayists has no place in the histor-

ical narrative he borrows from MacIntyre. Nor does he ask what the historical relationship among these genres might be.

John Lyons's *Exemplum*, a fascinating and learned study of the trope of example in early modern France and Italy, calls attention to a transition from characteristically medieval ethical genres, like the morality play, the novella, and the fable, to such works as the *Heptameron* and Montaigne's essays:

> The writers of the sixteenth and seventeenth centuries reacted to the changed horizon of belief by attempting to connect general statement with specific and purportedly convincing instances, calling attention to this gesture with frequent use of the term *example*. For many writers the rhetoric of example became less an illustrative technique, through which a general statement would be impressed upon an audience, than a process of discovery, in which the tension between instance and general statement forced modifications in that statement.[6]

As Lyons makes evident, example was a prominent topic for reflection in these centuries precisely because the relationship between examples and abstractions was becoming increasingly problematical.

I see the increasing tension between example and general statement as deeply indebted to two desires expressed repeatedly in Renaissance humanism. The first of these is the desire to take advantage of newly available scholarly means for learning more about the actual human beings whose lives have been heralded as exemplary. The second is the desire to employ newly fashioned literary means for rendering human character more fully in dramatic and narrative forms. Both of these desires are wholly in keeping with Hauerwas's complaints about the use of examples in quandary ethics. But the more attention the humanists gave to the narrative or dramatic details of putatively exemplary lives, the more trouble they had relating them to the virtues and general truths the lives were supposed to exemplify. When the amount of detailed information about an individual's character and situation contained in a story is drastically increased, it becomes harder to know what the story should be taken to exemplify. The now-richly described life or episode becomes more ambiguously related to the general ideas or abstractions it might otherwise have been taken to exemplify straightforwardly.

Lyons refers to the problem of *excess* that Renaissance authors identified in literary representation of exemplarity:

> Example is excessive because any element of historical reality and even any fiction adduced to support a generalization will have characteristics that exceed what can be covered by the generalization. . . . To make an example of an object is to account for only one limited aspect of that object. . . . [R]ecall that the

example is a dependent statement drawing its meaning from the controlling generality. As the dependent statements grow into complex narratives, however, the number of other concepts that can be illustrated by the narrative begins to threaten the control of the generality. The dependent statement may bring details that cast an entirely new light on the apparently simple generality being illustrated, or both writer and reader may be carried away by the richness of the concrete instance to the neglect of the concept to be illustrated. (*Exemplum*, 34)

The humanists wanted thick descriptions of the people their mentors taught them to admire. The thicker the descriptions became, however, the more ethically complicated they seemed. This is, clearly enough, the same logic Hauerwas and Burrell used to disrupt the systematic ambitions of ethical theory back in 1977. They proposed replacing the thin descriptions of a quandarist's cases by enriched narrative depiction of character and circumstance. The rhetoric of detail in the thicker descriptions makes it harder for a thinker to take them as exemplifying something. The pragmatic significance of the example, as an inferential link between the particular and the general, becomes unclear.

To put this point somewhat more philosophically, enriching descriptive detail in one's rendering of an example is a matter of adding assertions, and thus new commitments, to the ones already involved in the original rendering. But new commitments at the level of detailed description can have the effect of diminishing one's entitlement to the general conclusion licensed by the example in its original form. The reason for this is that the inferential license granted in practice by the original version of the example is defeasible. The license expires if new commitments undermine its authority. The general assertion that had been licensed by the old version of the example turns out to be incompatible with the new version. What, then, shall we do with the general assertion? Reject it? Qualify it? Restrict its scope? Or should we turn back to the example itself and modify the set of assertions that constitute its descriptive content? To ask these questions is to stand, as it were, between the commitments embodied in assertion of the example and the commitments embodied in the general assertion, reflecting on each.[7] It is, in Musil's terms, to stand "between example and doctrine." My historical claim is that certain genres of ethical discourse that arose in the early-modern period were designed to enable the pursuit of such questions. These genres turned out to be highly valued by the citizens of modern democracies.

An early-modern thinker once wrote an essay in which he qualified his admiration for his beloved Socrates. He did this because Socrates's virtues, as real as they may be, are not the whole story of a life that also includes obedience to the voice of a *daimonion*. The essayist was responding to the problem of excess created by the fullness of his knowledge of Socrates from both Platonic and non-Platonic sources. Another author, working in another genre, might create a similar tension between exemplifier and exemplified by enriching the depiction of characters from a medieval play to the point that the heroes and villains alike become mixtures of vice and virtue. Yet another might transform the narrative of a novella by making the central characters seem more like living, breathing human beings and less like stick figures clothed in a didactic label. Such were the means by which the culture of paideia became the culture of Montaigne, Shakespeare, and Marguerite de Navarre.

When Hauerwas and Burrell wrote in 1977 that they preferred a story "that does not issue in a determinate *moral*," they were unwittingly expressing a sentiment that did much, in the early-modern period, to shape the distinctively modern genres in which we still conduct much of our ethical discourse. But when this sentiment became part of the ethical life of modern societies, it did much to disturb the culture of paideia that Hauerwas now hopes to revive. We may desire perfectly clear distinctions between good and evil and equally clear exemplifications of each—explications of virtue to emulate or admire and exemplifications of vice to denounce or reject. But the essay, the Shakespearean play, and the novel represent forms of moral inquiry that constantly frustrate the desire for characters that straightforwardly personify abstractions, just as they frustrate the desire for stories that straightforwardly illustrate morals. Instead, these genres explore a world in which things are too complicated, morally speaking, for the culture of paideia to be sustained, at least in its original form.

The Gospels say to their readers: "Attend to the life of Jesus offered here and you will know the character of the living God." Lives of the saints say to their readers: "In this story you will find a genuine personification of holiness." Every classic life says to its audience: "In the life of this person lies a true exemplification of good character or virtue." All of these genres can have their own rhetorical complications, and specific narrative reconstructions of the lives of figures of virtue can prove much more complicated on analysis than a reader initially takes them to be.[8] But in none of these genres should we be surprised to discover a rhetoric of thin description, for that is the standard way for an author to keep the problem of excess under sufficient control to establish the desired relationship of exemplification. In contrast, as Milan Kundera writes, "Every novel says to the reader: 'Things are not as simple as you think.' "[9] That, I believe, is what Montaigne's essays and Shakespeare's plays are saying as well.

In this chapter, I have discussed Hauerwas's complaints about how examples are handled in modern ethical theory. I have also discussed his endorsement of an ethics of character, which turns out to be an ethics of discipleship centered on exemplary lives. One reason for juxtaposing these two sets of claims about the ethical uses of example is to notice a tension between them. The same formal characteristic that Hauerwas finds troublesome in the way ethical theorists write about cases also turns up in official retelling of lives of the saints and in Hauerwas's thinned-out versions of the Gospels. It happens, moreover, to be one of the main things that made the topic of example a major theme of Renaissance humanism—a theme of great concern to early-modern writers who helped create a moral culture in which novels, plays, and essays became prominent modes of ethical discourse. To recognize this, however, is to see that modern democratic culture contains resources of its own for resisting what the ethical theorists typically do with examples. Hauerwas's critique of formalist ethical theory, far from lending support to his account of modern ethical discourse, actually helps one see how little historical warrant there is for that account's assumptions about what modern ethical discourse has been like.

It is not my purpose to make essayists, novelists, and dramatists in general the heroes of modernity. I am simply trying to begin coming to terms honestly with the broader ethical culture they have helped create—a culture that neither formalist ethical theory nor the new traditionalism has bothered to study in its complexity. On the one hand, ours is a culture in which many people look upon ethical theory and the forms of ethical discourse it reflects as laughable or despicable or at least questionable enterprises. On the other hand, it is not any longer a culture in which moral education consists wholly in modeling oneself on a classic life. Modeling remains a crucial aspect of an individual's moral development. We still become who we are largely by responding to models. But we do not generally suppose that our moral education requires the kind of docile relation to models that Brown finds among the Greco-Roman elites. Emerson's famous dictum in "Self-Reliance," that "imitation is suicide," is a hyperbole.[10] Wise democrats know how to use Emersonian tonic in the way that it was intended to be used—as compensation for the excesses of paideia. It is effective spiritual medicine for any model-emulator, any disciple, of whom it can truly be said, "If I know your sect, I anticipate your argument."[11]

It is true that exemplary figures—saints, prophets, and other gifted spirits—are essential to education in virtue. Emersonian perfectionism insists on this truth no less than does Hauerwas's updated Wesleyan perfectionism. Emulation of excellence is an indispensable aspect of becoming excellent in one's own person. But emulation can easily become a form of slavish idolatry, in which we are dazzled and bound by the person we admire. We must therefore take care to emulate also the excellence of self-trust, which consists in freedom from such subservience. We struggle with our exemplars, so as to avoid being overwhelmed by them—as they were not in the long run overwhelmed by their exemplars, if they were truly worthy of our admiration in the first place. Those most worthy of emulation, according to Emerson's "Uses of Great Men," are those whose "genius seeks to defend us from itself."[12] No mere underling has fully succeeded in emulating genuine excellence. This is Emerson's democratic addition to the ethics of example.

In the days of my adolescent sublime, Martin Luther King, Jr., was the hero of my humanitarian cause, and Jesus was one of three personifications of my loving divinity. Nowadays things have become more complicated, because I have come to know more about these figures of virtue than their hagiographers and publicists wanted me to know. Now that I am less innocent of the complexities, I am no less moved by love and justice, no less cognizant of the place such traits have in a virtuous character, and no less able to put these concepts to work discursively than I used to be. King and Jesus remain persons of ethical interest, as before. I still spend much of my time thinking about them. Love and justice remain virtues, as well; but now the relation between the persons and the virtues is more complicated. It requires a different, less doctrinal, more improvisational kind of explication. To the extent that King and Jesus exemplify virtues in my imaginative life, they now do so imperfectly and defeasibly. I therefore need an open-ended way to think the relation through: as it were, from both sides at once. Neither doctrine, nor principle, nor system, nor overarching plot, knowable in advance, constrains the course of the thinking. Between example and doctrine, with Montaigne and Musil, is where most of us now stand. We all have our examples, after all, and we all make something of them sooner of later. We do not, however, make the same thing of them. Neither do they make the same thing of us.

THE CRITICAL THEORIST AND HER OTHER

Some readers will have found my description of Hauerwas's early critique of quandary ethics strangely reminiscent of arguments put forward independently by Seyla Benhabib. In this section, I want to consider the very different theoretical context in which Benhabib makes her Hauerwasian points. For Benhabib is not a theologian but a political theorist, and her primary concern is the ethics of democratic discussion. Brief consideration of her views will bring us back into the general vicinity of Rawls and Rorty, and help us frame the issues to be addressed in part 3.

When Benhabib refers, on the first page of *Situating the Self*, to the "fractured spirit of our times," she sets the tone of her book with a theme that has had remarkable longevity in modern thought.[13] Its roots can be traced back to the Romantic transformation of biblical prophecy into a secular vocation of social criticism. As the Romantics saw it, the critical task was to decipher the signs of the times in the hope of discerning the crisis or break from the past that defines both our present situation and the nature of the decisions modern individuals face as selves thus situated. The break from the past appeared in this sublime light as a result of the breakup or breakdown of an old spiritual coherence or as a rupture brought about when a new spirit breaks into history. The remarkable thing is how this cluster of Romantic ideas survived the passing of Romanticism. The imagery of fragmentation, fracture, and ruin and the concepts of critique, modernity, and crisis have been commonplaces in the rhetoric of social criticism ever since. One finds them in Hegel, Marx, and Nietzsche; in turn-of-the-century debates over nihilism and historicism; in Pound and Eliot; in Heidegger, MacIntyre, and West; in the critical theory of the Frankfurt School; in the clichés of modern journalism.

Benhabib inherits this cluster of ideas from her predecessors in the Frankfurt School. In her first book, *Critique, Norm, and Utopia*, she reconstructed the dialectical progression of this tradition by showing how and why such concepts as critique, modernity, and crisis changed as they passed from Hegel, to Marx, to Horkheimer and Adorno, and finally to Habermas.[14] As the argument moves from one thinker to another, subjecting each to rigorous questioning, it develops considerable momentum. It carries us initially to the claim that communicative interaction should serve as critical theory's model for social action, but ultimately beyond the elaborate framework in which Habermas enshrines this notion, toward Benhabib's modified version of communicative ethics.

The two most important charges Benhabib makes against Habermas's theory, for our purposes, are these: first, that he does not go far enough in integrating questions of the good life into his ethical theory; and second, that his ethical theory, by focusing on formal reciprocity with the "generalized other" as a bearer of rights and locus of dignity, leaves little or no room for consideration of the "concrete other" as an individual with a life history of her own. As Benhabib explains in her second book, these charges are important in part because they echo challenges that communitarians and feminists, respectively, have posed to critical theory. She does not remark that both charges echo major themes in Hauerwas's traditionalism. What, if anything, shall we make of this convergence? Does it offer any hope that the standoff between secularism and traditionalism can be overcome?

Benhabib says plainly that her communicative ethics "does privilege a secular, universalist, reflexive culture" (SS, 42). The juxtaposition of "secular" and "universalist" here suggests that a confrontation with Hauerwas may be in store. What do these notions mean in this context, and how do they fit together with her Hauerwasian points about the importance of focusing on the concrete other? We have seen that in Hauerwas's view, all standpoints are conditioned. No point of view can plausibly claim universality in the Kantian sense. That is why ethics always needs a qualifier, according to Hauerwas. He suspects that those who claim to have achieved an unconditioned standpoint for "the moral point of view" are actually grinding an axe for secularism.

If Benhabib's version of critical theory were "transcendental" in Kant's sense, it would aim to justify the normative claims of the theory by showing them to be necessary (or necessary for us)—in the sense of already being presupposed by anyone who wishes to offer reasons to other people.[15] This would give a clear sense to the universality she is claiming for her standpoint. But Benhabib is persuaded that no transcendental argument of this kind is available. She claims to have stripped away the transcendental scaffolding of Habermas's theory. If she has done this, however, it is no longer clear why the elaborate model of communicative ethics should be thought to justify the normative claims of the theory. Even if one accepted those claims, one could still doubt the usefulness of feeding them into one end of a fancy theoretical machine only to watch them come out the other end decorated in technical terminology. As a justification, the normative theory appears to beg the question. But if it isn't a justification, in what sense is it a normative theory?

Now consider the empirical component of the theory. Benhabib criticizes me for not making use of Habermas's social theory of modernity. She speculates that a more serious engagement with Habermas's sociological theory would give some of my views "a firmer basis in contemporary social theory" (SS, 147). I appreciate the offer and the friendly spirit in which it is made, but I have my own reasons for not wanting a firmer basis in a social theory like Habermas's. I am especially wary of its assumptions about the effects of rationalization, in Weber's sense, on religious worldviews.

Benhabib has a big Habermasian story to tell about the emergence of modern structures of consciousness—a story that includes the account of secularization criticized in chapter 4, above. My own model of secularization is a much more modest thing, and deliberately so. Its purpose is to explain how religious plurality can, under certain conditions, alter the presuppositions of discourse in specific institutional settings. What becomes secularized, according to my model, is a set of discursive presuppositions, not necessarily the worldview or state of consciousness of participants in the relevant form of discourse. Because my model does not predict increasingly generalized disenchantment, it does not break down in the face of facts to the contrary—such as the religious revivals of the last four decades.[16]

Benhabib makes clear that the "moral point of view," as she understands it, is partly a product of what Weber calls "the 'disenchantment' of the world" (SS, 41). To adopt the moral point of view is thus to leave behind "a conventional morality" in favor of a fully "reflexive" one. Those "who adhere to a conventional morality have a cognitive barrier beyond which they will not argue." They "invoke certain kinds of reasons which will divide the participants of the moral conversation into insiders and outsiders, into those who share their presuppositions and those who do not."

> Moral reflexivity and moral conventionalism then are not compatible; but in a disenchanted universe, to limit reflexivity is an indication of a rationality deficit. . . . In this sense, communicative ethics "trumps" other less reflexive "moral points of view." It can co-exist with them and recognize their cognitive limits . . . but it is also aware of the historical conditions which made its own point of view possible. (SS, 43)

In a disenchanted world, in other words, those who reason about ethical questions as Hauerwas does, by arguing from religious presuppositions some others do not share, are displaying their own deficiency as rational agents. The putative universality of Benhabib's standpoint, then, is intimately linked with a sort of secularism. Indeed, it presupposes a Weberian account of the historical conditions that made it possible.

This is an odd result, it seems to me, for a theorist who stands with Hauerwas on the need for a shift in our ethical thinking from the "generalized other" of quandary ethics to the "concrete other" of a narrative-centered normative theory. Hannah Arendt and the feminists have taught us, according to Benhabib, that we need to take seriously all of the dimensions of human lives that come to light when we tell rich stories about "situated selves." The point of emphasizing the role of narrative in ethics, for Benhabib (as for the early Hauerwas), is to complicate our conception of rational agency by setting it in the context of individual human lives. But suppose rationality and irrationality are indeed traits of situated selves, whose life histories need to be reckoned with before we judge them. How, then, can Benhabib be so sure on the basis of highly general—and dubious—historical considerations that those who want to argue from religious premises exhibit a rationality deficit?

Hauerwas would argue that two individuals can be justified in holding different beliefs, on religious or other questions, given their different life histories. This seems correct. We have taken note of a distinction between being justified in believing something and being able to justify a claim to someone else. If one is unable to justify one's beliefs to someone else— for example, in a public forum where no theological presuppositions are currently shared—this need not entail that one is unjustified in holding the belief. Must it, then, be "an indication of a rationality deficit" to go ahead and argue from one's own point of view? As we learned in chapter 3, above, it is by no means clear that all important questions can be settled on a common basis of ideals and principles that no reasonable people would reasonably reject. Benhabib has not shown that democratic discussion must be secular in the sense of presupposing the disenchantment of the world.

Her own reasons for placing situated selfhood at the center of her theory suggest why. If we are all situated selves, our reasons will not necessarily carry weight with someone differently situated—not, at any rate, unless the hypercontext called "modernity" is the only aspect of our situation that matters.

When discussing religion, Benhabib assumes just this. She situates the self by relating all of us to a single, ubiquitous, large-scale epistemic context. She neglects the possibility that there might be significant differences, with respect to what an individual is justified in believing, among modern people who are acculturated in different ways. She takes for granted that acculturation is not capable of rendering some individuals justified in holding beliefs not held by the majority of their neighbors. As I see it, however, it is precisely the coexistence of multiple subcultures, all of which succeed at some level in acculturating the young, that constitutes the all-important fact of pluralism in modern democratic societies. Such acculturation does, I think, often succeed in bringing it about that particular groups of individuals are justified in believing things that their neighbors either justifiably disbelieve or justifiably ignore. The relevant epistemic situation for such selves, in other words, turns out to be much more specific and variable than the hypercontext, modernity, allows us to account for.

The possibility that some of our neighbors might actually be justified in believing the strange (and perhaps unliberating) things they believe is one of the grounds of toleration in a democratic society. The respect we have for one another need not be a purely abstract regard for potential rational agency. It tends in fact to be much more specific than that. It is nourished by our recognition that much of what our neighbors believe is what any reasonable person would believe if situated in exactly the same way they are. One's situation, in this sense, would include the particulars of acculturation in a specific family and as someone involved in particular social practices and communities. This is what respect for the concrete other is largely about. Substantive respect of this kind can still be in place (and can still support democratic habits) in cases where I, as a social critic, have strong reason to conclude that my neighbor believes something that is false, against his or her own true interests, or unliberating.

Only as a last resort, when I have taken all situational particulars into account and done my best to interpret them charitably, should I adopt the hypothesis that a given person or group suffers from a "rationality deficit." Then and only then should I be prepared to explain away my neighbor's expressed reasons for action and belief by invoking the special interpretive tools of critical theory. When I am pressed that far, however, I ought to be conscious of the cost that my critique exacts from the reservoir of substantive respect on which democratic discourse among neighbors can draw.

Ideology critique is a hermeneutical ambulance. Calling upon it too often bankrupts the same democratic process it seeks to serve.

This, in the end, is the irony of critical theory as an across-the-board approach to modern democratic discourse. Critical theorists begin by embracing the hope that genuinely democratic discourse will flourish among us. They set out to serve this hope by systematically diagnosing the sources of distortion that arise within our discourse as it is. But they end by explaining away, instead of entering into conversation with, nearly everything that real people think, say, and feel. Even Benhabib's version of critical theory tends in practice to pass over the connections between selves and the concrete situations and historical traditions in which they acquire their beliefs and identities. When it employs the notion of "rationality deficit" as it does, it addresses those selves as something more like patients than as fellow citizens. Benhabib obviously senses this problem more clearly than do most other critical theorists. She has begun to rework the concepts of situation and judgment in ways that would help resolve it. But she has not yet managed to get to the root of the trouble.

There is no point in recommending that social critics keep their mouths shut when they suspect their neighbors of wishful thinking and other forms of irrationality or delusion. I am saying simply that the standard of proof for justifying such suspicions is much higher than most critical theorists imagine. Democratic hopes would often be better served if we used more respectful modes of interpretation as our means of first resort. Our fellow citizens might well hold many false beliefs. We might well be justified in taking them to be in error. But in many cases we ought to be content to explain our differences with them by pointing to differences in context, allowing that they might be justified in believing what they do, and then beginning or continuing the exchange of reasons with them in a charitable and democratic spirit. If all goes well, the discussion will itself alter our respective epistemic contexts in such a way that we can overcome some of our differences, or at least learn to live with them respectfully.

Whether we ought to change our minds, at a given point in the democratic exchange of ideas, is something to be decided case by case—by situated selves, reflecting critically on their own experience and on the various traditions and sources of evidence their situation makes available to them. It is not generally true, however, that we are obliged to abandon beliefs that have not been certified as "justified" in public discussion. Many interesting questions arise here concerning the relationships that can obtain between what individuals are justified in believing and the justificatory arguments of which they have become aware in the relatively generalized context of public discussion. Yet these questions are hard to raise, let alone to resolve, in terms of a theory that does not distinguish between being justified in believing something and justifying a belief or proposition to an audience.

When Benhabib ascribes a rationality deficit to those who differ with her religiously, she glosses over these questions entirely.

We can hardly claim at this point to have overcome the standoff between Benhabib's secularism and Hauerwas's traditionalism. But it seems clear that neither of these thinkers has imagined the possibility, let alone the desirability, of a loosely structured democratic conversation in which variously situated selves tell their own stories on their own terms. Neither accounts adequately for the complicated functions these stories can take on in ethical reflection. Both back away at a crucial moment from the full significance of their common insight that the different ways in which selves are situated in the world make a difference for ethics. Benhabib recognizes the difference one's gender can make in situating a self in the world, and rightly highlights the value that narrative can have in making explicit what that involves for a particular man or woman. Hauerwas recognizes the difference one's religious community can make in situating a self in the world, and rightly highlights the value that narrative can have in making explicit what that involves for a particular Christian or Jew. But Benhabib declares Hauerwas's kind of story deficient, as if this could be known before the tale is told and subjected to criticism from various points of view. And Hauerwas makes democratic story-swapping seem useless, unless everyone agrees in advance on a canon of classic lives as a framework for discussion.

Two points of *agreement* keep the standoff from being resolved. First, both of these thinkers view democratic modernity as the result of a break with tradition, after which a process of disenchantment places the religious believer at a fundamental disadvantage in public discussion. Benhabib considers this development progress, whereas Hauerwas considers it a catastrophe. Second, they both assume that *rational* discourse must proceed within a framework that accords their own point of view legitimacy over against its competitors. For Benhabib, this is the moral point of view, with its explicit commitment to secularism. For Hauerwas, it is the perspective of the community of Christian virtue, with its biblical metanarrative and its canon of classic lives. In part 2, both of these shared assumptions—the one about modernity and the one about discursive rationality—have come to seem dubious. In part 3, I will explore the consequences of rejecting them and, in doing so, I will try to account for the possibility of rational discussion among differently situated selves.

PART THREE

A Conditioned Rectitude

[A]lthough the commands of the Conscience are *essentially* absolute, they are *historically* limitary. Wisdom does not seek a literal rectitude, but an useful, that is, a conditioned one, such as the faculties of man and the constitution of things will warrant. . . . [T]he existing world is not a dream, and cannot with impunity be treated as a dream; neither is it a disease; but it is the ground on which you stand, it is the mother of whom you were born. Reform converses with possibilities, perchance with impossibilities; but here is sacred fact. This also was true, or it could not be: it had life in it, or it could not have existed; it has life in it, or it could not continue.

—Emerson

Chapter 8

DEMOCRATIC NORMS IN THE
AGE OF TERRORISM

THE ARGUMENT of part 2 has proceeded entirely by way of immanent criticism. I have closely examined the liberalism of Rawls and Rorty and the traditionalism of Milbank, MacIntyre, and Hauerwas, and found both of these approaches unable to provide a satisfactory account of the role of religious traditions in modern democracy. The task of part 3 is to work out an acceptable alternative to these approaches. A successful philosophical account of democratic political culture would overcome the weaknesses I have identified in these approaches while simultaneously inheriting their strengths. It would thus put us in a position to explain both the strengths and the weaknesses of the previous approaches. Liberalism and traditionalism thrive on exposing one another's weaknesses. Liberals have no trouble showing that traditionalism threatens to deprive us of the actual and potential benefits of exchanging reasons across the boundaries of enclaves. Traditionalists have no trouble showing that liberalism has failed to resolve a conflict between its commitment to freedom and its desire to dictate the terms of social cooperation. Both sides have gotten rather good at biting their respective bullets and at making their opponents seem despicable or foolish. But neither side has had much success at explaining the other side's strengths. Nor have critical theorists like Benhabib done any better on the crucial issue of religion.

There are, however, some hopeful signs that suggest a path beyond the current impasse. We have seen that Rawls, in an attempt to solve problems in a social-contract theory inspired by Locke, Rousseau, and Kant has introduced concepts derived from the pragmatic expressivism of Hegel and Dewey. The conception of conversation that Rorty develops in *Philosophy and the Mirror of Nature*—but then forgets about when discussing the role of religion in political culture—is also a product of pragmatic expressivism. It is this pragmatic expressivism that MacIntyre has in mind when he acknowledges that Rawls and Rorty have recently recognized that liberalism must be understood as a tradition. And Benhabib's critical theory is also indebted in various ways to the Hegelian strand of expressivism.

As for the traditionalists, Milbank openly avows a form of pragmatic expressivism influenced by Hegel and by various postmodernists. Both MacIntyre and Hauerwas stress the priority of social practices. While neither of them responds successfully to Hegelian criticisms of their positions, both have unacknowledged debts to Hegel that place them in the vicinity of pragmatic expressivism. MacIntyre wavers between two conceptions of tradition. One of these conceptions begs the question in favor of traditionalism by assuming that traditions require high levels of agreement on canonical authorities and the nature of the good. The other defines a tradition in Hegelian fashion, as a dialectical argument over goods and virtues in the context of shared social practices that endure over time. In both MacIntyre's and Hauerwas's writings, we can catch glimpses of how this second conception of tradition and the related notions of virtue and example can be creatively applied to contemporary society. MacIntyre sometimes makes modern ethical discourse seem hopeless, but he also explicates a notion of rationality that involves something like conversation in Rorty's sense. In Hauerwas's insistence that he is not a sectarian and in his praise for Dorothy Day, one can sense the possibility of a democratically engaged ethics of virtue that has been cleansed of antiliberal resentment. The same can be said for Milbank's brief references to Christian socialism.

The way beyond the current impasse, it seems to me, is to see both sides as converging on a form of pragmatic expressivism that takes enduring democratic social practices as a tradition with which we have good reasons to identify. By working out a defensible version of pragmatism, I hope to explain the strengths of liberalism and traditionalism, as well as their weaknesses. This means:

- resolving the internal tensions in Rawls's political liberalism by discarding his notion of a freestanding conception of justice and his loaded account of reasonableness, while retaining the idea that we owe reasons to one another when we take stands on important political questions;
- seeing our overlapping consensus on the legitimacy of constitutional democracy as involving a practical commitment to holding one another mutually responsible for our political arrangements and thus to keeping a democratic discussion going across the boundaries of ethnic, racial, and religious enclaves;
- working out an account of our discursive practices that takes seriously Rorty's ideal of conversation and MacIntyre's emphasis on the need to understand one's rivals on their own terms, while jettisoning the quest for principles that no reasonable person could reasonably reject;
- developing a conception of tradition centered on enduring social practices, without begging the question in favor of traditions that are hierarchically organized and insistent on doctrinal conformity as a criterion of membership;

- and redescribing modern democracy as a tradition of this looser sort by focusing attention primarily on the relatively freewheeling discursive practices it involves.

Splitting the difference is a tried and true strategy for overcoming dialectical impasse. Hegel and Dewey were both master practitioners of the art. Indeed, I believe Hegel took himself to be splitting the difference between earlier versions of liberalism and traditionalism, and Dewey self-consciously followed in his footsteps. So we are not exactly moving into uncharted territory. Moreover, this strategy puts me in close proximity to a number of my contemporaries: Robert Brandom, Sabina Lovibond, and Cheryl Misak in philosophy, Nancy Fraser in political theory, and Rebecca Chopp and Cornel West in religious studies, to name only a few obvious examples.[1]

The present chapter begins this more strictly philosophical part of the book by trying to explain the sense in which democratic norms are creatures of the practices of accountability in which we exchange reasons with one another. For purposes of illustration—but also with an eye toward contemporary political relevance—I consider a familiar dilemma known to philosophers as the problem of dirty hands. This is the question of whether political officials responsible for protecting the public from attack may, under conditions of emergency, do things that are commonly thought to be not only wrong but horrible. The problem is philosophically interesting because it forces us to clarify what norms of responsibility are, to what kinds of responsibilities they pertain, and how responsibilities of different kinds can conflict. The timeliness of the problem derives from its obvious relevance to the struggle against terrorism. My aim here is not to solve the problem, but to improve our understanding of what the problem is and why it resists a solution that would be likely to command assent from the entire citizenry. In the process, I hope to clarify certain features of the version of pragmatism I favor and to shed light on the limits of moral consensus in a society as religiously divided as ours.

BEWARE OF LEADERS PLEADING NECESSITY

Political officials everywhere do bad things. One mark of tyrants is their interest in doing *horrible* things, such as torturing political prisoners or murdering civilians, for the purpose of making opponents fear the *unscrupulous* exercise of power. The point of the exercise is to impress people with their unwillingness to be constrained, in the exercise of power, by moral considerations. In a representative democracy, however, we expect political officials to answer to the citizenry for the bad things they do. They are acting in our name, as our representatives, with the consent of the governed. So we demand reasons for their actions, not least for their bad actions. The practice of asking for reasons is an exercise in scrupulosity. The reasons we demand imply or impose constraints. When our officials do bad things, they are often acting in secret, hoping to avoid public scrutiny. They are not trying to impress us with their lack of scruples; they are trying to hide from us because they do not have justifying reasons to offer. They would prefer to duck our questions. They stonewall; they deny involvement.

When their dirty hands come to light, and there is no denying the bad things they have done, officials often plead necessity. They claim that they had to do bad things if they were to serve us well in dire circumstances. There was no choice. That, they say, is the way politics works in the real world. At one level, the problem of dirty hands is the question of how democratic citizens ought to respond when political officials make this excuse for admittedly bad acts.

Often the excuse turns out to be phony—another bad act. The circumstances are not what the dirty politician says they were. Perhaps they were not dire at all. Or perhaps they were dire relative to some set of personal concerns, like the desire to remain in power, but not relative to the citizenry's survival and well-being. In most cases where people plead necessity in ordinary life, there is more room for maneuver than they acknowledge. They say, "I had no choice," but what they really mean is that the alternatives they did consider seemed unacceptable at the time.[2] Often there are other alternatives that should have been considered, and it is not unusual for people to be mistaken about the unacceptability of the alternatives they do consider. The same is true in the political arena. The necessity excuse almost always turns out to be false.

Even when it is false, it often works. The desire to make it work therefore gives politicians an incentive to create a sense of emergency among the citizenry. Leaders who tend to act badly tend also to play upon our fears. They portray neighboring nations and domestic minorities as threats. Sometimes they even deliberately provoke their opponents to behave horribly, hoping then to be excused for responding in kind. The stronger the sense of emergency the leader can arouse, the more plausible the necessity excuse becomes. The more plausible the necessity excuse becomes, the greater the leader's temptation will be to act badly. The more scope we give our leaders to act badly by accepting the necessity excuse, the closer we move to unconstrained rule by the holders of power. The closer we move to unconstrained rule, the less reason some citizens will have to trust officials to protect them or otherwise serve their interests. In the absence of such trust, a democratic culture tends to dissolve. The necessity excuse belongs to a vicious cycle that has been detrimental to democracy in contexts as different as the final phase of the war against Japan, nuclear deterrence during the Cold War, the Balkans in the 1990s, the Israeli-Palestinian conflict, and the global struggle against terrorism. Politicians who plead necessity are usually enemies of democracy. They are not to be trusted.

But some leaders do find themselves in real emergencies. I grant that in some such situations conscientious leaders committed to maintaining the culture of trust essential to democracy face genuinely hard choices through no fault of their own. Even if they have surveyed all of the alternatives responsibly and understood the facts accurately, they might still find themselves having to choose between doing something bad to someone and allowing something bad to happen to the people in their charge. How shall we respond to choices like this?

One familiar answer is a simple form of consequentialism: everyone should always act so as to bring about the best consequences they can; hence, leaders should do so in cases like this. If the consequences of allowing something bad to happen to the people would be worse, on the whole, than the consequences of doing something bad to someone, then one ought to go ahead and do the bad thing, knowing that the end justifies the means. The principle invoked in this answer is too simple, however, to square with the rights characteristically recognized in democratic constitutions or with the claim of some prominent democratic thinkers that cruelty is the worst thing people do.[3] In practice we treat these considerations as constraints on the means leaders may select when deciding how to pursue their legitimate ends. Simple consequentialism leaves these constraints out of the picture. That is why it makes the problem of dirty hands seem easy to solve—too easy, from what I would want to call a democratic point of view. The next section offers an anatomy of the problem that puts these constraints back in the picture. The anatomy is carried out in terms borrowed from Robert Brandom's pragmatic analysis of practical reasoning in *Making It Explicit*.

An Anatomy of the Problem

One way to describe the problem of dirty hands is to speak of a dilemma created by conflicting desires. The first horn is the desire to protect the survival or well-being of the people. The metaphor "dirty hands" suggests that the second horn is concerned with the leader's moral purity. Other things being equal, decent political officials would like to keep their hands clean, and we would prefer that they do so as well. But when the desire for the official's moral purity comes into conflict with the desire for the people's survival and well-being, how can we reasonably prefer the former to the latter? Wanting to keep one's hands clean sounds selfish when compared with the desire to protect the people. It seems like the kind of desire one should desire not to be motivated by in such a situation. We do not want officials to concern themselves with their own purity at the people's expense. What we want, all things considered, are political leaders who are neither unscrupulous nor squeamish. Democratic leadership is no place for tyrants, but it is also no place for purists.

While this way of posing the problem dovetails nicely with the metaphor of dirty hands, it is not clear that the second horn should be interpreted as a desire for purity. If the problem were really about the conflict between the desire for purity and the desire for such goods as social survival, then most of us would not see it as a perplexing matter at all. Aside from a few genuine purists on the fringes, those of us who want to place rigid constraints on our political representatives are more interested in the victims than in the stain left on the hands of the official who does the bad thing. The value we have in mind is not moral purity but the importance, worth, or sanctity we attribute to individual human beings. I return to this thought later in the chapter.

Whatever we make of the point about purity, I doubt that the problem of dirty hands is best described as a conflict between desires. To see why, consider Brandom's distinction among three typical patterns of practical inference, which I will illustrate with examples modeled on his:

(a) Going to the store is my only way to get milk for my cereal, so I shall go to the store.
(b) I am a lifeguard on the job, so I shall keep close watch over the swimmers under my protection.
(c) Ridiculing a child for his limp would humiliate him needlessly, so I shall refrain from doing so.[4]

According to Brandom, each of the three examples is a material inference. To make any of them valid by virtue of its logical form, we would have to add a premise, but in another sense they are proper exactly as they stand. For they are materially good, in the sense that all competent participants in our evaluative practices treat such inferences as proper (and are not making a mistake by doing so). By taking these inferences as (materially) proper, we acknowledge the premises of these practical inferences as reasons for their conclusions.

Emphasizing that each of these inferences is (materially) in order as it stands is not a way of denying significance to the premises we would need to add to them to make them formally valid. It is rather a way of making clear what that significance consists in (MIE, 246–47). Suppose I added to (a) a statement expressing my *desire* to have milk for my cereal; to (b) the conditional that if I am a lifeguard, it is my *responsibility* to keep a close watch over the swimmers under my protection; or to (c) the principle that one *ought* not to humiliate people needlessly. In each case, according to Brandom, I would thereby make *explicit* the material inferential commitment *implicit* in the original example of practical reasoning. This has the advantage of putting the formerly implicit material inferential commitment in the explicit form of a claim, which in turn allows it to be challenged or justified inferentially in light of other considerations. This becomes especially important, of course, when conflicts arise among different material inferential commitments that we have undertaken.

The problem of dirty hands is a classic instance of such a conflict. But which types of material inferential commitment are at issue? They do not seem to be of the sort made explicit in the language of desire. The kind of inferential commitment expressed in (a) is only one typical pattern to be found in our practical reasoning. If you treat (a) as a materially good inference for me to make, this involves taking entitlement to the commitment expressed in the premise to be inferentially heritable by the commitment expressed in the conclusion. If you also treat in the same way a battery of other similarly structured inferences to the same conclusion, you are implicitly ascribing to me the desire to have milk for my cereal (MIE, 249). Desire talk is one way in which we explicitly attribute material inferential commitments in practical contexts, but there are others.

The problem of dirty hands seems to have more to do with inferential commitments of the kinds expressed in (b) and (c) than with commitments of the kind expressed in (a). When made explicit, the first horn of the dilemma clearly involves the political official's role-specific responsibility to protect the people. The second horn appears to be a role-independent responsibility to refrain from acts of a certain sort. Brandom refers to the explicit formulation of these two types of constraint, respectively, as "institutional" and "unconditional" obligations (MIE, 252).

Instrumentalist accounts of reasons for action follow Hume in assimilating both of these to the prudential "ought" associated with inferences of type (a). Kantians, on the other hand, tend to reduce all reasons for action to the third pattern. Brandom argues, however, that both Humeans and Kantians are too quick to reduce reasons for action to a single pattern.[5] A nonreductive account of practical reasoning has the advantage of allowing us to offer a deeper, more illuminating account of moral perplexity in cases of genuinely conflicting considerations. In the present case, it allows us to work through our intuition that the problem of dirty hands is genuinely problematic, rather than brusquely explaining it away.

Let us begin by thinking in more detail about institutional responsibilities. Lifeguards have an institutional role. By virtue of that role they have a responsibility to keep a close eye on the swimmers under their protection. We implicitly ascribe this responsibility to them whenever we treat (b) as a commitment-preserving inference for a lifeguard to make. Notice that the propriety of my inference in (b) does not depend on my desire to keep a close eye on the swimmers under my protection. Nor does it depend on my desire to be, or remain, a lifeguard—to occupy the role that entails the responsibility. To be a lifeguard is to have responsibilities of this kind. When I acknowledge the responsibilities, I treat inferences of type (b) as providing me, qua lifeguard, with reasons for action that are independent of my desires.

We can make the inferential commitment in (b) explicit in the form of a claim about my responsibilities as a lifeguard. The language of responsibility allows us to challenge or justify such a claim as the need arises. This need might arise, for example, in the event that my responsibility to keep a close eye on the swimmers conflicts with my desire to leave the beach (say, to buy ice cream) while I am on duty. It is also possible, however, for two of the responsibilities a given lifeguard has, qua lifeguard, to come into conflict. A given lifeguard's responsibilities, qua lifeguard, can also conflict with his or her responsibilities as a promise-keeper or as a spouse.

Heads of state hold an office that comes with unique responsibilities. If they were not responsible, in our eyes, for protecting the people from serious harm, then the problem of dirty hands they sometimes face would not capture our attention. If simple consequentialism were true, there would be no special problem of dirty hands pertaining to holders of high office as such. If the end of maximizing the balance of good over evil in the consequences of our acts entitled *everyone*, regardless of role, to do *anything* necessary in the pursuit of that end, we would not need to consider the political leader's predicament as a morally distinctive kind of case. This problem merits its own chapter in the ethics of democracy, if it does, only because holders of high office are in some respects unique. They are unlike the rest of us in being officially responsible for the exercise of coercive power on behalf of the people's survival and well-being. By virtue of their office they have powers and responsibilities the rest of us do not have. Their responsibilities can give rise to hard choices. These choices invite them to exercise power in ways that leave their hands dirty.

The most plausible appeals to necessity in such cases involve officials who are entitled to claim that they *must* do something bad *if* they are to fulfill the role-specific responsibility to protect the people's survival. If the necessity excuse isn't phony, and there really are no alternative means available, the question is whether officials thus situated are entitled to go ahead and fulfill the relevant responsibility, willing the bad thing as a necessary means toward that end. The problem is that by refraining from doing the bad thing, they know that this will leave the relevant responsibility unfulfilled.

Lifeguards are responsible for protecting the swimmers under their care from drowning. But suppose I am on duty in this capacity and notice a swimmer going down in violent surf for the third time. Suppose further that an old man in a wheelchair, through no fault of his own, is blocking my path on the jetty. I know that my only way to save the swimmer is to push the wheelchair aside with sufficient force to cause some harm to the old man. I have no doubt that this would be a bad thing to do to the old man. Yet if I refrain from doing it, I will be responsible for a drowning that it is my responsibility to prevent. What shall I do?

The case is artificial and abstract. Lifeguards do not confront cases of this kind very often. So while it does illustrate how a role-specific responsibility can come into conflict with another reason for action, our conception of a lifeguard's responsibilities does not make special provisions for it. Quandaries of this sort, when they do arise, are normally left to a lifeguard's discretion. A lifeguard caught in such a situation will be expected to assess the gravity of the harm likely to be inflicted on the old man if he is shoved out of the way and to weigh this against the life of the drowning swimmer. Especially if the harm to the old man is likely to be slight, the necessity excuse will be accepted. Some quandaries faced by political officials are like this. They involve the prospect of knowingly causing relatively slight harm to someone in unforeseeable, unusual circumstances where a judgment call needs to be made on a life-or-death matter. We are prepared to see the harm in such cases as regrettable but proportionate. We would not want to have either lifeguards or heads of state who were too squeamish to do this sort of thing when necessary.

Now consider another analogy. A Catholic priest has a role-specific responsibility to maintain the secrecy of the confessional. He is also responsible as a citizen or as a resident to provide information to the police that might lead to the apprehension of violent criminals. Suppose he has such information but refuses to provide it because he acquired it when hearing a confession. Catholics do not treat this kind of case as something priests have the discretion to resolve according to their assessment of the circumstances. Instead they have found it necessary to codify their conception of the priest's role with maximal explicitness in canon law and moral theology. The Roman Catholic code takes the priest's responsibility to hold confessions in confidence to be absolutely overriding with respect to other responsibilities. A priest who fails to fulfill this responsibility necessarily incurs guilt, according to the code. A priest who, in fulfilling this responsibility, withholds information that the police need if they are to prevent numerous murders, is not held responsible for those murders if and when they occur. He incurs no guilt for that consequence of his action, even if he has every reason to expect it to occur.[6]

It makes sense to give officials some discretionary authority to do bad things if the thing being done is bad only in the sense of wronging someone in a minor way and if it is a necessary means toward an end essential to the fulfillment of an important official responsibility. When, however, the wrong or harm would involve severe cruelty we are much more reluctant to give officials—or lifeguards—discretionary authority. When the bad things being done are horrible, it becomes more plausible to suppose that the second horn of the dilemma derives from an obligation that is not only independent of particular roles, but also absolutely binding. Political officials, it is said, are citizens and human beings before they assume their responsibilities as leaders. If there are indeed some unconditional obligations, they apply by definition to political leaders no less than they apply to the rest of us. And if some of these obligations override any role-specific responsibility with which they might conflict, then there are some things political leaders should never do, regardless of the circumstances. Nobody, even a politician, has license to do horrible things.

The Catholic code imposes an absolute constraint on priests to preserve the confidentiality of the confessional. It thus allows a priestly responsibility to override the responsibility all citizens have to give information to the police that might lead to the prevention of capital crimes. An analogous solution to the problem of dirty hands would treat the political official's responsibility to protect the people as capable in some circumstances of overriding the responsibility to refrain from acts recognized as absolutely wrong when committed by ordinary people. The Catholic rationale for the code of priestly confidentiality is the sacramental status of the confessional in Catholic theology. No one guilty of capital crimes would have reason to confess such sins to a priest not bound by such a code. The most compelling democratic rationale for the parallel solution to the problem of dirty hands is the claim that in situations of supreme emergency, the worst thing a political official can do is to allow the people to perish at the hands of its enemies.[7]

It seems foolish to insist that a lie or a bribe would not be justified if that is what it takes for a leader to extricate her people from such grim circumstances. But what about acts often cited by prominent democratic thinkers as the *worst* sorts of thing human beings do to one another—acts involving torture or murder of innocent civilians? Can we not agree that we are all obliged to refrain from such acts, regardless of our roles and however severe the emergency of the moment may seem? If our answer to the latter question is yes, we are thereby treating the responsibility to avoid committing moral horrors as both unconditional and capable of overriding a political official's other responsibilities. This is the possibility I wish to pursue in the remainder of this chapter. I will deal first with the issue of unconditional obligations and then with what it means for one "ought" to override another.

UNCONDITIONAL OBLIGATIONS AS EXPRESSIONS OF DEMOCRATIC CULTURE

An unconditional obligation, as I am using the term here, is universal in the sense that it is not role-specific or otherwise restricted to a specific group in its application. Some philosophers doubt that there are any such obligations. They see the belief in such obligations as an unwelcome by-product of what Hegel, in *The Phenomenology of Spirit*, denigrates as Kantian *Moralität*—the thinned-out, abstract point of view he contrasts with the "ethical life" or "substance" of prereflective custom, or *Sittlichkeit*. If I may transpose Hegel's categories into Brandom's terms, the prereflective ethical community treats material inferences of types (a) and (b) as proper but lacks the expressive resources to make these types of inferences explicit in the form of claims. Such a community also lacks inferential commitments of type (c), which is to say that it does not even implicitly acknowledge unconditional responsibilities. In Sittlichkeit no responsibilities are made explicit in the form of contestable claims, and whatever implicit responsibilities there are, are duties of one's station, not the obligations of a human being per se.

The ethical life of such a community is constituted in part by the material-practical inferential commitments it treats as proper—that is, by *something it does*. What it cannot yet do in the stage of Sittlichkeit is reflect on the adequacy of these commitments, because it lacks the concepts—the expressive resources—required to make them explicit in the form of claims. Students of ethics have sometimes observed that before a certain date, one finds no expressions in ancient languages that have the sense of our expression "morally ought" and little or no mention of desires as reasons for action. This is what Brandom and Hegel would lead one to expect—namely, that practical reasoning begins in implicit acknowledgment of material inferential commitments and evolves in time toward their explicit articulation in a normative vocabulary suitable for critical reflection. Hegel argues that implicitly acknowledged conflict involving role-specific responsibilities drives practical reasoning toward explicitness. Catholic teaching on priestly confidentiality is but one instance of what can result from this drive. Other communities have responded to similar conflicts in other ways.

A crucial turning point in the *Phenomenology* is Hegel's description of ancient Greek tragedy as a dramatic means of representing conflicts involving role-specific responsibilities. The norms of Sittlichkeit are implicit in the practical inferences of a people. They are ethically immediate in the sense that the practical reasoning transpiring under these circumstances is not mediated by explicit formulation of norms. Yet conflicts inevitably arise, as Sophoclean tragedies like *Antigone* make clear. Creon's role as a political leader carries with it responsibility for the proper administration of the state. Antigone's role as the sister of Polynices carries with it responsibility for burying his body after he dies. The two responsibilities come into tragic conflict when Creon, for reasons of state, orders that Polynices' corpse be consigned to the dogs and the vultures. Sophocles puts the spectator in a position to see what generates the conflict, thus inviting reflection of a sort in which neither of the main characters engages.[8] Reflection on such a spectacle allows an audience to infer that role-specific responsibilities can come into conflict not only for two people occupying different roles but for a single person who occupies roles in both the state and the family. Once such reflection gets going, however, it rapidly develops the expressive resources to allow agents to take responsibility, not only for their actions, but also for explicit claims about what their responsibilities are and claims about how those responsibilities should be conceived. These claims are well suited to play the role of reasons for action, but they are also inherently vulnerable to potential challenge insofar as reasons can be demanded for them. The norms that Creon and Antigone see as given are thus brought within the sphere of responsibility. For individuals can now be held responsible for treating some explicit formulation of these norms as a reason for action. To hold someone responsible in this way is to demand reasons for his or her explicitly acknowledged norms.[9] In a modern democratic culture, this sort of demand is made every day.

Tragedy, law, rhetoric, logic, dialectic, and democracy all signal the creation of the expressive resources required for reflective discourse about norms. The critical distance from a culture's normative inheritance that is made possible by these resources can also be experienced, however, as a form of estrangement from the roles and responsibilities in which one finds oneself. In its most extreme form this estrangement represents Moralität, the alienated condition in which moral reflection, once triggered by conflicts relating to socially recognized role-specific responsibilities, finds itself trying to make itself completely independent of the ethical life of a people. In Brandom's terms, this would involve trying to think normatively without relying in any way on the material inferential commitments in which the responsibilities now being critically scrutinized were initially implicit. Hegel argues persuasively that no such attempt can succeed, because only the ethical life of a people—what a people *does* discursively—can give substantive *content* to the norms in question.[10]

Right-wing Hegelianism identifies the ideals of modern democracy with the vacuity of Moralität, a move emulated by recent communitarians and traditionalists interested in criticizing modern democracy in the name of premodern Sittlichkeit. This move is intended to make the concepts of justice, rights, and decency that are central to modern democratic cultures seem inherently ill-suited for the discursive roles they are meant to fulfill. Democracy is pictured here in Burkean fashion as an essentially destructive force, directed against the ethical life of traditional cultures. It sets the unconditional obligations of pure practical reason against the role-specific responsibilities of traditional culture. Democratic ideals are diagnosed as symptoms of a self-defeating attempt to rise above *sittlich* communities or traditions to the perspective of universal reason.

But there is a dangerous confusion at work in this way of interpreting the moral of Hegel's story. An obligation can be universal in the sense of applying (as we see it) to everyone, without requiring a supposedly universal point of view (wholly independent of the ethical life of a people) for its justification. These two senses of universality are in fact distinct. An obligation that we attribute to everyone has what Rawls and Rorty call "universal reach." But an obligation that is universal in this sense need not possess what Rorty calls "universal validity."[11] The most promising defense of an unconditional obligation to avoid acts of moral horror would frankly acknowledge its expressive function in the ethical life of a democratic people. That is, it would purport to be making explicit a norm that is already implicit in the practical inferential commitments of a community that exchanges reasons democratically.[12] Once the norm is made explicit, it automatically becomes a candidate for critical inspection, because it now takes the form of a claim for which reasons may be requested. The background of material inferential proprieties, the expressive resources for making norms explicit, and the practice of exchanging reasons and requests for reasons with fellow citizens are, taken together, the discursive core of democratic culture. Democracy, far from being a freestanding set of institutional arrangements and abstract norms essentially opposed to culture, is a culture in its own right. Democratic norms are its expressive fruition. These norms allow us to ask such questions as whether there should be a role of master, whether women ought to have the opportunity to be political leaders, and whether some obligations should be attributed to the holders of any role whatsoever. We are fortunate to be able to ask these questions.

The fact that not everyone embraces our norms is no reason to think that such norms cannot include unconditional obligations. There is a distinction between those to whom democrats attribute the obligations and those—namely, the democrats themselves—who acknowledge the obligations by avowing them or attributing them to others. An unconditional obligation is one *attributed to* everyone, regardless of role. But this leaves open whether everyone acknowledges the obligation thus attributed. Sensible democrats understand that not everyone acknowledges the norms that they themselves avow. There is no paradox in supposing that some of these norms apply even to people who do not acknowledge them.

If I say that no one should torture another human being, I am avowing an obligation and attributing it to everyone else. This need not involve claiming that everyone else acknowledges it. Torturers who acknowledge the norm will be prone to secrecy, bad consciences, and hypocrisy. Other torturers, however, might do their dirty work openly, with clear consciences, and in ignorance of the norm I avow and the reasons I would offer for it. The ignorance of the latter group might be culpable or not, depending on the circumstances. Imagine a monk who turned the rack during the Spanish Inquisition. Suppose he was completely unfamiliar, through no fault of his own, with many of the considerations that lead me to condemn torture. (This is at least conceivable. I am not doing history at the moment.) The reason for concluding that the monk's ignorance is truly nonculpable would be that he made proper use of the evidence, concepts, and norms available to him—all factors that vary from one cultural setting to another. I am less inclined to excuse a contemporary right-wing dictator who tortures political prisoners some of the time, gives speeches on supreme emergency on other occasions, and burns books by his democratic opponents whenever it suits his purposes. If he is ignorant of the reasons for condemning torture, the chances are good that he is culpably so.

Endorsing an unconditional obligation to avoid torturing people has the significance of avowing that obligation oneself and attributing it to everyone else. The avowal involves treating the practical inferential schema "Torturing X would be cruel, so I shall refrain from torturing X" as materially proper. Attributing the obligation to everyone else involves treating the cruelty of torturing someone as a reason that would entitle anyone to refrain from torturing people. In the example of the imaginary monk, however, differences between my collateral commitments and his complicate matters. The unconditional norm I endorse implies that the monk *should not* have tortured human beings. But in saying so I do not claim that he had access to the reason I recognize as a decisive count against torture. When I endorse cruelty as a reason for refraining from torture, I am offering the reason to everybody and I implicitly express confidence in my reasons for acknowledging this reason. But in saying all this I am keeping track of ethical responsibilities in light of my collateral commitments (MIE, chap. 3). I am talking *about* what everybody should refrain from doing. I am saying *of* everybody that they should refrain from doing something. But I am speaking from my own social perspective, making use of reasons and collateral commitments native to my setting.[13] I need not suppose that the monk (given his social perspective) would in fact be able to acknowledge the force of the reason I acknowledge. There can *be* such a reason, and it can be a decisive reason when placed in the context of my collateral commitments, even if the monk and various others have no reason to treat it as a reason.[14]

The point might become clearer when put in terms of an image. A norm is a license for making inferences of a certain kind—in this case, inferences conforming to the schema mentioned in the previous paragraph. To endorse a norm implying an unconditional obligation is to *issue* a license to everyone to make inferences of that kind. But in issuing the license—that is, in *offering* the reason whose authority I myself acknowledge—I need not suppose that people outside my own discursive community can get their hands on it. Even if they came across it by accident, they might not be in a position to recognize it as a license, to acknowledge its authority. This particular license is on offer to all comers, even though I recognize that people who lack something like my conception of cruelty are unlikely to make use of it. Its intelligibility and authority derive from a background of material inferential commitments native to my environment, not from pure practical reason. It is universal only in one sense.

There is a simple way of finessing the issue by redefining unconditional obligations as a variety of role-specific responsibilities. Instead of saying that unconditional obligations apply to everyone (period), we could say that they apply to all holders of the (democratically basic) role of norm user. A norm user is anyone who possesses the expressive resources to exchange reasons for and against explicit normative claims. Then democrats can be seen as committed to conscripting everyone they can into this role: the young by educating them, the foreign by offering them reasons and asking them for reasons, the dead by imagining ourselves in conversation with them. But the role comes with responsibilities; we attribute the role and the responsibilities together. Some of these responsibilities are discursive; they pertain to the proprieties of reasoning about norms. Others impose restrictions on what may be done.

The idea that we are free to attribute this role and its attendant responsibilities to people outside our own culture is no more puzzling than the Roman designation of someone as a barbarian or the Jewish designation of someone as a gentile. It is simply our way of beginning the process of holding them responsible to us and ourselves responsible to them. Ancient, sittlich cultures had their ways of coping conceptually with people who were not friends, neighbors, or members of the family. They called them strangers or enemies—roles differentiated from each other by the presence or absence of hostile behavior, each with its distinctive role-specific rights and responsibilities. A stranger who spat on the sandals of a native official would be held responsible for his act. If the offense seemed grave enough, he might be reclassified as an enemy and treated accordingly. The spitting in this context might give license for what we would call a cruel response. We have our own ways of holding strangers and enemies responsible. One of these ways is by attributing to them the obligation to avoid torturing people. Strangers and enemies, like the rest of us, employ norms. We therefore press them for reasons and in various other ways hold them accountable for indecencies and cruelties.

The foregoing discussion suggests, then, that one can endorse an unconditional obligation while also standing with Hegel in rejecting pure practical reason. For the notion of pure practical reason, in the pejorative Hegelian sense I am using here, is that of practical reason operating independently of the ethical life of a people. In attributing to such people as the monk and the dictator the obligation to avoid torture, I have not adopted the standpoint of pure practical reason in this sense. But at least in the dictator's case, I have begun a process intended to expand my own discursive community to include him as a fellow norm user, as someone I might hold responsible for his actions and as someone who might hold me responsible for mine. The unconditional obligation to avoid torture that I invoke against him has two things going for it. It is expressive of commitments implicit in our own practices, and it has thus far withstood criticism in the give-and-take of democratic discourse. Anyone who has mastered the relevant normative vocabulary can of course challenge the norm by questioning our entitlement to it or offering reasons against it.

My examples raise another complication worth mentioning. There is more than one way of becoming committed to a norm. The most obvious ways are by acknowledging it, explicitly through avowals or implicitly in action. But I can also be committed to a norm that follows from other commitments I have made. When I acknowledge a normative commitment, it directly implies other commitments, which I implicitly undertake whether I am aware of the implications or not. Together with my previous beliefs and practical commitments, the new commitment implies many more, which I also implicitly undertake. In this way the inferential significance of my acknowledged normative commitments can far exceed my awareness.[15] And the same holds for the monk and the dictator.

As a result, it is possible that even the monk is committed unawares to considerations that deprive him of what should count, *from his point of view*, as entitlement to the policy of torturing people. The rudiments of my conception of cruelty might already be present among the unacknowledged commitments he has undertaken, waiting, so to speak, to be articulated and put together. If that is so, there may be a fairly strong sense in which he did have access to my reason for opposing torture after all. The relativity of entitlement to context does not necessarily get any torturer who is unfamiliar with the explicit articulation of democratic norms and arguments off the hook (as inculpable for his or her moral ignorance). Whether it does or not in a given case is something that can be determined, if at all, only through meticulous historical inquiry and immanent criticism. But even if our monk turns out to be on the hook, in the sense of being culpable through negligence for his moral ignorance, it would not take an appeal to pure practical reason to put him there. For in concluding that torturing people is in tension with some of his own unacknowledged commitments, we would still be appealing to the ethical substance of a culture, namely his. We need not suppose that everyone who engages in practical reasoning—or who engages, as Habermas would have it, in communicative acts— has implicitly undertaken commitment to the normative conclusions a democrat would like to see explicitly endorsed.

OVERRIDING OBLIGATIONS AND QUESTIONS OF IMPORTANCE

The previous section attempts to make sense of the idea that there is an unconditional obligation to avoid some sorts of especially bad acts—horrible acts—such as the act of torturing people. That analysis does not resolve the problem of dirty hands, however. Its first purpose is to bring the problem into focus as a conflict between a responsibility we attribute to those holding a certain role and an obligation we attribute to everybody. The second purpose is to show that even the latter can be interpreted as an expression of commitments implicit in democratic culture, rather than as a theorem in transcendental philosophy. The question that remains is which of these two norms *overrides* the other in cases where a political official cannot fulfill both.[16] This is the crux of the problem of dirty hands.

The first point to grasp is that whether one norm overrides another is distinct from the question of their status as role-specific or unconditional. In the Catholic code, as we have seen, the priestly responsibility to maintain the confidentiality of the confessional overrides the obligation we all have to provide information to the police in certain circumstances. It is perfectly coherent to suppose that a role-specific responsibility can trump an unconditional obligation, or vice versa. The reason for this is that the distinction between role-specific and unconditional constraints has nothing to do with the question of how important these constraints are—with how and why we care about having them fulfilled. Judgments about whether one norm overrides another express commitments about the relative importance of the norms being compared. An obligation can, in theory, be both unconditional and trivial. The problem of dirty hands is as problematic as it is, however, because both of the concerns that constitute the problem are obviously very important to most democratic citizens and because we ascribe importance to those concerns from somewhat different points of view.

The Catholic stand on priestly confidentiality reflects an underlying commitment to the importance of confession in the sacramental system for saving souls from damnation.[17] In the grand scheme of things, an obligation Catholics attribute to everyone need not be more important than a responsibility they attribute to the occupant of a particular role. But Catholicism has a view of the grand scheme of things. This view authorizes a definitive stand on the problem of priestly confidentiality—and also, for that matter, on the problem of dirty hands. Modern democratic culture, in contrast, does not have a single view of the grand scheme of things; it opens up space in which many such views can be held and acted upon. It is not vacuous in the sense that Hegel thought Moralität was, for the ethical life of democratic peoples clearly commits them to the importance of such matters as the people's survival and the decent treatment of others.[18] It does not, however, entail a single ranking of the most important things, for most of its citizens have agreed to disagree on questions of ultimate importance. They have not been able to settle these questions by rational argument so far, and do not expect to do so in the foreseeable future. They are therefore prepared to grant one another considerable latitude in answering them.[19] They cannot decide which of their highly important moral concerns is the most important to them *as a society*. (All of them agree that bombing a civilian population is very bad, but not all of them think that such a horror would in all circumstances be literally inexcusable.) It should come as no surprise, then, that they are of several minds on the problem of dirty hands, that the problem remains problematic for them.

Nor should it come as a surprise that this is one of the issues on which some citizens feel compelled, in conscience, to express their religious commitments in public. Questions about the relative importance of highly important values are for most people so intimately connected with religious commitments that they would be hard-pressed to defend their answers to them without employing such commitments as premises.[20] This fact counts heavily against any theory that proposes to exclude the expression of such premises from the public sphere. These are things we need to talk about with one another, even at the risk of conflict, awkwardness, and a good deal of stuttering.

I, for one, aspire to belong to a society that would treat the commission of horrible acts like the intentional bombing of civilian populations as literally inexcusable, even in situations where such a tactic is thought on plausible evidence to be necessary in fending off terrorist destruction. I fear that anything less than an absolutely overriding prohibition of such acts will tempt our leaders to commit moral horrors in situations that only seem, at the time, to be emergencies. So I worry that endorsing the supreme-emergency exception would weaken democratic culture by undermining its ability to sustain a genuinely democratic politics, here and now. I am also prepared to bite the bullet in the event of an actual emergency. A society resolutely committed to avoiding the infliction of moral horrors would rather go down in flames, while treating this commitment as a matter of integrity, than survive by instructing its leaders in advance to perform such acts on its behalf if an emergency arises. I would defend this commitment as an apt expression of the importance we ought to attribute to human beings as unique, irreplaceable individuals with the capacity to love, exchange reasons, repent of wrongdoing, and suffer. As I see it, the issue is what kind of people we are going to be—a matter of self-definition and integrity. It is about what we care about most, of what we deem sacred or supremely valuable or inviolable, not the desire to have clean hands.[21]

I don't expect to change the minds of those who feel that in an actual supreme emergency they would attach more importance to the people's

survival than to the people's identity and integrity as a community dedicated to removing moral horrors from the list of permissible political
means.[22] Nor do I think philosophy has the means to discredit as irrational
either absolute intolerance of horrible acts or a willingness to grant rare
exceptions. While I aspire to live in a society that shares my convictions
about the moral limits of war, I understand that the utopia I am projecting
asks more of my actual fellow citizens than many of them are prepared
to give when they are threatened by potentially massive terrorist attacks.
Moreover, one of the things that is highly important to me is living in a
society where I am free to decide what is most important to me and in
which others are similarly free. So there are limits on what I am willing to
do to bring others into perfect agreement with me on the morally most
important things.

But I still abominate the bombing of civilian targets, the torture of prisoners, and various other things my government is either ordering or contem-
plating. And because of this, I am necessarily left in severe tension with
those of my fellow citizens who today authorize our leaders, albeit condi-
tionally, to do things which horrify me. Living with such tension is not an
easy task, because it borders on complicity in horrible things. That is why
Thoreau, a profound modern democrat, so often felt like resigning symbol-
ically from his country. One needn't be a sectarian to have such feelings.

It is because modern democratic discourse does not proceed from ante-
cedent agreement on how the most important values should be ranked, but
nonetheless invites citizens to express their own reasons for their commitments on important public questions, that democratic culture tends to
evoke ambivalence even from its defenders. The sectarian temptation is to
allow the ambivalence, which is appropriate, to turn into alienation, which
only makes things worse. Sectarians propose to withdraw from the broader
community of discourse, convinced that it would be a violation of their
commitments on matters of high importance even to exchange reasons and
requests for reasons with those who do not share those commitments.

I have just been portraying the debate over the problem of dirty hands
in the age of terrorism as an argument over the relative importance one
ought to assign to two conflicting prima facie responsibilities—one role-
specific, one not. But it would be misleading to leave the impression that
reasoning on this issue within religious traditions like Judaism, Christianity, and Islam has generally proceeded from uncertainty about how much
the relevant prima facie responsibilities weigh. That is not in fact how
the reasoning always—or even very often—has worked in those traditions
historically. Within such traditions, the overriding importance of the responsibility to avoid committing certain injustices has often been taken for
granted in such a way that the problem of dirty hands does not even arise.
For those committed to the resulting forms of absolutism, practical reason-

ing typically *begins* by classifying actions as either intrinsically prohibited or not, so that "weighing" the relative importance of conflicting responsibilities comes into play explicitly *only* for actions falling into the latter class.[23] One of the deepest worries about modern democratic society, from the perspective of those committed to such absolutism, is that this society does not take absolutist commitments for granted as a premise from which all practical reasoning proceeds. In this context, absolute dedication to justice, or even to the avoidance of moral horrors, is a commitment for which reasons are constantly being requested, not a premise on which all implicitly agree. This means that our ethical discourse does not take the shape that many of us would like to see. So long as this remains the case, the problem of dirty hands will remain with us, and some of us will remain ambivalent, at best, about participating in our common life at all.

Without pretending to solve the problem of dirty hands per se, I want to conclude by offering two contextually specific arguments for placing especially rigorous constraints on the political officials who are leading us in the struggle against terrorism. The first argument is simple and appeals to consistency. What we condemn in terrorism is precisely the moral horror it involves—its intentional targeting of civilian populations. We cannot maintain consistency without holding our leaders to the same standards of conduct we apply to the leaders of Afghanistan and Iraq. If we are not prepared to make exceptions for our enemies, we should not make them for ourselves.

The second argument is prudential. The struggle against terrorism is not only military, but also ideological. We are unlikely to win it on the ideological front if we cannot persuade people who are tempted to side with the terrorists that we are not essentially hypocritical in condemning the terrorism that threatens us. If we show callous disregard for the lives of innocent civilians—or, for that matter, intentionally frustrate the legitimate democratic aspirations of other peoples—in order to protect our own country from terrorism, then our country will not be seen as a champion of justice and democracy. The outcome of this struggle depends largely on the perceived sincerity and rigor of our ideals and principles—on what people all around the world take our character to be. We will win only if we gradually earn the trust of those people. We can do that only by proving ourselves true to our principles even at those moments when we are sorely tempted to forgive our leaders for violating them. If we cannot manage to attain the moral high ground and stay there over the long haul, we are going to lose the ideological battle. And if we lose that, the flow of terrorist recruits will never cease.

Chapter 9

THE EMERGENCE OF MODERN
DEMOCRATIC CULTURE

MODERN DEMOCRACY came into existence by defining itself over against its predecessors and competitors as a revolutionary departure. Its champions often claimed that in criticizing traditional mores and institutional arrangements they had broken completely with a feudal and ecclesiastical past. One hears echoes of this claim in Paine's *The Rights of Man*, in Emerson's "Self-Reliance," and in many lesser texts. The claim exaggerates a real difference.

Modern democracy was in some sense a revolutionary break with the past. Its emergence was intertwined with the English, American, and French Revolutions, and the use its early defenders made of such concepts as the rights of man was indeed an innovation. But the rhetoric of revolution obscures the slow, *evolutionary* process of a transition that actually took place over the course of many centuries and has yet to unfold its full implications. If not used with caution, revolutionary rhetoric also generates a good deal of perplexity over how the champions of modern democracy could have been rationally justified in urging some of the changes they brought about. A complete break with tradition would seem to require either a transcendental point of view, wholly independent of what I have called the ethical life of a people, or a point of view so discontinuous with that of the traditional past as to be incapable of arguing with it.

I will begin by giving a thumbnail sketch of the emergence of rights-talk in the modern period. Thereafter, I will examine some of the pitfalls surrounding the idea that modern democracy eliminates deference to authority. The early defenders (and opponents) of modern democracy who made this idea seem essential to it were wrong. I will then turn to the debate between Edmund Burke and Thomas Paine over the French Revolution. My analysis of that debate will lead, finally, to an account of the role that observational social criticism has played in the emergence and development of modern democratic culture. Each section of the chapter contributes something to the case I am making for the conclusion that democratic culture is best understood as a set of social practices that inculcate characteristic habits, attitudes, and dispositions in their participants. Because those practices do involve a sort of deference to authority (as well as much defiance of authority) and have achieved enough stability to be transmitted from one generation to another, it makes sense to call them a tradition in their own right. But in working out what it means to say this, we are transcending oppositions that Burke and Paine took for granted. This, I take it, is what American pragmatism has long sought to achieve—an antitraditionalist conception of modern democracy as a tradition.

THE VOCABULARY OF RIGHTS: A JUST-SO STORY

Once upon a time, there were feudal kingdoms. In those days, rights were mainly treated as if they belonged to persons identified with particular roles. What are rights? All rights are normative social statuses. To have the status of a right is to have a legitimate claim on others for the enjoyment of a good. In the feudal past such statuses were determined by a hierarchically arranged set-up of persons, each of whom had his or her place in the providentially designed order of things. Because the basic social order was thought to be divinely ordained, human beings were not responsible for determining what the available roles should be. The question of who gets to play which roles was also to be answered by discerning God's will. Occasionally, a group of religious purists would press demands for universal poverty and equal standing, but the need for some variant of the hierarchical framework was mainly taken for granted. There was ample room for reflection, in the form of political theology, but such reflection tended to reinforce the inequalities of the entrenched hierarchical arrangements.

Questions about rights tended in this setting to be of the following form: "What claims may you legitimately assert against those to whom you are bound by relations of obligation, given the stations to which you and they have been assigned by God?" The question assumed that the basic order is fixed: prince, king, father, mother, first son, second-born, mere daughter, commoner, peon, outcast, priest, bishop, pope, and so on. Your assigned roles constituted your ethical identity, your vocation. Your roles plus the relations they involved determined your obligations. The relations of role-determined obligation in which you stood determined your rights. In this linguistic setting, "dignity" was a term associated with the bearing appropriate to a nobleman, the sort of person who rarely, if ever, had to beg or grovel when acting appropriately within hierarchically defined relationships. There were, in the feudal era, basically two ways of managing social conflict that could not be resolved by recourse to political theology. One of these was physical coercion, in which one party forcibly pushed another into a subordinate role in a hierarchy. The other was submissive behavior on the part of a weaker party, which established the hierarchical equilibrium more peaceably.

Eventually, however, church councils began to strike many Catholics as a model for more collegial, less hierarchical, exercise of authority within the church.[1] And in certain places, including England, the demand of Protestant radicals for egalitarian social and political relationships made significant headway. Increasingly, people started asking about the whole set-up. They began to think of the set-up itself as something for which a social group, and not just the divine source of all things, bore responsibility.[2] So they began posing hard questions, not just about, say, whether a specific prince should be deposed or a specific priest defrocked or a specific lady respected, but about whether there ought to be such a role as that of a king, or a priest, or a lady. In *The Rights of Man*, Paine is out to show that present-day kings are merely the descendants of another age's "bands of robbers."[3] In *Democratic Vistas*, Whitman remarks on the "fossil and unhealthy air which hangs about the word *lady*."[4] Remarks like these gradually shifted the burden of proof so that nowadays anybody who affirms or proposes a hierarchically defined role needs to bear the burden of proof in a debate where objections will be allowed from all sides. The argument, if made, will be expected to acknowledge that we are going to settle the question, if at all possible, by talking things out. We will not simply assume that a hierarchy of fixed roles is given in the nature of things.

The net effect of such developments was the creation of what amounted to a new basic role, that of rights claimant and responsibility holder. This role would henceforth be open to everybody who could talk and display enough civility to listen, avoid groveling, abide by the results of deliberations conducted by fair and agreed-upon rules, and so on. There are still role-specific rights. That is to say, there are legitimate claims that a role-occupant can make for the enjoyment of a good, given what other role-occupants owe him or her as a matter of duty. But now there are also widely recognized rights of another kind. In other words, there are legitimate claims one can make on behalf of oneself or one's group at those points in the discussion where the set-up of available roles and the procedure for assigning individuals to roles are up for grabs. In this sense rights are statuses involving legitimate claims to a social arrangement of a certain kind, a set-up capable of ensuring "that one will not be deprived of the enjoyment of the good in question by ordinary, serious, or remediable threats."[5] The linguistic innovation was to use the old word "rights" to stand for statuses involving these new sorts of legitimate claims. A parallel innovation (there were many others) was to say that everybody with the level of linguistic competence and civility needed to participate in the discussion had something called dignity. In both of these cases, a "fossil and unhealthy air" might cling to the old word for a while, eventually to be dispelled by the vigor of its new uses.

The contemporary feminist philosopher, Annette Baier, makes a profound point when she associates modern rights-talk with an unwillingness to beg. Here is a passage from an essay of hers called "Claims, Rights, Responsibilities":

The social device of dominance itself avoids mutually disadvantageous in-fighting, but its cost is high for the dominated. The various rituals of defer-ence, and of begging and response to begging, reduce this sort of cost. We are a species who recognize status (and so avoid the war of all against all) and who have a strictly limited willingness both to beg and to give to those who beg. The conditions of the form of human justice that recognizes universal rights include not only moderate scarcity, vulnerability to the resentment of one's fellows, and limited generosity, all of which Hume recognized, but also a lim-ited willingness to beg, a considerable unwillingness to ask, even when—if we did ask the powerful for a handout—it would perhaps be given to us. What we regard as ours by right is what we are unwilling to beg for and willing only within limits to say "thank you" for. We seem to be getting less and less willing both to beg and to give to beggars. The increasing tendency to talk of universal rights and the extension of their content correlates with the decreasing ability to beg.[6]

Baier does not defend rights-talk in the usual, highly theoretical, meta-physical way. She does not make excessive claims on behalf of such talk, and she is careful to say that rights are less basic, even in our modern moral discourse, than responsibilities. Moreover, she candidly analyzes the problems that rights-talk can get into, especially when it is not supple-mented by other ethical and political concepts. But she does have a clear sense, it seems to me, of what rights-talk does for us. The problems come from asking rights-talk to do too much. When it comes time to appraise character, for example, we need to speak of virtues and vices, not of rights. But there are other linguistic tasks that are hard to accomplish without speaking of rights in the way citizens of modern democracies tend to speak of them, as legitimate claims about matters that are not merely by-products of other people's role-specific duties.

MacIntyre has proposed that we drop rights-talk in favor of an older moral vocabulary focused mainly on the virtues. In defense of this proposal he argues that questions of rights are inherently arbitrary and that there is no reason to suppose that basic human rights even exist.[7] Belief in rights, he concludes, is on a par with belief in unicorns. The practical worry about such proposals can be expressed in the question, "When the powerful try to shut us out or hold us down, what are we supposed to do, beg?" In a democratic culture begging and certain other expressions of deference come to seem responses unbecoming of a human being or fellow citizen. The language of rights arises in such a culture as an alternative to begging, on the one hand, and to certain kinds of coercion, such as torture and religiously motivated warfare, on the other. But it does not arise alone. Accompanying it is a significant alteration in the character traits held up for praise and blame. The members of such a culture do not stop talking about the virtues. But they are more likely than their ancestors were to look kindly on the traits in common people that would allow them to stand up before power-holders and participate in the practices of claim-making and reason-giving. Their participation in turn demands from them respect for other claimants and a willingness to be constrained by the reason-giving that occurs in the discussion.

One institutional constraint that matters in this context is that everybody who satisfies the minimal conditions of being able to speak and remain civil deserves a hearing. If they can avoid the posture of subordination, the conclusions they urge upon us will have some hope of being treated as the (perhaps legitimate) claims of fellow citizens, not as beggary. The virtues, postures, moods, and gestures that become habitual in this culture are easily recognizable, provided that an ethnographer like Whitman calls them to our attention. Speaking of the common people, Whitman writes: "The fierceness of their roused resentment—their curiosity and welcome of novelty—their self-esteem and wonderful sympathy—their susceptibility to a slight—the air they have of persons who never knew how it felt to stand in the presence of superiors—the fluency of their speech—. . . their good temper and openhandedness." All of these, he says, are "unrhymed poetry."[8] They reveal the ethical life of democracy.

Of course, it is not always so easy, even in relatively ideal circumstances, to discern the difference between legitimate and illegitimate claims to the enjoyment of goods. But then it isn't always easy to discern the difference between legitimate and illegitimate claims of other kinds. Factual claims, for example, are claims *about* what is the case. We know what some of the legitimate factual claims are, but others remain in dispute. This is no reason to conclude that there is no such thing as a fact or that all fact-claiming is arbitrary. If facts are legitimate claims about what is the case, then if we know that there are claims about what is the case and that some of them are legitimate (that is, true), we know that there are facts.[9] And if we know that the legitimacy of some claims about what is the case can be settled beyond a reasonable doubt by appeal to available evidence, then we have reason to deny that all fact-claiming is arbitrary. Rights involve legitimate claims *to* the enjoyment of certain goods. We know that there are claims to the enjoyment of certain goods. People make such claims all the time. If some such claims are legitimately made on behalf of everyone—such as the claim not to be tortured and the claim to be free from humiliation— then there *are* human rights, and human rights are not *essentially* arbitrary. For rights are just statuses conferred by legitimate claims of this sort. I grant, however, that the legitimacy of some claims to the enjoyment of goods can be hard to determine. The reason for the difficulty in the hard cases is that there are conflicting considerations to take into account when settling what the basic social set-up should be. (Similarly, a claim about what is the case counts as legitimate only if it belongs to the best overall account of the matter being investigated, but the best overall account of the facts can be hard to determine.)

Who will know better what some of the relevant considerations will be than the one on whose behalf a right is claimed? All the more reason, then, to highlight one class of legitimate claims or rights, namely the ones that have directly to do with who gets to talk and with what the conversation is going to be like. Suppose the talking that went on in a given community were principally a matter of mere coercion, from which the weak could save themselves only by assuming a posture of submission. Suppose the "discussion" were essentially analogous to the decision making and conflict resolution that goes on in a pack of wolves. We would not then be prepared to count it as discourse. As democrats we would object to it unconditionally, without regard to the substance of what had been decided. A democratic claim is not something one asks for by assuming a prone position before a superior. One need not say "pretty please" or "I beg of you." The claimant is not meant to be assuming all the while that of course it would be legitimate for the real decider, in his superior place, to decide whatever he wants, regardless of the reasons one might give.

Our sense is that there ought to be a discussion. Anybody who bullies other people into exclusion or into submission is someone we tend to blame. We encourage the weak, the likeliest victims of exclusion or domination, to stand up and speak in a way that can be clearly distinguished from begging or beseeching. The ideal of equal voice implicit in these aspects of democratic culture is itself, of course, something one can justify, if need be, in the discussion. But as long as it does stand justified, as long as it withstands critical scrutiny in our common discussion with one another, it imposes unconditional demands—not unconditioned demands, unconditional ones. They are obviously demands shaped by actual historical conditions in which people came to be suspicious of begging and coercion as modes of conflict resolution. But they are unconditional in the sense that they help constitute, in this time and place anyway, what we are justifiably prepared to count as democratic discussion.

No doubt, the foregoing story oversimplifies the historical emergence of rights-talk in the modern period, as anything this brief would. But it does begin to suggest why our ancestors saw recognition of "the rights of man"— and shortly thereafter, "the rights of woman" and "the rights of slaves"— as a sort of revolution or reorientation in moral thinking. Edmund Burke called it an "innovation." Burke's democratic opponents, like Thomas Paine, were for the most part pleased to agree, thus transforming Burke's pejorative term into a positive one. But what shall we make of the contrast Burke and Paine both drew between ethical discourse in feudal and democratic settings? Is it true that democratic discourse, with its talk of rights, essentially eliminates deference to authority? Burke and Paine both thought of the innovation in this way; they differed over whether this made the innovation horrific or wonderful. Burke held that a society without deference to genuine authority could not last more than a generation. Paine saw Burke as an apologist for a corrupt order of power and privilege. To determine where the truth lies, we will need to take a brief philosophical detour.

Exchanging Reasons: Deference, Challenge, and Entitlement

The reasons exchanged in ethical discourse pertain to commitments that individuals undertake and attribute to one another. The commitments pertain to such topics as conduct, character, and community. They make essential use of evaluative concepts. They distinguish between right and wrong, justice and injustice, decency and indecency, virtue and vice, the excellent and the horrible, the good and the bad, the responsible and the irresponsible. And they often employ notions that are more specific than these, but clearly belong to the same conceptual family, such as the idea of murder or courage. Ethical reasoning, when fully expressed, involves claims, questions, arguments, narratives, examples, and various other linguistic units in terms of which ethical topics can be specified.

Ethical discourse in any culture bears on reasons for action. It is a *discursive* practice because reasons, in the form of asserted claims, are among the things being exchanged in it. It is a *social* practice, first, because the reasons being exchanged pass from one person to another and, second, because each participant needs to keep track of the discursive process in terms of his or her own commitments. By exchanging reasons and requests for reasons with one another, participants in the practice hold one another responsible for their commitments and actions. To be able to exchange reasons for this purpose, they must be able to do certain other things as well. They must be capable of undertaking both cognitive and practical commitments. They must be able to express such commitments, by avowing them and acting on them. They must know how to attribute commitments to others on the basis of what those others say and do. And they must have a grip on the distinction between being entitled to a commitment and not being entitled to it (MIE, 157–68).

"[F]or someone to undertake a commitment," Brandom says, "is to do something that makes it appropriate to *attribute* the commitment to that individual" (MIE, 162; emphasis in original). Accordingly, attributing commitments to other people is one way in which we explain their behavior, including their verbal behavior. For example, if my brother is packing his bags frantically, I might infer that he is committed to the cognitive judgment that the train will be arriving shortly and that he is also committed practically to boarding the train. If he then says to me, "The train will be

leaving shortly," I will be inclined to interpret this as an assertion expressing his judgment. But as an assertion, this utterance has significance beyond
the confirmation it affords me concerning his cognitive commitments, for
it also serves to *authorize* me (and anyone to whom I repeat it) to employ
it as a premise in reasoning. If I proceed to make use of the claim in a
practical inference that leads me to begin packing, I will be relying on the
authority conferred by my brother's claim. I also have the authority to
challenge his assertion, either by requesting reasons for accepting it or by
making claims of my own that are incompatible with it. It will then be up
to my brother to interpret what I say and do. Any such interpretation will
need to attribute commitments to me and assess those commitments in
terms of entitlement.

If my brother sincerely says to me, "You ought to start packing," this
assertion also expresses a commitment he has undertaken, authorizes me
to attribute this commitment to him, and authorizes me to employ the
claim as a premise in my own reasoning. But in this case the issue is slightly
more complicated, for reasons that emerged in chapter 8. The function of
an "ought-to-do" judgment is to make explicit a commitment to the material soundness of a practical inference. Which kind of material inference is
at issue here? Perhaps my brother simply assumes that I share his desire to
board the train. In that case, the "ought" is prudential. But we can easily
imagine other scenarios. If my brother has employed me as his valet, he
might be making a claim about my role-specific responsibilities. If he is a
member of the resistance, and the train he is about to board is carrying a
tyrannical leader, he might be asking for my help in packing our bags with
the explosives he is planning to use in blowing up the train. In that event,
his "ought" statement might very well make a claim about the implications
of my unconditional obligation to assist in the fight against tyranny. Notice
that on any of these interpretations, my brother's "ought" statement entails
a *discursive* responsibility on his part, for he is implicitly vouching for the
claim as a sound premise fit for use in my practical reasoning. Again, if I
request reasons for accepting the claim or issue a counterclaim, I can challenge his entitlement to it. But to know which claim I would then be challenging, I would need to know which commitment he was expressing in
the first place.

Holding one another responsible for commitments involves keeping
track of the commitments we attribute to each other and of the entitlements we attribute to or withhold from the commitments thus attributed.
Commitments and entitlements are socially tracked normative statuses.
Participating in a discursive social practice is in part a matter of keeping
track of oneself and one's fellow participants in terms of these normative
statuses (MIE, 180–98). It is an exercise in what Brandom calls normative
"scorekeeping." Anything we say or do can have significance in the reason-

giving practice we are engaged in insofar as it affects the various scorecards of discursive commitments and entitlements that each participant keeps from his or her own point of view on participants in the discursive game.

Cognitive commitments are commitments to a claim or a judgment, whereas practical commitments are commitments to act.[10] We may refer to these as beliefs and intentions, respectively.[11] The point of calling them commitments is to draw attention to the appropriateness of being held responsible for them, of being deemed entitled to them or not. What is it to be entitled to a belief or an intention? It is not the same thing as being able to justify the commitment to someone else, let alone being able to justify it compellingly to all rational agents. Sometimes one is entitled to a commitment by default, without needing to offer an argument for it, provided that no one who has the authority to challenge the commitment does so (MIE, 176–78). Sometimes one is entitled to a commitment because someone else (with the appropriate sort of authority) has authorized it by expressing it in the form of a claim. But there are many circumstances in which one does need to justify a commitment discursively to achieve or maintain the status of being entitled to it. And there are also cases in which one needs to justify treating other claim-makers as authorities if one wants to become or remain entitled to the commitments they have authorized.

When studying the ethical life of any community it is important to take note of its (implicit or explicit) way of distributing discursive authority and responsibility. Within a given discursive social practice, under what conditions is someone normally held to be entitled to certain sorts of commitments by default? Under what conditions is someone normally assumed to need to justify a commitment discursively in order to secure entitlement to it, even if no one challenges it? Who is entitled to issue challenges? Conversely, who is excluded from the roles of claim-maker and challenger? Under what conditions are challenges deemed appropriate? And when does a challenge suffice to deprive someone of entitlement to a commitment? In other words, what suffices to shift the burden of proof?

Suppose my sister comes into the hotel room in which my brother and I are packing the bags. She asks me, "Why are you in such a hurry?" "The train is coming shortly," I say. She says, "But why do you think that?" I might respond by referring to the train schedule that is lying on the night table, committing myself to what it says as a reason for expecting the train to arrive shortly. This would implicitly attribute authority to the schedule. Or I might appeal directly to my brother's authority: "Ralph says that the train is coming shortly." In accepting his claim at the outset of the conversation, I deferred to his authority on the question of when the train is coming. Now I am invoking his authority in responding to my sister's challenge. By invoking his authority, I implicitly attribute to him responsibility for the claim about the train's arrival. At this point, my sister can defer to his authority on the matter or challenge my implicit attribution of authority to him. She might do the latter by saying, "Why do you think he can read a train schedule?" If I then say, "Because I have relied on him many times before, and he hasn't been wrong yet," I will be giving grounds for an explicit attribution of authority.

My family happens to be a discursive community in which a younger sister is considered entitled to challenge brothers about practically anything if she has reason to do so. She need not hold her tongue about when the trains are likely to arrive, what my role-specific responsibilities might be, or what I am obliged to do in the struggle against injustice, simply because she is female or because she is the youngest of the three siblings. That the three of us challenge one another on many occasions does not mean, however, that deference is wholly lacking from our discursive practice. We defer to one another's authority on a regular basis whenever we have reason to think that doing so provides access to sound claims that will prove useful in our reasoning. Each of us considers the others to be competent readers of train schedules and skillful trackers of rights and responsibilities to which we pay close attention. Whoever has read the train schedule most recently (when alert and sober) is likely to be trusted by the others on the question of when the train is probably going to arrive. And whoever has given the most careful and disinterested thought to a particular moral issue is likely to be trusted by the others to be entitled to his or her commitments about it. We are entitled to defer in such cases because our siblings have proven their reliability in the relevant domains, and we reserve our right to challenge one another if we discover sufficient reason to doubt a claim in a particular case.

All discursive practices involve authority and deference to some extent. The notion that ethical discourse in democratic societies is "nondeferential" therefore requires qualification. It is more accurate to say that such discourse is *relatively* nondeferential. The difference is a matter of how, when, and why someone defers or appeals to authority, not a matter of whether one does so at all.

Some early defenders of modern democratic ideals wrongly sought to eliminate deference and authority from ethical discourse altogether. The theoretical consequence of this move is known as foundationalism, a doctrine that unjustifiably takes the default status of all claims to be "guilty until proven innocent." Ascribing this default status to all claims triggers a regress of reasons that can be stopped, if at all, only in a foundation of certitudes. The best way to avoid this doctrine and the problems associated with it is to say with the pragmatists that many claims are "innocent until proven guilty—taken to be entitled commitments until and unless someone is in a position to raise a legitimate question about them" (MIE, 177). This involves treating some claims as having authority by default, which means being prepared to defer to those claims, other things being equal.

But this authority is, according to the pragmatists, defeasible, because other things are not always equal. At any given moment, some claims must be treated as having authority by default. But any claim may be questioned if a relevant reason for doubting it can be produced. As Sellars put it, a discursive practice "is rational, not because it has a *foundation* but because it is a self-correcting enterprise which can put *any* claim in jeopardy, though not *all* at once" (SPR, 170; emphasis in original). This central thesis of American pragmatism is sometimes presented as a free-floating epistemological truth. But it is best viewed as a modern democratic principle for the governance of discursive practices, for in fact most discursive communities have implicitly rejected it. By granting that some claims must have authority by default, and simultaneously insisting on the defeasibility of all claims, pragmatists have endeavored to reconceive the authority relations of ethical discourse democratically. This alternative to foundationalism is pragmatism's most important contribution to democracy. For other leading alternatives to foundationalism tend to be *authoritarian* in the sense that they promote uncritical acquiescence in the allegedly authoritative claims of some practice, tradition, institution, person, text, or type of experience. American pragmatism differs from the version of pragmatism that Martin Heidegger accepted when he embraced Nazism precisely in its principled scorn for unquestioning acquiescence in authority of any kind.[12] The new traditionalism that I examined in chapters 5–7 combines an emphasis on the priority of social practices with a kind of authoritarianism. Some varieties of Wittgensteinian fideism use the concept of "forms of life" to arrive at a similar result.

Where do Burke and Paine fit into this array of alternatives? Burke's traditionalism explicitly endorsed a type of authoritarianism, whereas Paine's antiauthoritarianism implicitly committed him to foundationalism. From a pragmatic point of view, neither of these positions can survive criticism. Burke and Paine were therefore both wrong in the positions they tried to maintain and both right in identifying the flaws in the other's position. Pragmatism splits the difference by reconceiving authority in nonauthoritarian terms. It acknowledges that all societies involve deference to authority while insisting that deference and defeasibility can go hand in hand. It thereby aims to make explicit what a *democratic tradition* involves.

How Burke and Paine Argued Their Cases

If modern democracy were completely discontinuous with the traditions that preceded it, then Edmund Burke and Thomas Paine would have been wasting their time in trying to win over the other's followers by arguing over the language of rights. But these men were not wasting their time, for they did succeed, now and again, in converting those one would expect to be most firmly tied to the opposition's commitments. Burke was, after all, nearly driven to distraction by hearing Paine's arguments and conclusions from the lips of the English noblemen for whose privileges Burkean Whiggism was meant to provide the ideal justification. And the reasoning Paine offered seems, as a matter of historical fact, to have played some role in the process of conversion. Has not the same been true for other great writers working in the midst of dramatic conceptual change—writers like Plato, Augustine, Montaigne, Wollstonecraft, and Whitman? If they had not found ways of arguing their cases at least somewhat persuasively, we would not still be reading them.

The debate between Burke and Paine over democratic ideas was in fact a conceptually intimate affair, fought on the ideological plane between parties who were bending much the same ideas in different directions. In the heat of the moment, the defenders and critics of representative democracy often depicted it as a complete break with the past. But a retrospective view teaches that this is not so, at least if the debate between Burke and Paine is any indication. Both of these men saw modern democracy as utterly discontinuous with what had gone before. In fact, we may owe the theme of revolutionary discontinuity to them. Looking back, however, it is easy to locate them both within the same broad tradition of European thought—Burke struggling to hold several different strands of that tradition together, Paine convinced that the democratic-republican strand he favored was ultimately incompatible with the others. The two men shared more assumptions and concepts than anyone could enumerate. Recall in this connection the surprise and shock Paine felt when Burke, the man who had written the "Speech on Conciliation" with the American colonies, a work that contributed to Burke's reputation as a great critic of British imperial rule, published *Reflections on the Revolution in France*.

Interestingly, both Burke and Paine recognize the authority of traditional just-war criteria, despite their other differences. In the *Reflections* Burke claims that the "Revolution of 1688 was obtained by just war." He quotes Livy's version of the criterion of necessity or "last resource," and applies that criterion to the French Revolution. He inquires into the intentions and putative authority of the Jacobins, declares that the "punishment of real tyrants is a noble and awful act of justice," and reflects at length on the disproportionality of revolution in the French case.[13]

In *The Rights of Man*, Paine tries to refute Burke on many of these points, but he assumes throughout that just-war criteria are pertinent. He invokes them more explicitly in *Common Sense*. On the question of last resort, Paine refers to "the peaceful methods which we have ineffectually used for redress." He defends the justice of his own intentions as a revolutionary by claiming that "I am not induced by motives of pride, party, or resentment to espouse the doctrine of independence." His appeal to the norm of proportionality maintains that "the object contended for, ought always to bear some just proportion to the expense." The cause is just, he argues, because "thousands are already ruined by British barbarity." And he concedes the need to establish just authority by declaring independence and adopting plans for just self-government: "While we profess ourselves the subjects of Britain, we must, in the eyes of foreign nations, be considered as Rebels."[14] His solution to this problem, of course, is to declare independence.

No doubt, something of great importance was at stake in the debate between Burke and Paine. The proposed change in received conceptions of rights was important enough to be termed a conceptual revolution in some sense. Suppose we grant the need to be wary of using the term as Burke and Paine used it, lest we think that the two sides were separated by complete conceptual discontinuity. What does the "revolutionary" conceptual change consist in, then? Where exactly shall we look to find it? Obviously, the two authors differ over the courses of action they are committed to and over *some* of the explicit norms they endorse. Paine supports the French Revolution, while Burke opposes it. Paine's norms clearly attribute normative statuses of a certain kind—rights—to all men.[15] Our discussion of how the two authors appeal to just-war criteria shows that they also share some explicitly stated norms, but they apply them differently. Their competing applications of just-war criteria reflect differing material inferential commitments concerning the connections between claims about justice and claims of certain other kinds.

What else is at issue here, ethically speaking? The first section's just-so story about rights suggests that part of the answer has to do with patterns of deference. The culture Burke is defending is one in which pomp and circumstance function as marks of authority and excellence as well as privileges of rank and symbols of power. "We fear God; we look up with awe to kings, with affection to parliaments, with duty to magistrates, with reverence to priests, and with respect to nobility. Why? Because when such ideas are brought before our minds, it is *natural* to be so affected" (*Reflections*, 76). He means that the intuitive, noninferential response to being in the presence of such things is to judge them excellent and thus to admire them and feel awe or reverence. The authority he attributes to persons of high rank in the state and the church correlates with a disposition to defer to such persons on matters to which their authority is relevant. Bad behavior of certain kinds can deprive such persons of their authority and of their legitimate claim to their office. But even the removal of a genuine tyrant from office must be carried out, according to Burke, with pomp and circumstance, above all with proper acknowledgment of the respect due to the office. It is crucial, he thinks, to maintain a culture in which admiration of excellence and deference to authority are not only possible but central to the habits of the populace. Democracy, he thinks, is the opposite of such a culture, a mere destructive force. This issue appears in Burke's *Reflections* under the rubric of the loss of chivalry, and it is of great moment to him.

Paine, of course, is out to debunk the culture of chivalry as a set of props designed to mask the operations of tyranny. "It is by distortedly exalting some men," he writes, "that others are distortedly debased, till the whole is out of nature. A vast mass of mankind are degradedly thrown into the background of the human picture, to bring forward with greater glare, the puppet-show of state and aristocracy" (59). Where Burke enjoins deference, Paine typically requests a reason or asserts an objection. It is crucial from his point of view to create a citizenry that is not disposed to bow and scrape before the holders of high office. The thousands of ordinary people in England who learned to read in order to read the radical pamphleteers of the 1790s and early 1800s had before them unmistakable models of non-deferential behavior. That they revered these writers for their eloquence and courage—and ascribed moral weight to their pronouncements—shows, however, that the emerging democratic culture made room for admiration and attributions of excellence and moral authority. The practical upshot was not to rid the moral world of such things but to dissociate them from the presumptions of hereditary rank.

We have seen that Burke opposed the Revolution and deferred to certain figures of authority, while Paine differed from him on both points. These are differences in *action*. The two men also endorsed somewhat different norms, attributed somewhat different normative statuses to people, and committed themselves to somewhat different material inferences. These are differences in practical and inferential *commitment*. But it now becomes clear that they were also disposed to have different *noninferential moral responses* to the events, persons, and actions of their time. In short, they *perceived* or *experienced* things differently. In terming these responses noninferential, I do not mean to imply that they were incorrigible, beyond the pale of rational scrutiny and revision. I simply mean that they were not arrived at initially as the result of reasoning.

The most famous passage in the *Reflections* is Burke's vivid description of the revolutionaries' treatment of the Queen of France, which calls upon his recollections of having met her when she was "the dauphiness, at Versailles," seventeen years earlier (66). The point of the passage is to portray a scene that any morally competent observer would regard intuitively as horrible. It is, he says in a passage quoted above, "natural to be so affected." The failure to respond noninferentially in this way must, from Burke's point of view, be the result of an improper use of reasoning that effectively strips us of a natural responsive disposition essential to social order.

Paine remarks in *The Rights of Man*, equally famously, on "the tragic paintings by which Mr Burke has outraged his own imagination" and complains that Burke "pities the plumage but forgets the dying bird" (51). Paine is concerned to offer his own picture of the events of October 1789, a picture designed to elicit moral responses unlike Burke's horror at abusive treatment of the Queen. In other passages he portrays the oppressed, above all the poor, as victims of a tragedy. *Their* condition, as he sees it, is horrific. That it is horrific warrants not only pity for them—the dying bird of his metaphor—but also action on our part to change their condition. No less than Burke, he is busy trying to provide occasions for noninferential, as well as inferential, responses on the part of his readers. Both authors buttress or even initiate some of their arguments by saying, in effect, "Look at this! What do you see? Is it not horrible (or excellent)?" The responses they are trying to elicit are noninferential, but they are inferentially connected to moral passions, like awe and pity, and the actions for which they serve as warrant.

While both Burke and Paine are officially prepared to submit their "moral perceptions" or intuitive responses to critical scrutiny, neither of these men finds sufficient reason to abandon them. These perceptions may be noninferential, but they undoubtedly exercise a strong influence over the ethical and political inferences these men make and over the actions they endorse and perform. What is at issue between them is as much a matter of perception as it is a matter of inference and action. It is because their noninferential moral responses to events are to some extent outside of their control and are closely connected with what they care about that the language of conversion can get a foothold here. There is a strong sense in which both men are in the grip of moral visions. Their writings are designed in part to cause others to see what they see. Here is a word-picture of someone—a queen or a pauper—being maltreated. Do you not intuitively take this to be horrible, the violation of something precious? If not, there is no hope for you as an observer of moral affairs. Either you see it, or you don't. Coming to see it is the process of conversion that each side is trying to initiate in its opponents. What is involved in such a conversion? The parties of Burke and Paine appear to be divided primarily on *examples of the excellent and the horrible*.

ETHICAL PERCEPTION

While inferential moves are clearly essential to practices centered on giving and asking for ethical reasons, these moves are not the only sorts of moves made in such practices. There are also noninferential moves in which a participant in the practice responds to something he or she observes by becoming committed to a perceptual judgment or claim. That a judgment was arrived at noninferentially does not guarantee its truth. Many such judgments turn out to have been mistaken. Observation is an indispensable source of knowledge, but a fallible one. Because things are not always what they seem, observers sometimes retreat from their reports about what they saw to reports about how things seemed at the time. Observation reports are no more immune from challenge than claims of other kinds. They can be challenged because they conflict with the observation reports of other witnesses. And they can be challenged on theoretical grounds if someone has reason to suspect that the alleged event probably did not happen, given what else we know.

Observations come into play in ethical reasoning in two different ways. The first way, which is emphasized in the work of Sellars and Brandom, is by supplying straightforwardly factual information that has a bearing on ethical questions when combined with considerations of other kinds. Suppose two witnesses—one sympathetic to Rosa Parks, the other her enemy—observed her being arrested by the Montgomery police. We can imagine them making use of this observation theoretically by constructing competing explanations of the tensions between whites and blacks in Montgomery. We can also imagine them making use of the same observation practically when deciding whether to support or oppose the boycott to which Ms. Parks's action led. Anyone properly situated, whether her friend or her foe, was equally able to observe her being arrested. To report that this had happened to her was not in itself to take a side on an ethical question. Nonetheless, the observational premise has a bearing on an ethical topic in both the theoretical and practical contexts just mentioned—the question of what causes racial tension in the former context, the question of whether one ought to support the boycott in the latter. The observation report is relevant to ethical questions without being explicitly value laden.

It seems clear, however, that some observations land the observer immediately (that is, noninferentially) in an ethically charged or value-laden position. Imagine that you are at this moment witnessing the arrest of Rosa Parks. One of your prereflective, intuitive responses to such a spectacle might very well be to say, "That is unfair!" Another might be to whisper to your companion, "Such splendid courage she shows." If you said these things in appropriate circumstances, you would be making observations that essentially employ evaluative terms. This shows that observations need not be relevant to ethical questions only by virtue of the role they can play as premises in inferences that *lead to* ethical conclusions, for they can also *directly commit* the observer to an ethical stance. This is the second way in which observations can come into play in ethical reasoning.[16] One crucial factor in winning public support for the Civil Rights movement in its heyday was the televised spectacle of demonstrators under attack by fire hoses and police dogs. What viewers saw were acts of brutality endured with moral courage. We need not assume that they saw only streams of water hitting bodies and dogs straining at leashes and then used criteria of brutality and courage to construct inferences from what they saw to reach explicitly ethical conclusions. There is no reason to think that moral responses to such events are normally that complicated. Some ethical terms find their way into the vocabulary in which we observe the events transpiring around us. Some of our observations are ethical perceptions.

Observational social criticism is a major genre of democratic nonfiction, and has done much to shape modern democratic sensibilities. Writers like William Cobbett, Harriet Martineau, George Orwell, James Agee, and Meridel Le Sueur reported what they perceived with their own senses. From them their readers learned what life was like for the rural and urban poor, for the homesteaders of the American West, for the coal miners of England. As Irving Howe once pointed out, in Orwell's case the nose sometimes mattered as much as the eyes and ears. Martineau, being hard of hearing, had to rely on her eyes all the more. At times these writers give us bare facts, leaving us to infer the ethical conclusions to which they are hoping to lead us. Sometimes, however, their observations are cast in an ethical vocabulary that makes explicit their revulsion at the conditions they are reporting and their commitment to the improvement of those conditions. Their stylistic differences reflect the full spectrum of observational diction in ethics, ranging from the most austere to the most morally charged. It would be foolish to think that such artful writers give us nothing but the first thoughts that crossed their minds (noninferentially) when they witnessed the people and events they describe. But the authority of their reports depends on our trust in their reliability as witnesses. A reliable witness is disposed to respond to the conditions he or she is observing by making appropriate noninferential judgments and expressing those judgments appropriately. We do not fault witnesses for expressing those judgments in fresh words that would not have occurred to them immediately, but we do expect them to remain true to what they originally observed (unless, of course, they find sufficient reason to believe that they had been deceived). The cognitive value of an observation report as testimony resides ultimately in the reliability of the original noninferential judgment of the observer.

Agee's descriptive prose in *Let Us Now Praise Famous Men*, with its biblical and liturgical echoes, mainly falls on the morally charged end of the spectrum. Agee always emphasized, however, that Walker Evans's photographs were as essential to the book's observational authority as were his own words. Readers were meant to see through the lens of Evans's camera the same conditions and people Agee had described in prose. Here we have another example of how photographic images enter into ethical discourse. At one level they function in the way most testimony does, as a report of what someone saw. The claim they are used to make is that things looked as the photographic image makes them look. But they also put the public in a position to mimic the eyewitness' moral experience. Once we begin to focus on the role of observation and observation reports in ethics, it becomes plain that the study of ethical discourse must take the full range of media into account, not merely those that are primarily verbal. It is obvious that the printing press, newspapers, pamphlets, books, and now the Internet have all played important roles in modern democracies as vehicles for the exchange of arguments. But the story of ethical discourse in modern democracies is also tied up with the history of photography, moving pictures, radio, and television—with all of the ways in which we have come to record and disseminate our observations of the world.

Observation involves conceptual skills that one can acquire only through initiation into a discursive practice. While some of these skills are inferential, others are not. The noninferential skills are as much the result of training as the inferential ones. We are trained to respond noninferentially to cats with the word "cat" and to dogs with the word "dog." Similarly, we are conditioned to respond noninferentially to instances of cruelty by using the term "cruelty" and to instances of courage by using the term "courage." But the social conditioning of observation does not stop there. Our social practices prescribe not only what sorts of linguistic responses are appropriate in response to what sorts of circumstances, they also often prescribe actions for us to perform if we want our observations to count as those of a reliable observer. Lifeguards are trained to keep a close eye on the swimmers under their protection. They are taught when to reach for their binoculars, how to avoid being distracted by irrelevancies, and what posture improves their chances of seeing what they need to see. New parents have to learn to tell the difference between the ominous and the innocuous sounds that come from a newborn's crib, between a fever that requires medical attention and one that does not, between a bath that is too hot and one that is just right.

Athletes, referees, chefs, poets, painters, musicians, biologists, police detectives, nurses, and journalists all learn their own highly sophisticated perceptual regimens. In all of these areas, individuals invest a great deal of effort to acquire observational skills that many people lack. They learn to make specific kinds of reliable noninferential judgments. Some of these noninferential judgments are clearly normative. The soccer referee can see whether a slide tackle is fair or a foul. The chef can taste whether a dish is properly seasoned. The musician can hear whether a note is on or off pitch. All such judgments presuppose some set of norms, but this does not mean that the person making the judgment needs first to perceive something in a non-normative way and then apply norms inferentially by determining, through a series of steps, whether certain criteria have been met. In fact, if someone does have to move through a series of inferential steps when making a judgment, this is often a sign that he or she has not yet mastered the skills essential to the role.

I once took a three-day course for soccer referees, and got the top score in my class on the final examination, but I have done very little refereeing. I can apply the rules of soccer properly to any given case if I am allowed a moment or two to consider the relevant facts. As a result, I am a reliable retrospective critic of referees. But I am a very poor referee, because my judgments come too slowly to keep up with the rapidly unfolding events of a game. The reason my judgments are too slow is that I reach too many of them inferentially. Good referees are able to make nearly all of the normative judgments they need to make in a soccer match without inferring those judgments from premises. When challenged, of course, they are also able to defend their decisions inferentially. It is a mistake, however, to think that their retrospective arguments reflect the perceptual process that led them to their judgments in the first place.

Ethical theory has thus far given little attention to the ways in which ethical communities inculcate habits of moral observation. Some religious and philosophical traditions have devised stories, catechisms, rituals, and spiritual exercises that shape how their members perceive people, actions, and events. In some communities special regimens of perception are reserved for those who occupy specialized roles of moral authority. Sages, imams, spiritual advisors, rabbis, and confessors are subjected to specific forms of training. If the training is effective, they acquire a structure of appropriate emotions, a set of approved inferential habits, and a collection of reliable observational dispositions for reaching moral judgments. Moral authorities, in turn, train other members of their communities not only to reason in a certain way, but also to see some people or actions in a certain moral light. Periodic retelling of the lives of the saints within a given community can, for example, create a widespread disposition to respond, noninferentially, to particular people or actions by judging or saying that they exemplify courage in the face of persecution. Repeated exposure to narrated instances of courage prepares individuals to know courage (noninferentially) when they see it, at least some of the time. Perhaps the process of moral development includes an intermediate stage, analogous to my soccer example, in which the initiate is able to reach reliable moral judgments inferentially, but still lacks the sage's capacity for noninferential, intuitive response to the relatively clear instances he or she witnesses first-hand.

In modern democracies the exercise of observational moral authority tends not to be restricted to individuals who have undergone a highly specialized course of moral training. Moral authority belongs not to a class of ordained experts, but rather to anyone who proves his or her reliability as an observer and arguer in the eyes of the entire community. Religious and academic subcultures may ascribe special authority to clergy or to ethicists, and that authority may be recognized in particular institutional settings (like the local hospital's ethics committee), but give-and-take in the broader community is officially open to all comers. The authority of moral observation is widely dispersed. Anyone who demonstrates over time the ability to make reliable moral observations is in a position to become recognized as someone to whom others should defer as a reporter of moral affairs. The dispositions of the reliable moral observer are not acquired mainly through highly specialized, professional forms of training. They belong to the ethical life of the people as a whole, and are acquired through the same process of moral acculturation that nearly everyone in the community undergoes—in the nursery, around the dining room table, in the classroom, on the playing field, and so on. The process is formal and purposeful only to some degree, for we learn the skills of moral observation largely by expressing moral judgments in the presence of peers who, though neither parents nor teachers in charge of our development, are no less eager to correct us. The challenge of making observations that can withstand the criticism of ordinary interlocutors is itself a stern instructor, and a suitable one for the formation of democratic citizens.

Explicitly moral observations involve undertaking or acknowledging a prima facie normative commitment to respond to the observed action or event in certain ways—for example, by coming to the aid of the victim of cruelty or by praising the exemplar of courage. Like all observations, they are noninferential, but also potentially defeasible. And they depend on discursive skills of various kinds. Full mastery of ethical concepts involves the acquisition of observational as well as inferential skills. That is, it involves acquiring the ability to respond differentially but noninferentially to the persons, actions, and states of affairs one perceives and to do so in accordance with the norms of the relevant social practice—the practice within which the ethical concepts in question acquire their inferential significance.

How, then, might the standoff between Burke and Paine be resolved through reasoning, if *conflicting* noninferential responses to examples play such a major role? One promising opening, it seems to me, comes in a passage in the *Reflections* where Burke is defending the role of monks in the grand scheme of things. Suddenly, he interrupts his reasoning by expressing heartfelt pity for the lot of ordinary people who work

> from dawn to dark in the innumerable servile, degrading, unseemly, unmanly, and often most unwholesome and pestiferous occupations to which by the social economy so many wretches are inevitably doomed. If it were not generally pernicious to disturb the natural course of things and to impede in any degree the great wheel of circulation which is turned by the strangely-directed labor of these unhappy people, I should be . . . inclined forcibly to rescue them from their miserable industry. (141)

Here we can see Burke having the sort of noninferential moral response that disposed Paine to draw democratic practical inferences. He has seen these people. His intuitive response is an inclination to rescue them. No doubt, they remind him of other oppressed people—American colonists, Irish Catholics, the Indian victims of Warren Hastings—whom he has spent years of his life defending. What holds him back? His assumption about the perniciousness and impracticality of "imped[ing] in any degree the great wheel of circulation." He cannot imagine altering the working conditions of the wretches without threatening the "great wheel of circulation" on which the rest of us depend for our happiness. To attempt to rescue these people from their misery would be to "disturb the natural course of things." It is not within the realm of imagined possibility. Everything we hold dear would collapse.

This assumption goes hand in hand with his conception of democracy as an essentially destructive, leveling force—as the opposite of a culture. Burke cannot imagine an articulate democratic culture evolving among the working people who will soon be gathering to read Paine, let alone among the wretches he would be inclined, in some counterfactual world, to rescue from their wretchedness. For him democracy is simply a deceptive banner carried by the mob, not a civilizing practice capable of shaping individuals into articulate, reasoning beings who care about excellent things and abominate moral horrors. He suspects that it is really the pretext by means of which an urban elite of talented men seizes power for itself in the name of, and at the expense of, the people. There is truth in this suspicion, a truth forcefully restated in our day by Michel Foucault. But Burke's conception of democracy also represents a failure of *imagination*. He and Paine do not only have differing moral perceptions of what is present to them (noninferentially) in their experience, they also differ in how they imagine what is not yet fully present in their experience—the possible futures that may be in the process of becoming actual. If moral perception is a capacity to respond to experiential presence, moral imagination is a capacity to respond to experiential absence, to what is not present (noninferentially) to the senses. Both of these capacities are, of course, inextricably intertwined with the *emotions*—in this case, with fear and sympathy—and with such *virtues* as discernment and hope.[17]

If I am right about the considerations holding Burke back from endorsing democratic commitments, it is clear what the most promising argumentative strategy for his opponents would have been. They needed a way of attacking Burke's picture of the natural order of things that went beyond Paine's style of debunking. Ironically, Burke supplied ammunition for this attack by describing symbolic and ritual aspects of this deferential order in Humean terms as artificial. He referred to these aspects as a "well-wrought veil," as drapery "furnished from the wardrobe of a moral imagination," and as "the fictions of a pious imagination."[18] His most discerning radical readers, like Wollstonecraft and Hazlitt, inferred that any such veil or drapery, being artificial in the first instance, could be reimagined democratically if the wardrobe of *the people's* moral imagination were rich enough.

After *Leaves of Grass* and *Walden*, why wouldn't it be? The need for some sort of cultural covering may belong to human nature, but once we think of this covering as the product of our artifice, we are in a position to take responsibility for it. When we do, we will be embarked on the creation of a democratic culture. And if the social division of labor in the workplace and in the family is something in which we are all complicit, and thus for which we are all responsible, then we had better test Burke's assumptions about the inevitability of miserable conditions for the least well-off. The only way to do this without begging questions is empirical. It is an exercise in social experimentation that involves trying out new arrangements on a limited basis to see what comes of them. It can be carried out, however, only if the people claim responsibility for the condition of society and take action on behalf of those in misery.

Two centuries after Burke and Paine, democratic discourse in the West no longer seems like a revolutionary innovation. Its defenders have an established, if deeply flawed, tradition to point to, and a modest record of social experimentation to argue over. It has its own habits of deference, challenge, ethical perception, material inference, and moral imagination— habits that have now managed to be transmitted, with some success, from generation to generation. But what pride can we take in our accomplishment if the wretches are still with us? Democracy remains an empty ideal so far as they are concerned. Our inaction invites them to mock it—and to affiliate themselves with antidemocratic social forces, including the reactionary theocratic movements now actively recruiting them into terrorist cells. If we now lack Burke's excuses, the responsibility of rescue is ours. The truth of the matter is that we also lack Paine's will. We acknowledge the responsibility in the principles we avow but only rarely in the actions we undertake.

Chapter 10

THE IDEAL OF A COMMON MORALITY

DEMOCRACY came into the modern world opposing the representatives of a feudal and theocratic past. Among its opponents on the global scene today are terrorists, dictators, and crime lords, who use cruelty, intimidation, and extreme poverty to infuse populations with fear and hopelessness. Meanwhile, some multinational corporations strike deals with thugs wherever this advances their economic interests. In return they receive a supply of docile workers, most of them women, willing to work for low pay, as well as the freedom to run sweatshops and abuse the environment as they please. In nominally democratic states, they buy elections, break unions, and attempt to control the flow of information. They strive to create a workforce that is anxious to curry favor with the boss and willing to work for unjust wages. As marketers, they specialize in appeals to greed and envy. What they want is our cash and our tolerance of what they are doing to the land, the ozone layer, their employees, and their customers. Their plan for the latter group, which includes our children, is to turn them into consumers who identify mainly with costly emblems of lifestyles that can be merchandized to specific enclaves—Armani suits and espresso machines for one set, rap music and basketball shoes for another. Ethnic and religious strife abounds, racial divisions deepen, the gap between rich and poor widens, and millions are now enslaved to outlaws who traffic in people.

When international communism fell, pundits were smug enough to declare global victory for democracy. In fact, however, democracy is losing more ground in most settings than it is winning in others. In the era of a globalized economy and widely shared concerns about international terrorism, the need has never been greater for democrats to assert claims and exchange reasons with people here and there around the world who show no sign of being committed to democracy. And yet it seems painfully evident that one thing we cannot take for granted in this effort is the existence of a common morality, a single way of talking and thinking about ethical issues that is already the common possession of humankind. The failure of democratic movements and institutions in settings where fear, hatred, greed, and docility are the rule makes this clear. Oppressed peoples have often been in a position to find democratic ideals attractive from a distance, but those ideals are first of all expressions of a democratic culture. They are meaningless when abstracted from the inferential practices and behavioral dispositions of a people in the habit of trusting one another and talking things through in a certain way. Writing democratic ideals into a constitution or a treaty without first initiating a people into the relevant social practices accomplishes little.

The first part of this chapter defends a piecemeal, pragmatic approach as the only realistic means of building a common democratic morality. Part of the democratic project is to bring as many groups as possible into the discursive practice of holding one another responsible for commitments, deeds, and institutional arrangements—without regard to social status, wealth, or power. Because the entire practice is involved, not merely the ideals abstracted from that practice, a common morality can only be achieved piecemeal, by gradually building discursive bridges and networks of trust in particular settings.

Some philosophers who are friendly to democratic principles think this approach underestimates the moral resources all human beings have in common. They also worry that my approach, despite its affirmation of unconditional obligations and human rights, makes democratic commitments seem too contingent, too relative, too dependent on a particular culture's perspective. They appeal directly to a morality that is already, in their view, the common property of humankind. And this morality, they say, is not simply a common way of thinking and talking about moral issues (that is, a discursive practice) but a body of moral truths that need only be applied to yield concrete moral guidance on the questions currently under dispute. It is a law higher than, better than, the mores of any people. Traditional natural-law theorists take it that we all have cognitive access to this law, at least to some significant degree. If they are right, the democratic project will prove easier than it now seems. Later in the chapter I will argue that they are not. The argument leads quickly into deep philosophical waters, where questions arise about the nature of justification and truth in ethics. These are daunting questions, and will occupy us in the next chapter as well, but they must be faced if the argument is to be pursued very far. The point of the argument, as I see it, is to help us return in the end to the practical tasks of community building with our moral confidence intact. As a character in Edward Albee's *The Zoo Story* says, "Sometimes it is necessary to go a long distance out of your way in order to go a short distance correctly."

WHAT ARE THE PROSPECTS FOR A COMMON MORALITY?

The place is Bosnia, Jerusalem, Zimbabwe, or Chicago. Two groups are in conflict over some issue, and we would like to see the conflict resolved reasonably and peaceably, if possible by appeal to democratic principles. One thing we will want to know is the extent to which the moral vocabularies and patterns of reasoning employed by the two groups resemble or can be made to resemble one another. If the extent of similarity is great, we say that the groups in question have a common morality. If high similarity can probably be brought about by acceptable means, and members of the groups are willing to employ such means, we say that the prospects for a common morality are good. In this context, a question about the prospects for a common morality expresses a practical concern; for democrats on the scene, it may be an urgent one.

The same question can express another sort of concern as well. We notice that not everybody thinks and talks about moral topics in precisely the same way, and we would like to explain the differences philosophically. Nobody doubts that there are differences. But if the differences extend too far, we may feel compelled to become nihilists, skeptics, or radical relativists. The nihilist abandons the idea that there are moral truths. The skeptic abandons the idea that we are justified in believing whatever moral truths there may be. The radical relativist abandons the idea that we can justifiably apply moral propositions to people, deeds, and practices outside of our own culture. With these alternatives in view, good prospects for a common morality would offer consolation. If moral diversity occurs within a single framework globally shared, and the differences in how people think and talk about moral matters can be explained in terms of deeper similarities, then confidence might be restored in moral truth, in justified moral belief, and in the possibility of cross-cultural moral judgment.

Practical and philosophical concerns can arise independently, but they often become intertwined. Doubts about how to respond in practice to a specific instance of moral conflict can induce philosophical reflection on the nature of morality, and philosophical reflection can influence one's practical approach to the conflicts one faces in life. Yet it is worth distinguishing the two sorts of concern when we can. Otherwise, we risk confusion over what ought to count, in a given context, as a common morality. Where we are concerned to resolve a conflict between two groups, we will mean one thing by the prospects for a common morality. Where we are concerned to assess nihilism or skepticism, we will usually mean something else.

Our question about the prospects for a common morality is a daunting one, too unwieldy to answer well. It needs deflation. What makes it so unwieldy? It is really a congeries of questions, each of which can be put in the same words. It needs division. How to proceed? By distinguishing various questions in the congeries, tracing each to the concern that makes it matter, and then seeing whether answers come more easily: by means of analysis, but with pragmatic intent.

It goes without saying that two groups would share a common morality if their ways of thinking and talking about moral topics were exactly similar in all respects. But there is obviously no such pair of groups to be found. In a trivial sense, each group's morality is unique, differing in some respect from everybody else's. No ethical theorist denies this. When we make com-

parisons among moralities, we count some respects of similarity and difference as relevant and others not. Which respects count as relevant in a given
context depends on which concerns motivated the comparison. By the
same token, we count varying degrees of similarity in relevant respects of
comparison sufficient to establish that two or more groups hold a morality
in common. Again, the relevant degree of similarity depends on the concern at hand.

Not everybody thinks and talks about moral topics. Newborns do not,
nor do some of the insane or the comatose. Perhaps some societies do not.
But it goes without saying that for any two people who think and talk about
moral topics, their ways of doing so (in short, their moralities) will resemble
each other in some respects. Anybody's morality resembles everybody
else's in some respects. The fact that all of the moralities are ways of thinking and talking is itself something they have in common, something that
guarantees formal and functional similarities of various sorts. The fact that
all moralities are about roughly the same kind of topic is also something
they have in common, such that the substantive moral commitments of any
two groups can be expected to resemble each other in some degree. Let us
say that a uniformity is some respect in which all moralities resemble each
other closely. Theorists differ on what the actual uniformities are, the
closeness of the similarities in which they consist, and the relevance they
have to various practical and explanatory concerns. They do not differ on
whether there are any uniformities.

"Moralities," as I have been using the term, are ways of thinking and
talking about a particular kind of topic. Even if I were to specify precisely
what a way of thinking and talking is, the term "moralities" would still be
vague, given the fuzziness of the boundaries around the topics we call
moral. For the most part, the vagueness is tolerable, and for two reasons:
first, because it rarely comes into play, since most cases we discuss are some
distance from the fuzzy boundaries; and second, because when it does come
into play, it is usually resolved by context. When we confront an alien
group and its strange ways of thinking and talking, we take our initial cues
from the habitual uses of the term "moral" that are embedded in our ordinary discourse at that time. If some of the topics the strangers think and
talk about exhibit overall similarity to the topics we habitually call moral,
we can, for most purposes, safely designate their way of thinking and talking about those topics a morality. Overall similarity is itself a vague notion,
consisting as it does "of innumerable similarities and differences in innumerable respects of comparison, balanced against each other according to
the relative importances we attach to those respects of comparison."[1] The
vagueness derives from the fluctuation of relative importance across contexts. We can resolve the vagueness, if need be, by specifying which respects
of comparison are important given our current concerns.

Suppose our concern is practical and quite limited. We ask what the prospects are for a common morality in Belfast. What we want to know, ultimately, is whether the conflict among the Catholics and Protestants who live there can be settled through democratic discussion and what can be done to achieve that end. The scope of the relevant comparison-class is relatively narrow. We need not concern ourselves, in this context, with distant tribesmen, ancient Egyptians, or humanity as a whole. What respects of comparison matter? Mainly, the differences most responsible for creating or sustaining the conflict and the similarities most likely to facilitate settlement.

Most of us are concerned about many different moral conflicts. It would be fortunate if the theorists could show that all such conflicts are capable of being adjudicated in terms of one set of moral uniformities. (Presumably, these will involve either a very large set of truths about particulars together with some certain means of knowing them or a small set of principles together with some determinate means of subsuming cases under them.) Then we could say that there is a common morality in a very strong sense— a sense relevant simultaneously to a wide range of practical and philosophical concerns. Many theorists have tried to prove the existence of a morality that possesses these powers of adjudication. But even if they have all failed, as I suspect they have, and even if they will all continue to fail, as I suspect they will, it remains possible to proceed piecemeal. This might mean taking each conflict as it comes and trying one's best to find the means of adjudication in whatever makes the moralities in question similar. (If that fails, one can always attempt the more painstaking approach denoted by the term "conversation" in chapter 3.) The possibility of adjudication in a given case does not depend on a guarantee of adjudication in all cases. And it seems likely that adjudication will succeed in more cases if it allows itself to rely on local similarities, not merely on the ones that are also global uniformities. Of course, not all types of similarity will help, and some will hinder.

Some moralities are *akin* to each other. Kinship is a special kind of similarity, the kind brought about by sharing a common history of development up to a certain point and then separating. Protestantism and Catholicism are members of the same ethical family. Their moralities branch off from the same stem. Their kinship helps determine the character of conflict in Belfast, both for good and for ill. It engrains many close similarities in vocabulary, attitude, and inferential commitment that could turn out to be useful in adjudication. It also means, however, that each group defines itself over against the other, thus hardening whatever differences there might be. In comparative ethics, as in folk-genealogy, a family tree is especially rigid where branches diverge from the stem.

The moralities of two groups in conflict are *parallel* to each other just in case they have developed along closely similar lines without branching

from the same stem. Many rural societies have parallel moralities structured around a hierarchical system of roles. The moral world consists of
fathers, mothers, eldest sons, younger sons, daughters, friends, neighbors,
strangers, enemies, and so on. To know how to respond to others in such
a world, you need to know what roles you occupy, what roles they occupy,
and what relations obtain between your roles and theirs. Duties and entitlements are all specific to roles and pertain mainly to the distribution of
honor, which is recognized as the dominant good. Conflicts between such
groups often start with an insult, move through a cycle of violent vengeance, and end at times in a negotiated settlement designed to limit disproportionate bloodletting. Parallel distinctions between strangers and enemies, accompanied by parallel rules requiring hospitality for the former,
can keep such groups out of conflict over prolonged periods. But parallel
commitments to honor as the dominant good and to vengeance as a means
of protecting it can keep conflict going.

Two groups with independent histories and relatively dissimilar moralities can come into conflict when one conquers or subjugates the other. If
Antonio Gramsci and Michael Walzer are right about such cases, the dominant group virtually always tries to justify its dominance to the oppressed.[2]
In the course of making its justificatory arguments, the dominant group
introduces its victims to unfamiliar moral concepts, principles, and ideals
that, when applied in new ways, may be used by the oppressed themselves
to justify rebellion. Let us say that when this happens, one morality acquires *Gramscian similarities* to another. Anticolonial and revolutionary
struggles are nowadays defended mainly in terms of borrowed ideas, detached from one morality and grafted onto another. Gramscian similarities
can increase rather than decrease the likelihood of conflict between two
groups. They have also, however, significantly increased the overlap among
existing moralities in a way that is beneficial to the prospects of democracy.
One unwitting result of imperialism and global capitalism is that many
emerging groups on the periphery of the world-system justify themselves
in a language of rights, liberation, and self-determination—a modern European scion grafted onto to many varieties of native stock. The moralities
of these groups are to some extent parallel with each other while each has
Gramscian similarities with the moralities of the colonial powers.

Cases of moral conflict, then, come in kinds. I have mentioned only a
few, but even this limited sample suffices to show that the task of adjudication takes very different forms from one kind of case to another. Anybody
who really cares about resolving moral conflicts had better proceed on an
ad hoc basis, keeping the scope of comparison as narrow as can be. This
policy maximizes the similarities available for adjudicatory work on each
occasion by minimizing the number of groups to be compared. If we knew
in advance what the moral uniformities are, we would always be in a posi

tion to call on them, if they are relevant, no matter what the setting. That would be welcome. But we can get by without such knowledge, for practical purposes, trusting that whatever uniformities there are will necessarily turn up locally among the similarities obtaining in the case at hand. If we are unable to tell which are which, so what? In real-life adjudication, it does not matter. The more similarities that help, the better.

JUSTIFICATION

Philosophers have their own reasons for wanting to tell which from which. One reason is that they would like to know what resources there are for responding to moral skepticism. Those resources would be very powerful indeed if there were a common morality in something like the "very strong sense" mentioned in the preceding discussion. Any set of uniformities among moralities able to adjudicate all moral conflicts should also be able to refute all moral skeptics. It would do so by showing skeptics not only that they are justified in holding moral beliefs but what some or all of those beliefs are. I reject moral skepticism. I affirm that many of us are justified in holding some of the moral beliefs we hold. Whatever reasons make the skeptic feel compelled to deny this leave me unswayed. Yet affirming that many of us are justified in holding some of the (nontrivial) moral beliefs we hold is not the same thing as affirming that somebody has established a set of (nontrivial) moral beliefs that any human being or rational agent, regardless of context, would be justified in accepting. Doubting the latter claim does not, therefore, make me a moral skeptic, as defined here. It only makes me skeptical of one especially grandiose attempt to refute moral skeptics.

Behind my doubt is the idea that being justified in believing something—being entitled to believe it—is a status that can vary from context to context. Because one context differs from the next, not everybody is justified in believing the same claims. This goes for nonmoral and moral claims alike. Quine was justified in believing Gödel's Theorem, that a complete deductive system is impossible for any fragment of mathematics that includes elementary number theory. Euclid believed no such thing, though through no fault of his own. Quine, unlike Euclid, was trained to think and talk in the language of twentieth-century logic, so he was able to entertain claims Euclid did not have the conceptual wherewithal to entertain, including some that figure in the reasoning that led Gödel to his Theorem. Quine also had the advantage of access to Gödel's proof itself, which was not worked out until 1931. The proof served as Quine's evidence, justifying his acceptance of its conclusion. Once he had studied the proof and understood it, Quine would not have been entitled to disbelieve its result. If you could travel backward in time to visit Euclid, and you induced him to entertain the conclusion of Gödel's proof without otherwise altering his epistemic context, he would not be justified in believing it. If he disbelieved it, you would not fault him by judging him unjustified, for you understand that two people can be justified in holding different beliefs, given the vocabularies, styles of reasoning, and evidence available to them in their respective contexts.

Now consider Ignazio Silone's novel, *Bread and Wine*, which is set in Italy in the 1930s.[3] The novel's protagonist is Pietro Spina, a socialist who returns from exile, disguised as a priest, to live among the peasants of his native Abruzzi, whom he hopes to organize into a revolutionary movement. The Abruzzi peasants adhere to a morality of the type described briefly in my discussion of parallel moralities among rural groups. Despite its assimilation of certain Christian beliefs about unconditional obligations, it remains for the most part a morality of role-specific duties and one in which honor dominates other goods. Spina has travelled in circles the peasants have not. His epistemic context differs from theirs. He entertains claims couched in moral vocabularies they do not know, his reasoning follows different patterns, and he therefore disbelieves much of what they believe.

Spina's time among the peasants changes him. It, too, contributes to the context of his ethical reasoning. He therefore abandons some moral beliefs he held in exile, acquiring others in their place. But he does not simply convert to the peasant morality. Silone is no Romantic. He is careful to show that someone with Spina's life history would not be entitled to accept certain peasant beliefs—for example, about the causal efficacy of using ox horns to ward off evil, the moral consequences of resignation to fate, or the just treatment of unmarried pregnant women. Spina rejects such beliefs and is justified in rejecting them. He does not, however, fault the peasants for believing what they believe. They are justified in believing even many of the falsehoods they believe, given the limitations of their context.

It may be, of course, that Silone was giving an untrue picture of who was justified in believing what in Italy circa 1935. What matters, for my purposes, is simply that there are differences among moralities like the ones described in Silone's novel and that they make the kind of difference to our judgments about entitlement to ethical commitments that I have been suggesting. Silone's novel illustrates the fact that there are important differences in what moral beliefs people in various contexts can justifiably accept. Could it not still be, however, that there are *some* (nontrivial) moral claims everyone is justified in believing, a common morality for philosophers? For all I have said so far, it remains possible that there are, though I assign a low probability to the prospects of showing that there are.

I have been speaking of "everyone." It would seem that the scope of comparison could not be broader. Yet not every human being need be included. In this context, we may ignore newborns, the insane, and the comatose. To exclude them, let us say that we are confining our attention to rational users of norms. Can we not, then, define rationality strictly, so that anyone who fails to accept certain moral claims falls outside of the comparison class? We can indeed. We can achieve a similar result by defining the term *moral* narrowly, so that human rights or respect for persons as ends in themselves are the only moral topics. Nothing prevents us from defining such terms as we please. But if the definitions are arbitrary, designed solely to exclude potentially relevant counterexamples to the theses we are testing, they accomplish nothing.

The only relevant notion of rationality would be one that we could use in making defensible normative judgments about the various human beings who actually engage in moral reasoning, ourselves included. It is perfectly conceivable that we will someday be justified in deviating significantly from the beliefs we are currently justified in believing. It would therefore be foolish to define rationality in such a way that our future selves, with all their possibly good reasons for deviating from our path, would nonetheless be disqualified by definition from the class of rational agents. Our future selves deserve better treatment from us. So do Abruzzi peasants, distant tribesmen, and ancient Egyptians. Anybody—past, present, or future—might turn out to be less than fully rational, human beings being what they are. But our normative verdict on someone's rationality cannot sensibly be settled by definition a priori, and it needs to proceed in any case by attending to details of context, with the burden of proof falling to the prosecution.

I see no way of telling what new moral vocabulary, style of reasoning, or form of evidence might turn up next, either in the findings of anthropologists and historians or in the handiwork of creative geniuses and moral reformers still to come. Nor do I see a way of telling in advance how such novelties will affect the list of commitments people are entitled to accept. Euclid would have been very surprised to be told about Gödel's Theorem. Kant would have been very surprised to be shown the bearing of Einstein's theory of special relativity on the status of some claims he deemed universally justified. Neither Euclid nor Kant had any way of knowing how later developments would alter the standing of the relevant commitments. We are in no better position in ethics. Perhaps our distant ancestors had no way of anticipating some of the considerations that make us diverge from their moral conclusions. Chances are, our distant descendants will discard some moral claims that we find deeply intuitive or that a clever philosopher has "proven" to the satisfaction of his followers; which claims, we cannot say. Humility is the best policy.

Humility, I say; not skepticism. For I am not denying that we are justified in holding various moral beliefs, as moral skepticism does, by the definition assumed here. How can we claim to be justified in believing something and also suitably humble in what we claim to know? By saying that being justified is relative to context and that the relevant features of context might change in unexpected ways. Until they do change, we remain justified in believing certain things. The possibility of change is not yet a reason to abandon any particular belief. But it is a reason to consider our moral knowledge fallible. If being justified in believing something depends on context, and context can change, perhaps for the better, then we should do our best to remain open to the possibility. Democratic discursive practices are designed to hold themselves open in this way.

The line of reasoning that counsels humility with respect to our own beliefs also counsels charity toward strangers. People from distant times or places are apt to believe some things we deem false, even if they and we are equally justified in holding our respective beliefs. That is what we should expect if being justified in believing something is a contextual affair. Unless we are prepared to give up our own beliefs at the points of conflict, we shall have to say, on pain of self-contradiction, that some of their beliefs are false. But unless we can show that they have acquired their beliefs improperly or through negligence, we had better count them as justified in believing as they do. And while we are at it, we had better consider the possibility that their context affords them better means of access than we enjoy to some truths.

Earlier I remarked that being justified in believing a claim is not the same thing as being able to justify it or to justify believing it.[4] The idea requires further explanation here. There are many legitimate ways of acquiring beliefs. Accepting the conclusion of a sound justificatory argument is only one of them. Many beliefs are acquired through acculturation. I say, with Wolterstorff and others, that we are justified in holding such beliefs, except in those cases where we have adequate reason to doubt or reject them or where for some other reason (like culpable neglect of evidence) we are not doing our best as inquiring minds.[5] I say, with Wittgenstein and others, that many of these beliefs are such that we would not know how to justify them in a noncircular and informative way even if we tried, and that life is too short for us to supply arguments in support of many of them. I say, with C. S. Peirce and others, that if we ceased taking the vast majority of them for granted, far from enhancing the capacity to think scrupulously, we would lose the capacity to think at all. It makes sense to say that we can be justified in accepting a belief acquired through acculturation even in the absence of a justifying argument. It is unreasonable to demand justifying arguments across the board. Skeptics have been wrong in making this demand, their opponents wrong in trying to meet it.

Justifying a claim, unlike being justified in believing one, is an activity. The result of the activity is a justification. Let us say that a justification of the claim that P is an answer to the question, Why believe that P?[6] If the answer is successful, we say that the claim in question is justified. In what, then, does the success of a justification consist? In eliminating relevant reasons for doubting that *P*. What reasons for doubting *P* are relevant and what suffices for their elimination? That depends on context, in particular, on the people to whom the justification is addressed. Call the class of such people the justification's *audience*. Reasons for doubting *P* are relevant if they prevent or might prevent an epistemically competent and responsible member of the audience from being justified in believing that *P*. Relevant reasons for doubting *P* have been eliminated when everyone in the audience is justified in believing that *P*.

We sometimes speak of justifying a claim *to* someone, either oneself or someone else. In such cases, the audience of the justification is specified. I justify a claim to myself when I construct or rehearse an argument that makes me justified in believing it. I justify a claim to someone else, *S*, when I construct or rehearse an argument that makes *S* justified in believing it. More often, we speak simply of justifying a claim, allowing context to specify the audience. Philosophers have long tried to discover, in abstraction from any context in particular, what conditions a successful justification of a moral claim ought to satisfy. In doing so, they have usually attended exclusively to features of ethical justification qua argument, and often ended in puzzles about the status of first principles or the logical transition from nonmoral premises to moral conclusions. We are now in a position to see why they have met with little success. If my analysis is correct, abstraction from context in a theory of justification is bound to end in frustration. Justifications are answers to why-questions of a certain sort. As such, they are dependent on context: first, because conversational context determines the question to which a justification counts as an answer and thus the sort of information being requested; second, because conversational context determines a justification's audience; and third, because a justification's success can be appraised only in relation to its audience, including their relevant reasons for doubting and the commitments they are entitled to accept.[7]

Now consider a bit of ethical fiction. Someone proposes a candidate for the title of supreme moral principle. Being newly minted, it is not already accepted currency, and we have our doubts. So the question arises, Why believe it? A brilliant philosopher constructs a justification. The justification consists of a relatively complicated argument, but not so complicated that the philosophically astute cannot follow it. Suppose that, after diligent study, we accept its premises as true. We find no mistakes in the proof, no reason to question its validity. We are prepared to say, as Gödel's fellow logicians were in the case of his Theorem, that the justification is successful. We therefore come to accept the new proposal as the supreme moral principle, and we are justified in believing it true.

I do not deny that this could happen. I do want to insist, however, on the importance of considering the limits on who might plausibly be expected to look upon such a justification as a reason for accepting its conclusion. Otherwise, we shall be tempted to exaggerate what will have been shown by the justificatory argument. Let us distinguish a justification's intended audience from its actual audience. Whatever a justification's intended audience may be, its actual audience cannot extend beyond the class of people who understand the vocabulary in which it is cast and have mastered the patterns of reasoning required to follow it. The limits of an actual audience are not set; they can be expanded by pedagogical means or by missions to the heathen. But it is worth reminding ourselves that the actual audiences of all justifications produced so far in human history have been limited, the philosophical justifications especially so. Saying to ourselves that we are addressing our justifications to all rational agents does not by itself affect what other people are justified in believing. We can increase the membership of a justification's actual audience only up to a point.

The democratic ethical analogue of Gödel's Theorem, even if it were justified to the satisfaction of all living philosophers, would not thereby become the common moral property of humankind. Many people, including Abruzzi peasants and (in all likelihood) members of the great philosopher's own family, would still recognize no real reason to accept it. The reasons there would be for accepting it would be other people's reasons, not theirs. It would be uncharitable on our part to fault them for not accepting it, just as it would be uncharitable of Quine to fault Euclid for failing to anticipate Gödel or Kant for failing to anticipate Einstein. If Pietro Spina's favorite peasant or my nonphilosophical relative accepts a belief at odds with our newly justified supreme moral principle, they might still be justified in believing what they do. Our proof has no place in their epistemic context.

There is another sense in which our justifications ought to be addressed to a limited audience, a sense related to the policy of humility. Future generations will find themselves in epistemic contexts unlike ours. We do not know what the respects of dissimilarity will be, so we cannot know what their reasons for doubting will be or what they will be justified in believing. It follows that we cannot know how successful our justifications will be for them. So it would be foolish to address our justifications to the audience of *all* rational agents, regardless of time or place.[8] All we would accomplish by doing that would be to make the success of our justifications impossible to determine, thereby making the question of success pointless. We know from experience that justifications are fallible. To require that they be infallible to count as successful is to misunderstand the indispensable role they play in our lives. Justifications are successful if they eliminate relevant reasons for doubting. The reasons future generations might have for doubting, being necessarily unknown to us, hardly count as relevant in our context.

No logician is tempted to reject Gödel's Theorem simply because there are some people who would dismiss Gödel's reasoning as gobbledygook. Yet many philosophers devote serious attention to the question of what one would say to the philosophically inclined Nazi. Their worry seems to be that if one cannot justify one's moral beliefs to the imaginary Nazi, then one is not justified in holding those beliefs. The worry might derive from any number of sources. One of these might be a tendency to confuse being justified in believing something with being able to justify it; another might be the mistaken idea that successful justifications must be addressed to a universal audience. We are now concentrating on the latter, so perhaps we should ask whether any philosopher seriously intends to say that Nazis are morally competent. If not, why should a Nazi's reasons for doubting be considered relevant to the appraisal of our moral beliefs? People whose lives prove them unwise, and especially the extremely vicious, are obviously not good judges of moral truth. Nazis are extremely vicious in ways that can be expected to corrupt their responsiveness to our reasoning. If *they* doubt our moral conclusions, we should expect to have trouble in persuading them by rational argument. Their reasons for doubting need not be eliminated before we consider ourselves justified in rejecting their beliefs as false. Of course, if we found ourselves strongly tempted by Nazi reasoning, we might feel that we needed to refute their conclusions in order to be justified in holding ours. But this wouldn't necessarily be a matter of persuading actual Nazis, who might dig in their heels and spit on our perfectly valid refutation.

My mother is no philosopher and no Nazi. She may not be a competent judge of sophisticated philosophical proofs, but she is a wise woman, a competent judge of moral truths of many kinds. So if she doubts the truth of a supposedly supreme moral principle because it obviously conflicts with her settled convictions about specific cases, her reasons for doubting may be relevant to the principle's epistemic status. If the principle conflicts with her view of the wrongfulness of murder, for example, that is something the philosopher will need to take into consideration. The task will be to explain how she could have come to believe a claim incompatible with the truth of the proposed principle. Her competence as a judge makes her reasons for doubting relevant. When other people differ with us over the truth of matters they are competent to judge, we often need to justify our own view by explaining how they came to believe a falsehood. Failure to work out a good explanation of their apparent error sometimes leaves us unjustified in believing a claim we would otherwise have adequate reason to accept. It may be more reasonable for us to change our minds on the disputed point than to assume that our disputants believe wrongly and let that go unexplained.

Truth

The epistemologist's interest in refuting or assessing skepticism is only one of the concerns that make philosophers debate the prospects of a common morality. It is one thing to ask whether there are moral claims everybody is justified in believing or whether we need to seek a universal audience for our justificatory arguments. It is another to ask whether there are moral truths, whether in calling them true we can sensibly mean more than that they are true *for us*, or whether some moral claims apply to everybody. Doesn't the contextual view of justification defended in the previous discussion require me to answer these questions negatively by committing me to a relativistic conception truth?

The first thing to be said is that I have used the notion of moral truth liberally throughout this chapter. Far from denying it, I have been presupposing it. For example, at one point I said that Pietro Spina *disagreed* with the Abruzzi peasants on what constitutes just treatment of unwed pregnant women. In saying this I meant to imply that Spina and the peasants entertain the same claim, that the claim is either true or false, and that in disagreeing on the issue either he believes a falsehood or they do. So long as Spina remains committed to his view on that topic, he is logically committed to rejecting the conflicting peasant view on that topic as false. Nihilists, who dismiss the very idea of moral truths, could not describe a case of moral conflict in this way. They would have to redescribe it without relying on the notion of moral verity, most likely construing Spina and the peasants as mistaken about the nature of their conflict. But I see no adequate reason for redescribing it in that way, let alone one that derives from my contextualist account of justification.

Someone might want to claim that the peasant view is true for them, just as Spina's is true for cosmopolitan Italian socialists. If this means only that the peasants accept their view as true and Spina accepts his view as true, there is no point in discussing the claim, for it merely paraphrases what I have already granted. We do sometimes use the expression "*P* is true for *S*" as a synonym for the expression "*S* believes *P*" or "*S* accepts *P* as true." What if the claim were intended to imply that we should take "*P* is true" to mean "*P* is true relative to *M*," where *M* names the morality of the speaker? This would make the claim more interesting, but it would also put it in conflict with my account of moral diversity. At no point have I introduced a relativist conception of truth in describing a moral conflict. Nor would I want to do so.[9]

A relativist conception of truth erases disagreement among groups rather than making it intelligible. To say that Spina's view is true relative to his group's morality and that the peasant's view is true relative to theirs would imply that both views could be right simultaneously and that neither party's view entails rejection of the other's. But Silone does not describe the relation between Spina's moral beliefs and the peasants' in this way. If he did, his novel would lack moral tension: Spina would be neither genuinely at odds with the peasants on the issues where he eventually holds his ground, nor able to learn from them on matters where he eventually changes his mind. I stand with Silone in holding that there are such cases of genuine moral conflict in life. Nazis and I differ in many respects. We belong to different groups, each with its own way of thinking and talking about moral topics. I also differ with Nazis in another respect, for I reject various moral commitments they accept, including their view of what constitutes just treatment of Jews. The fact that we have different moralities should not be allowed to obscure the equally important fact that we disagree about the moral truth. If I am right about justice, then the Nazis are wrong. Using a relativist conception of truth to redescribe our differences would be to dissolve the conflict in which we take ourselves to be engaged.

Yet have I not been defending a version of relativism throughout the first two subheadings of this chapter? And if so, is it not too late for me to be distancing myself from a relativist conception of moral truth? The first section does imply that the prospects of adjudicating a moral conflict between two groups depend upon what their respective discursive practices are like. Say, if you like, that this makes adjudication relative. The second section does argue that being justified in believing a moral claim is a relational status and that the success of a justificatory argument is a contextual affair. Say, if you like, that this makes both entitlement and the activity of justification relative. But do not assume that these doctrines commit me to a relativist conception of moral truth, for they do not.

Adjudication, justification, and truth are distinct concepts, requiring separate explications. The first two are very closely related, for the obvious reason that rational adjudication of a moral conflict typically involves offering justifications to people in the hope of changing what they are justified in believing. If justification (in both senses) is relative, it should not be surprising that adjudication is, too. None of this implies, however, that every concept we encounter in ethics (and other cognitive endeavors) will exhibit a similar relativity. My claim is that the concept of truth does not. It would therefore be misleading to summarize my position as the claim that morals are relative. "The thesis of moral relativism," like "the thesis of a common morality," is not in fact a thesis at all, but an intersection in conceptual space where distinct ideas tend to be run together and need to be disentangled before thought can responsibly proceed.

When Spina believes that a given practice is unjust and the peasants disbelieve it, either he accepts a falsehood or they do. It is not possible for a claim and its negation to be true simultaneously, in ethics or anywhere else. But when Spina believes the claim and the peasants believe its negation, they can both be justified. Similarly, Spina can be justified in believing a moral claim at one point in his life and justified in rejecting precisely the same claim at a later point, whereas the truth-value of the claim has remained the same all along. By considering these possibilities, we can see how differently the concepts of truth and justification behave. It is because they behave so differently that it makes sense to combine a contextualist account of justification with a nonrelativist account of moral truth. This is exactly what my version of pragmatism does. In the next chapter I will respond further to the worry that there is something paradoxical about this combination of theses.

Contextualist epistemology is compatible with the idea that there is a moral law in this sense: an infinitely large set consisting of all the true moral claims but not a single falsehood or contradiction. Being infinitely large and including truths cast in myriad possible vocabularies we will never master, this set boggles the mind. We will never believe, let alone be justified in believing, more than a tiny fraction of the truths it encompasses. Most of them are inaccessible to us—and therefore not truths it would be wise for us to pursue. If the God of the philosophers exists, he believes them all, and is justified in believing them all, but nobody else could come close.[10] Notice that the moral law in this sense is not a morality in the sense under discussion earlier in this chapter. It is merely a set of truths, not a way of thinking and talking (that is, a discursive social practice).

There is no harm in granting that there is a set of truths like this, provided that we rigorously avoid treating it as something we could conceivably know and apply. This conclusion ties in closely with what Mark Johnston has called "the practical element" in pragmatism. This, he says, "is best presented as a normative claim, the claim that our interest in the truth should always be a practically constrained interest, an interest restricted in principle to accessible truth (at least to this and probably to something more practically accessible)."[11] Notice that this normative claim, as Johnston nicely formulates it, is not a definition of truth. It does not define truth as inherently accessible, so it does not lead to the problems associated, for example, with Dewey's definition of truth as warranted assertibility. I am happy to grant that accessible truths are not the only truths that there are. But Johnston's formulation does have strong implications for the governance of our cognitive and justificatory practices. The main reason for confining attention to accessible truths is simply that taking an interest in truths that are inaccessible is at best a waste of time and at worst a source of seriously confused cognitive strategies. One need not define truth as Dewey did to support this conclusion.

THE HIGHER LAW AS AN IMAGINATIVE PROJECTION

Human beings are less than perfect in knowledge and virtue. It should not surprise us that they construct imperfect moral codes. The beliefs their codes embody are all too often untrue. We therefore honor women and men who, in the name of moral truth, have risked their lives in defiance of imperfect codes and the powerful people intent on enforcing them. But much of what these heroes say in their own defense is hard to believe. Antigone, in the Sophoclean tragedy that bears her name, defended her defiance of the mortal Creon by invoking the "unwritten and unfailing laws" of the gods. Speaking of the decree that her brother be left unburied, she said: "For me it was not Zeus who made that order. Nor did that Justice who lives with the gods below mark out such laws to hold among mankind."[12] Thomas Jefferson, declaring independence from British tyranny, appealed to the "laws of nature and nature's God." The God in question was deism's. The laws, which he held to be self-evident, were largely Locke's. Martin Luther King, Jr., writing as a Baptist preacher from a Birmingham jail, claimed that an "unjust law is no law at all" and defined an unjust law as "a human law that is not rooted in eternal and natural law." His authorities for this doctrine were Augustine and Aquinas, but the content of the moral law he envisioned derived from the personalism he learned while earning his doctorate at the Boston University School of Theology: "Any law that uplifts human personality is just. Any law that degrades human personality is unjust."[13]

The theologies of Antigone, Jefferson, and King could hardly be further apart: pagan polytheism, Enlightenment deism, and Trinitarian Christianity. When they claim that there is a law higher and better than the artificial constructions of human society, they differ drastically over the source and substance of that law. Is there anything left of the idea they had in common once the hubris and the dubious metaphysical trappings are stripped away? Let us see.

F. P. Ramsey once hypothesized that laws are "consequences of those propositions which we should take as axioms if we knew everything and organized it as simply as possible in a deductive system."[14] Ramsey's hypothesis belonged to philosophy of science. The laws he had in mind were laws of nature in the natural scientist's sense. He held this conception of lawhood only briefly, in March of 1928, but in 1973 David Lewis revived and revised it. Lewis's modified version does not rely on the idea of what we would know if we knew everything:

Whatever we may or may not ever come to know, there exist (as abstract objects) innumerable true deductive systems: deductively closed, axiomatizable sets of true sentences. Of these true deductive systems, some can be axiomatized more *simply* than others. Also, some of them have more *strength*, or *infor-mation content*, than others. The virtues of simplicity and strength tend to con-flict. Simplicity without strength can be had from pure logic, strength without simplicity from (the deductive closure of) an almanac. Some deductive systems, of course, are neither simple nor strong. What we value in a deductive system is a properly balanced combination of simplicity and strength—as much of both as truth and our way of balancing will permit. (*Counterfactuals*, 73; empha-sis in original.)

An ideal deductive system achieves a best possible combination of simplic-ity and strength—if not the one and only best combination, one of the combinations tied for first place in the ranking of all such systems. The notion of an ideal deductive system allows Lewis to reformulate Ramsey's explication of lawhood: "a contingent generalization is a *law of nature* if and only if it appears as a theorem (or axiom) in each of the true deductive systems that achieves a best combination of simplicity and strength" (*Counterfactuals*, 73; emphasis in original).

It should be possible to develop similar conceptions of lawhood for eth-ics. Imagine an infinitely long list including all of the true moral sentences that human beings could possibly devise.[15] Assume that these sentences can be organized into innumerable deductive systems of moral truths. Assume further that these, like Lewis's systems of empirical truths, achieve varying degrees of simplicity and strength. Of them, one or more achieves a best combination of simplicity and strength. Now we can define *the moral law*. It is precisely those generalizations appearing as theorems or axioms in each of the best moral systems.

To employ the notion I have just defined, you need not be a theist. But you do need to have an active imagination. First, you need to imagine the possibility of all the various conceptual improvements that could be made in the ways we think and speak about moral matters. Second, you need to imagine the possibility of the various sentences that could appear in the resulting language games. I do not mean that you need to be capable of knowing in what all of these possibilities consist. There are too many of them for that—infinitely many, in the case of the sentences. And there is no way of knowing the conceptual improvements we could adopt until somebody invents or discovers them. If we knew in what any possible im-provement consisted, we could instantaneously make it actual by changing our ways. The point of the present exercise is to imagine the full range of possible improvements not yet actualized, while remaining agnostic about the details. In addition to performing these acts of imagination, you need to accept the standard apparatus of deductive logic and grant that systems of moral sentences can be more or less simple and possess varying degrees of strength. Finally, and most importantly, you must be prepared, as I am, to apply the concept of truth to moral sentences.

Call the concept of the moral law just defined the minimal version. The minimal version is metaphysically austere. Its definition explicitly treats the moral law as an imaginative projection. The improvements it projects above and beyond the already existing moral codes are indefinite. To speak of the moral law in this sense does not commit us to a view of what those improvements would look like. It merely holds out for the possibility that improvements are possible. Of course, many philosophers are less parsimonious than this. By adding commitments not presupposed by the minimal version, you can get increasingly controversial versions of the concept. If you are a theist, for example, you might wish to add that God is the author of the moral law. You might go on to describe the moral law as promulgated providentially, as an ordinance of divine reason for the common good. By making these additions, you would be taking the moral law closer to what Aquinas calls the "eternal law."

Even so, the two notions will not be identical. To see why, consider a remark Lewis makes when elucidating his concept of scientific law: "Imagine that God has decided to provide mankind with a *Concise Encyclopedia of Unified Science*, chosen according to His standards of truthfulness and our standards of simplicity and strength" (*Counterfactuals*, 74). A published version of the moral law would be like Lewis's imaginary *Encyclopedia*. God's standards of truthfulness would prevail in that He, being omniscient, would be in a position to edit out all traces of falsehood. But our standards of simplicity and strength, vague as they are, would also constrain the resulting system. Because these standards tend to conflict, it is likely that our need for reducing complexity to manageable levels will lead to significant sacrifices in strength. In contrast, there seems to be no such concession to human standards in Aquinas's concept of the eternal law.

The Thomistic eternal law satisfies God's standards of truthfulness, but what standards of simplicity and strength does it satisfy? In a word, God's. Aquinas would not presume to know what such standards are, but he does at various points seem to assume that the eternal law is maximally strong. No moral truth falls outside it. It forbids all of the sins there could ever be, including those secreted away in the human heart. It encompasses all of the moral truths and none of the moral falsehoods. Is the eternal law also maximally simple? Assuming that God is omniscient, there is no need for simplicity in this system. An omniscient being would know every detail of an infinitely long almanac of moral truth. If the eternal law is simpler than that, the simplicity must come without loss of strength. If God prizes simplicity for its own sake, then the eternal law may tentatively be defined in terms of the generalizations appearing as axioms or theorems in each of the simplest of the maximally strong deductive systems of moral truth. How simple that might be we have no way of knowing. God only knows, if anybody does.

We have seen that the minimalist definition of the moral law does not presuppose commitment to theism. We can similarly strip the theology from the Thomistic concept of the eternal law by settling for the tentative definition just given while dropping the requirement that the standards to be satisfied are God's. Even if we accepted this formulation as our definition of the eternal law, it would remain distinct from the moral law in my nontheological senses. The reason is this. If a system is the simplest of the strongest systems of its kind, it is not necessarily a system that achieves a best combination of simplicity and strength for systems of that kind.

Suppose a logic professor has given you several deductive systems of moral truths and the assignment of judging some of them ideal in the two senses just distinguished. The method for finding the simplest of the strongest systems is to begin by isolating the strongest and then to select the simplest of those. The method for finding a best combination of simplicity and strength is to begin by isolating systems that are both simple and strong in high degree and then to select the ones that strike an ideal balance overall. It is possible but not necessary that the two methods would yield the same result. Given sufficiently various systems to pick from, the second method is likely to pick out systems that are simpler and weaker than the first.

What good will the minimalist definitions of these notions do me? They will allow me to use such phrases as "the moral law" and "the eternal law" in good conscience should I ever want to do so. Hereafter I shall know what I mean when I echo Sophocles, Jefferson, or King and refer to a law higher and better than the codes of my peers. I will know how to mean what I say about that law without meaning too much.

Why preserve these locutions at all? They have long been a rhetorically effective means of emphasizing that the all-too-human codes we confront in society are always likely to include moral falsehoods and conceptual deficiencies. This fact makes room for conscientious objection to such codes. It underscores the need for social criticism. It assures us that a lonely dissenter or critic, taking a stand against the crowd or the powers that be, might be right.

Admittedly, the same point can be made without the concept of a higher law. What matters most in this context is the underlying concept of truth and resistance to any reductive definition of it. If truth were a function of what the powerful dictate or what one's peers accept—or even what we, in our humble epistemic condition, are justified in believing—then we would have less reason to give dissidents a hearing or to entertain the possibility of becoming critics ourselves. But truth, I have claimed, cannot be reduced to any of these things. On the minimalist reading, the rhetoric of a higher law is little more than an imaginative embellishment of the gap between the concepts of truth and justification, between the content of an ideal ethics and what we are currently justified in believing. It evokes a picture of what some of our codes would be if they were perfect. It thereby gives the project of discovering particular imperfections an imaginative ideal to strive for. The picture is less diffuse than the image of an infinitely long list of true moral sentences, and more inspiring than the image of an ideal moral almanac. Since our codes are sometimes expressed systematically in law-like form, the image of a higher law encourages striving for something of the same kind but better.

Natural-law and divine-command theories become mystifications whey they assume that an ideal system or its axioms can function—or is already functioning—as *our criterion* for deciding which moral claims are true.[16] How could we ever know that the standard we were actually applying belonged to the ideal system? To know this would be to know that there was no possibility of improvement in our cognitive capacities and inferential commitments. Being finite and aware of the long history in which our fallibility makes itself manifest, we have reason to believe that even if we had achieved *the* ideal system, we could never be justified in believing that we had. To believe this would close our minds to the possibility that further rational revision of our moral outlook might well prove necessary. We have no way of knowing what it would be like to be at the end of ethical inquiry.[17] At any time, the ideal system (if there is such a thing) might differ in some respect from what we justifiably believe.

This does not add much to my earlier remark that truth and justification are distinct, that the two concepts behave differently—in ethics, as elsewhere. To say that some of the moral propositions we are justified in believing might not be true is to remind ourselves that no matter how well we now think and talk about moral topics, it remains possible, so far as we can tell, to do better. To strive for moral truth as finite beings conscious of our finitude is to keep that possibility in view, to keep alive the struggle for this-worldly betterment of our commitments, not to wish for a final revelatory moment, a moral philosopher's eschaton.

The *Concise Encyclopedia of Ethical Truth* is merely the philosophical imagination's variation on three themes: the notion that the totality of moral truths would not embrace a contradiction, the hope that the fraction of it we care about is not infinitely complicated, and the realization that it cannot be reduced to what we already know. It is not a handbook anyone can use, even at the end of inquiry. Therefore, it is not something we can expect to do justificatory work when we are trying to resolve disputes. Our practice of thinking and talking about moral topics will continue as long as we do. It will not be brought to conclusion by the discovery of an ideal moral system.

Chapter 11

ETHICS WITHOUT METAPHYSICS

NOTHING in the previous chapter entails striking the locutions of Sophocles and King from the lexicon of pragmatic democrats. When a great poet or social critic decks out the distinction between justification and truth in a memorable image, and by speaking of a higher law empowers a search for the betterment of our actual codes, the pragmatic philosopher is wise to leave well enough alone. But some readers might worry that my pragmatic approach to the prospects for a common democratic morality and my metaphysically austere treatment of "the moral law" would, if accepted and fully understood, have a strongly demoralizing effect on the culture of democracy.

They might argue that democratic culture needs something more solid to depend on for the justification of its commitments than I am supplying when I refer to the ethical life of a people. Perhaps they will suspect that my discussion of moral truth and the moral law leave ethical discourse without something sufficiently determinate or independent of us to be true *of*, to be *about*. For I have taken norms to be creatures of discursive social practices. Moral principles, according to chapter 8, make explicit the material inferential commitments implicit in the practical reasoning that transpires when people hold one another responsible for their actions. Given that the only sense of "the moral law" that I have been able to take on board is an idealized imaginative projection, it is hardly the sort of thing one could appeal to directly in justifying an answer to a moral question. As a regulative ideal, it names something that always transcends our grasp. Have I not, then, implicitly admitted that our reason-giving cannot succeed here and now in holding our attitudes answerable to anything more than our own subjective creations?

The previous chapter anticipated these questions by opposing all attempts to reduce moral truth to a function of what the powerful command, what one's peers accept, what one is justified in believing, or what one is warranted in asserting. But perhaps these attempts to distance myself from Dewey are more perplexing than reassuring, given my points of agreement with him. For in previous works I have affirmed Dewey's claim that there is no explanatory value in the notion of truth as "correspondence" to the "real." I have not changed my mind on this point. I remain committed to Dewey's criticisms of such "realism" as metaphysical in the pejorative sense, as a bad set of props for our practices.[1] And throughout this book I have repeatedly echoed his pragmatic insistence that democratic ideals and principles depend for their conceptual content and justification on contingent social practices. My position may therefore appear to alternate paradoxically between realism and pragmatism—two positions that have long understood themselves to be at odds.

A preliminary rejoinder to these concerns can be cast in terms of the distinctions I have introduced in the first three chapters of part 3. This rejoinder would claim that the standard menu of options in moral philosophy results from conflating a series of distinctions that need to be carefully observed:

- between obligations or rights that we attribute to everybody, regardless of role, and obligations or rights that everyone already has reason to acknowledge;
- between being justified in believing something (in the sense of being entitled to believe it) and being able to justify a claim to someone else (in the sense of producing an argument that successfully undermines someone's relevant reasons for doubting it);
- between being able to justify a claim to one's actual audience and being able to justify it to all rational beings;
- between a claim that is justified (in the sense that no relevant reasons for doubting it remain standing within a given discursive context) and a claim that is true;
- between a claim that one is entitled to accept and a claim that is true;
- between the moral law understood as a regulative ideal projected by an active philosophical imagination and a morality understood as a way of thinking and talking about moral topics (a discursive practice);
- and, finally, between the idea that the terms "true" and "false" are appropriately used in reference to moral claims and the idea that a particular theory of truth, such as natural-law realism, offers an informative explanation of their significance in moral language.

If these distinctions are well drawn and have the significance I have attributed to them, the standard array of options in moral philosophy will have to be reconceived. We are not faced with a choice between two package deals, one of which is metaphysically realist with respect to truth, anticontextualist with respect to justification, and cosmopolitan with respect to rights and obligations, the other being metaphysically antirealist with respect to truth, contextualist with respect to justification, and parochial with respect to rights and obligations. A principal objective of chapters 8–10 has been to pick apart these packages, thus putting us in a position to take or leave their various contents as we see fit.

Of course, this analytical work does not by itself explain how the obligations, rights, virtues, and other normative statuses attributed to people by the members of democratic communities can be assessed *objectively*. Both the statuses and the norms governing their attribution, I have argued, are creatures of a social practice. How, then, can our attempts to apply and perfect the norms also be objective? If the norms are constituted by our social interactions, what sense can there be in saying that everyone in our society might be wrong about what those norms are and what they imply?

Is Truth-Talk Metaphysical?

Let us return for a moment to the distinction between truth and justification. When we attribute knowledge to someone, we take that person to believe something that is true, and we take him or her to be justified in holding that belief. But someone who believes a truth might not be justified in doing so. And someone who is justified in believing something might well turn out to have accepted a falsehood. Despite being joined together in our concept of knowledge, the notions of truth and justification can readily swing free of each other. This is what we should have expected. If the two concepts had the same entailments in all contexts, it would have been redundant to combine them by saying that knowledge requires belief that is *both* justified *and* true.

Dewey held that truth, like justification, is a relative concept. He identified it with warranted assertibility. Other pragmatists have identified it with utility—with what is useful to believe, which is also a relative notion. But if truth is not a relative concept, must it not be an absolute one? And if it is an absolute concept, don't I need to account for its absoluteness by defining truth as correspondence to the real, the very kind of theory I have praised Dewey for criticizing?[2] I am happy to say that truth is absolute if this is understood strictly as a remark about how the term "true" behaves in our language. But I still hold that defining truth as correspondence has no explanatory value. Furthermore, I have no other definition of truth to offer in its place.[3] I propose neither to analyze the concept into more basic ideas, nor to specify the content of truth attributions in what philosophers call an implicit or a contextual definition.[4]

It might be objected that this refusal to define truth leaves me unable to make clear, in a sufficiently positive way, what I take truth to be.[5] If I accept neither the metaphysical realism of correspondence theory nor the truth-relativism of the familiar pragmatic theories, it seems that I still need to say in positive terms what I think truth is. It is not enough to say simply that it is not identical with justification. I must show, at the very least, that my denials leave open the possibility of an acceptable philosophical alternative. Fair enough. But what kind of philosophizing is needed here?

Let us begin by taking note of a few standard uses of the term "true," and asking what sort of account tells us what we need to know about the meaning of the term in these contexts.

One familiar use of the term "true" may be called the *inferential* use, as when we declare that the conclusion of a valid inference is true insofar as its premises are true. The second I will call the *acceptance* use of "true," as in the sentence, "The claim that racial segregation is unjust is true." A speaker who asserted this sentence would be expressing acceptance of the claim named by the that-clause. The third use may be called the *equivalence* use, as in the remark, " 'Courageous acts deserve praise' is true if and only if courageous acts deserve praise." A fourth use is the one Rorty calls the *cautionary* use, as in the sentence, "We may be justified nowadays in believing *P*, but *P* might not be true."[6]

Realists typically focus mainly on the equivalence use, construe it as expressing a substantive, nontrivial relation of correspondence, and then try to account for other uses of "true" in terms of that. I do not reject the equivalence use. In fact, I think it is of great practical and theoretical value. My complaint about realism is that I do not see any explanatory value in the notion of correspondence that realists lay over it. If the explanation is genuinely needed, it had better be more intelligible than the thing being explained; yet I find substantive notions of correspondence much less clear than the concept of truth they are meant to explain. So I cannot credit them as explanations, as informative answers to a question about the concept of truth. The harder realists work at trying to elucidate what it is for a proposition to correspond to reality, the murkier things get.

To play its role in the wanted explanation, reality must be taken to come in units that are apt counterparts for the propositions that are supposed to correspond to them. But what might these units be? And how can we specify them without introducing a fatal equivocation into the notion of reality? If the notion of correspondence is going to capture the absoluteness of truth, "reality" will have to mean something like the world as it is in itself— a metaphysical conception if there ever was one. But this conception seems ill-equipped to become involved in a relationship of correspondence that could explain substantively what property one attributes to a proposition by calling it true. To be the sort of thing to which a proposition could correspond, reality has to be divided up into units that bear some resemblance to propositions. Specifying what these units are appears to involve placing reality under a description. But how can one do this without losing one's theoretical grip on the independence of the world?

The metaphysics of realism wavers between two conceptions of reality, one of which is designed to capture the absoluteness of truth in a theory of the independence of the world, the other of which is designed to find units of a kind to which propositions could correspond. To give up the latter is to abandon the project of explaining in the realist's terms what the (substantial) property of truth is. To give up the former is to begin the process in which realism mutates into the antirealism of idealists like Berkeley and pragmatists like Dewey, for whom correspondence to reality becomes coherence among ideas, beliefs, or assertions that we accept. Hoping to avoid both of these outcomes, the realist typically tries to have it both ways with "reality," while coping with recurring charges of equivocation. Meanwhile, the antirealist firmly grasps the inferential and acceptance uses of "true," and tries to get by without the independence of reality prized by realism. But this move appears to undermine the cautionary use of "true" and to collapse truth into justification. In the more aggressively postmodern versions of antirealism, justification is then collapsed into power, thus yielding the reduction of truth to power.

Hilary Putnam responds to these troubles by focusing on the acceptance use of "true" and then enriching the notion of acceptance so that he can account for other uses of the term as well. Taking inspiration from another classical pragmatist, C. S. Peirce, Putnam argues that truth consists neither in plain old acceptance nor in currently justified acceptance but in idealized rational acceptance.[7] This move allows truth and justification to be related—in that rational acceptance is a near-synonym of justified belief— without the two concepts being identical. Putnam's account is superior to most acceptance-oriented explanations of truth because it does some justice to the cautionary use of the term. It is therefore less reductive than Dewey's notion of truth as warranted assertibility. If forced to choose between Putnam's Peircean definition and Dewey's, I would certainly select Putnam's. But Horwich, Michael Williams, and others have made telling arguments against it, so I cannot accept that either.[8] The notion of idealized rational acceptance turns out to be too close to that of justified belief. If we assimilate truth to idealized rational acceptance, we will not be able to account adequately for the differences between truth and justification. In particular, we will lose our grip on the possibility that there may be some truths we could never, even with access to all of the evidence, capture within a net of justified beliefs. As Mark Johnston has put it, there is something narcissistic about the resulting conception of truth. The truth about some subject matter pertains to that subject matter, yet on Putnam's view even the truths natural science teaches us about the properties of atoms are actually about what *we* would be justified in believing under ideal conditions. Johnston rightly asks, "How did *we* get into the picture?"[9]

The moral that Arthur Fine draws from these difficulties is that attempting to *define* truth as a "substantial something" has proven to be a fruitless enterprise.[10] He does not claim to have refuted the whole lot of definitions currently on offer, but neither does he find sufficiently good grounds for committing himself to any of them. He therefore suspects that there was something wrongheaded about trying to cast our theorizing about truth in this form. It remains unclear, he thinks, why the truth theorists think truth needs an explanation of the sort they are seeking. Once you have figured out how the term "true" behaves in all of the relevant contexts, what remains to be explained? We should content ourselves with accounting for its characteristic nonphilosophical uses—the ones that do not presuppose a metaphysical picture.

Fine is not denying the intelligibility, value, or legitimacy of the concept of truth. His attitude toward truth—he calls it "the natural ontological attitude"—is permissive with respect to ordinary usage and offers no philosophical grounds for hesitating to speak of truths in any domain where ordinary speakers apply the term "true" to claims and beliefs. Given that ordinary speakers routinely refer to moral claims as true or false, the natural ontological attitude would entail no invidious distinction between ethics and other domains manifestly concerned with discovering truths. Truth-talk in ethics, as in science, is intelligible without help from the metaphysical theories that purport to explain it.

Fine does not himself offer a theory of the concept of truth. But a number of theories are compatible with what he calls the natural ontological attitude. These theories differ on whether truth is a property, on whether propositions are the primary bearers of truth, and on various other topics, but they can all be classified as forms of "minimalism." Johnston defines minimalism in general as the view that whereas "ordinary practitioners may naturally be led to adopt metaphysical pictures as a result of their practices, and perhaps a little philosophical prompting, the practices are typically not dependent on the truth of the pictures. Practices that endure and spread are typically justifiable in nonmetaphysical terms." While metaphysicians often present their pictures as an essential buttress for our practices, "we can do better in holding out against various sorts of skepticism and unwarranted revision," according to the minimalist, "when we correctly represent ordinary practice as having given no crucial hostages to metaphysical fortune."[11] Minimalism can be given a pragmatic twist if one adds that the wanted justification of our practices is to be found, if at all, "in showing their worthiness to survive on the testing ground of everyday life."[12] My own approach to the concept of truth is both minimalist and, in the sense just specified, pragmatic. I prefer to call it *modest pragmatism*. It rejects any form of pragmatism that proposes, immodestly and unwisely, to reduce truth to some form of coherence, acceptance, or utility.

In *Understanding Truth*, Scott Soames takes a minimalist approach (in Johnston's sense) to the analysis of truth. He follows Alfred Tarski and Saul Kripke in claiming that "truth is not a contentious metaphysical notion" and that "a successful analysis of it should not be laden with controversial philosophical consequences."[13] He takes the equivalence use to be the key to the meaning and value of the concept. The utility of the notion of truth, according to Soames, derives largely from the fact that "the content of the claim that a putative truth bearer is true is equivalent to that of the truth bearer itself." But this is already plain to anyone who reflects on nonparadoxical instances of the equivalence use of "true." No metaphysical gloss is required:

> [S]weeping, philosophically contentious doctrines about reality and our ability to know it cannot be established by analyzing the notion of truth. Examples of such doctrines are the thesis that a statement is true [if and only if] it corresponds to a mind-independent fact that makes it true and the rival thesis that a statement is true [if and only if] it would be rational for beings like us to believe it under ideal conditions of inquiry. These are independent philosophical doctrines that cannot be derived from an adequate analysis of truth. (231)

Soames proceeds to survey and criticize several varieties of minimalism (232–51). He rejects so-called "redundacy" theories, which oppose the idea that truth is a property of any sort. His own version of minimalism aims to improve on the detailed semantic analyses of Tarski and Kripke. He ends up with a view that is not distant from Horwich's minimalism.[14]

It would be tedious to go into the details of these theories here. For our purposes, there is no need to declare one of them correct. All that matters is that they represent a plausible and promising theoretical alternative to the metaphysical approaches from which Soames distinguishes them. If some version of minimalism is correct, then we do not have to choose between realism, antirealism, and no theory at all. On the question of which variety will prove strongest, I remain agnostic. My claim is that recent developments in the philosophy of language have vindicated the plausibility of pursuing a nonmetaphysical approach to truth, an approach that makes the notion of truth seem like an inappropriate focal point for large-scale cultural angst. As Soames points out, the minimalist positions that he and Horwich defend do not by themselves entail an answer to the question of whether "normal indicative sentences containing evaluative terms" can be true or false (250). But they supply no reason for suspecting that such sentences lack truth-value. So minimalism as such does not appear to undermine the "objectivity" of ethical discourse. What it does, instead, is to put the burden of proof on those who hope to show that ethical discourse does not involve genuine truth-claims. It also provides encouragement to anyone who, in keeping with the spirit (but not the letter) of Dewey's pragmatism, hopes to reduce his or her metaphysical commitments to a minimum. The metaphysics of realism is more likely to render the concept of moral truth precarious than to save it from its cultured detractors.

Minimalism is not an attempt to debunk or reform ordinary usage. I favor preserving all four uses of "true" that I have distinguished; they are no less intelligible in ethical contexts than in scientific contexts. In particular, I want to preserve the cautionary use. Because I am sure that some of our currently justified beliefs must be false, but do not know which ones these are, I want to preserve a spirit of self-critically open-ended inquiry. Drawing attention to the gap between truth and justification helps in this effort, because it cautions against cognitive complacency. No less than the realists, I hope that I might someday hold more true beliefs and fewer false beliefs than I do now. In light of the equivalence use of "true," what this comes to is the hope that (with respect to important topics) I shall believe P if and only if P.[15] Does it add something to say that we should strive to bring our beliefs into correspondence with the facts (including the moral facts)? If taken nonmetaphysically, this seems to add nothing. If the point of realism is simply to stress that whether a given proposition is true or false depends not only on its conceptual content, but also on the objects, events, properties, relations, values, and so forth being referred to, then again I have no problem accepting the point.[16] I just do not see that this gets us beyond the basic implications of the equivalence use. The equivalence involved in "it is true that P if and only if P" may be trivial in the logician's sense. But it already serves as a sufficient reminder that inquiring into the truth or falsity of P involves directing one's attention to what P *refers to* and holding one's beliefs and claims answerable to that.[17] The metaphysics of correspondence hardly makes the reminder more impressive.

I have been using "realism" strictly as the name for a metaphysical theory that defines truth as correspondence to reality. But, as Horwich says, "The term 'realism' is an over-used, under-constrained piece of philosophical jargon, and one can no doubt invent senses of it such that the minimalist approach qualifies either as 'realist' or 'anti-realist' " (*Truth*, 56). It is not hard to see why David Fergusson calls me a realist.[18] In the first place, I do *employ* the term "true" in the way the realist does in ordinary moral discourse—cautionary use and all. Second, I share the realist's suspicion of what Johnston calls philosophical narcissism. Third, I hold that the truth can transcend our ability to know it, even under ideal conditions of inquiry. And fourth, I accept that whether a belief is true or false depends in part on the objects, events, properties, relations, values, and proprieties to which reference is made. If that is all it takes to be a realist, then I am one, too. This appears to be all Scott Davis means by the "minimal realism" he attributes to Davidson, and it is all Sabina Lovibond seems to mean by the "realism" she attributes to Wittgenstein in *Realism and Imagination in Ethics*.[19] Many people mean more by the term "realism" than that, so I have been reluctant to adopt the label. But it is a mistake, in any event, to get hung up on the labels.

You can have the concept of moral truth and an ethos of fallibility and self-criticism, it seems to me, without adopting a theory that makes moral facts or "the moral law" capable of explaining what it is for true moral propositions to be true. Some realists think a definition of truth is needed to keep the democratic culture of moral seriousness and its spirit of self-criticism intact. I see no evidence that this is so. I fear that persuading people to consider a metaphysical theory essential to democratic culture invites them to give up on that culture when the theory comes to seem unpersuasive. Citizens are better advised to keep their commitment to democracy free from the unresolved disputes of the metaphysicians.

Part of my motivation for favoring a minimalist (as opposed to an antirealist) version of pragmatism is the hope of vindicating the continued use of "true" in moral contexts by freeing it from metaphysical interpretations of its significance that have proven exceedingly difficult to sustain. The concept of moral truth entered modern philosophy like one of the knights who clang their way awkwardly through Robert Bresson's *Lancelot du Lac*— wearing enough protective gear to be rendered clumsy and vulnerable. There is no point in rearranging the armor if it ends up being too heavy to wear. The solution is to retain the concept of truth while shedding the weighty armor the metaphysicians have designed for it. Pragmatism prefers to travel light.

Thus far, I have been discussing the meaning of "true," and I have accounted for this strictly in terms of the uses of the term, without feeling compelled to reduce its meaning to a definition. I have followed Soames and Horwich in beginning with the equivalence use, while acknowledging that other versions of minimalism have started elsewhere. A complete account would cover all of the paradigmatic uses.[20] An acceptable form of minimalism would not merely catalogue uses at random, but would rather confer a sort of explanatory order on those uses, thus rendering them more fully intelligible. As an approach to the concept of truth, minimalism proposes to provide this intelligibility without reducing it to a definition. It also promises to shed light on what makes the concept useful—a sticking point for redundancy theories.[21]

Does modest pragmatism provide an answer to the question of what truth is? I am inclined to grant that truth is some kind of property but not that it is a naturalistic property. Truth does not belong, in my view, to the furniture of the natural world (as conceived by natural science). So we cannot provide an account of it by turning our attention to some feature of the natural world and describing empirically in what that feature consists.[22] The concept of truth is normative. It belongs to practices in which we assess claims and beliefs as possessing or failing to possess a sort of status.[23] What status do we attribute to a claim by declaring it true? The status that is preserved in valid inference, as the inferential use of "true" indicates. This is the same status that is implicitly imputed when we endorse a claim, as the acceptance use of "true" shows. This status does not involve a relation to evidence, so it is not relative to epistemic context. Truth pertains to the conceptual content of a claim, not the epistemic responsibility of the person who accepts or asserts it. Truth, or accuracy, is an objective status as well as a normative one. We attribute this status willy nilly to the beliefs we currently accept, in accordance with the acceptance use of "true." But whether our beliefs and claims actually enjoy the status of being true is not up to us.[24] Believing that someone has a particular obligation, right, or virtue does not make it so.

Truth-talk has a place wherever we take the subject matter under discussion—and not simply the evidence pertaining to it—as the object of our inquiry. By engaging in truth-talk, we implicitly view our subject matter as something we might get wrong, despite our best cognitive efforts. Adopting this orientation toward our subject matter is the antinarcissistic core of "the natural ontological attitude" and "minimal realism"—"realism" in the nonmetaphysical sense. "Realism" in the metaphysical sense combines this praiseworthy attitude with a dubious doctrine that is meant to legitimate it. Fortunately, the attitude needs no such legitimation.

"Accuracy with respect to the subject matter" does not by itself explain what the property of truth is. It is, in most contexts, an acceptable paraphrase for "truth." But truth is the more basic concept. We know what it means to speak of an accurate proposition because we know how to use the term "true." No near-synonym of truth gives an informative answer to the question of what status is attributed to beliefs and claims in truth-talk. "Correspondence to reality" is no better. Is it a rough synonym for truth? Yes. Does it clarify the property we are trying to understand? No.

Most ordinary people, including many children, exhibit a practical grasp of what truth is in their day-to-day speech. It does not appear to be a difficult thing to acquire. How do they acquire it? By mastering paradigmatic uses of "true." Not by having the property explained to them metaphysically. Their teachers and parents do not introduce the term "true" to them by defining it as accuracy or correspondence. These near synonyms come later in the learning process, and they don't explain much once they arrive. Building a metaphysical theory around these words, hoping to make them perform explanatory tasks they cannot perform on their own, is to seek clarification in an area of philosophy infamous for its lack of clarity. The order of explication needs to move in the opposite direction—out of the bog where philosophies whole have sunk, onto the solid ground of actual language use. Truth-talk is not an implicitly metaphysical affair, standing in need of metaphysical articulation and defense. It is an aspect of ordinary language use, to be made sense of in terms of an empirically oriented linguistic theory.

The main targets of modest pragmatism are a dubious realist project of legitimation, which aims to identify and firm up the metaphysical basis of truth-talk, and a similarly dubious project of delegitimation that reacts against realism in the wrong way. The latter project includes "postmodern" attempts to unmask truth-talk as implicitly committed to realistic meta-physical ideas that are demonstrably incoherent. Postmodernism of this sort often begins with a high quotient of moral seriousness. Its political instinct is to align itself with ordinary people against the system of power relations that surrounds them. But the narcissistic and self-refuting impli-cations of the antirealist metaphysics it adopts eventually reduce the critical enterprise to a somewhat farcical academic melodrama. The central char-acters are ironical dandies and their natural enemies, the self-righteous, truth-loving prigs. But what if ordinary truth-talk has been innocent of metaphysics all along? Then disclosing the incoherence of metaphysics might deflate the pretensions of a few metaphysically obsessed professors, yet it hardly promises to uncover a nasty secret about the civilization as a whole. The pragmatic remedy is to drop the identification of truth with power, cut out the narcissism that goes with it, and recover the democratic instinct that fueled the critical project in the first place.

THEOLOGY AND METAPHYSICS: TRUTH, OBLIGATION, AND EXCELLENCE

It might be objected that pragmatism, pursued as a general antimetaphysi-cal strategy within philosophy, is inherently antitheological. But this objec-tion ignores the fact that there are numerous theologians and theologically committed philosophers who hope to free themselves and the culture as a whole from the compulsion of pursuing metaphysics in the pejorative sense.[25] Their work is not only intellectually adventurous and rewarding, but also an apt reminder that theological commitments need not be seen as a subset of metaphysical commitments.

The etymology of "meta-physics" is apt to cause confusion in this con-text. My opposition to metaphysics is not intended to rule out a class of claims simply because they refer to something *beyond* or *above* the ontologi-cal framework assumed in the natural sciences.[26] To see what I am getting at here, consider Timothy Jackson. As a Christian thinker, he affirms (a) that God the Father Almighty made heaven and earth; (b) that Jesus Christ, His Son, is the perfect embodiment of divine love; and (c) that Christ's love of others is intrinsically good, indeed the most important intrinsic excellence there is. These are theological claims. Jackson's meditations on (b) and (c) in particular plumb their ethical significance with a degree of eloquence and insight uncommon in recent Christian ethical writing. I would not imagine that these claims came into Jackson's life as conclusions of a metaphysical argument about how to construe the objectivity of discur-sive practices.

But Jackson does have such an argument to offer. He proposes "a correspondence theory of truth" and "an objectivist theory of value."[27] These doctrines imply (d) that a substantial metaphysics of correspondence is implicit in both Christian and secular practices of making truth-claims in ethics. He therefore concludes (e) that the primary principle of ethics, which enjoins love of the actual neighbor, would be transformed into mere narcissism if removed from the context of a realistic metaphysics. Solidarity, according to Jackson, is impossible outside "a community that fosters objective self-scrutiny and attention to others as they are in themselves." For this reason, he fears that abandonment of realism would eviscerate civilization itself, rendering likely a "decline into the . . . war of all against all."[28] Putting the same point more delicately, he cites "the danger that liberal virtues will not be sustainable under an ironist sky." We "can't cultivate kindness in the first place, we don't know fully what it means to be kind, without attending to the intrinsic worth (and vulnerability) of others."[29] *Attending to* the intrinsic worth of others must not be reduced to a process in which we *project value* onto them. As one can tell from the references to solidarity and irony, Jackson is criticizing Rorty in these passages. He offers realism as an antidote to Rortian narcissism.

What in Jackson's critique of Rorty does a modest pragmatist have a stake in denying? Only such claims as (d) and (e) and the fear of civilizational collapse associated with them. The dispute has nothing to do with claims (a) through (c) unless one grants the truth of (d), which the minimalist does not. In defending (d), Jackson presupposes that we all are bound to accept something like his metaphysical conclusions on pain of incoherence, simply because we use the term "true" as we do. But no one, including Jackson, has yet shown that a metaphysical theory is implicit in ordinary truth-talk. As for (e), Jackson's arguments are merely variations on the same themes. His arguments for both (d) and (e) make a controversial assumption. They assume (f) that metaphysical realism and antirealism are the only alternatives worth considering.[30] Because the latter alternative is obviously narcissistic, he infers that the former must be preferred by anyone who wishes to avoid narcissism. But if minimalism is correct, then (f) is false, and the arguments for (d) and (e) collapse. I have tried to show that minimalism is perfectly compatible with a wholehearted rejection of a narcissistic attitude toward truth.

Jackson and I both endorse the cautionary use of "true." This is what expressively reinforces the emphasis we both give to epistemic humility and fallibility. It might be supposed that Jackson's realism provides a stronger emphasis on fallibility than I am able to provide because it makes room for the hope for full-fledged correspondence.[31] My problem is that I do not yet understand what we are supposed to be hoping for beyond believing *P* if and only if *P*. Jackson sees other-regarding, self-sacrificing love as the single most important value in ethics. While I see no need to give primacy to one form of excellence in this way, I have no trouble acknowledging the value and importance of such love. In the domain of ethics, valuing truth and loving others do typically require us to clear our minds of illusions generated by prejudice and selfishness; to appreciate the needs, pain, and concerns of other people for what they are; and to adjust our evaluative beliefs and claims accordingly.[32] Jackson affirms this, and so do I.

Let us now turn to another example of theological metaphysics—namely, Robert Merrihew Adams's book, *Finite and Infinite Goods*.[33] Like Jackson, Adams is concerned to account for the objectivity of ethical discourse in Christian terms, but he expresses this concern mainly in connection with his accounts of excellence and obligation. While the concept of love plays a major role in the former, Adams is more concerned with love of the good (erotic love in the broad sense) than with self-sacrificial love per se. His theory of excellence identifies it with likeness to the transcendent Good, which he interprets theologically. He offers a social theory of obligation, but one that includes essential reference to God's commands. A main benefit claimed for these theories is the especially strong sense in which they buttress the objectivity of ethics. If obligation is a matter of what God commands, this makes it "more unqualifiedly objective than human social requirements" (256). If excellence is resemblance to God, then it is a property that "things have or lack objectively, independently of whether we want them to or think they do" (18).

Consider first the distinction Adams draws (15–18) between the question of what the terms "obligation" and "excellence" *mean* and the question of what obligation and excellence *are*. The former question is about what conceptual role the terms play. But in his view what obligation and excellence *are* must be stated metaphysically. Adams and the pragmatist are not at odds on the conceptual issue. What the terms mean in a given language depends on how they are used in that language. It is not a metaphysical matter. Individuals who differ over what we are in fact morally obligated to do and which persons, acts, and things exhibit moral excellence are able to communicate successfully with one another because they use the relevant terms in roughly the same ways. The same holds for individuals who differ over what the nature of obligation or excellence is. Disagreement over this metaphysical question need not prevent us from understanding what it means when a speaker attributes an obligation or a moral excellence to someone. One can know what such utterances mean, and even know how to appraise them as true or false, without knowing what obligation and excellence, as such, are.

To clarify the contrast between semantics and metaphysics, Adams uses the example of water, as discussed by philosophers like Putnam and Kripke. People who are ignorant of chemistry are ignorant also of the nature of water, of the kind of stuff it really is, but many of them have mastered the uses of the term "water" that arise outside of the laboratory. They still know what it means when you ask them for a glass of water or when you say that the water you are swimming in is warm. "But," says Adams, "the nature of water is to be discovered in the water and not in our concepts" (15). Similarly, even if we were all unable to say what the nature of obligation is, we might still be able to say what the term "obligation" means (a semantic question). We might even be able to reach agreement on what a given person's obligations are (a moral question). Where, then, is the nature of obligation to be discovered, if not in the use of the term "obligation"? Clearly not in chemistry, or in physics, or in some other natural science. "Metaphysics" is Adams's term for systematic inquiry into "natures" that fall outside of the scope of the sciences. The metaphysician of ethics does for such topics as obligation what the chemist does for water. Is this activity benign, or is it metaphysical in the pejorative sense?

It is clear that the chemist's question about the nature of water is about what water is made of, what constitutes it. What constitutes water is a good question.[34] We have known for millennia to look for the answer in the water. Where else would one look for its constituent parts? And we have in recent centuries made great progress in improving the methods we use when carrying out such investigations. We are now confident that water is made of hydrogen and oxygen, two parts to one. But the metaphysician's question about the nature of obligation is not about what it is made of, because obligation is not a kind of stuff. So what is being asked here? Where and by what means are we supposed to look for an answer?

The theory of obligation that Adams presents in chapter 10 implies that we should be looking for an answer by attending to certain aspects of social life and our experience of it as individuals involved in social relationships. This is where a pragmatist would expect an illuminating answer to be found. Social relationships tend to impose requirements on those involved in them. Valuing such a relationship "gives one, under certain conditions, a reason to do what is required of one by one's associates or one's community" (242). An obligation, Adams says, is a reason of this kind. Thus, obligations are constituted by social relationships, although not in the same sense that the right mixture of hydrogen and oxygen constitutes water. This just means that social relationships and the activities they involve *give rise* to obligations. This is what it means to say that obligations are creatures of social practices. They consist in a kind of reason that arises in valued social relationships that impose requirements on their members. Some relationships are wrongly valued, however; some are "downright evil." So we distinguish between obligations that are undermined, as reasons, by defects in the relationship they involve and obligations that can withstand rational, fully informed criticism of the relationship they involve. The latter are morally valid obligations. This strikes me as a very promising theory. Up to this point, I see nothing in it that a pragmatist should find objectionable. If it is metaphysical, it must be in some innocuous sense. I would prefer to call it simply philosophical.

If a personal God exists and chooses to interact with us, then our relationship with God, according to the theory just given, should be capable of giving rise to obligations. If God issues commands to us, these will qualify as a kind of social requirement. The theory holds that the goodness of the social bond is essential to giving obligations their force. A central claim of theism is that divine commands arise within the context of a continuing relationship that can be recognized as good—as excellent—by the human beings involved in it. If God takes an interest in the full range of human relationships, he is free to command that human beings fulfill all of the obligations arising from those relationships that are properly valued. This would transform all morally valid obligations into religious obligations. All of this follows if we begin with a social-pragmatic theory of obligation and then factor in a theistic view of what the relevant relationships are like and who is involved in them. Nontheistic pragmatists will not accept the additions, but that goes without saying. Still, the controversial additions need not involve metaphysics in the pejorative sense, just some questionable ontological claims.

Adams is careful to keep his account of divine commands from having undue influence on the epistemology of moral judgment he proposes. In deciding what to view as a moral obligation, according to Adams, we need consider not only what we think God has commanded us to do, but also whether the content of the putative command survives rational criticism. Such criticism must take into account our best understanding of God's goodness. A command that we initially take to be from a divine source, but which cannot plausibly be viewed as the sort of edict that a wise and loving God could have issued, should not be viewed as a divine command. This aspect of Adams's theory makes it vastly superior to most divine-command theories at both the theoretical and practical levels.

Theoretically, it permits him to sidestep Socratic objections to the kind of theological ethics advocated by Euthryphro in the Platonic dialogue that bears his name. Furthermore, it makes the theory much less prone than it would otherwise be to ideological abuses, fanaticism, and cruelty on the part those who attempt to live according to it. For example, Adams forthrightly denies in chapter 12 that the killing of Isaac is something that a loving God would actually command Abraham to do (Genesis 22:1–19). So anyone who believes himself to have received such a command from God is not thereby licensed to obey it, but rather required to change his mind about what the true God commands. Would that all believers subjected their assumptions about divine commands to this sort of testing![35]

Adams's theological conception of moral obligation is a humane vision, which leaves ample scope for self-criticism.

In chapter 11, Adams underscores the theoretical importance of including God in the account of moral obligation. The explanatory advantage of doing so, he claims, is to strengthen the sense in which obligations are held to be an objective matter. Assuming that God's commands cover everything that is required in every sort of genuinely wholesome relationship, all obligations turn out to be objective in the strongest possible sense. Because divine commands are not, by definition, human artifacts, they would secure a point of reference for the genuinely obligatory outside the realm of merely human social practices—although not outside of social practices altogether. This is the one point in his reflections on obligation where one might suspect that Adams is indulging in metaphysics in the pejorative sense. For God is being called on here precisely to buttress our sense of the objectivity of our evaluative practices.

Adams does not deny that obligations are creatures of social relationships and the practices of accountability they involve. Nor does he deny that rational criticism of those relationships can often disclose the difference between defective and good relationships, thus funding a distinction between defective and morally valid obligations. But he would prefer not to rely solely on an appeal to a human practice of rational criticism in defining this difference. Because morally valid obligations are identified as those arising from good relationships, the objectivity of moral obligation depends on the objectivity of goodness. This is what Adams means when he says that the good is prior to the right in his framework for ethics. The type of goodness at issue here is excellence. So it matters greatly, from Adams's point of view, that excellence be made out to be objective in a strong sense.

What, then is excellence? What type of goodness is it? Unlike usefulness, but like well-being, it is something that human beings value for its own sake. Adams distinguishes it from well-being by describing it as "the goodness of that which is worthy of love or admiration, honor or worship" (83). The distinction is nicely drawn, and Adams makes effective use of it in an argument designed to show that our interest in our own well-being should lead us to an interest in enjoyment of excellence. Once we have specified the property of excellence in this way, by placing it accurately among the types of goodness, don't we already have the nature of excellence within our grasp?

The terms "excellent" and "true" have parallel uses. Declaring something excellent normally expresses approval of it. This parallels the acceptance use of "true." The term "excellent" also has a use analogous to the cautionary use of "true," as in: "X conforms to our highest ideals as they now stand, but X might not be excellent."[36] With these uses in mind, we can conclude that the action-guiding and objective dimensions of excellence-talk, respectively, are built into the term's conceptual role. We do not need help from metaphysical theorizing to do what the cautionary use of "excellent" already accomplishes on its own behalf. Excellence, roughly, is the goodness of something worthy of love or admiration; and, given the cautionary use of "excellent," this kind of goodness must be understood as a normative status about which we can be wrong. There is much more to be said one level below this, in accounting for the types of excellence, such as beauty and virtue, and the sorts of thing that can exemplify them. And these details do enrich our sense of what excellence is. It consists in manifold types, each of which must be understood in the context of the practices in which we acquire and express our interest in and concern for it—the arts, child rearing, and so on. But what more is there to be said in the abstract about excellence as such?

Adams wants more than this, and his reason once again has to do with objectivity. He thinks that the nature of excellence must be described in such a way that its independence from human valuing is guaranteed metaphysically. Something must be done, Adams thinks, to keep excellence from collapsing into *what human beings love and admire*. Excellence, properly understood, must turn out to be as independent of our responses to things as truth is. Appreciating the parallel between the cautionary uses of "excellent" and "true" does begin to lend credence to the idea that excellence-talk is objective in some fairly strong sense. But this, from Adams's point of view, is mere semantics. What we need is an account of the nature of excellence. If excellence consisted simply in what human beings love and admire, it would lack the sort of independence that would allow us to speak meaningfully of being wrong in our judgments of excellence. Sometimes we love and admire people who abuse us. We pathologically treasure the relationship that binds us to them, and accept the requirements they impose on us as genuine obligations. Such people do not deserve our love and admiration; such relationships are not properly treasured. To make sense of this, we need an account of excellence as an objective property, independent of what we actually love and admire. The same concern arises, for both Jackson and Adams, in connection with the intrinsic worth of human beings.[37]

Excellence of a given kind normally manifests itself to competent judges of the relevant sort. What such judges steadily love or admire, when given full information and ample opportunity to reflect critically, is our best guide to excellence.[38] A competent judge is someone who has become adept at the patterns of approval and disapproval essential to a social practice involving kinds of thing taken to be worthy of love or admiration. A person who is deeply familiar with jazz, cares about it in the way jazz buffs do, and is capable of reflecting critically on jazz performances would qualify as a competent judge. He or she could tell the difference between a saxophone solo played by a beginner and one played by the mature Lester Young. Indeed, listeners who could not tell the difference, under conditions where they could experience both performances without distortion and reflect on them critically as long as they wished, would immediately be disqualified within the jazz world as competent practitioners.

Moral excellence can be approached along similar lines. Again a competent judge is someone who has mastered a repertoire of appropriate noninferential responses (ranging from revulsion to admiration) and the inferential habits involved in reflecting critically on such responses. Take the practice of child rearing, where talk of moral excellence has its firmest footing and clearest function. One thing we do when engaging in this practice is to correct children who bully their siblings. Suppose, in a given case, the correction is effective. A little boy seems to have overcome his previous tendency to bully his little sister. He no longer screams with rage and punches her when she touches his toys. His parents express their approval by praising him: "What a nice boy!" Such talk attributes to him an elementary form of the virtue of temperance, a cardinal moral excellence. This type of excellence is a status in a process of moral development with which we are all familiar. The boy either has this status or he does not. His parents might be wrong in attributing it to him. Perhaps they have excessive pride and are disposed to approve of everything he does. Surely, the boy possesses the excellence in question only if their approval of it, in their capacity as participants in the practice of child rearing, can withstand critical scrutiny in light of increasingly complete information about the boy's behavior in particular and child development in general.

I have stopped short of equating the boy's excellence with his newly acquired disposition to elicit approval from competent practitioners "under conditions of increasing non-evaluative information and critical reflection."[39] Taking that additional reductive step, for excellence in general, is a controversial move, which Adams resists. And I have my own reasons for resisting it. Suppose, in a galaxy far away, there exists an advanced civilization whose excellences would not even register on the scales employed in any human evaluative practice. Or, to take an example more to Adams's liking, suppose that God exists and that his greatness surpasses the understanding that any finite being could acquire. Then there might well be some forms of excellence that cannot be reduced to a disposition to elicit approval from human beings, even those operating under what, in human terms, would have to be counted as hyperbolically idealized conditions. The term "excellence," when employed in such thought-experiments, has an intelligible use. There could, it seems to me, be a form of excellence that transcended even an idealized human capacity to recognize it. This would be something sufficiently analogous to our more mundane forms of excellence to merit being classified with them (for the purposes of the thought-experiment) but sufficiently superior to them to surpass human understanding.

Nonetheless, the reason that thought-experiments about distant galaxies place strain on the concept of excellence they employ is that the concept has its natural home in down-to-earth human practices in which the evaluation of persons, traits, and so on has an evident point in relation to our earthly concerns. When theists engage in the practice of doxology, and praise God as one whose greatness surpasses human understanding, they know that they have an excellence in mind, but they admit that they cannot give the idea much positive content. We would not have a grip on what excellence is if this were the only context in which we used the term "excellence." We understand what excellence is, practically speaking, because we interact constantly with finite things that satisfy the interests in excellence that arise in the context of practices like child rearing, spiritual counseling, philosophy, science, the arts, athletics, and politics. These are all practices in which we are trying to improve on something: a child's behavior, our grasp of a concept, a set of institutional arrangements, or whatever. And we mark the difference between things we have reason to modify and things we have reason to deem satisfactory or laudable, given the overall point of a practice, by selectively attributing specific forms of excellence to them. Our grasp of excellence—of what it is—consists in our ability to reflect meaningfully on our experience of normative ascent within a number of particular practices. To understand excellence is thus to possess a kind of wisdom that is difficult or impossible to state propositionally. The metaphysical temptation, in this area of philosophy, is to think that an explicit, highly general propositional formulation would represent an advance on the practical understanding gained through experience of particular excellent things.

We must still come to terms, however, with what may be Adams's deeper worry, the existence of conflicting communities of competent judges. Most of us would know how to tell the difference between a Lester Young performance and a beginner's. We would respond approvingly to the former but not the latter as a piece of improvisational music. We are also ready to stand shoulder to shoulder with parents everywhere in approving of the child who overcomes his tendency to bully his sister. Unfortunately, however, there are many conflicting communities of competent judges claiming jurisdiction over questions of excellence. Assume, for the moment, that jazz buffs find disco revolting. They might be willing to grant disco fans jurisdiction over the relative worth of disco performances (as music to dance to), but not over the question of whether the best disco performances are excellent. Disco fans might be willing to acknowledge Lester Young's superiority to a novice, but not the greatness of John Coltrane's *A Love*

Supreme as a musical performance. Similarly, Emersonian democrats and Nazi officers would hardly respond in the same way to such traits as compassion for one's enemies and submissiveness to one's military commander. Who is to decide who counts as a competent judge of these matters?

The pragmatist sees this query more as a practical question than as a philosophical puzzle about objectivity. The relative merits of jazz and disco have been transformed into a matter for objective inquiry by the creation of a social practice, music criticism. In this practice various forms of musical expression are studied deeply, both in relation to their social functions and the higher aesthetic aspirations they bring into play. Over time a class of competent judges has established its authority to make disciplined judgments of relative artistic worth, with jazz faring rather better than disco. By the same token, the way to transform the relative merits of Nazi and Emersonian valuations into a matter for objective inquiry is to create a critical practice in which various human ethical practices can be judged comparatively. The hope once again is that the claim to be a competent judge of such matters can at some point honestly be presented as an earned entitlement. Without the construction and development of such a practice, all we have are various communities making ill-informed, biased judgments of each other's valuations. Until some standards are developed for evaluating these judgments, the judgments themselves are likely to be biased and unreliable. This does not mean that they lack truth-value, for some of them are plainly mistaken. But calling some of them "mistaken" expresses an earned entitlement, according to the pragmatist, only in relation to the incipient metapractice. Making such a claim may or may not be to speak truly, but it does not belong to an objective cognitive endeavor unless it is being presented as a claim for which reasons may be requested.

When one says that *A Love Supreme* really is excellent, as compared with any performance by the Bee Gees, one is either expressing one's cultural snobbery in an undisciplined way or implicitly gesturing toward a critical practice in which this judgment could be vindicated. Because this practice exists, I have grounds for my confidence that Coltrane's performance would elicit steady admiration from fully informed, critically reflective judges who experienced it. Even if this dispositional trait does not exhaustively characterize the excellence in question, it still tells me where to look for it. If I want to experience it, I shall need to approximate, at least to some degree, the characteristics and circumstances of ideally situated, competent practitioners of the relevant kind. A similarly emergent metapractice in the area of ethical criticism has definitively eliminated Nazi claims about the virtues from serious consideration. But as in music criticism, so, too, in disciplined cross-cultural ethical inquiry: there are many alleged examples of ethical excellence and inadequacy that have yet to elicit a stable response from the best-informed, most reflective judges. There are many more arising every day. Still, one can get a reasonably clear sense of what ideally competent judges would have to know and what sort of critical reflection they would be inclined to practice. So there is no reason to suppose that we are dealing here with a merely subjective matter.

Adams, however, is pressing for a propositional statement that will name the substantial something in which the excellence of any excellent finite thing consists. Anyone not already persuaded that this effort is necessary will be disposed to suspect unwarranted reification at work as Adams passes from ordinary uses of "good" and "excellent" to talk of God as the transcendent Good. God, for Adams, is the actual, unchanging paradigm of excellence. The excellence of a finite thing, he concludes, is its resemblance to this paradigm. It is not clear that this explanation works, even if one accepts Adams's theological premises. In the first place, the value of many types of excellence derives from their roles in the lives of finite, fallible, physical beings situated in a natural world. It is not obvious what parallel some of these types of excellence would have in the life of God.[40] Second, as Adams admits, philosophers since antiquity have doubted that the varieties of excellence can be accounted for on a model as unitary as the Platonic one he endorses (38–41). But there are other problems as well.

When we value the excellence of finite things, we are (implicitly or explicitly) applying our norms to those things. Sometimes the norm takes the form of an exemplar with which we compare other instances of the same kind. But it isn't typically their resemblance to something else that we are valuing when we value their excellence. Usually what we value in them is simply their excellence, or some particular aspect of their excellence, such as the inventive expressivity of the guitarist's riff or the steadfast courage of the protestor's defiance. It is not their resemblance to a higher, paradigmatic instance, let alone a being (real or imaginary) nothing greater than which can be conceived.

Suppose that an atheist performs the same act of heroism in two possible worlds and that these worlds are very similar, except that God exists in only one of them.[41] Suppose further that in both of these worlds, you witness the act of heroism and come to value its moral excellence. In the God-inhabited world, the act turns out to resemble God in certain ways. Its practical wisdom images God's own wisdom; its compassion for people in suffering images God's love; and so forth. Even so, the act's resemblance to God need not be what you value in deeming it excellent. Is resemblance to God, then, *identical* to excellence? What you value as the excellence of the act, presumably, is a property that the act and God supposedly share— the very property the sharing of which constitutes the resemblance. This would seem to be a property the act could have in the godless possible world as well. In that world, the act would still have the property but it would lack the relation of resemblance to divinity. Why assume that excellence would be *a different property* in that world?

It is unclear, in any event, how resemblance to divinity would explain what the property is—what it is that we value when we value excellence—in either world. Whichever possible world we are in, our practical understanding of excellence will depend on the various forms of excellence we experience. That is one reason for trying to experience great art or great philosophy; it deepens our understanding of excellence, thereby orienting us toward enjoyment of excellence in our lives as a whole. By the same token, interaction with a *supremely* good being would make an enormous difference to our understanding of excellence—even though we might still find it impossible to state this understanding in the form of an informative, workable (metaphysical) explanation. If there is such a being, we should praise its excellence to the highest and hope to deepen our understanding of excellence by interacting with it (or participating in it).

We might then follow Barth in redescribing all finite forms of excellence as pale reflections of God's excellence. In that event, we might well affirm as an article of faith that God's excellence is the analogue and any finite instance of excellence is the analogate. Taken out of context, this might seem to be exactly what Adams is affirming. But Barth would be anxious to deny that our mundane conception of excellence, built up from experience of excellent finite things, is capable in itself, without God's gracious help, of bearing adequate witness to God. Barthian affirmation of God as the archetype of excellence belongs to the theological enterprise in which faith seeks understanding. It takes faith as its absolute presupposition. Theology properly conceived, according to Barth, shatters all attempts to argue on strictly philosophical grounds from the experience of finite things to a God posited as a metaphysical *explanans*. The contrast between Barth's conception of analogy and Adams's conception of resemblance brings the metaphysical provenance of the latter into sharp relief.[42]

How do we come to grasp the concept of excellence? By participating in evaluative practices. In these practices we interact with instances of excellence, and learn to apply such expressions as "good," "better than," "eloquent," "beautiful," and "virtuous" in accord with the norms of our community. There is also an important role for the imagination, as we learn to project ideals of excellence on the basis of experience of actual finite things that are good in some respects but not others. The monotheistic traditions unify these ideals in a single conception of divinity—a personal being who not only exemplifies excellence perfectly but is also causally responsible for the creation and destiny of the universe. The alleged actuality of this divinity is then said to explain many things, including the excellence of finite things that resemble it. The prior unification of the ideal and the actual, however, is obviously controversial. Feuerbach,

Freud, Santayana, and Dewey denigrate it as wishful thinking. Without denying the element of wish, Pascal and William James affirm it as a reason of the heart. Especially for those on the verge of despair, it might well be a saving comfort to believe that our highest ideals are instantiated in an actual being—not only a perfect paradigm of goodness but a power capable of seeing to it that everything will eventually turn out well.[43] I do not gainsay people of good will and common decency who accept faith in such a God. Who am I to judge them? Yet I do question the wisdom of treating the objectivity of ethics as if it depended, in effect, upon a faith shared by only some of the people.

It would be foolish to pretend that religious commitments do not play a major role in shaping intuitions about what a philosopher ought to be aiming for in this area. If God created the earth and immediately declared it excellent, and only then proceeded to create human beings, it makes little sense to insist that excellence, as a normative status, is a creature of *human* practices.[44] But this just means that *God* has a creative practice the point of which is to improve on something—in this case, the formless void. An improvement-oriented practice gives content and point to a distinction between things that qualify as excellent and things that are relatively inadequate. Assuming that the divinity is either multiple (as the plural Hebrew form suggests at Genesis 1:26 and as the Christian doctrine of the Trinity implies) or has an audience of angelic beings, the practice of creation might even have a *social* dimension from an orthodox point of view.

Pragmatism, understood strictly as a critique of metaphysics in the pejorative sense, need not be troubled by any of this, taken simply as a story faithfully believed. Its quarrel is not with the God of Amos and Dorothy Day, or even with the God of Barthian theology, but with the God of Descartes, and with the God of analytic metaphysics. Its account of excellence, like its account of obligation, can accommodate whatever persons, social relationships, and practices there happen to be. Its purpose should not be to put theologically inclined citizens on the defensive. The purpose served by pragmatic ethical theory is rather to make clear that a society divided over the nature and existence of God is not thereby condemned to view its ethical discourse as an unconstrained endeavor. If the God of the philosophers is dead, not everything is permitted. There can still be morally valid obligations to constrain us, as well as many forms of excellence in which to rejoice. Pragmatism comes into conflict with theology in ethical theory mainly at those points where someone asserts that the truth-claiming function of ethics depends, for its *objectivity*, on positing a transcendent and perfect being.[45] Metaphysics asserts the need and then posits the divine explainer to satisfy it. Pragmatism questions the need and then doubts the coherence of the explanation.

Our grasp on the objectivity of obligation is firmest in those ordinary contexts where we fully understand the point of requiring one another to live up to the demands of the decent relationships in which we take part. Outside of the context of faith, our grasp on the objectivity of excellence is firmest in those down-to-earth—but still uplifting—moments when we experience a finite thing that is significantly better than others of its kind and our heart spontaneously fills up with admiration. In thinking otherwise, we risk alienating ourselves from the very activities in which evaluative properties and proprieties normally manifest themselves to us. The nature of obligation and excellence is something we lay our hands on in our practices. Their capacity to transcend the awareness of competent judges is disclosed to us when we undergo social and spiritual crises, and are forced to abandon long-cherished rules and exemplars as idols. Such reversals teach human beings something important about our intimations of morally valid obligation and genuine excellence: metaphysical consolation notwithstanding, we have this treasure in earthen vessels, and must make of it what we can.[46]

"Where do we find ourselves?" writes Emerson. "In a series of which we do not know the extremes, and believe that it has none. We wake and find ourselves on a stair; there are stairs below us, which we seem to have ascended; there are stairs above us, many a one, which go upward and out of sight."[47] The stair I am on is higher than the one below me. It affords a better view. This view excels the other. I declare it excellent—but not perfect, for I can imagine a better one. Does this judgment depend, for its objectivity, on whether the uppermost actual stair affords a perfect view? If I cannot yet see to the top, don't I still know what I'm talking *about* when I assert the excellence of the view I now enjoy?[48]

Chapter 12

ETHICS AS A SOCIAL PRACTICE

THE PREVIOUS CHAPTER argued that even if one does not adopt a metaphysical explanation of what moral obligation and excellence are, it remains reasonable to view ethical discourse as an objective affair. I will now give additional support to this conclusion by reflecting on Brandom's account of the ways in which we all keep track of the beliefs and intentions we undertake and attribute when conversing with other people. A game, as Wittgenstein realized, is a relatively perspicuous example of a social practice—a relatively simple species of the genus to which ethical discourse belongs. Brandom develops the analogy between discursive practices and games in a way that sheds light on the objective dimension of ethics as a social practice. My main purpose in discussing Brandom is to show how pragmatism can best resist degenerating into something like conventionalism, according to which the tyranny of the majority effectively determines what obligation and excellence are.

OBJECTIVITY IN THE CONTEXT OF A SOCIAL PRACTICE

In sandlot baseball, there are no umpires. In street soccer, there are no referees. The players keep track of runs or goals and how well everyone played. Similarly, in forms of discourse that include a dimension of objective inquiry, players make commitments and attribute commitments to one another. They give credit to one another for being entitled to commitments and occasionally blame one another for commitments undertaken irresponsibly. They also award points, so to speak, for commitments they deem correct. Any participant can withdraw a point once awarded if he or she thinks that subsequent developments in the practice of inquiry warrant such a change in the awarding of endorsement status to propositions. The way to withdraw a point once awarded is to say something like, "I thought Smith's belief about X was true, but it isn't." When this happens, no aspersions need be cast on how Smith played the game, on his entitlement to his commitment. He may still count as a responsible inquirer or even be ranked among the best. A person who thinks so will be inclined to excuse Smith for failing to commit himself to views that we now accept. The way to excuse him is to say something like, "What Smith believed about X wasn't true, but he was justified in believing it."

It would not improve the rules of baseball if we appended to them a chapter on the nature of scoring runs, explaining that a player who touches home plate after rounding the bases has scored only if he or she has *really* touched it. We would be no more enlightened if we were told that scoring a run within the game *corresponds* to the physical state of affairs in which the player actually touches home plate. But sandlot baseball would be a much different game if players did not feel constrained to award runs by adhering to a rigorous discipline. At a minimum this discipline involves attentiveness to evidence and an attempt to avoid being wrongly influenced by wishful thinking. These non-narcissistic features of scorekeeping discipline contribute to the objective dimension of baseball as a practice. Objective scientific inquiry includes similar features, and endeavors to extend and perfect them. Its objectivity is a matter of the constraints the practice imposes on its practitioners when they make commitments and when they keep track of normative statuses involving other practitioners and the propositions to which they commit themselves. The constraints are object-directed in the sense that they involve attentiveness to something being investigated as well as disciplined avoidance of wishful thinking, rationalization, and related intrusions of "merely subjective" factors.

Ethical discourse has an objective dimension insofar as it involves constraints of this kind. Why does it make sense to draw a distinction between being justified in believing a moral proposition and the truth of that proposition? Because our way of keeping track of one another's commitments and entitlements pertaining to ethical topics includes the same implicit distinction between the "how-you-play-the-game" factor and the *correctness* of commitments. The fact that ethical topics are themselves often practice-dependent normative statuses (and not natural properties) does not diminish the need to earn entitlement to one's commitments about them by attending to matters other than one's own subjective states. And whether one's commitments, attributions of commitments, and attributions of entitlements in ethical discourse are correct is not a matter of willing or wanting them to be so.

A divine-command theorist might want to insist that an adequate model for tracking the attitudes of our interlocutors in ethical discourse would *have to* include a single ultimate authority figure. The rules of major league baseball and major league soccer designate the head umpire or the referee as the only scorekeeper. A run or a goal can then be defined as having been scored when and only when the officially designated scorekeeper says so. Brandom's theory shows that a discursive practice can be objective in the sense at issue here without being construed on an authoritarian model of scorekeeping. If Brandom is right, in a democratic society, where no monolithic authority is recognized by all those engaging in ethical discourse, it should still be possible in principle to make sense of being entitled to commitments and of making commitments that are correct in content. For the same reasons that baseball can be played on the sandlots and soccer can be played in the streets, ethical discourse can retain an objective dimension without there being a single authority on questions of truth and falsity. In ethics, as in most other forms of objective discourse, we are all keeping track of our interlocutors' attitudes, as well as our own.[1]

Let us consider the example of soccer a little more closely. Before human beings invented this practice, there was no such thing as the normative status that soccer people refer to as "having committed a foul." This normative status is a creature of a social practice in which people take one another to have committed a foul or not when competing with their opponents on the playing field. But this dependence of a normative status on a social practice does not in the least deprive claims about fouls in soccer of *their* status of being true or false. Everybody who cares about soccer, and understands how it works, behaves as if claims about this status have a truth-value. They treat inquiry into the truth-value of such claims as an objective affair, to be settled by the testimony of trustworthy eyewitnesses, the evidence of instant-replay videos, and so forth.

Before the officials of British public schools began formalizing the proprieties of soccer in explicitly stated rules, the norms governing the sport were entirely implicit in what soccer players did. By the middle of the nineteenth century, some people hoping to reduce the mayhem of their recreational activities had become disposed (a) to stop play when an especially brutal "hacking" occurred in a game of soccer and (b) to award the ball to the side that had been "hacked." The implicitly recognized impropriety of hacking was later made explicit in a rule against fouling, which formally mandated (a) and (b) as a penalty for fouling. Once the "Laws of the Game" had been formulated, this rule was subject to critical review and rational revision. The tackle from behind has recently been formally prohibited as a result of this critical process. The reasons for introducing this particular rule happen to be good ones. Just as the application of established rules is an objective affair, so, too, is the rational revision of the rules in light of the pleasures, excitements, and other goods to be enjoyed when playing (or watching) the game.

"Norms," according to Brandom, "are not objects in the causal order" (MIE, 626). He immediately adds, however, that normative *attitudes* are in the causal order. Kant was right, according to Brandom, in holding that normative attitudes institute normative statuses. Hegel agreed with this central Kantian thesis, but he criticized Kant for explaining the process of norm-institution as a matter of self-legislation and for modeling society on a contract among independent rational agents. Hegel argued that social-contract theory is insufficiently sociological or historical to account for the institution of ethical norms. Norms do not arise because solitary individuals, already in full possession of practical rationality, commit themselves to a social contract. They emerge out of the mutually recognitive activities through which a people comes to share a culture. Ethical norms are instituted, according to Hegel, not by something analogous to a contract (among already rational independent operatives) but by a form of ethical life (which shapes the subjectivity and rationality of the individuals who participate in it). This form of life gives birth simultaneously to ethical norms and to the rational individuals who use, scrutinize, and revise such norms.

Democratic ethical norms were instituted, then, in the same way that soccer players instituted the normative statuses associated with fouling. Before there was a rule against fouling, soccer players acquired a habit of stopping play in response to instances of hacking. By the same token, democratic ethical norms originally took shape in shared dispositions to respond in certain ways to behavior of certain kinds. It is a small but momentous step from this humble beginning to the explicit statement of rules and then to the critical scrutiny and rational revision of rules in light of the purposes they serve (the rationally self-conscious form of life they make possible). This conception of ethical norms as creatures of a social practice may originate in Hegel, but it is reformulated, without the obscurities of Hegelian diction, in American pragmatism. While this conception stops short of the objectivist picture of norms as wholly independent of human activity, it nonetheless allows us to affirm that ethical discourse is an endeavor in which truth-claims are put forward and entitlements to them are assessed by attending to objective considerations.

The normative claims soccer players make about who fouled whom can clearly be true or false. Whether it is true that Beckenbauer fouled Charlton in the fifty-third minute of the 1966 World Cup Final depends on the physical relationship obtaining at that time between the relevant body parts of Beckenbauer and Charlton. Clearly, this is not a question about our subjective states. If we set out to determine responsibly whether Beckenbauer fouled Charlton, we will need to position ourselves advantageously within the physical world and interact causally with such physical objects as the shins, ankles, feet, and elbows of the two players. Of course, in doing so we will be taking for granted, at least for the time being, what it means for something to be a foul. We will be taking for granted that the proprieties of soccer are what they are (in a way that makes us complicit in the valuations of the relevant social practice). But nothing prevents us, a moment later, from subjecting the Laws of the Game, as they now stand or as they stood in 1966, to critical scrutiny. Whether a particular rule should be changed is itself obviously a question on which objective considerations have a bearing. So there is every reason to suppose that talk about soccer fouls and norms has a truth-claiming, objective dimension.

There is also much talk in soccer about excellence, and this too has an objective dimension. Beckenbauer and Charlton are both universally acknowledged as excellent players, and Beckenbauer is admired as one of the four or five greatest players the sport has seen. The esteem these players enjoy is either merited or not. Either they actually possessed the excellence attributed to them or they did not. Anyone who spoke of Charlton as a poor or mediocre player would be speaking falsely—and also exhibiting either ignorance of Charlton's play or incompetence as a judge of such matters. Truth and falsity are at issue here. In declaring Charlton excellent, one makes a normative judgment. It is possible to make the relevant norms explicit by stating a standard of excellence for soccer players or for players of a certain type. In some cases this will involve treating a particular player as an exemplar. In other cases it will involve projecting an ideal in which the virtues of several good players are imaginatively enhanced and combined in a way not yet instantiated. But the standards change over time. One thing that counts in favor of Beckenbauer's greatness is the way in which his play as a defender transformed the standards by which defenders have subsequently been judged.[2] The standards changed in response to specific features of Beckenbauer's play—his skill as a passer, his ability to join in the attack without weakening the team's defensive configuration, and so forth. These were objective considerations. The need to rely on conditioned norms, which evolve along with the game itself, does not make judgments about excellence a merely subjective matter.

Needless to say, ethical norms are much more important in most contexts, and much harder to assess critically, than the proprieties and ideals of soccer are. But if ethical norms and soccer norms are, from a point of view like Hegel's, Dewey's, or Brandom's, instituted in roughly the same way, then there is no reason to suppose that the adoption of this form of pragmatism deprives ethical discourse of its title to objectivity.[3] Pragmatism does not reject the objective dimension of ethics, but it does doubt the adequacy of two sorts of philosophical theorizing about it. The first of these are objectivist accounts of moral objectivity, which fail to do justice to the responsibility we bear for the object-oriented norms we apply in ethics. The second are a series of subjectivist reactions against objectivism, which either try to pull the objective rabbit out of a subjective hat or abandon the ideal of objectivity altogether. What I am calling pragmatism here is not to be interpreted as a form of subjectivism, but as a third way. It offers a *social* theory of moral objectivity—according to which both objective ethical norms and the subjectivity of those who apply them are made possible in part by social interactions among individuals. But if it is crucial to distinguish pragmatism from subjectivism, it is no less crucial to specify what kind of social theory it involves.

Consider the impropriety, other things being equal, of hitting somebody over the head with a sledgehammer. On the account being presented here, this moral impropriety was initially implicit in the dispositions of people to respond negatively to one sort of harmful behavior, to take it as having harmed or breached the relationship among persons, as well as the person harmed. There are various ways in which a community can make this normative status explicit. We might, for example, attribute to everyone the right not to be treated in this way. Once this right is recognized, we are in a position to ask whether, in any given case, it has been violated. This question is obviously every bit as objective as the question of whether Beckenbauer fouled Charlton in a soccer match. But what about the question of whether individuals really have the right we have attributed to them?

This question gets us on the wrong track if we take it as an invitation to do an inventory of everything there *really* is. Pragmatism construes rights and obligations as creatures of social practices. Does not anything *created* by a social practice *exist?* Of course it does, but some thinkers have wanted to contrast social phenomena with, say, physical objects, concluding that the former are merely subjective or ontologically queer, whereas the latter alone should be counted as first-class entities. Pragmatism involves no such contrast. The use of "really" in the question, "Do individuals really have this right?" is cautionary. First, it helps us raise the possibility of a revision in our norms or even in the vocabulary in which we state our norms. This is not a question to be settled by doing an ontological inventory or a typology of first-class and second-class ontological categories. Second, the term helps us focus on the possibility that we might all be wrong to attribute this particular right or to embrace the underlying norm.

For practical purposes, we can often replace the previous question by asking, "Do we (really) have sufficiently good reason, all things considered, to attribute the right not to be smashed on the head with a sledgehammer?" The question is analogous to the question, "Do we have sufficiently good reason to remain committed to the rule against tackling from behind in soccer?" Both of these questions have the merit of directing our attention explicitly to reasons, to rational considerations that would count for or against the rule being discussed. The answers to both of these questions happen to be clear, for we have every reason to remain committed to our conception of these particular proprieties. We know this because we can easily survey all of the considerations that are likely to prove relevant. When we do so, we find that they all line up on one side of the question. There is nothing arbitrary about our answers at all.

In controversial cases, however, we sometimes feel tempted to say that the decision of whether or not to revise a norm is a matter of subjective choice. This feeling can induce the worry that the entire practice is, at bottom, a reflection of arbitrary will, a subjective affair. But in such cases what we are actually faced with is a conflict or balance of rational considerations, not an absence of such considerations. The endeavor of weighing those considerations can be an objective affair (in the only sense worth bothering with in this context), even if it does not lead to an unambiguous result. Why? Because the considerations we are weighing direct our attention away from our subjective states to how things and persons are in the world and how things and persons would be if we revised our norms. As responsible subjects we must still weigh these considerations in light of what we have come to care about as a result of participating in our evaluative practices. And the considerations themselves, the reasons that guide us when we undertake our ethical commitments, cannot be understood apart from the norm-instituting social practices in which we offer and ask for them. For it is those practices, not a lonely subject's arbitrary act of will, which confer on our reasons whatever content and force they have.

At this point in the argument, worries over the distinction between truth and justification are bound to resurface. For it might appear that even if my pragmatism accounts successfully for the relativity of justification to social context, the nonrelativity of truth could never be made consistent with the priority of social practices. Does not my emphasis on social practices require me in the end to view truth as a matter of communal agreement? Am I not proposing to substitute *the community of competent ethical judges* for the eternal law and the self-legislating Kantian will as an indefeasible authority on ethical truth? And would this proposal not just collapse truth into justification all over again, thus threatening the social critic's cautionary use of "true"?

The answer to all three of these questions is no. To see why, consider the following passage from Lovibond's defense of Wittgenstein against similar charges:

> [A]lthough (in Wittgenstein's view) it is an agreement, or congruence, in our ways of acting that makes objective discourse materially possible, this agreement does not itself "enter into" the relevant language-game: when we ask a question about some aspect of reality, we are not asking for a report on the state of public opinion with regard to that question, we are asking to be told the *truth* about it. . . . The idea of rationality as resting upon a consensus, then, does not imply that the *fact* of consensus need carry any weight with us in any particular piece of thinking about the objective world: a point which is demonstrated by the absence of any logical (or "grammatical") objection to statements of the form: "I'm right and everyone else is wrong."[4]

There is indeed a sense in which our use of the term "true" rests on agreement within a social practice. But the agreement that matters in this context is not agreement specifying *which* substantive ethical claims are true, as if the community as a whole could decide such things by fiat. It is rather a practical agreement that we exhibit when we use the terms "true" and "justified" differently. What we have agreed to do, in effect, is to treat truth in practice as something that cannot be settled simply by communal agreement. It is this underlying social agreement on the use of certain words in the process of self-criticism that gives the term "true" its nonrelative sense. When I insist on the importance of the underlying social agreement, I am not saying or implying that in deciding which ethical claims to accept as true, one must ultimately bow to the will of the community as a whole or to the majority of its members.[5] The agreement at issue here operates on a different, more basic level.

Brandom makes the same point by denying the adequacy of what he calls "I-we construals of the social practices in which conceptual norms are implicit."

> Such construals fund a distinction between what particular individuals *treat* as or *take* to be a correct application of a concept, on the one hand, and what *is* a correct application, on the other, by contrasting individual takings with communal ones. This is the standard way of understanding objectivity as intersubjectivity. The cost of adopting this way of understanding the significance of the social dimension of discursive practice is, unacceptably, to lose the capacity to make sense of the distinction between correct and incorrect claims or applications of concepts on the part of the whole community. (MIE, 593f.; emphasis in original)

It is very important to see that in endorsing the view that norms are creatures of social practices, I am not endorsing a reduction of truth or objectivity to what some community takes to be true or objective. Our socially instituted conceptual norms do not in fact permit such a reduction.

Brandom specifically rules out what he calls an "I-we" account of discursive social practices for the following reason:

> I-we accounts mistakenly postulate the existence of a *privileged* perspective— that of the "we," or community. The objective correctness of claims (their truth) and of the application of concepts is identified with what is endorsed by that privileged point of view. The identification of objectivity with intersubjectivity so understood is defective in that it cannot find room for the possibility of error regarding that privileged perspective; what the community *takes* to be correct *is* correct. (MIE, 599; emphasis in original)

According to an I-we theory of discursive social practices, ethical truth can be defined as that to which one's community agrees. It "is settled in advance that any perspective from which a distinction appears between how things seem from [the community's] privileged point of view and how things in fact are is itself without any authority at all" (MIE, 600). Brandom's I-thou theory, in contrast, treats each individual's perspective as "at most *locally* privileged in that it incorporates a structural distinction between objectively correct applications of concepts and applications that are merely subjectively taken to be correct." As Brandom puts it, what is shared by the discursive perspectives of each "I" and each "thou" is "*that* there is a difference between what is objectively correct in the way of concept application and what is merely taken to be so" (MIE, 600; emphasis in original). Interlocutors do not, however, necessarily share a view of what this difference is. What they share is a structural distinction implicit in the cautionary use of "true," not the content of any particular belief about what is true.

It should be clear, I hope, that this is the same point Lovibond was making when she said that the agreement that makes objective discourse materially possible "does not itself 'enter into' the relevant language-game." What Brandom adds to this point is an analysis of the perspectival structure of objectivity.

Individual and Community

Brandom's account of the social dimension of discursive practice "focuses on the relation between the commitments *undertaken* by a scorekeeper interpreting others and the commitments *attributed* by that scorekeeper to those others." The "crucial feature" of this relation, he says, "is the *symmetry* of state and attitude" between I and thou—between the person who is ascribing commitments and the one to whom those commitments are ascribed (emphasis in original). Conceptual contents, Brandom says, "can be specified explicitly only from some point of view, against the background of some repertoire of discursive commitments, and how it is correct to specify them varies from one discursive point of view to another."

> Mutual understanding and communication depend on interlocutors' being able to keep two sets of books, to move back and forth between the point of the view of the speaker and the audience, while keeping straight on which . . . commitments are undertaken and which are attributed by the various parties. Conceptual contents . . . can be genuinely shared, but their perspectival nature means that doing so is mastering the coordinated system of scorekeeping perspectives, not passing something nonperspectival from hand to hand (or mouth to mouth). (MIE, 590)

For this reason, each scorekeeper must exercise his or her own authority, on a strictly local basis, to distinguish between what is correct and what is merely taken by someone else to be correct. For any two interlocutors, this relation will be symmetrical. I draw the distinction from my point of view, in light of my collateral commitments, taking my specifications of the conceptual content of commitments as authoritative. You, as my interlocutor, draw the distinction from your point of view, in light of your collateral commitments, taking your specifications of the conceptual content of commitments as authoritative. The authority each of us exercises in this process is defeasible, in the sense that we are both free to change our minds with respect to these specifications and also in the sense that neither of our perspectives holds sway over the discourse that transpires between us. But we cannot get by without taking a specific point of view, and when we do this, we are bound to draw a distinction between "what is correct and what is merely taken to be correct, between objective content and subjective view of it" (MIE, 601). If I did not draw such a distinction, I would be utterly incapable of keeping track of how other people's commitments differ from mine, in content and in entitlement, and thus incapable of participating in the social exchange of reasons that confers significance on my own attitudes. Once I do draw this distinction, however, I am already well on the way toward being able to grasp the difference between truth and justification.

Democratic ethical discourse is social, then, not in the sense that the community of committed democrats functions as an ultimate authority, which no individual can in principle oppose. Rather, it is social in the sense that it needs to be understood in terms of what the individual members of a group do *when they keep track of their interlocutors' commitments from their own perspectives.* "This symmetric pair of perspective types, that of attributor and attributee, each maintaining this fundamental normative distinction [between what is correct and what is merely taken to be correct] is the fundamental social structure in terms of which communities and communal practice are to be understood" (MIE, 601). As in street soccer or sandlot baseball, all of the participants have the authority to "keep score," and each of them necessarily does so in light of his or her already-adopted commitments. That I have the authority to track commitments and entitlements, and thus to draw the fundamental normative distinction from my own point of view, does not make my commitments correct; nor does it make me entitled to them, in the sense that entails being epistemically justified in holding them. It simply puts me in the democratic game of giving and asking for reasons. "Sorting out who should be counted as correct, whose claims and applications of concepts should be treated as authoritative, is a messy retail business of assessing the comparative authority of competing evidential and inferential claims" (MIE, 601).

What does an ethical community share that makes it an ethical community? My answer thus far has been: a way of thinking and talking about ethical topics, or more precisely, a discursive social practice. One danger in this answer is that it can easily be interpreted in communitarian, conventionalist, or contractarian terms—that is to say, in terms that ascribe perfect, unassailable authority to something communal that the individual must obey on pain of rational incoherence or unreasonableness. We can avoid this danger by adding to my initial answer a claim about what makes a discursive social practice social. It is not the indefeasible authority of the community, its conventions, or a social contract that makes such a practice social. It is rather the need for each participant in the practice to keep track of other participants' commitments and to assess those commitments from his or her own point of view.

No ethical community could sustain a discursive practice without imposing on each of its members the necessity of keeping track of the normative attitudes and entitlements of their interlocutors, because without this there would be no communication—and therefore no exchange of reasons—among them. But, as we have seen, ethical communities have different ways of going about their discursive business. They employ different concepts, which implicate them in different material inferential commitments and dispose them to have different noninferential responses to things going on around them. They also distribute discursive authority very differently. Adopting an I-thou model of sociality for all discursive practices allows us to make room for the full range of variation in the "default-and-challenge structure of entitlements" in different sorts of ethical communities. Where the default position in a given community is that the ethical judgments of those in ecclesial or political office are correct, we have a pattern of deference to one kind of authority. The authoritarian extreme is reached whenever such a default position is treated as indefeasible and the authority is treated as self-interpreting. As one approaches this extreme, ethical truth is reduced in practice to what the highest authority says. When the reduction is total, it no longer makes sense to claim that the highest authority says P, but P might not be true.

One should not assume, however, that all religious communities are huddled near the authoritarian extreme of the spectrum. Many religious traditions and movements have developed relatively flexible structures of authority, and even those best known for their official rigidity are rarely able in practice to stamp out critical questioning of allegedly indefeasible authorities. In most cases, the indefeasibility asserted in doctrine reflects the wishes of a particular well-placed faction more accurately than it reflects the practice of the rank and file. Roman Catholicism, for example, is not only the tradition of Vatican I, Pius IX, and Cardinal Ratzinger, but also that of Vatican II, John XXIII, and Lord Acton. The official doctrine of papal infallibility is itself treated by many Catholics as a defeasible teaching—as something to be subordinated to the Spirit that is manifest in the life of the church as a whole. Many Protestants, Jews, and Muslims who begin by attributing indefeasible and unique authority to a revealed law end up interpreting that law in a highly flexible way. All of these traditions have been more pluralistic and less authoritarian in practice than some of their officials and intellectuals have wanted them to be. Religious recognition of the faithful as a common body and of the need to conform oneself to the best available understanding of what membership in that body involves can be fleshed out in many ways, only the most extreme of which deserve to be impugned as inflexible and uncritical. What Brandom calls the "I-we" model of sociality applies only to communities at the authoritarian limit where the distinction between what the group holds and what is true melts away, and individuals disappear without remainder into the collectivity. The "I-thou" model is preferable because it allows us to see how the "notion of a discursive *community*—a we—is built up out of" the actions and reactions of the individuals involved (MIE, 508; emphasis in original). Deferential activity on the part of individuals is what confers authority as a normative status on those who exercise it. Communities take shape only insofar as their members perform the work of mutual recognition, whether they are aware of this or not.

Many critics of democracy portray it as a tendency to attribute indefeasible authority to the ethical opinions of the citizenry taken as a whole or on average. That modern democratic culture can devolve into this sort of authoritarianism is both clear and cause for grave concern, especially when the people are corrupted by fear and resentment of their enemies and by a relentlessly homogenizing stream of mass entertainment, manipulative advertising, and political pandering. Perhaps an essentially conformist type of sociality—absorption into the demos—is the one most likely to result from the dissolution of older communities in the age of capitalism and counterterrorism. But this is precisely what Whitman was warning against, not arguing for, when he spoke of the people as "canker'd, crude, superstitious, and rotten."

The only defensible form of democratic community is one in which ethical authority is treated as an entitlement (to deference) that one must earn by repeatedly demonstrating one's reliability as an ethical judge. This is not achieved by conforming one's opinions to those of the majority, but rather by expressing judgments that withstand critical scrutiny in a discussion open to all. The "default-and-challenge structure of entitlements" in a genuinely democratic ethical community is not to be understood in purely procedural terms. It is intimately connected with substantive commitments to mutual respect, equal voice, and the value of critical discussion. But aren't these substantive commitments held by democrats to be indefeasible? No, they are not; nor need they be. They certainly enjoy a default status as presumed correct until or unless devastating considerations are brought to bear against them, and no committed democrat expects such considerations to emerge. But this does not mean that these commitments have been removed from the agenda of discussion. To the contrary, the tradition of democratic reflection subjects them to relentless critical scrutiny. The question of whether central democratic commitments can withstand such scrutiny is always in order, and has been discussed in earnest in every modern democracy throughout the last two centuries. If this question had been taken off the agenda, Whitman could easily have ignored the challenge of Carlyle's *Shooting Niagara* in the 1860s, Baldwin and Ellison could have ignored the challenge of Black Nationalism in the 1960s, and we could ignore the challenge of the new traditionalism today.

A democratic ethical community at least permits and at best encourages its members to express their normative stocktaking in public and to include the wealthy and powerful among those who are publicly held responsible for what they say and do. Ideally, it also invites its members to resist their own absorption into the social mass and to cultivate whatever virtues are required to foster the development of novel forms of action, speech, association, and selfhood. Whitman calls this the "principle of individuality."[6] A self-consciously democratic ethical community is aware of itself as a community of *individuals*: each of whom has evaluating to do that no one else can do on his or her behalf; each of whom stands in a potential relation of dialogical exchange with each other; each of whom can be challenged to offer reasons to the rest; and each of whom is ultimately responsible not only for actions taken and commitments undertaken, but also for the self he or she has become through the exercise or neglect of expressive freedom.[7] It is no less a "we" for that.

The notions of democratic individuality and expressive freedom bring us back, once again, into the area in which Emersonian perfectionism has staked out its strongest claims in ethics and political theory. Modern democracy began in a series of protests and revolutionary upheavals driven by resentment of specific injustices and the reasoned insistence on holding rulers discursively and politically responsible to the people for their actions. This was primarily what philosophers call a deontic matter, an issue of principle. It involved the assertion of entitlements against monarchical and theocratic orders intent on denying them. Its first preoccupations were expressed in terms of negative freedom, of rights against the established order.

But the political consequences of democratic moralizing eventually transformed the received ethical culture by opening up a space in which the ideals of democratic individuality and expressive freedom could be self-consciously pursued. Writers like Emerson and Whitman pursued these ideals in such a way that both democratic moralizing and democratic political arrangements came to seem subservient, in their eyes, to the positive freedom that results from self-cultivation. They were therefore attracted to the idea that the authority of any state to exercise political constraint depends on the success with which it protects or cultivates the expressive freedom of its citizens.[8] This thesis in political theory has an ethical counterpart, which is the notion that how to make appropriate use of expressive freedom in the development of one's character and individuality is the central question of ethics. Preoccupation with rights and wrongs, however important this may be when horrible injustices need to be opposed, threatens to engulf individuals in resentment and to distract them from taking full responsibility for what they have become as human beings. The most challenging democratic thinkers care at least as much about character and selfhood, about what the philosophers call "aretaic" questions, as they do about the rules of proper conduct. As theorists of virtue they are anything but levelers. What they want to promote in society generally and hope to exemplify in their own lives is excellence—and, if possible, spiritual greatness. The mere conformity to custom or convention exhibited in the life of the average citizen is something they abhor, and seek to disturb, in the name of democracy.

Appendix: Method in Comparative Ethics

The process of reason-exchange in any discursive community is constrained by socially engrained (but defeasible) assumptions about discursive authority and responsibility. These assumptions specify the circumstances in which one is, by default, entitled to a commitment or entitled to raise a challenge. They also specify the circumstances in which entitlement to a commitment or a challenge must be earned through reason-giving. Against the background of these assumptions, we engage in the inferential activity of reason-giving. That is, we make claims and assemble them into argumentative form by treating some claims as premises and others as conclusions. And by exchanging claims and arguments with one another, we bring about changes in the normative statuses—the commitments and entitlements—we have reason to attribute to one another.

The inferential activity of reason-giving is hardly the whole of ethics as a social practice, but it is central to it. Indeed, it is because the claims in which we express our commitments can play the role of premises or conclusions in inferences that they have conceptual content (MIE, 214). If we did not have inferential commitments, if we were not committed to treating one claim as a reason for another, the claims themselves would lack significance. To mean something in particular, they need to be taken to *imply* something and *not to imply* something else. Their inferential relations confer significance—conceptual content—upon them.

How do we know, for example, that a given community possesses the concept of cruelty that I have attributed to modern democracies? One bit of positive evidence would be acceptance of a constitution that treats the cruelty of a form of punishment as sufficient reason for declaring it unacceptable. A group—for example, a gang, a wayward military platoon, or a sports team—that never treated the claim that an act is cruel as a reason against performing the act would not attribute the same significance to cruelty that modern democratic constitutions do. In other words, they would not endorse the modern democratic *concept* of cruelty. The claim that an act is cruel, then, has the conceptual content it has within a discursive practice at least in part by virtue of what can be appropriately inferred from it, according to the norms implicit in that practice. Clearly, it is not formal logical relations that are at issue here. No one supposes that "I shall not do X" follows from "X is cruel" simply by virtue of logical form. What matters is that participants in the discursive practice treat the inference from "X is cruel" to "I shall not do X" as *materially* sound in the sense introduced in chapter 8. Material inferential commitments involving moral expressions like "cruel" confer conceptual content on those expressions.

Jewish, Muslim, and Christian communities have often treated anyone who is committed to "X is against God's commandments" as entitled by default to infer "X is morally wrong." It is beside the point to object to this practice by saying that no "ought" statement can validly be inferred from an "is" statement, for the inferential commitment at issue here is obviously a material one. No one supposes that the inference from "X is against God's commandments" to "X is morally wrong" is good by virtue of its logical form. Theologians can make their material inferential commitment explicit in the form of a claim by asserting the conditional, "If X is against God's commandments, then X is morally wrong." Or they can achieve a comparable degree of explicitness by asserting the principle, "Morally speaking, thou shalt not act against God's commandments." The conditional and the principle codify the underlying commitment and reflect a conceptual connection, in the linguistic practice of these communities, between God's commandments and moral wrongness. One type of divine-command theory in ethics consists of the claim that "morally wrong" *means* "against God's commandments." If material inferential commitments do confer conceptual content on the expressions caught up in them, as Sellars and Brandom argue, then this sort of divine-command theory can be seen as a perfectly legitimate attempt to make explicit the conceptual content of the relevant terms.

But two points need to be kept in mind here. First, the theory accounts semantically only for communities where the underlying material inferential commitments are already operative. It does not give an accurate account of how the expression "morally wrong" behaves in religious communities where God is not conceived as a commander or in secularized discursive practices where nothing can be taken for granted about the existence, nature, or acts of God. Hence, it does not give an account of what "morally wrong" means *simpliciter*. According to the approach I am defending, the meaning of a concept is always the meaning of a concept *in a particular discursive practice*. The semantics of ethical expressions must be done for one community at a time. Second, the role of a semantic explication like the one we are considering is expressive. It makes explicit in a semantic idiom precisely what conditionals and principles make explicit in slightly different ways—namely, the underlying material inferential commitments of the community being investigated. It does not tell us what the underlying commitments ought to be. So even if the semantic analysis correctly explicates a given community's inferential commitments, this does not show that some other community should change its inferential commitments to conform to the expectations of a divine-command theory. Nor does it show that a Jewish, Muslim, or Christian community should remain committed to its current inferential habits.[9]

If I am right in affirming the expressive role of principles, then it is a mistake to think that any community's ethical discourse can be reduced to the most general norms accepted by its members. My approach does not assume, as David Little and Sumner Twiss did in a book that has become the standard methodological text in comparative ethics, that "all codes of conduct can be reduced to a basic norm, or set of norms."[10] This sort of reduction could be carried out only if ethical reasoning proceeded in but one direction—as Little and Twiss originally put it, in an "appellate pattern," with the most basic, general rules serving as the final court of appeal.[11] But in fact, as Little now grants, much ethical reasoning uses considerations other than basic norms to call such norms into question.[12] If "basic norms" are held accountable to other sorts of ethical commitments, as well as vice versa, there is no way to reduce codes of conduct to basic norms, as Little and Twiss originally proposed. Little's subsequent admission that ethical reasoning is not unidirectional should not, then, be viewed as a minor adjustment to the method for which he and Twiss are known. It opens the door to an inferentialist pragmatism of the sort I am defending here.

Another point worth keeping in mind is that the explicit codes and semantic theories officially promulgated in a given community do not always accurately reflect the actual inferential commitments of its members. There are several reasons for this. First and most obviously, not all official spokespersons possess the skill, time, or conceptual resources to explicate the inferential commitments of their communities in an accurate or revealing way. Second, actual inferential commitments are constantly being revised in response to new circumstances, while officially promulgated codes change slowly or not at all. So even in the best of circumstances, there is often a time lag to be taken into account. Third, the inferential, cognitive, and practical commitments of a community can have implications that escape the notice of most or all of its members. Where such implications are at odds with the official codes or semantic doctrines of the community, the resulting contradictions or tensions are often of great interest to ethical inquiry. In some cases they are the as-yet-unnoticed seeds of revolutionary change. They can also provide evidence of wishful thinking, rationalization, or other forms of ideological distortion that effectively insulate the group from critical questioning. Finally, the codes and doctrines of a community are typically the work of elites that have their own axes to grind as explicators. Any elite has an interest in projecting its own commitments as normative for the larger community for which it claims to speak. Such an elite can easily be tempted into declaring that a particular office holder's edicts or a particular text—as interpreted by the elite itself—possesses indefeasible authority. It is one thing for such authority to be asserted, and another thing for the members of the community to defer accordingly. We should therefore always be wary of the biases that are expressed in codes and doctrines, as well as the possibility that codes and doctrines represent unsuccessful attempts to enforce uniformity against the grain of communal practice. The question "Whose commitments are actually being expressed here?" is always worth asking.

For all of these reasons, then, it is unwise to take established moral codes, the officially endorsed "action guides" of ethical communities, at face value (as Little and Twiss appear to do in *Comparative Religious Ethics*). I am arguing for an approach that interprets codes expressively, contextually, and suspiciously. The ethical concepts of a community reside largely, according to my approach, in the material inferential commitments of the group's members, and to get at these we need to treat codes as a limited, sometimes severely misleading, source of evidence. If codes of conduct are understood in relation to the material inferential commitments they make explicit, then it is a mistake to identify norms (as Little and Twiss tend to do) with rules or law-like principles stated in the form of propositions or prescriptions. The pragmatic approach being pursued here assumes, on the contrary, that norms are initially implicit in practice. Material inferential commitments are fully capable of guiding action, of functioning normatively, without taking the explicit form of a rule. Hence, norms are not to be identified with rules.[13] Rules do not have the primacy in my approach that they have for Little and Twiss, who see the ethical reasoning of a community as essentially an expression of commitment to an explicitly stated basic rule or set of such rules. From my pragmatic point of view, their approach not only pays insufficient attention to the criticism of basic rules in terms of other ethical considerations, it also gets the expressive relations between inferential practice and rules exactly the wrong way around. Hence the importance of focusing on *discursive practices* rather than simply on *codes* in comparative ethics.

CONCLUSION

Sacredness is unveiled through your own experience, and
lives in you to the degree that you accept that experience
as your teacher, mother, state, church, even, or perhaps
particularly, if it comes into conflict with the abstract received wisdom that power always tries to convince you to
live by. One of power's unconscious functions is to rob
you of your own experience by saying: we know better,
whatever you may have seen or heard, whatever cockeyed
story you come up with; we are principle, and if experience contradicts us, why then you must be guilty of something. Power—whether church, school, state, or family—
usually does this at first in a charming way while feeding
you chocolate cake, bread and wine, advanced degrees,
tax shelters, grant programs, and a strong national defense. Only when contradicted does it show its true face,
and try to kill you. Instead, kill it inside you fast, and do
it whatever damage seems practical in the outer world.
Next, put your arms around everything that has ever happened to you, and give it an affectionate squeeze.
—Bill Holm, *The Music of Failure*

DEMOCRACY AND MODERN EVILS

Eminent writers have recently been inviting us to choose sides on the modern age, as if they knew the essence of modernity and whether, on the
whole, it has been a good or a bad thing. The ones who say that modernity
has mainly been a good thing tend to think of democracy as its essence.
The ones who imply, at least in their tone and their selection of examples,
that modernity has mainly been a bad thing tend to see talk of democracy
as a sort of smoke screen, designed to draw attention away from modern
evils. Both sides tend to describe modernity as an essential underlying structure. They differ over what that structure is and how democracy relates to
it. The temptation seems strong to find something in particular that stands
for modernity itself, some set of necessary and sufficient conditions the
absence of which would make a form of life pre- or postmodern, some basic
trait or structural feature in terms of which modernity can be judged.

Beginning in this way tends to block the path of moral inquiry and social
criticism. It does so by narrowing one's focus too quickly, reducing one's
ability to recognize complexity and ambiguity or to experience moral am-

bivalence. Disbelieving in essences gives no certain protection against this habit of thought. If you doubt this, consider the antiessentialist who commits himself to the doctrine that modern thought, the history of philosophy from Plato to Hegel, or perhaps even the "Western project" itself, is (in essence) the history of essentialism or the metaphysics of presence. In one breath he tells us that there are no essences; in the next he describes an entire age or epoch as if it had one. And from what point of view does the postmodern oracle speak? At times he claims to speak from the perspective of the emerging future, the character of which he cannot specify; at others he seems to hover in midair above the epoch he describes. He is prepared to think through any position but his own. When pressed he merely repeats the hard sayings of his postmodernist masters. Delineating an alternative to the system of the now-vanishing present, he says, is mere complicity in that system, so he must excuse himself from defending a "position." Yet his descriptions of the age are obviously saturated with moral outrage.

His opposite number typically responds, first, by pointing out the implicit contradiction, and second, by defending everything his postmodernist opponent wishes to destroy or deconstruct. He claims to understand and represent what makes Western culture or the modern period worth caring about, and that, for him, is the whole story. On what basis can he defend the achievements of an entire age or culture? It would be viciously circular, he thinks, to appeal to parochial values in defending his conclusions. So he goes transcendental. He feels he must rise above the age and look down upon us, judging us from afar. Like his opponent, he has trouble explaining the point of view he claims to occupy.

When writers set out to instruct us about the essence or deep structure of modernity, and we take their claims at face value, at most one writer or school of writers can be correct. But suppose we take them—against their stated wishes, if necessary—to be saying simply that the so-called essence or deep structure is something about modernity worth studying in detail. Then we can go on to ask how a detailed description of *that* might be integrated into our understanding of other things within the same temporal field. Mere comprehensiveness of detail, of course, would be debilitating if taken as an end in itself. There are too many details to assimilate and more coming in all of the time. Do we not, then, need to be told which are essential? Yes we do, but here the word *essential* does not mean "of or pertaining to an essence." It means "the sort of thing you need to know about, given acceptable ends and concerns." Many things can be essential in this pragmatic sense. The distinction that matters is not the one between essences and accidents or that between deep structures and the phenomena to which they give rise, but rather the distinction between the trivial and what is worth caring about.

Needless to say, drawing the distinction between triviality and significance in a study of modern democratic culture is in part a moral and political task, and it can generate heated controversy. Not everybody writing about modernity shares the same ends or concerns. When a writer says that some X is essential to our understanding of modernity, it is wise to ask: relative to what ends? What concerns make sense of this writer's descriptions and evaluations, and what reason might we have for sharing those concerns or rejecting them? It would not be worth asking our descriptive questions about modernity unless something were at stake, something about the modern age that makes us want to bury it or resurrect it, to condemn it or mourn its passing. If we knew what was at stake, we might know which details were essential in the relevant sense.

In this book, modern democratic practices and ideals are the objects of my concern. I have been spending many pages trying to understand them. But I am not claiming that democracy is the essence of modernity. Nor am I claiming that the social practices in which democratic ideals are embedded live up to those ideals themselves. Far from it. The so-called democratic societies—though often preferable, on the whole, to their predecessors and competitors—are in fact severely deficient when judged from the perspective implied by their own best thinking. So my ambivalence is not only directed toward modernity, conceived as an epoch that includes much else besides democracy, but also toward modern democracies, understood as societies officially yet imperfectly committed to democratic ideals.

Assuming, as I do, that democratic individuality is a good thing, not to be confused with atomistic dissolution of social life, does not mean that it compensates for the evils of alienation and exploitation, still less for the horrors of racism, slavery, and mass death. "The evil cannot be willed or wanted or philosophically tolerated, whatever good it may lead to unintentionally," as George Kateb rightly says.[1] We can praise the genuine achievements of modernity, according to Kateb, "and still believe that no amount of greatness can weigh as much, or outweigh, the horrors. There is no commensurability, no wish to strike a balance. The horror of totalitarianism is unforgivable: incommensurate with other evils and with all greatness. Still, there is a life, a life in modernity. Political theory must try to take it in, in its vast indefiniteness" (*Hannah Arendt*, 170). Not only political theory, I would add, but critical thought in general.

Postmodernism is apocalyptic in tone. It prepares the way for something radically new—something, utterly beyond modernity, which has heretofore appeared, if at all, only at the margins or in the fissures of official Western culture. Traditionalism, on the contrary, tends toward nostalgia. It is trying to find its way back to premodern traditions in the hope of reconstructing and defending them anew. The difference between the two is often summed up in a question like the one MacIntyre poses halfway through

After Virtue: "Nietzsche or Aristotle?" It is as if our troubled journey beyond modernity had finally brought us all, after much strife and destruction, to the same crossroad, where we must turn either right or left, certain only that modernity itself lies in ruin behind us.

But there is something wrong with this picture, and not merely with its stark and misleading disjunction. There can be little doubt that many influential modern thinkers have attempted to escape history and tradition. Elsewhere I have tried to contribute to the historiography of their effort and to the diagnosis of their failures. Yet I see no good reason to suppose that modernity, even as we know it in the West, is the expression of a single project, the career of a single ambition. There is more to modernity than that. There is a life, a complicated network of practices and institutions and goods and evils to be taken in.

Declaring modern democratic aspiration a good thing need not lessen our capacity to recognize modern evils: alienation, racism, anti-Semitism, the horrors of mass death, the prospect of nuclear war, the suffering of the poor, the subjugation of women, the banality of political discourse, and so on. It does, however, make the now-familiar reductive slogans of our social critics seem irresponsibly one-sided: that modernity is simply the Enlightenment project in collapse; an enterprise of logocentric self-deception, the death of authentic political action, the triumph of instrumental reason; or "nothing more than discipline concealed."[2] There is truth in each of these slogans. They are not, however, the whole truth, and if they were nothing but the truth, we would all be too far gone to know it. Yet in making this point one can easily appear to be implying that we should disregard our misgivings about modern evils.

George Orwell, in a commentary on the "twilight-of-the-gods" mentality expressed in "Sweeney Agonistes," remarked sardonically that T. S. Eliot had achieved "the difficult feat of making modern life out to be worse than it is."[3] By now our critics have practiced Eliot's difficult feat so many times and with such zeal that they have made it look easy. Any graduate student can perform it at a moment's notice. More demanding and more worthy of respect is the kind of ambivalence Orwell worked into the crack about Eliot. It can be found throughout much of his best social criticism— sometimes directed toward features of his own society, at others toward features of British socialism. Few writers can hold together contempt for and appreciation of different aspects of a single object so successfully. I think especially of his various commentaries on mass culture. Orwell can sound like Adorno when he talks about tinned food or the decadence of a life dominated by machines, but he can also make us see an ordinary bourgeois paperweight or a cup of properly brewed tea as a fitting object of love. How many writers could work all of this, and much more, into a picture of our culture without seeming insincere or hopelessly incoherent?

More common is the rhetoric of half-hearted concession, in which one first concedes the truth of a proposition, utters the word "but" emphatically, and then immediately introduces another proposition designed to drain away the force of the first. When we hear certain intellectuals say that blacks have been terribly mistreated *but* . . . , we know what to expect next and are right to suspect an urge to excuse inaction in the face of injustice. Nothing could be further from the sort of ambivalence I propose. Not everyone will look kindly on my ambivalent praise of democracy. But then some people, as Orwell once said, think "half a loaf is the same as no bread."[4]

If we decide to use democratic ideals to help us get critical leverage on some of the bad and horrific things around us, we will be using concepts our own age makes available to us to criticize it. We are, I believe, entitled to these concepts, and the early champions of modern democracy were rationally justified in introducing them. But it is self-deceptive to imagine, as they often did, that democratic norms are free-floating products of pure reason, wholly independent of tradition. Like all norms, ours are embedded in contingent, fallible social practices. The sad truth is that these practices have themselves often been used to buttress unjust institutions, turned to bad ends, and defended by horrific means.

Emerson once remarked wisely on our incompetence "to solve the times. Our geometry cannot span the huge orbits of the prevailing ideas, behold their return, and reconcile their opposition." The question of the times finally resolves "itself into a practical question of the conduct of life. How shall I live?"[5] Even when phrased in the first person singular, the practical question has a political dimension, because each of us bears some responsibility for the condition of society and the arrangements that govern it. The question is not whether ours is an age we would prefer, all things considered, into which to be born. None of us has a choice in that. So our question had better be how to live here and now, under the circumstances in which we actually find ourselves.

THREE CONSTITUENCIES

In a passage worth quoting at length, the historian David Hollinger has distinguished three "formidable constituencies" that are currently contending for control of the American state:

> One is a business elite that, in an age of international corporations, finds more and more of its employees and factories abroad. This elite has some need for the American state, but it can get along without attending very carefully to the needs of the nation, the people who constitute the community of American citizens. The second constituency identifies with one or more diasporas and sees the United States more as a site for transnational affiliations than as an

affiliation of its own. The proponents of diasporic consciousness sometimes look to the state for entitlements, but, like the business elite, they have little incentive to devote themselves to the welfare of the [civic] national community. In the meantime, a third constituency has claimed America with a vengeance. This third constituency is made up of a great variety of Middle Americans, evangelical Christians, advocates of family values, and supporters of Newt Gingrich and of Rush Limbaugh. Many of these Americans are suspicious of the state except as an enforcer of personal morality, but they claim the nation as, in effect, their own ethnic group.[6]

It takes only a little reflection to realize that none of these already-mobilized constituencies is currently behaving in accordance with a substantively democratic conception of justice. To some significant degree, they all lack the virtue of justice as democrats define it. The business elite is busy hoarding wealth, depressing tax rates, exploiting foreign workers, breaking unions, dismantling arrangements that offer hope to the poor and the insane, and preventing reform of the electoral process. The cultural Right—not to be confused with Middle America as such—reinforces sexist hierarchy in the family while struggling in other social arenas to maintain privileged status for men, whites, and conservative Christians. Some leaders of the diasporic communities have used the ideology of multiculturalism to secure entitlements from the state, but they often actively discourage the broader identifications that would allow effective democratic coalitions to come together.

Associated with the three constituencies we have a set of stock characters: the jet-setting executive, the Bible-thumping evangelical, and members-in-good-standing of the cult of ethnicity in all of its forms. Those who play the roles can purchase the requisite uniforms, gear, and preferred sources of infotainment from multinational corporations, which have discovered how to fill their coffers by multiplying and merchandising identities. But be warned; anyone who buys in is agreeing to conform to a type. The process of conscription starts early. The main choice that many young people think they face today is which type in a standard menu of types to conform to. This choice first presents itself to children in schoolyard options like jock, nerd, babe, Goth, straight edge, homeboy, and skateboarder—each with its own costly emblems and accoutrements. Boys can be like their favorite sports hero, girls can be like their favorite pop star, if only they fork over the cash. But none of these options provides a means of escaping an essentially docile role in one of the three main adult constituencies unless the activities and role models they involve happen to awaken a desire for excellence and self-cultivation—for individuality.

Democracy will face unpromising odds at the national level so long as the three entrenched constituencies jointly control the political landscape and behave as they have been behaving. Its ideals can achieve political expression only when people learn to think of themselves as individuals while identifying with a broader ethical inheritance and political community. On the issue of democratic individuality I stand with Emerson, Whitman, and Thoreau, and against the communitarians and traditionalists who have cast aspersions on this ideal. Theorists have given individuality a bad name by misconstruing it as essentially atomistic and possessive. The democratic ideal of individuality is not a fiction of complete independence from influence.[7] It is a set of interlocking virtues—including courage and self-trust—that are required to resist conformity to socially mandated types. The only way to acquire such virtues is to participate in social practices of a kind that direct one's attention to intrinsically valuable goods and away from goods that can be selfishly pursued and hoarded. In our circumstances, as in most others, all social practices directed toward excellence—including crafts, arts, sciences, and sports—are threatened by greed and docility. If we fail to protect such practices and the modes of identity-formation, self-transcendence, and reason-exchange they sustain, it is foolhardy to expect concerted democratic action to remain possible for long. A nation of selfish conformists—entirely uncommitted to the self-enlarging, other-regarding, excellence-oriented demands of individuality—would be a nation inherently incapable of citizenship.

The social practices that matter most directly to democracy, as I have argued at length, are the discursive practices of ethical deliberation and political debate. The discursive exchange essential to democracy is likely to thrive only where individuals identify to some significant extent with a community of reason-givers.[8] At the local level, this may be the community constituted by arguments over who does the dishes, what to do with the garbage we produce, how the police are behaving, and what should be covered in a high school curriculum. But at the national level it must be the people as a whole, attending to the concerns and well-being of the people as a whole. The phrase "as a whole" here is not intended to reify the people into something that will itself become the object of mystical attachment or awe. It is meant simply to rule out implicit definition of the people in terms of a constituency. In the present context, this means at a minimum the avoidance of implicitly ethnic or racial specifications of who the people really are. Yet an implicitly racist usurpation of the concept of the people is only one obstacle to the creation of a democratic politics. Another is an inability or unwillingness—on the part of diasporic communities, workers, the poor, and others who would benefit most directly from democratic social change—to identify with any group larger than their own faction. It is by no means clear how the friends of democracy can overcome this obstacle, especially in the face of the business elite's strategies for reinforcing ethnic identification through the merchandising of life-styles. It will be a formidable challenge, to say the least, and well worth our best efforts in the coming decades.

BEYOND SECULAR LIBERALISM AND THEOLOGICAL TRADITIONALISM

Hollinger's three constituencies should be kept in mind when one evaluates the behavior of the intellectuals who have acquired positions of influence in our major institutions of higher education. The social-contract theorists have become a dominant force in law schools, ethics centers, and philosophy departments—thanks mainly to the intellectual and moral authority of John Rawls's *Theory of Justice*. Rawls saw utilitarianism as his principal opponent in normative theory. But the ease with which his social-contract theory established itself as *the* philosophical position most worthy of serious attention had as much to do with the absence of strong competitors as it did with the theoretical ingenuity and argumentative power with which Rawls developed his position. In the decades immediately preceding the publication of Rawls's masterwork, American normative philosophy had largely confined itself to something called metaethics, the second-order analysis of moral language (carried out for the most part without answering the first-order questions of how a person should live or a state should behave). So Rawls was stepping into a near-vacuum, and doing so at a moment when the students who had come of age during the controversies over Civil Rights and the Vietnam War were demanding that normative inquiry be given a central place in the curriculum. In the philosophy departments, the most important effect of Rawls's work was simply that normative inquiry became a respectable philosophical specialty again. On the other hand, because it initially occupied the philosophical stage almost by itself and encouraged its audience to think of utilitarianism as its only worthy competitor, Rawlsian philosophy did not at first foster discussion of the full range of theoretical alternatives in social and political theory. And the extremely abstract nature of the discussion it has engendered has limited its impact on the behavior of Hollinger's three constituencies.

The sons, daughters, and future members of the business elite who read *A Theory of Justice* in college or law school are at least confronted, if only momentarily, with serious reasons for supposing that their actions are constrained by fairness and by the rights of the least well-off. It is a very good thing for such people to spend a few weeks of their young adulthood imagining themselves behind "the veil of ignorance" in "the original position." It is good for them and good for the rest of us that they have at least once had to ask themselves what sort of social ground rules they would select if they did not know they were about to occupy positions of power and wealth. But as Rawls gradually came to realize, the egalitarian arguments of *A Theory of Justice* were themselves expressions of a comprehensive view of life not widely shared by the general population—a view disparaged by the cultural right as secular liberalism.

For some time Rawls struggled, with only modest success, to reformulate his liberalism as a *political* doctrine designed to appeal to citizens holding various reasonable comprehensive views. The goal was to show that one need not be a Kantian liberal, like Rawls himself, to accept his reformulated theory as a basis for political order and social cooperation. It was a noble project, and Rawls deserves credit for the intellectual honesty as well as the patience and philosophical skill with which he pursued it. But for reasons hinted at in chapter 3, I doubt that the project can be made to work on its own terms. The sticking point, the issue that reveals the implausibility of his contractarian premises, is the question of what role religious reasons are permitted to play in political argument. On this issue Rawls started off with a doctrine that prohibited citizens from relying essentially on such reasons when deliberating on constitutional essentials and certain other basic matters. This allowed writers like Neuhaus and Hauerwas to portray him as the enemy of everything they stand for and as the symbol of secular liberalism's triumph in the elite educational institutions. Rawls's subsequent attempt to soften his stand on this issue brought it somewhat closer to the intuitions of the American public on the ethics of citizenship. But the concessions it made to those intuitions do not seem to emerge naturally from the contractarian premises with which Rawls began. Hence Rawls was left, at the end of the day, in an awkward stance. He was a secular liberal who realized, quite rightly, that secular liberalism could not successfully play the expressive role that it originally sought to play in American democratic politics. He hoped to modify social-contract theory into something distinct from secular liberalism as a comprehensive view of life. Yet the modifications, which incorporated a few lessons from Dewey and Hegel, seem finally to have gone against the grain of the theory's premises.

Richard Rorty has performed a great service to American democracy by reviving interest in the tradition of Whitman and Dewey and by formulating an unambiguously expressivist account of philosophy's role in the culture. Democratic and egalitarian ideals have had few more eloquent defenders in our period. Yet, like Rawls, Rorty tends to waver between a form of pluralism that in principle ought to welcome the expression of religious as well as secular outlooks in political contexts and a relatively aggressive form of secular liberalism that appears to exclude views unlike his own from public life. His style is livelier than Rawls's and more accessible to people trained in neither philosophy nor legal theory. But in the many passages where Rorty seems to be emulating Nietzsche rather than Dewey as his model social critic, he becomes too naughty, too much the violator of what his fellow citizens recognize as common sense, to perform the expressive function he has limned in his best work. To the proponents of diasporic communities, he often seems too smug about the benefits of liberal society. To the cultural right, he is a symbol of the aestheticism and decadence to which secular liberalism leads.

A traditionalist like Hauerwas obviously has no desire to perform an expressively reflective function on behalf of democratic culture. He styles himself as an external critic of that culture, which he addresses as a "resident alien." He speaks as a member of the "Christian colony" within liberal society.[9] This has not, however, prevented him from being named "America's Best Theologian" by an authority as dedicated to the status quo as *Time* magazine.[10] One suspects that his antiliberal screed may be more comforting to the Christian members of Hollinger's three constituencies than Hauerwas intends it to be. We are, after all, in an era when any self-described liberal stands little chance of getting elected to national office. If one wants to be prophetic in this time and place, why choose liberalism as one's chief ideological target? The Republican Party and the Fox News Network tell American Christians on a daily basis that they are a beleaguered minority in an evil, liberal order. Why confront the fact of being a majority complicit in injustice if you can believe something like this?

Many of Hauerwas's readers seem to have taken consolation from the idea that strengthening one's identification with the church at the expense of identification with the nation is the most important step one can take toward membership in a community of true virtue. The leading political beneficiaries of Hauerwas's revival of virtue ethics appear to have been not some latter-day Dorothy Day but Pope John Paul II and former Secretary of Education, William Bennett. Hauerwas has not seen fit to remind American Christians forcibly that, as a majority in a wealthy world power with a democratic constitution, they constantly display the character of their community in part by discharging their responsibilities as citizens well or poorly.

It is largely with Rawls, Rorty, and Hauerwas in mind that I have tried to develop an alternative public philosophy in this book. In the last several chapters, I have defended a type of pragmatism that appropriates the most promising features of Rorty's work while steering clear of its philosophical and stylistic excesses. Throughout the book, I have tried to define an acceptable path between the liberalism of Rawls and Rorty, on the one hand, and the traditionalism of MacIntyre and Hauerwas, on the other.

In Rawlsian terminology, my position might be termed a sort of "modus vivendi" pluralism, for the public philosophy I propose does not insist on the need to ground political discussion in a set of rules no reasonable and rational citizen could reasonably reject. I am trying to articulate a form of pluralism, one that citizens with strong religious commitments can accept and that welcomes their full participation in public life without fudging on its own premises. But I see this pluralism primarily as an existing feature of the political culture, not as a philosophical doctrine needing to be imposed on it. Our political culture is already pluralistic in the relevant sense. What I have tried to supply is a philosophical statement of what this pluralism involves. It is a remarkably widespread and steady commitment, on the part of citizens, to talk things through with citizens unlike themselves. This commitment is there, prior to all theorizing, in the habits of the people. The burden of proof is on those who want to change it. Because it is an aspect of our substantive commitment to the ethical life of democracy, because it coheres with the widely (but not unanimously) held conviction that no merely human perspective has a monopoly on the truth, it seems inappropriate to think of it as a mere modus vivendi. It is not something we "settle for" in the absence of a real social contract or authentic communitarian unity.[11]

To the members of Hollinger's three constituencies this book serves primarily as a reminder that they are also members of a civic nation. It is a nation that needs their active help and concern if it is to endure as a people committed to democracy, let alone as a people capable of living up to democratic ideals. The terms "nation" and "people" here are synonyms, and are not to be confused with the nation-state, considered as a sprawling bureaucratic apparatus for conducting the business of government. Hauerwas is quite right to say that the call to sacrifice oneself for one's country today sounds a lot "like being asked to die for the telephone company."[12] But this is partly because we tend to confuse the civic nation—the people—with the nation-state. In this book, I have been encouraging identification with the civic nation, with the community of reason-givers constituted by the democratic practice of holding one another responsible. This implies no affection for the massive institutional configuration of the nation-state, of which we should always remain suspicious. The American nation-state has proven itself especially worthy of suspicion in recent decades. And as chapter 10 makes clear, identification with the civic nation implies no reluctance to construct discursive communities that transcend national boundaries. I am not recommending that we become *preoccupied* with our identities as members of a civic nation. In my view, this is merely one important concern among others. Indeed, a life lived solely or even largely as an expression of this concern would hold no attraction for me.

In part 2, I have sought to persuade seriously committed religious citizens, especially those members of the Christian majority who have half-acknowledged democratic commitments in their hearts, that identifying with the civic nation in a democratic republic like ours need not conflict with their theological convictions. First, I argued against the notion that Rawlsian liberalism offers a descriptively adequate account of our political culture. One can reject the liberal theory without rejecting the culture.

Second, I offered an account of the benign sense in which our political discourse is secularized. Hence, one can participate in it wholeheartedly without implicitly discounting one's theological convictions. Third, I offered a good deal of immanent criticism of the new traditionalism, with the aim of showing that its case for rejecting modern democratic societies is deeply flawed, even on its own terms. I have not denied that *some* coherent theological outlooks are at odds with democracy. This goes without saying. Theocratic theologies are plainly inconsistent with democracy, as are radical forms of separatism that depict participation in any religiously plural society as essentially vicious or sinful. But one of the most important findings presented here is that Christian theological orthodoxy is not the source of the new traditionalism's antidemocratic sentiments or tendencies. Robert Merrihew Adams, Karl Barth, George Hunsinger, and Nicholas Wolterstorff are all orthodox Trinitarians who have played prominent parts in these pages; each of them takes an attitude toward the world outside the church that exhibits a commendable commitment to democracy. The politically worrisome aspects of the new traditionalism derive from sources quite distinct from any doctrine shared by the major varieties of Trinitarian theology. At a moment when orthodox Judaism in Israel and orthodox Islam around the world are struggling to sort through analogous issues, study of Christian thinkers who have connected theological orthodoxy with democratic practice is an academic topic of global significance. It would be a good thing if the relevant parts of Barth's *Church Dogmatics* came to hold a prominent place in the seminary curricula of all the desert faiths. So much the better if voices seeking to democratize religious institutions were heard there as well.

Democracy involves substantive normative commitments, but does not presume to settle in advance the ranking of our highest values. Nor does it claim to save humanity from sin and death. It takes for granted that reasonable people will differ in their conceptions of piety, in their grounds for hope, in their ultimate concerns, and in their speculations about salvation. Yet it holds that people who differ on such matters can still exchange reasons with one another intelligibly, cooperate in crafting political arrangements that promote justice and decency in their relations with one another, and do both of these things without compromising their integrity. Cooperating democratic citizens tend also to be individuals who care about matters higher than politics, and expect not to get their way on each issue that comes before the public for deliberation. It must be said, however, that there are times when anyone with a conscience will be hard-pressed to say why one ought to identify with a nation willing to adopt a policy inconsistent with what seems patently right and true. For me, our use of capital punishment and our excessive use of military force are among the issues that make me wonder whether paying taxes to the state is a form of complicity from which I ought to extricate myself, regardless of the cost. For many others, abortion raises similar doubts. But even if I were to refuse paying my taxes, thus following Thoreau's noble example, I would intend the gesture as an act of communication, as a signal to other members of my community that I intend to hold them responsible for their injustices. So long as I am thinking along those lines, I am still identifying with that community, even as I express my alienation from it. This sort of ambivalent membership has a notable lineage in democratic culture.

It is worth keeping in mind that similar issues arise concerning one's membership in any sizable group, not least of all a religious one. The Christian churches are now torn on numerous doctrinal, practical, and institutional issues, including many of the same issues that divide the rest of us politically. Many Christians have faced hard decisions over whether they could continue in good conscience to remain members in good standing of a group that, say, bans women from the priesthood or permits same-sex couples to marry. It is easy to see how these issues can come to have such a strong bearing on the question of continued identification with the group. But this should remind us that no social body, including the church, provides immunity from the dilemmas and conflicts of membership. Retreating from identification with the American people while intensifying one's identification with the people of God leaves a Christian with roughly the same dilemmas, the same ambivalence, with which he or she started. The only alternative is full-fledged separatism, which involves commitment to a group that is small enough and uniform enough to eliminate ambivalence altogether, at least for a while. But why would I want to confine my *discursive* community to the people who already agree with me on all essential matters? Isn't part of the point of trying to hold one another responsible discursively that we do not agree on everything and therefore *need* to talk things through?

Secular liberals, sensing the demise of the religious Left, might want to argue that the only way to save our democracy from the religious Right is to inhibit the expression of religious reasons in the public square. Aside from whatever theoretical errors might lie behind this argument, it is foolhardy to suppose that anything like the Rawlsian program of restraint or what Rorty calls the Jeffersonian compromise will succeed in a country with our religious and political history. So the practical question is not whether religious reasons will be expressed in public settings, but by whom, in what manner, and to what ends. Secular liberals underestimate the role they themselves have played in shifting the balance between the religious Left and the religious Right in American politics. The rise of the religious Right is in some measure a backlash against the perceived dominance of secular liberalism over certain important institutions and professions. In the 1960s, Neuhaus and MacIntyre were prominent figures on the Left, and Hauerwas was a young Niebuhrian liberal. Secular liberalism has unwittingly fostered the decline of the religious Left by persuading religious intellectuals that liberal society is intent on excluding the expression of their most strongly felt convictions. The new traditionalism portrays the religious Left as *a mutation of secular liberalism* that is infecting the churches like a deadly virus.

This picture gets all of the relevant historical patterns wrong. The first modern revolutionaries were not secular liberals; they were radical Calvinists. Among the most important democratic movements in American history were Abolitionism and the Civil Rights movement; both of these were based largely in the religious communities. Religious colleges and seminaries provided strong support for both movements. If religious premises had not been adduced in support of them, it is unlikely that either movement would have resulted in success. The Christian majority needed to be persuaded in both cases that commitment to scriptural authority was at least compatible with the reform being proposed. If the religious Left does not soon recover its energy and self-confidence, it is unlikely that American democracy will be capable of counteracting either the greed of its business elite or the determination of many whites to define the authentic nation in ethnic, racial, or ecclesiastical terms.

COMMUNITY

In my town an institution that calls itself a medical center—my neighbors and I call it a hospital—has gone to court, hoping to gain an exception to zoning regulations so that a block of residential housing can be converted to bureaucratic offices. The community is fighting back, fighting for its life as a community, and searching for words and reasons to use in making its case. It is a collection of little neighborhoods, all within a ten-minute walk from a meeting ground known as Community Park. Closest to the hospital lies a mainly Italian neighborhood, founded by skilled stone carvers who came here many decades back, when the university that employs me chose to build Gothic buildings that ape the architecture of Oxford and Cambridge. The house my wife and I lived in as newlyweds in our early twenties was in the Italian section, and then overlooked the entrance to the emergency room. That house and the garden behind it, which our landlord used to raise vegetables and rabbits, have long since given way to a parking garage. To one side is our neighborhood, mostly Anglo and professional. To the other is a lower-class neighborhood for many years populated only by blacks and now home also to many immigrants arriving from Latin America.

In what sense do these neighborhoods, which I have just defined in terms of ethnicity and class, constitute a community? A community is a group that holds something in common.[13] What, then, do the people living in these little neighborhoods hold in common, besides a geographical space I could arbitrarily define? Communitarians refer to communities as constituted by common ends, common ethnic roots, and common narratives. By communitarian standards, I suppose my interlocking neighborhoods are not a community at all. Perhaps the Italian neighborhood, taken by itself, might come close to qualifying, but not all three neighborhoods, taken together. Many social critics would probably say that what I call my community is in fact nothing but a collection of atomistic individuals. According to such critics, if my neighbors and I imagine that we are fighting for the existence of our community, we must really be fighting for our rights or self-interest as property holders and renters. And if the hospital has rights and interests, too, and now owns the property in the block it has gradually bought out, our dispute is just a clash of conflicting wills.

Participating in the ethical life of this place while reflecting on the issues treated in this book has led me to see my community differently—to see it as a community, but not in the communitarian sense. One way of viewing this book is as an answer to the question of what my neighbors and I hold in common. We share activities. For example, we play basketball, baseball, and soccer in one another's company. Sometimes we play next to one another in games that do not cross ethnic or racial lines. Sometimes we play against one another on teams that represent our differences. And sometimes we play with one another on teams that mix things up. Soccer has done a good deal to bring us together, because it was brought here initially by the Italians, and Anglo and black children began playing it at about the same time the Latin Americans began to arrive. On one banner day, the latter group appeared en masse, faces painted in school colors, to cheer on the high school girls in a state tournament game. On another important day, not long after Latinos began to join a soccer club founded back in the 1970s by suburban whites, a boys team called the Latin Power offered membership to a handful of Anglos. Not long thereafter, the high school boys won the state championship with a team that included Latino, African-American, Anglo, and Asian members.

We all understood what community those teams represented. Now, I don't mean to idealize that community. Racism and ethnic animosity flare up among us on a regular basis. The Guatemalan who organized and later integrated the Latin Power, and who has probably done more for our children than any other individual, was once beaten to a pulp for holding his ground on one of the basketball courts at Community Park. He has also been exploited and mistreated in many other ways by upper-middle-class whites pretending to be his friends. Three years after the state championship, the tensions between Latinos and Anglos at the high school had grown significantly. There is a local politics of ethnic identity, and it is not always pleasant or uplifting. There are also fathers among us who beat their wives and children. Many of my neighbors lack medical insurance, fear the police, and notice their incomes shrinking. Some of our children use drugs or commit suicide.

In the midst of all this, what we hold in common, what we have going for us as a community, are valued social practices and the forms of excellence they involve. We care about soccer, about how the pizzas and tortillas are made, and about having our voices heard in town hall. We want to hold each other responsible for commitments and actions, so we talk about them. We debate the merits of center forwards, anchovies, and school board candidates. Those of us who have voted at least once have begun to feel that we need not quake or bow in the presence of school superintendents, hospital executives, or other members of the professional class. Because of all of this, we are able to sense personally and say publicly what the hospital threatens to take away from us if it clumsily destroys the Italian neighborhood that links our little community together. And we are beginning to realize that if we fail to behave as if we identify with our community, a large corporation in our midst will have its way, and we will lose something we care about.

It would be foolish to think that this level of political interaction encompasses the whole of politics, but it should count for something. A correspondent in Sweden tells me that the notion of a national community as a group that holds activities in common has influenced governmental policy there on the funding of projects designed to overcome ethnic divisions resulting from a recent wave of immigration. What a commitment to democratic culture implies, so he tells me, is that governments at all levels had better make it their business to foster common activities if civil society and identification with the community as a whole are to survive the increasing awareness of ethnicity and race. No doubt, there is much to be done to fine-tune our understanding of how to provide effective support for civil society, but we already know enough, it seems to me, to experiment boldly and prudently with this end in view.

A recent book by Cornel West and Roberto Mangabeira Unger sets the need for such experimentation within a broader vision of political and economic reform.[14] One can debate the details of its proposals, but if we are to achieve anything like the reforms West and Unger advocate, it seems to me that great urgency attaches to the general project of cultivating identifications that transcend ethnicity, race, and religion—at the local and national levels. It is becoming obvious to the members of my local community that if we do not behave as a group that holds valued practices in common, including the discursive practice of holding one another responsible, we will lose something we care about. To survive as a community, we need to identify with the group we constitute and behave accordingly. Must an analogous practical inference remain beyond the reach of the civic nation?

Only, I think, if our muckrakers, novelists, poets, essayists, filmmakers, painters, singers, and professors fail to nourish the public's imagination in the right way.

There are, of course, several reasons that they might fail. The first and most obvious of these is that they might not try. They might keep themselves busy doing something else that does not advance the cause of democracy. This could be something narrowly aesthetic or academic that does not make much connection with the cause of democracy at all. Or it could be something that is meant to advance the cause of democracy but is actually misconceived and counterproductive, like the Rawlsian position on the public expression of religious reasons. Still worse, it could be something likely to weaken commitment to democracy in the public at large, like the traditionalist program of Hauerwas and MacIntyre. This book expresses my concern that the current dominance of social-contract theory in law schools, philosophy departments, and ethics centers and the rising influence of the new traditionalism in seminaries and divinity schools are mutually reinforcing tendencies in American intellectual life that spell trouble for American democracy. And I have hinted that the postmodernists in our literature departments have not made things much better. The main audience I hope to address is a younger generation of intellectuals now in the process of deciding how to define its vocation, its task. They can use a reminder, I suspect, of their own half-conscious commitment to a form of free expression and exchange of reasons that is not adequately accounted for in Rawlsian, traditionalist, or postmodernist terms.

But even if highly gifted intellectuals choose to embrace a vocation of improving the prospects of democratic community, there is no guarantee that things will go well. It would be a grave mistake, for example, if they came to believe that a nation like ours could become a community in the communitarian sense. No nation the size and complexity of ours can realistically imagine itself as a group bound together by agreement on a ranking of its highest values, a religious vision of the good, or a big story about the origins and destiny of a people. This would be an unrealistic self-image even for the collection neighborhoods around Community Park. And it would quickly become dangerous if pursued through legislation that either inhibited the free expression of religious belief or effectively established one set of religious commitments as the presuppositions everyone is expected to take for granted when exchanging reasons with their peers.

The kind of community that democrats should be promoting at the local, state, and national levels of politics is the kind that involves shared commitment to the Constitution and the culture of democracy. In America, this culture consists of a loose and ever-changing collection of social practices that includes such activities as quilting, baseball, and jazz. But its central and definitive component is the discursive practice of holding one another responsible for the actions we commit, the commitments we undertake, and the sorts of people we become. The expressive vocation of a democratic intellectual involves identifying with the community constituted by this practice, attempting to make its various features explicit, and subjecting those features to critical scrutiny and revision.

Hegel worried that intellectuals in his own day were responding in essentially debilitating ways to the social situation in which they found themselves. Among the types he had in mind were the Kantian formalist who estranged himself from that situation by trying to rise completely above it in thought, the proponent of premodern virtue who opposed the way of the world, and the Romantic enthusiast for a community of racial or religious fervor. Of these three types, only the third overcomes alienation from the group immediately around him, but he does so by alienating himself from his own implicit claim to have reasons for his stance. Hegel's philosophy was intended to overcome the forms of alienation represented by the first two types while overcoming the irrationalism of the third. I have attempted something similar in relation to my interlocutors in philosophy, political theory, and religious thought.

The key to being able to reconcile oneself responsibly to one's social situation, Hegel thought, is to identify with what is *rational* in it. A social situation devoid of rationality would of course be hopeless; there would be no *reason* to reconcile oneself to it. If I were actually in such a situation, I would be incapable of knowing it, because I would not know anything. A social situation devoid of rationality would be one in which I would have no way to acquire the conceptual skills required to criticize it. But if rationality is itself necessarily embodied in a social practice, as Hegel argued, then I who think critical thoughts about my own society am actually dependent as a critic on what is rational in my social situation. I think, therefore I belong to a community of reason-exchangers. This is Hegel's version of the Cartesian *cogito*. If I am truly conscious of what is going on when I perform acts of social criticism, the proper object of my identification will be neither disembodied reason, premodern virtue, nor my ethnic roots, but an actual community of reason-givers.[15] The community at issue, then, is that constituted by our mutual recognition of one another as those to whom each one of us is responsible in the practice of exchanging reasons about ethical and political questions.

Brought down to the level of Community Park, this is just a way of saying that my neighbors and I do not need to agree with one another on some sort of philosophical or narrative framework to be a community in the relevant sense. We are already members of such a community insofar as we are disposed to hold one another responsible in the exchange of reasons. To declare our reasons to the hospital administrators and demand reasons from them for their policies is to treat *them* as potential members of the same community. And if they choose to respond to us by *giving reasons* and holding themselves responsible to *act reasonably*, they will be members of that community.

Framing the issue in this way immediately draws attention to a deeper threat that democracy faces. For it is clear, in the case of the neighborhoods around Community Park, that the exchange of reasons might well be undermined in any number of ways, even if the community becomes conscious of itself as a community and if its spokespersons and officials behave wisely. For example, much depends in this case, as in so many other similar ones, on the independence, courage, and decency of the local press and judiciary. Only time will tell whether the hospital has already acquired a degree of power and influence over the relevant media and decision-making organs that permits it to have its way without having to give good reasons for its further acquisition of property. A single bad decision by a single fallible official could easily bring it about that there is no discursive community left that is capable of mounting resistance on its own behalf.

If we move above the local level, it is obvious to any fair-minded observer that corporate influence over the electoral and legislative processes now threatens to circumvent a politically effective and open public exchange of reasons on issues of concern to the citizenry. One cannot honestly call our mode of government democratic if corporate influence on it is so strong that the reasons offered by the public against its decisions have little bearing on legislative outcomes. It is now hard to claim with a straight face that either the Supreme Court or the press retains its traditional independence of the political process. A severely worrisome development is the rapid shrinkage of the number of corporations controlling the means of public communication, both in the United States and internationally. "Six firms dominate all American mass media."[16] Not long ago the number was fifty. Globally, the communications system "is dominated by three or four dozen large transnational corporations . . . with fewer than ten mostly U.S.-based media conglomerates towering over the global market."[17] It will take all of the intellectual and organizational creativity that the next generation of democrats can muster to sustain recognizably democratic forms of public discourse in contemporary circumstances.

I do not suppose that democratic rule is a simple matter, to be achieved by some sort of unmediated popular uprising. There is an indispensable role for "small dedicated groups" of committed democrats to play in the revival of democracy. No sensible democrat can be opposed to "elites" in this benign sense.[18] Whitman must have been conscious of his own dependence on the circle of literary radicals that had gathered around Emerson.[19] The social structure of a healthy modern democracy would include a plurality of such groups, several million serious activists, and a broader body of professionals and citizens prepared to hear signals of alarm, exchange reasons in their local settings, donate some time and money, and cast their votes accordingly.[20] Despite our evident vices, this is not beyond the bounds of reasonable hope. In a narrowly political context, the question of character thus becomes the question of whether and how we can go about shaping people who have the virtues required to play these roles.

Over the next several years these virtues will probably be much needed and sorely tested in determining the course of the struggle against terror. The struggle will be against our own fear and resentment as much as it will be against terrorism itself. Democratically committed intellectuals and journalists have a crucial role to play in articulating and reinforcing the people's latent desire for justice over against the other passions that tend to arise when a nation is under attack. It is also their duty to make clear to our political and military leaders that not a single injustice against the civilian populations of our own country and other countries will go unnoticed or unopposed. The struggle against terror—against the fear and resentment that turn democracies into imperial tyrannies—will last as long and face as many obstacles and setbacks as the struggle against terrorism itself.

The struggle against terrorism must be joined simultaneously on three fronts—one involving the disciplined use of armed force against terrorists and their supporters, a second involving the building up of international law, and a third involving persuasive argument on behalf of democracy. I have grave doubts about our conduct on all three fronts. On the military front, we have taken insufficient care to protect civilian life and shown little interest in committing ourselves to restraint in the use of force in the future. On the legal front, we have often ignored and otherwise undermined existing international law. On the ideological front, we have foundered at nearly every turn.

We rightly declare terrorism an abomination. And why is that? Because the terrorist takes deliberate aim at innocent civilians. We denounce regimes that make and use weapons of mass destruction. Right again. But we are not prepared to come to terms with the implications of these claims. The world remembers what we would like to forget. We are the ones who bombed Hiroshima and Nagasaki. And we did it on the premise that inducing *terror* in the civilian population of Japan would achieve unconditional surrender more quickly and at less cost than would otherwise have been possible. This has always been Islamic radicalism's most effective ideological weapon against us, and Osama bin Laden used it with relish in his most influential arguments. We have made and used weapons of mass destruction; we have yet to repent for this. Instead, we have retained them, tested them, and often aimed them at cities. More recently, our arrogant use of massively destructive military power announces that one nation, unconstrained by international law, will henceforth decide which regimes stand or fall. When our leaders oppose or support tyranny as it suits them, why suppose them to be interested in justice? They deliberately confuse the public about their reasons for war and the facts that justify resorting to it. They pretend to know the price of their policies in dollars, in the goodwill of other nations, and in human life. They extol humility, tradition, compassion, and democracy, while laying plans to rule the world. They propose their own will as the standard of right and wrong.

Do these objections justify terrorist attacks against us? Of course not. Nothing could justify such behavior. But until we sincerely and persuasively renounce the callous taking of civilian life and the casual tolerance of dictators and princely tyrants, we will be seen as both hypocritical and terrifyingly dangerous. It is foolish to expect the world to believe on the basis of little more than our saying so that we are committed to democracy and justice. The world suspects that we believe in technological might, oil, money, and entertainment. Our deepest apparent commitment is simply to having our way. It is one thing to have just cause to wage war, another to have the moral authority to do so.

In the long run, the ideological-moral front is the one on which the struggle against terrorism will be won or lost, and we are now losing it very badly. In truth, there is only one way to win it. That is by applying our ideals and principles to our own conduct with the same sense of purpose and courage that we demonstrated when denouncing Taliban thugs. In this rhetorical engagement, the character exhibited in the conduct of the arguer will determine who believes and trusts what is said. We will be sorely tempted in the months ahead to make exceptions on our own behalf. Yet we must somehow find it in us to become the people we are claiming to be. To win the struggle against terrorism, we must win the struggle against terror within our own political community.

Where These Waters Flow

I want to conclude by briefly considering a version of the question of character that was recently posed by the Augustinian political theorist, Jean Bethke Elshtain, at a conference I attended in Richmond, Virginia. As she put the question, "How long before the stream runs dry?" The stream, I take it, is a metaphor for the sources of ethical and religious virtue that sustain our democracy. Her worry was that citizens of democracies are in the process of losing the virtues needed for having a democracy at all. It is only a matter of time, she feared, before the stream runs dry. I believe many sensible citizens are asking themselves something like this version of the question of character today.

Now, how does Whitman respond? In fact, he offers no answer to it. He does not say how long it will be before the stream runs dry. His real interest, I think, is in the prior question of where we imagine those waters to flow. His answer, in "Autumn Rivulets," was this:

> In you whoe'er you are my book perusing,
> In I myself, in all the world, these currents flowing . . .[21]

The import of this answer is that we should not imagine the life-giving sources on which we depend as something essentially alien to American democratic modernity. That stream is in us and of us when we engage in our democratic practices. Democracy, then, is misconceived when taken to be a desert landscape hostile to whatever life-giving waters of culture and tradition might still flow through it. Democracy is better construed as the name appropriate to the currents themselves in this particular time and place. In *North Star Country*—a "history of the people of the Midwest, told from their dimension in their language"—Meridel Le Sueur imagines the people as

> a river that winds and falls and gleams erect in many dawns; lost in deep gulleys, it turns to dust, rushes in the spring freshet, emerges to the sea. The people are a story that is long incessant coming alive from the earth in better wheat, Percherons, babies, and engines, persistent and inevitable. The people always know that some of the grain will be good, some of the crop will be saved, some will return and bear the strength of the kernel, that from the bloodiest year some survive to outlive the frost.[22]

NOTES

INTRODUCTION

1. For defenses of the doctrine of neutrality, see John Rawls, *A Theory of Justice* (Cambridge, Mass.: Harvard University Press, 1971) and Ronald Dworkin, *A Matter of Principle* (Cambridge: Harvard University Press, 1985). It is interesting that many of the critics of this doctrine describe themselves as liberals. See Amy Gutmann, *Democratic Education* (Princeton: Princeton University Press, 1987); Stephen Macedo, *Liberal Virtues* (Oxford: Oxford University Press, 1990); Joseph Raz, *The Morality of Freedom* (Oxford: Oxford University Press, 1968); and George Sher, *Beyond Neutrality: Perfectionism and Politics* (Cambridge: Cambridge University Press, 1997) . I discuss the reason-tradition dichotomy in *Ethics after Babel*, expanded ed. (Princeton: Princeton University Press, 2001), pt. 2.

2. I explain all of this Rawlsian terminology and give the relevant references to Rawls's works in chapter 3 (page 65 and following).

3. Notice that I do not define modern democracy simply as rule by the people. Nor do I place emphasis primarily on the electoral process. "The heart of the matter is a principle about access to public deliberation" see (Oliver O'Donovan, *The Desire of the Nations: Rediscovering the Roots of Political Theology* [Cambridge: Cambridge University Press, 1996], 269–70).

4. O'Donovan, *Desire of the Nations*, 270.

5. John Dewey, *The Public and Its Problems* (Athens, Ohio: Swallow Press, 1927), 144, 146.

6. Dewey, *The Public*, 143.

7. Rebecca S. Chopp, "From Patriarchy into Freedom: A Conversation between American Feminist Theology and French Feminism," in *The Postmodern God: A Theological Reader*, ed. Graham Ward (Oxford: Blackwell, 1997), 237.

8. Dewey, *The Public*, 149.

9. On Emerson's deliberate use of this tactic in *Representative Men*, see Robert D. Richardson, Jr., *Emerson: The Mind on Fire* (Berkeley: University of California Press, 1995), 415.

10. The conception of religion I am taking for granted here and throughout part 1 is indebted to George Santayana, *The Life of Reason* (Amherst, N.Y.: Prometheus Books, 1998), and to the excellent exposition of Santayana in Henry Samuel Levinson, *Santayana, Pragmatism, and the Spiritual Life* (Chapel Hill: University of North Carolina Press, 1992).

11. For an explanation of what I mean by "expressive rationality," see Robert B. Brandom, *Making It Explicit: Reasoning, Representing, and Discursive Commitment* (Cambridge: Harvard University Press, 1994), 105–11, 130. This usage differs from George Lindbeck's use of the term "expressivism" in *The Nature of Doctrine: Theology and Religion in a Postliberal Age* (Philadelphia: Westminster John Knox Press, 1984). Lindbeck distinguishes "propositional," "experiential expressivist," and "cultural linguistic" theories of religion. The last of these types approximates the form

of expressivism one finds in Wilfrid Sellars and Brandom, neither of whom is an expressivist in Lindbeck's sense. The form of expressivism Lindbeck has in mind is the essentially subjectivist form associated with the Romantics; it views religious language as the expression of a prelinguistic dimension of human experience. The Sellars-Brandom form of expressivism began to take shape in Hegel's reaction against precisely this aspect of Romantic antirationalism, which he diagnosed as *"Begeisterung und Trübheit"* (ardor and muddiness) early in the preface to *The Phenomenology of Spirit*.

12. Whitman was also influenced to some extent by Hegel, as Richard Rorty points out in *Achieving Our Country: Leftist Thought in Twentieth-Century America* (Cambridge: Harvard University Press, 1998), 20–21.

CHAPTER 1
CHARACTER AND PIETY FROM EMERSON TO DEWEY

1. Walt Whitman, *Democratic Vistas*, in *Whitman: Complete Poetry and Collected Prose*, ed. Justin Kaplan (New York: Library of America, 1982), pars. 15, 14. Hereafter cited as "DV," with paragraph number.

2. Harold Bloom, *The American Religion: The Emergence of the Post-Christian Nation* (New York: Simon and Schuster, 1992), 22–25.

3. Montanus, who lived in the second century, claimed that the Holy Spirit spoke through him during his trances. His followers advocated more spontaneous liturgical celebration and emphasized that the Spirit might speak through anyone. The Montanist heresy was their claim that speech directly inspired by the Holy Spirit possessed more authority than the official pronouncements of any church official or even the scriptural record of Christ's teachings. Pelagius was a British monk who argued that if God holds human beings responsible for their sins, they must be free to behave responsibly. Augustine argued against the Pelagians that we are always already in a state of sinfulness, a condition for which we are nonetheless accountable as the result of our choices and from which only God's grace can save us. See William Placher, *A History of Christian Theology: An Introduction* (Philadelphia: Westminster Press, 1983), 50–51, 115–20.

4. Michael Lind, *The Next American Nation* (New York: Free Press, 1995), chaps. 4 and 5.

5. Of course, Robert Bellah and many others pose it in terms borrowed from Tocqueville. For an extended treatment of Bellah and his associates, see *Ethics after Babel*, expanded ed. (Princeton: Princeton University Press, 2001), pt. 3.

6. Edmund Burke, *Reflections on the Revolution in France*, ed. J.G.A. Pocock (Indianapolis: Hackett, 1987), 79.

7. Augustine of Hippo, *City of God*, trans. Henry Bettenson (London: Penguin Books, 1984), bk. 19, chap. 4.

8. Stanley Cavell, *Conditions Handsome and Unhandsome: The Constitution of Emersonian Perfectionism* (Chicago: University of Chicago Press, 1990).

9. Cavell borrows the term "perfectionism" from John Rawls, who uses it to name a position rejected in *A Theory of Justice* (Cambridge, Mass.: Harvard University Press, 1971). But Cavell appears not to mean by it what Rawls does. For Rawls, perfectionism is committed to arranging political institutions so as "to maximize

the achievement of human excellence in art, science, and culture" (325). Cavell sees the achievement, enjoyment, and respect of excellence as values that matter deeply to a democratic sensibility, but he does not set out to maximize them in a consequentialist spirit. In this respect, his position is closer to the one Robert Merrihew Adams defends in *Finite and Infinite Goods: A Framework for Ethics* (Oxford: Oxford University Press, 1999), chap. 14, than to what Rawls calls perfectionism. Adams adopts Rawls's usage, and so rejects perfectionism in this restricted sense. I will employ the term in Cavell's looser sense—according to which perfectionism need involve neither the consequentialist aim of maximizing excellence nor the notion that there is a fixed goal of perfection that all human beings should aspire to attain.

10. Ralph Waldo Emerson, *Emerson: Essays and Lectures*, ed. Joel Porte (New York: Library of America, 1983), 458; emphasis in original.

11. Emerson, "The Divinity School Address," in *Emerson: Essays and Lectures*, 83. By "the gift of tongues," he meant the inspiration to stand up and speak eloquently for oneself, not "as the fashion guides."

12. Consider this sentence from Whitman's "Letter to Ralph Waldo Emerson": "To me, henceforth, that theory of any thing, no matter what, stagnates in its vitals, cowardly and rotten, while it cannot publicly accept, and publicly name, with specific words, the things on which all existence, all souls, all realization, all decency, all health, all that is worth being here for, all of woman and all of man, all beauty, all purity, all sweetness, all friendship, all strength, all life, all immortality depend" (*Whitman: Poetry and Prose*, 1335). This is the language of pious acknowledgment of dependence, but the topic he is discussing is sex.

13. Preface to the 1855 edition of *Leaves of Grass*, in *Whitman: Poetry and Prose*, 24.

14. Ibid., 233.

15. Ibid.

16. John Dewey, *A Common Faith* (New Haven: Yale University Press, 1934), 53. Hereafter cited as "CF."

17. Emerson, *Emerson: Essays and Lectures*, 88, 302, 268. These words come from "The Divinity School Address," "Compensation," and "Self-Reliance," respectively.

18. A more plausible story is the one Robert McKim tells at the beginning of *Religious Ambiguity and Religious Diversity* (Oxford: Oxford University Press, 2001): "Once upon a time the religious traditions were distanced from each other, both geographically and mentally. The typical member of the typical tradition would learn about other traditions from travelers' tales, for example. There was us and there was them. Now they are our neighbors, and we are no longer at a distance. If they are our neighbors, and we are no longer distanced from them, then what can we do but try to find out what they think? What can we do but ask what is the appeal of their point of view?" But this, as McKim says, is the rub: "Taking other traditions as seriously as they ought to be taken may shake one's tradition to the core: in particular, it may require a different attitude toward one's own beliefs" (vii). McKim hopes for the emergence of "some awareness that the traditions represent a number of honest attempts to grapple with something obscure" (viii), but he wisely makes no predictions.

19. "Thoughts on the Cause of the Present Discontents" (1770), in *The Works of the Honourable Edmund Burke*, vol. 1 (Boston: John West and O. C. Greenleaf, 1806), 388.

20. Sabina Lovibond, *Realism and Imagination in Ethics* (Minneapolis: University of Minnesota Press, 1983), 227.

21. " Love," in Emerson, *Emerson: Essays and Lectures*, 337.

22. Meridel Le Sueur, *North Star Country* (Minneapolis: University of Minnesota Press, 1984), 11. This book, originally published in 1945, has chapter titles that are pure Whitman: "They Shall Come Rejoicing," "The Light Is Sweet," "Woe to My People," "Thunder On, Democracy," "Rise, O Days," "Struggle," and "Stride On, Democracy."

23. David Bromwich, *A Choice of Inheritance: Self and Community from Edmund Burke to Robert Frost* (Cambridge, Mass.: Harvard University Press, 1989), 168.

24. "Shall I say, then, that as far as we can trace the natural history of the soul, its health consists in the fulness [sic] of its reception,—call it piety, call it veneration—in the fact, that enthusiasm is organized therein" (Emerson, "The Method of Nature," in *Emerson: Essays and Lectures*, 125).

25. *Whitman: Poetry and Prose*, 1208f.

26. Emerson, *Emerson: Essays and Lectures*, 491.

27. Emersonians go further than this, expressing similar reservations about the capacity of churches to exercise authority over individuals in spiritual affairs.

28. *Whitman: Poetry and Prose*, 475.

CHAPTER 2
RACE AND NATION IN BALDWIN AND ELLISON

1. James Baldwin, *Collected Essays* (New York: Library of America, 1998), 319, 315.

2. Ellison's remark on style and ideologies appears in "A Very Stern Discipline," in Ralph Ellison, *Going to the Territory* (New York: Vintage, 1986), 294. Larry Neal discusses Ellison in his essay, "Ellison's Zoot Suit," reprinted in *Speaking for You: The Vision of Ralph Ellison*, ed. Kimberly W. Benston (Washington, D.C.: Howard University Press, 1990), 105–24. The quotations given here all appear on 115, the reference to Ellison's remark on 114.

3. *Going to the Territory*, 21f.

4. This is the approach to such controversies recommended by William James in *Pragmatism* (Buffalo: Prometheus Books, 1991), 22–38. For a more technical treatment of the same sort of approach, see W. V. Quine's classic discussion of explication as elimination in *Word and Object* (Cambridge, Mass.: MIT Press, 1960).

5. Baldwin, *Collected Essays*, 333.

6. Ibid.

7. Bernard Yack, *The Problems of a Political Animal: Community, Justice, and Conflict in Aristotelian Political Thought* (Berkeley and Los Angeles: University of California Press, 1993), chaps. 1 and 2.

8. Baldwin, *Collected Essays*, 308.

9. Ibid., 325.

10. Ibid., 17.

11. See Bethel Eddy, "The Rites of Identity: The Religious Naturalism and Cultural Criticism of Kenneth Burke and Ralph Ellison," (Ph.D. diss., Princeton, 1998), chap. 5, for a superb discussion of Ellison's treatment of "the vernacular

pieties of an American identity." Chapter 2 of the same work offers an interpretation of Kenneth Burke's conception of piety, which forms part of the background against which Ellison's treatment of piety can be understood. Eddy shows that Ellison needs to be seen, in part, as belonging to a tradition of cultural criticism that descends from Emerson and includes Santayana and Burke. I am here only skimming the surface of an aspect of Ellison's work that Eddy has considered in depth.

12. Roland Barthes, *Mythologies*, trans. Annette Lavers (New York: Noonday Press, 1972), 16. Hereafter cited as "M."

13. Scapegoating and various other forms of sacrifice are major themes in Ellison. See, for example, *Shadow and Act* (New York: Vintage Books, 1972), 124, and the treatment of lynching in *Going to the Territory*, 177ff. For a discussion of Ellison on sacrifice, see Eddy, "Rites of Identity," chap. 6.

14. Cornel West, *Prophetic Thought in Postmodern Times* (Monroe, Maine: Common Courage Press, 1993), 72.

15. Ellison, *Going to the Territory*, 53; my emphasis.

16. Ellison, *Going to the Territory*, 185. Ellison understands that comparable motives were at work in both Emerson and Whitman, two authors who have often been dismissed, as Ellison often is today, for being either too optimistic or insensitive to evil; see, for example, 311.

17. Ralph Ellison, *Shadow and Act*, 120; see 252 for a similar argument against Amiri Baraka (then called LeRoi Jones).

18. Ellison, *Invisible Man* (New York: Vintage, 1990), xviii. Compare Baldwin's discussion of the blues in "Down at the Cross": "In all jazz, and especially the blues, there is something tart and ironic, authoritative and double-edged. White Americans seem to feel that happy songs are *happy* and sad songs are *sad*, and that, God help us, is exactly the way most white Americans sing them. . . . Only people who have been 'down the line,' as the song puts it, know what this music is about" (*Collected Essays*, 311; emphasis in original). I am saying that readers of Baldwin and Ellison who complain that these authors fail to come to terms with black rage and the systemic evils of racism are making the mistake of wanting their sad songs to be *sad*. Both of these writers had been "down the line." Ellison, who thought Emerson and Whitman had developed a lyrical sensibility analogous to the blues, discerned the sadness in their happy songs. He credited them, too, with having been "down the line." For a discussion of the blues and the theme of comic transcendence in Ellison, see Eddy, "Rites of Identity," chap. 7: "I believe Ellison chooses the blues, in part for piety's sake, because he knows where he comes from and the sources of his being, but also because he believes that the blues, with its comic component, has more resources for coping with the absurdities [of life] . . . than does tragedy" (266).

19. Ellison, *Invisible Man*, xx, 581. My emphasis on the reference to "the lower frequencies" in the novel's last line is influenced by conversations with Al Raboteau.

20. Kenneth Burke, *The Philosophy of Literary Form*, 3d ed. (Berkeley: University of California Press, 1973), 160; emphasis in original.

21. Ellison, *Going to the Territory*, 21.

22. See Cornel West's *The American Evasion of Philosophy* (Madison: University of Wisconsin Press, 1989), esp. 232ff.

23. See especially his contribution to Henry Louis Gates, Jr. and Cornel West, *The Future of the Race* (New York: Knopf, 1996), which is entitled, "Black Strivings in a Twilight Civilization." For a much more hopeful book and one more in keeping with my democratic instincts, see Roberto Mangabeira Unger and Cornel West, *The Future of American Progressivism* (Boston: Beacon Press, 1999), where the authors invoke what they call "the American religion of possibility," and leave out the extreme highs and lows of West's prophetic Christian rhetoric. I believe this is easily West's best book so far, but given that the book is coauthored, it is hard to tell how fully it expresses his own perspective on the grounds for democratic hope. The book is also commendable for its elegant style, the specificity and imaginativeness of its practical proposals, and for allowing the rhetoric of reform and democracy to displace West's early rhetoric of revolution and socialism.

24. I started thinking seriously about Ellison while reading West's first book, *Prophesy Deliverance!* (Philadelphia: Westminster John Knox Press, 1982), where Ellison functions as a moral hero.

25. Emerson, "Man the Reformer," in *Emerson: Essays and Lectures*, 145. He adds: "But I think we must clear ourselves each one by the interrogation, whether we have earned our bread to-day by the hearty contribution of our energies to the common benefit? and we must not cease to *tend* to the correction of these flagrant wrongs, by laying one stone aright every day" (emphasis in original).

CHAPTER 3
RELIGIOUS REASONS IN POLITICAL ARGUMENT

1. John Rawls, *Political Liberalism* (New York: Columbia University Press, 1993; paperback ed., 1996). Hereafter cited as "PL." For a detailed account of the social contract as a set of principles "that could not reasonably be rejected, by people who were moved to find principles for the general regulation of behavior that others, similarly motivated, could not reasonably reject," see Thomas M. Scanlon, *What We Owe To Each Other* (Cambridge: Harvard University Press, 1998), 4 and passim.

2. Nicholas Wolterstorff, "The Role of Religion in Decision and Discussion of Political Issues," in *Religion in the Public Square: The Place of Religious Convictions in Political Debate* (New York: Rowman and Littlefield, 1997), 94; emphasis in original.

3. John Rawls, *Collected Papers*, ed. Samuel Freeman (Cambridge: Harvard University Press, 1999), 573–615. Hereafter cited as "CP."

4. For useful criticism, see Kent Greenawalt, *Religious Convictions and Political Choice* (Oxford: Oxford University Press, 1988) and *Private Consciences and Public Reasons* (Oxford: Oxford University Press, 1995); and Wolterstorff, "The Role of Religion," 67–120. The most thorough and powerfully argued treatment of the general topic is now Christopher J. Eberle, *Religious Conviction in Liberal Politics* (Cambridge: Cambridge University Press, 2002). See also Ronald F. Thiemann, *Religion in Public Life: A Dilemma for Democracy* (Washington, DC: Georgetown University Press, 1996).

5. Wolterstorff briefly discusses the relationship between entitlement and the Rawlsian sense of "reasonableness" in "The Role of Religion," 91.

6. Wolterstorff, "The Role of Religion," 105; emphasis in original.

7. Wolterstorff makes a related point about respect and particularity in "The Role of Religion," 110f.

8. Notice that even on the amended version of Rawls's position, this would not be enough.

9. For illuminating remarks on the importance of attending to the "concrete" other, see Seyla Benhabib, *Situating the Self: Gender, Community, and Postmodernism in Contemporary Ethics* (New York: Routledge, 1992), esp. chap. 5. In chapter 7, I will discuss this theme in Benhabib's work. In chapter 12, I will clarify what a dialogical model involves by discussing Brandom's distinction between "I-we" and "I-thou"conceptions of sociality.

10. Wolterstorff, "The Role of Religion," 109.

11. I am not addressing the distinctive issues surrounding the roles of judge, juror, attorney, or public official.

12. I will consider Hauerwas's arguments and give relevant references to his works in chapters 6 and 7.

13. One could also reasonably complain that the now rather baroque theory is simply too complicated to serve its intended public purpose as an action guide. If these scruples were to be followed by the masses, we would all need catechetical instruction from the Rawlsians.

14. The term "public" is to be understood here in its ordinary sense. Hauerwas was not speaking at a campaign rally or before a congressional committee. So Rawls might say that this case does not involve the "public forum," and that his scruples would therefore not apply. But why should this matter? Suppose another Christian pacifist did speak at a campaign rally for a political candidate representing the Green Party. Wouldn't it be good, all things considered, for her arguments to circulate publicly? How can we know in advance that they won't be persuasive? Suppose the speaker resists translating her arguments about the sanctity of human life into a Rawlsian vocabulary. Must we then condemn her for failing to satisfy the proviso?

15. The phrase appears as the title of chapter 4 in Stanley Hauerwas, *Dispatches from the Front: Theological Engagements with the Secular* (Durham: Duke University Press, 1994), where Hauerwas portrays Walter Rauschenbusch and Reinhold Niebuhr as complicit in "the exclusion from the politics of democracy of any religious convictions that are not 'humble' " (104). Hauerwas asks: "Does that mean I do not support 'democracy'? I have to confess I have not got the slightest idea, since I do not know what it means to call this society 'democratic'. Indeed, one of the troubling aspects about such a question is the assumption that how Christians answer it might matter" (105). In this book, I am trying to say what it might mean to call this society "democratic" and why it might matter how Christians answer that question.

16. John Rawls, *Lectures on the History of Moral Philosophy*, ed. Barbara Herman (Cambridge, Mass.: Harvard University Press, 2000), 329–71.

17. In the next several paragraphs, I will be relying on Robert Brandom, "Freedom and Constraint by Norms," in *Hermeneutics and Praxis*, ed. Robert Hollinger (South Bend: University of Notre Dame Press, 1985), 173–91. Brandom mentions arts and sports on 187.

18. Robert Brandom, "Some Pragmatist Themes in Hegel's Idealism: Negotiation and Administration in Hegel's Account of the Structure and Content of Con-

ceptual Norms," *European Journal of Philosophy* 7, no. 2 (1999): 164–89; emphasis in original.

19. Brandom, "Some Pragmatist Themes," 179.

20. Ibid., 166; emphasis in original.

21. These expressivist considerations explain why Wolterstorff is right to say that we do not need a political basis of the kind that Rawls is seeking: "We aim at agreement in our discussions with each other. But we do not for the most part aim at achieving agreement concerning a political basis; rather, we aim at agreement concerning the particular policy, law, or constitutional provision under consideration. Our agreement on some policy need not be based on some set of principles *agreed on* by all present and future citizens and *rich enough* to settle all important political issues. Sufficient if each citizen, for his or her own reasons, agrees on the policy today and tomorrow—not for all time. It need not even be the case that each and every citizen agrees to the policy. Sufficient if the agreement be the fairly gained and fairly executed agreement of the majority." ("The Role of Religion," 114, emphasis in original.)

22. Brandom, "Freedom and Constraint," 189.

23. Compare Wolterstorff, "The Role of Religion," 112f.

24. Richard Rorty, "Religion as a Conversation-stopper," in *Philosophy and Social Hope* (London: Penguin Books, 1999), 168–74. Hereafter cited as "PSH."

25. Robert B. Brandom, *Making It Explicit: Reasoning, Representing, and Discursive Commitment* (Cambridge, Mass.: Harvard University Press, 1994), 228; *Articulating Reasons: An Introduction to Inferentialism* (Cambridge, Mass.: Harvard University Press, 2000), 105; hereafter cited as "AR."

26. Greenawalt, *Religious Convictions*, chaps. 6–9.

27. Richard Rorty, *Contingency, Irony, and Solidarity* (Cambridge: Cambridge University Press, 1989), 73.

28. Richard Rorty, *Philosophy and the Mirror of Nature* (Princeton: Princeton University Press, 1979).

29. Johanna Goth made a similar point in her senior thesis for the Department of Philosophy at Princeton University (spring term, 2000).

Chapter 4
Secularization and Resentment

Personal correspondence, quoted with permission of John Bowlin.

1. From the introduction to *Radical Orthodoxy*, edited by John Milbank, Catherine Pickstock, and Graham Ward (London: Routledge, 1999), 1, 14, 3; hereafter cited as "RO." See also John Milbank, *Theology and Social Theory: Beyond Secular Reason* (Oxford: Blackwell, 1990); hereafter cited as "TST."

2. Richard John Neuhaus *The Naked Public Square: Religion and Democracy in America*, 2d. ed. (Grand Rapids: William B. Eerdmans, 1995), 25, 80, 82; emphasis removed.

3. Christopher Hill, *The English Bible and the Seventeenth-Century Revolution* (London: Penguin Books, 1994), 413. Hereafter cited as "EB."

4. See EB, 407–9, 420.

5. See Stout, *Ethics after Babel* expanded ed. (Princeton: Princeton University Press, 2001), chap. 3.

6. In this context, the term "liberal" does not imply that the society in question is committed to a version of "liberalism," which is a philosophical view.

7. I do think that it is dangerous to bring religion into political discourse in countries where religious hatred is severe, but the United States is no longer such a place.

8. Victor Anderson opens his book, *Pragmatic Theology* (Albany: State University of New York Press, 1998), by attributing to me the claim that theology is essentially obsolete, a casualty of secularization, a lost cause. The epigraph of his first chapter is a passage from my *Ethics after Babel*, 165, that appears to commit me to this claim. But Anderson omits two crucial sentences from that passage in which I make clear that "the language spoken in the public arena" is "compatible with belief in God." So he ends up attacking a position I do not hold. In *Wilderness Wanderings: Probing Twentieth-Century Theology and Philosophy* (Boulder, Colorado: Westview Press, 1997), Stanley Hauerwas complains that, according to *Ethics after Babel*, "no good reason can be given in 'our' kind of world for holding [religious] beliefs" (108). But I explicitly reject this view on 187 of that book. I did once argue for a negative conclusion on the rationality of modern religious belief, but *Ethics after Babel* withdrew both the argument and the conclusion. The old argument had two major flaws. First, it wrongly posited modernity as a more or less uniform megacontext in which all modern persons should be assessed epistemically. Thus it ignored many factors, of the sort typically mentioned in spiritual autobiographies and conversion narratives, that separate one individual's epistemic context from another's, even in the same epoch. Religious differences need not be explained by saying that only one group is justified in believing what they believe, while the others are not. This bears on the second flaw in the old argument. For my early work employed an implausibly rigorist standard of justification, which did in effect stack the deck against the possibility that a modern individual could be epistemically responsible in holding religious beliefs.

9. William T. Cavanaugh, "The City: Beyond Secular Parodies," in Milbank, Pickstock, and Ward, *Radical Orthodoxy*, 182–200; I am quoting from 190.

10. For a spirited refutation of the standard form of secularization theory, see Mary Douglas, "The Effects of Modernization on Religious Change," in *Religion and America: Spirituality in a Secular Age*, ed. Mary Douglas and Steven M. Tipton (Boston: Beacon Press, 1982), 25–43.

11. I owe this phrasing to John Bowlin.

12. See especially R. A. Markus, *Saeculum: History and Society in the Theology of St. Augustine* (Cambridge: Cambridge University Press, 1970). Milbank argues his case against Markus in *Theology and Social Theory*, chap. 12. For excellent critical discussions, see John R. Bowlin, "Augustine on Justifying Coercion," *The Annual of the Society of Christian Ethics* 17 (1997): 49–70, and James Wetzel's paper on Milbank and Augustine, forthcoming in the *Journal of Religious Ethics*.

13. I have learned much about Ruskin and about the limitations of Milbank's interpretation of him from David Craig.

14. George Hunsinger, *Disruptive Grace: Studies in the Theology of Karl Barth* (Grand Rapids: Eerdmans, 2000), 74–75.

15. Hunsinger, *Disruptive Grace*, 80.

16. I am quoting directly from Karl Barth, *Church Dogmatics*, I/1, trans. G. T. Thomason (Edinburgh: T. & T. Clark, 1936), 60; hereafter cited as "I/1." Hunsinger quotes this line in *Disruptive Grace*, 80.

17. George Hunsinger, *How to Read Karl Barth: The Shape of His Theology* (Oxford: Oxford University Press, 1991), 234–80. Karl Barth, *Church Dogmatics*, IV/3, trans. G. W. Bromiley (Edinburgh: T. & T. Clark, 1961), 3–165. Hereafter cited as "IV/3."

18. Hunsinger, *How to Read Karl Barth*, 279.

19. Recall that I am not using the terms "expressive" and "expressivist" as some theologians do. As I explain in note 11 to the Introduction to this book, what I am saying here does not put me at odds with what George Lindbeck calls a "cultural-linguistic" approach.

20. Cass R. Sunstein, *Republic.com* (Princeton: Princeton University Press, 2001).

21. On the connection between the small group and rituals of this kind, see Mary Douglas, *Natural Symbols: Explorations in Cosmology* 2d ed. (London: Routledge, 1996), chap. 7.

22. The nostalgic note is struck in the first paragraph of the first chapter of Milbank's *Theology and Social Theory*: "Once, there was no 'secular'. And the secular was not latent, waiting to fill more space with the stream of the 'purely human', when the pressure of the sacred was relaxed. Instead there was the single community of Christendom, with its dual aspects of *sacerdotium* and *regnum*. The *saeculum*, in the medieval era, was not a space, a domain, but a time" (TST, 9). The utopian note is especially prominent in Cavanaugh, "The City: Beyond Secular Parodies," 182, 194–98.

23. See John Milbank, "Postmodern Critical Augustinianism: A Short *Summa* in Forty-two Responses to Unasked Questions," in *The Postmodern God: A Theological Reader*, ed. Graham Ward (Oxford: Blackwell, 1997), 269.

24. See William Werpehowski, "Ad Hoc Apologetics," *The Journal of Religion* 66, no. 3 (July 1986): 282–301.

25. Barth, *Church Dogmatics* I/1, 61.

26. Hunsinger, *Disruptive Grace*, 86–87.

CHAPTER 5
THE NEW TRADITIONALISM

1. Milbank, whom I have described in the previous chapter as the leading proponent of radical orthodoxy, refers to chapter 11 of TST, as "a temeritous attempt to radicalize the thought of MacIntyre" (327).

2. *After Virtue*, 2d ed. (Notre Dame: University of Notre Dame Press, 1984), 253, 255. Hereafter cited as "AV." Neuhaus refers to the line about modern politics as a form of civil war no fewer than four times in *The Naked Public Square*, 21, 99, 111, 163.

3. Alasdair MacIntyre, *A Short History of Ethics* (New York: Macmillan, 1966). Hereafter cited as "SH."

4. *Marxism and Christianity* (New York: Schocken, 1968).

5. I allude of course to another of MacIntyre's books from this period, *Against the Self-Images of the Age* (Notre Dame: University of Notre Dame Press, repr. 1978).

6. *Herbert Marcuse: An Exposition and a Polemic* (New York: Viking, 1970), 70. Hereafter cited as "HM."

7. In the remainder of this paragraph, I am echoing David Bromwich's discussion of the sublime in *Hazlitt: The Mind of a Critic* (New York: Oxford University Press, 1983), 191.

8. William Hazlitt, *The Complete Works of William Hazlitt*, ed. P. P. Howe (London: J. M. Dent, 1930–1934), vol. 4, 124–25.

9. Alasdair MacIntyre *Whose Justice? Which Rationality?* (Notre Dame: University of Notre Dame Press, 1988). Hereafter cited as "WJ."

10. For my earlier criticisms of the narrative, see Stout, *Ethics after Babel*, expanded ed. (Princeton: Princeton University Press, 2001), chaps. 9–10, and "Virtue among the Ruins," *Neue Zeitschrift für systematische Theologie und Religionsphilosophie* 26, no. 3 (1984): 256–73.

11. In a review of George Forrell's *History of Christian Ethics*, vol. 1, *Ethics* 91, no. 2 (1981): 328–29.

12. Stout, "Virtue among the Ruins," 267–68.

13. I do not mean to imply complete agreement with MacIntyre's reinterpretation of Aquinas. For example, I believe he is overly impressed by Aquinas's rigorist account of truth-telling. He is overly impressed, I suspect, because he is insufficiently attentive to differences between Aquinas's approach to that topic, where "natural law" influences predominate, and his approach to such topics as violence, where he is more nearly Aristotelian. To describe these differences properly, MacIntyre would have had to give a more detailed account of Aquinas's conception of practical reasoning, especially his account of the moral species of an act, and then ask whether Aquinas adhered to that conception in treating truth-telling and sexuality. The person who first drew my attention to these differences was Victor Preller.

14. This difficulty mars his treatment of anything English and especially of Scottish and Irish thinkers, like David Hume and Edmund Burke, who acquired sufficient empathy with English modes of thought to adopt them as their own and raise them to new heights. Consider, for example, the long quotation from Roy Porter that MacIntyre uses to smear the English social order (WJ, 215), and ask yourself whether it shows a rare gift of empathy. Or, review the sentences I have already quoted about the "savage and persistent conflicts of the age," and ask yourself whether Hume's views on religious fanaticism and enthusiasm are given a fair hearing (WJ, chaps. 15–16).

15. Alasdair MacIntyre, *Three Rival Versions of Moral Enquiry: Encyclopedia, Genealogy, and Tradition* (Notre Dame: University of Notre Dame Press, 1990). I discuss this book in more detail in the postscript to the Princeton edition of *Ethics after Babel*.

16. MacIntyre's most recent book, *Dependent Rational Animals: Why Human Beings Need the Virtues* (Chicago: Open Court, 1999), is refreshingly free of his usual rhetoric about liberalism and liberal society. But the contrast between Aristotle and Nietzsche with which it ends echoes the partition first introduced in chapter 9 of

AV. And his criticisms of both "recent social and political philosophy" and "the modern state" (130–31) show that he has not changed his mind on these points.

17. E. P. Thompson, *The Making of the English Working Class* (New York: Vintage, 1966), 746–61.

18. Christopher Lasch, *The True and Only Heaven* (New York: Norton, 1991), 181–84.

19. William Cobbett, *A History of the Protestant Reformation in England and Ireland* (London: C. Clement, 1824).

20. William Cobbett, *Rural Rides* (London: Dent, 1913; originally published in 1830).

21. William Cobbett, *Thirteen Sermons* (New York: John Doyle, 1834).

22. Wendell Berry, *The Unsettling of America: Culture and Agriculture* (San Francisco: Sierra Club, 1986) and *The Hidden Wound* (San Francisco: North Point, 1989).

23. Susan Moller Okin, *Justice, Gender, and the Family* (New York: Basic Books, 1989), 60–61; emphasis in original.

24. MacIntyre is, at this point, clearly assuming the need for what Brandom calls an "I-we" model of discursive rationality. The "we" in this case is constituted by a traditional consensus on the good. I will discuss Brandom's alternative to such models in the final section of chapter 12 below.

25. WJ, 8, 217–18, 353. To MacIntyre, Burke essentially sold out his Irish compatriots by becoming complicit in English imperial rule. Politically and socially, he personifies what MacIntyre has always tried not to be. But for Burke to play this role in the story being told here, MacIntyre needs to omit reference to his writings on the Irish question, on the wisdom of conciliation with the American colonies, and on the misdeeds of Warren Hastings. Before we discard Burke too quickly and without ambivalence, it may be worth recalling what the radical critic William Hazlitt wrote of him in 1807: "It has always been with me a test of the sense and candour of any one belonging to the opposite party, whether he allowed Burke to be a great man."

26. Richard Bernstein, *Philosophical Profiles* (Philadelphia: University of Pennsylvania Press, 1986), 138, 140.

CHAPTER 6
VIRTUE AND THE WAY OF THE WORLD

1. Stanley Hauerwas, *A Better Hope: Resources for a Church Confronting Capitalism, Democracy, and Postmodernity* (Grand Rapids: Brazos Press, 2000), 10. Hereafter cited as "BH."

2. Hauerwasian perfectionism resembles Emersonian perfectionism in that both are rooted in a reaction against austere forms of Protestantism in which justification eclipses sanctification. And to a large extent, these two forms of perfectionism propose similar remedies in emphasizing excellence, virtue, self-cultivation, the value of exemplary figures and spiritual guides in the ethical life, and a conception of sanctification according to which individuals are swept up into some kind of divine abundance. But these parallels are not merely coincidental. Emerson and his followers were self-consciously radicalizing the kind of sanctification- and virtue-

centered Protestantism that Wesley and various others had set in motion. Historically, these forms of perfectionism represent two phases in the development of religious Romanticism. The Emersonian phase, of course, moves outside the ambit of Christianity.

3. The dissertation eventually appeared in revised form as *Character and the Christian Life: A Study in Theological Ethics* (San Antonio: Trinity University Press, 1975). Chapter 2 discusses Aquinas and Aristotle. Chapter 5 explicates the doctrine of sanctification.

4. Personal conversation.

5. In addition to the published dissertation, see two highly influential essay collections: Stanley Hauerwas, *Vision and Virtue: Essays in Christian Ethical Reflection* (Notre Dame: Fides, 1974) and *Truthfulness and Tragedy: Further Investigations into Christian Ethics* (Notre Dame: University of Notre Dame Press, 1977). Hereafter cited as "VV" and "TT," respectively.

6. Edmund Pincoffs, "Quandary Ethics," in *Revisions: Changing Perspectives in Moral Philosophy*, ed. Stanley Hauerwas and Alasdair MacIntyre (Notre Dame: University of Notre Dame Press, 1983), 92–112. The quotation is from 104.

7. For the purposes of argument, I am not going to dispute Hauerwas's interpretation of Yoder. But Scott Davis has persuaded me that Yoder probably had a more subtle position on justice than Hauerwas thought he did. See John Howard Yoder, *The Original Revolution* (Scottdale, Pa.: Herald Press, 1972), 76–84. When I speak of Yoder in the remainder of this chapter, I mean Yoder as understood by Hauerwas.

8. Stanley Hauerwas, *A Community of Character: Toward a Constructive Christian Social Ethic* (Notre Dame: University of Notre Dame Press, 1981), and *The Peaceable Kingdom: A Primer in Christian Ethics* (Notre Dame: University of Notre Dame Press, 1983). Hereafter cited, respectively, as "CC" and "PK."

9. See Stanley Hauerwas, *Against the Nations: War and Survival in a Liberal Society* (Minneapolis: Winston Press, 1985), and *Dispatches from the Front: Theological Engagements with the Secular* (Durham: Duke University Press, 1994), esp. chap. 4, "The Democratic Policing of Christianity."

10. Stanley Hauerwas, *Christian Existence Today: Essays on Church, World and Living In Between* (Durham: Labyrinth Press, 1988), 3–21. Hereafter cited as CET.

11. Oliver O'Donovan, *The Desire of the Nations: Rediscovering the Roots of Political Theology* (Cambridge: Cambridge University Press, 1996), 216.

12. See Stanley Hauerwas, *After Christendom? How the Church Is to Behave If Freedom, Justice, and a Christian Nation Are Bad Ideas* (Nashville: Abingdon Press, 1991), 45. Hereafter cited as "AC."

13. For an example of a book that sets out such reasons in detail, see Nicholas Wolterstorff, *Until Justice and Peace Embrace* (Grand Rapids: Eerdmans, 1983). It is a pity that Hauerwas chooses to focus his critical remarks so often on Rawls rather than on Wolterstorff, whose theologically conservative but politically radical Calvinist outlook offers a more challenging alternative to his own position. In *A Better Hope* (26–27), he discusses Wolterstorff briefly, but only for the purpose of borrowing from Wolterstorff's critique of Rawls. But see also Nicholas Wolterstorff, "Christianity and Social Justice," *Christian Scholars Review* 16, no. 3 (March 1987): 211–28; Stanley Hauerwas, "On the 'Right' to be Tribal," *Christian Scholars Review* 16, no. 3 (March 1987), 238–41; and Nicholas Wolterstorff, "Response to Nash,

McInerny, and Hauerwas," *Christian Scholars Review* 16, no. 3 (March 1987), 242–48. In this exchange, Hauerwas criticizes Wolterstorff for relying on the language of rights when discussing South African politics, but to my mind Wolterstorff's response to Hauerwas on this point is conclusive. As far as I know, Hauerwas has not responded further. For a response to Hauerwas's criticisms of the language of rights, see chapter 9, below.

14. Gloria Albrecht, *The Character of Our Communities: Toward an Ethics of Liberation for the Church* (Nashville: Abingdon, 1995).

15. Hauerwas's critique of liberation theology echoes the account of "absolute freedom" that Hegel offers in chapter 6 of *The Phenomenology of Spirit*, where he argues that the ideals of the French Revolution, pressed to their logical conclusion, led inevitably to the Terror. Hauerwas seems unaware that here, as in his critique of formalist ethics, he is recycling ideas and arguments from the *Phenomenology*. As in MacIntyre's case, Hauerwas fails to acknowledge his indebtedness to a *tradition* of modern thinking—a tradition that includes the feminism and expressivist pragmatism that I am advocating as well as his version of the new traditionalism. By presenting his arguments as if they did not have a history, Hauerwas is able to reinforce the impression that modern thought is essentially bankrupt.

16. See, for example, the following passage from Virginia Woolf, *Three Guineas* (San Diego, New York, London: Harcourt, Brace, Jovanovich, 1938), 33: "Surely . . . you must consider very carefully before you begin to rebuild your college what is the aim of education, what kind of society, what kind of human being it should seek to produce. At any rate I will only send you a guinea with which to rebuild your college if you can satisfy me that you will use it to produce the kind of society, the kind of people that will help to prevent war." If Hauerwas and MacIntyre were right about modern ethical discourse, the existence of this passage and countless others like it in the writings of major democratic authors would be very hard to explain.

17. George Hunsinger, *Disruptive Grace: Studies in the Theology of Karl Barth* (Grand Rapids: Eerdmans, 2000), 84.

18. Stanley Hauerwas, *With the Grain of the Universe: The Church's Witness and Natural Theology* (Grand Rapids: Brazos Press, 2001), esp. 145, 191–204.

19. Stanley Hauerwas, *In Good Company: The Church as Polis* (Notre Dame: University of Notre Dame Press, 1995), 12f. Hereafter cited as "IGC."

20. It is hard to imagine Hauerwas feeling anything but excitement and joy under such circumstances.

21. Scott Davis pointed out the parallel in correspondence.

22. See especially Stanley Hauerwas, "Virtue, Description, and Friendship: A Thought Experiment in Catholic Moral Theology," *Irish Theological Quarterly* (1998): 170–84. I thank Gene Rogers for providing this reference and for criticism of an earlier draft of the arguments offered in this chapter.

23. As Oliver O'Donovan points out in his perceptive discussion of Hauerwas in *The Desire of the Nations: Rediscovering the Roots of Political Theology* (Cambridge: Cambridge University Press, 1996), 216.

24. In a poignant exchange in the February 2002 issue of *First Things*, Hauerwas responds to an editorial published in the December 2001 issue, which claimed that "those who in principle oppose the use of military force have no legitimate part in the discussion about how military force should be used." He infers that he is being

"silenced" in the wake of 9/11, and wonders aloud whether his friendship with Neuhaus and the other editors has been brought to an end.

25. On the divorce question, see PK, 132, where Hauerwas suggests that perhaps "the prohibition against remarriage . . . was more rigorous than it needed to be to maintain the Christian commitment to fidelity in marriage." Hauerwas briefly addresses what Jesus says to the rich man in a sermon entitled, "Living on Dishonest Wealth," which can be found in his book, *Sanctify Them in the Truth: Holiness Exemplified* (Nashville: Abingdon Press, 1998), 249–52. He treats this teaching as a hard saying, but without drawing any costly practical implications from it. He says, "Being generous with our wealth is a good. But our generosity will not save us" (251). The first sentence does not say that Christians are *obliged* to give away their wealth to the poor. And the second sentence deflects attention from the ethical question to the doctrine of justification by faith. This is not the way Hauerwas addresses the pacifism issue. The sermon ends with a comforting thought: "Our salvation is that God has given us one another and in that giving we discover that we are no longer slaves, but friends of one another and of God and perhaps even friends with those who suffer because we are wealthy. That does, indeed, seem to be 'good news.' Amen" (252). See also Stanley M. Hauerwas and William H. Willimon, *The Truth about God: The Ten Commandments in Christian Life* (Nashville: Abingdon, 1999), 115.

26. There are also many questions concerning the biblical basis for Hauerwas's pacifism. God's way of dealing with evil is said to be revealed definitively on Good Friday. Hence, Christians are called to deal with evil nonviolently. Who, then, authorizes the killing of the Hittites, Amorites, Canaanites, Perizzites, Hivites, and Jebusites in Deuteronomy 20? Who ordains in Matthew 25 and Revelation 20 that the accursed shall be cast into the fire on judgment day? And who says in Matthew 10:34 that he has "come not to bring peace, but a sword"? See PK, 163 n. 11, where Hauerwas emphasizes that Yahweh, as portrayed in the Old Testament, does not fight through the armies of his people, but rather by means of miracle. Here he seems to acknowledge that God does sometimes deal with evil violently. The point Hauerwas wants to insist on is that God's people are not authorized to do so. But this way of formulating his position is in tension with the claim in the main text that "the very heart of following the way of God's kingdom involves nothing less than learning to be like God" (PK, 75). Well, is God nonviolent or not? And if so, then why does the Bible repeatedly portray him as using violence to separate his chosen people or the members of the kingdom from the accursed? Perhaps Hauerwas feels that Yoder dealt with these questions decisively, but I, for one, have never found Yoder's biblical scholarship persuasive.

27. For an example of an antimilitarist political theology that neither neglects the struggle for democratic justice nor gets distracted by polemics against liberalism, see part 1 of Hunsinger's *Disruptive Grace*. I would urge readers to compare Hunsinger's critique of Neuhaus in chaps. 2 and 3 with Hauerwas's critique of Neuhaus in *Against the Nations: War and Survival in a Liberal Society* (Minneapolis: Winston Press, 1985), chap. 7. It seems to me that this comparison allows the deficiencies in Hauerwas's rhetoric to stand out in sharp relief.

28. In this and the following paragraph, I am borrowing the quoted phrases as well as my argumentative strategy from the discussion of "Virtue and the Way of

the World" in G.W.F. Hegel, *Phenomenology of Spirit*, trans. A. V. Miller (Oxford: Oxford University Press, 1977), 228–35; emphasis in original. Hegel was criticizing a position—namely, Shaftesbury's—that resembles the new traditionalism only in some respects. The most important thing the two positions have in common is that they both attempt to recover an ancient conception of virtue in modern conditions. See Terry Pinkard, *Hegel's Phenomenology: The Sociality of Reason* (Cambridge: Cambridge University Press, 1996), 105–11.

CHAPTER 7
BETWEEN EXAMPLE AND DOCTRINE

1. Robert Musil, *The Man without Qualities*, trans. Sophie Wilkins (New York: Alfred A. Knopf, 1995), 273. Hereafter cited as "MWQ."

2. Peter Brown, "The Saint as Exemplar in Late Antiquity," in *Saints and Virtues*, ed. John Stratton Hawley (Berkeley and Los Angeles: University of California Press, 1987), 3–14; I am quoting from 4.

3. Stanley M. Hauerwas and William H. Willimon, *Resident Aliens: Life in the Christian Colony* (Nashville: Abingdon, 1989), 98–103.

4. Throughout this paragraph, but especially here, I am indebted to Oliver O'Donovan, *The Desire of the Nations: Rediscovering the Roots of Political Theology* (Cambridge: Cambridge University Press, 1996), 268–71.

5. Stanley Hauerwas, *Dispatches from the Front: Theological Engagements with the Secular* (Durham: Duke University Press, 1994), 31–57.

6. John D. Lyons, *Exemplum: The Rhetoric of Example in Early Modern France and Italy* (Princeton: Princeton University Press, 1989), xi.

7. My accounts of "example of" and "example for" rely in a general way on Brandom's inferentialist theory of language, but Brandom does not himself discuss these concepts. In fact, he claims that "there is nothing corresponding to the authority of testimony in the practical case" (MIE, 239). But this seems wrong. The authority of testimony in theoretical reasoning does have a parallel in the realm of practical reasoning, namely, the authority someone enjoys as an example *for* someone to follow, which authority a person often acquires when his or her life is taken to be an example *of* certain virtues.

8. For an attempt to unveil such complications in the Gospel of Mark, see Frank Kermode, *The Genesis of Secrecy* (Cambridge, Mass.: Harvard University Press, 1979).

9. Milan Kundera, *The Art of the Novel*, trans. Linda Asher (New York: Harper and Row, 1988), 18.

10. Ralph Waldo Emerson, *Emerson: Essays and Lectures*, ed. Joel Porte (New York: Library of America, 1983) 259. See David Bromwich, *A Choice of Inheritance: Self and Community from Edmund Burke to Robert Frost* (Cambridge, Mass.: Harvard University Press, 1992), 22–23.

11. Emerson, *Emerson: Essays and Lectures*, 264.

12. Ibid., 623.

13. Seyla Benhabib, *Situating the Self: Gender, Community and Postmodernism in Contemporary Ethics* (New York: Routledge, 1992), 1. Hereafter cited as "SS."

14. Seyla Benhabib, *Critique, Norm, and Utopia: A Study of the Foundations of Critical Theory* (New York: Columbia University Press, 1986).

15. For a discussion of transcendental arguments in Habermas and Karl-Otto Apel, see Cheryl Misak, *Truth, Politics, Morality: Pragmatism and Deliberation* (London: Routledge, 2000), 35–47.

16. Nor is it implicated, as Benhabib's appears to be, in the so-called philosophy of consciousness she spends much of her time dismantling.

CHAPTER 8

DEMOCRATIC NORMS IN THE AGE OF TERRORISM

1. I will be referring to Brandom and Lovibond, from whom I have learned much, but my debts to these and other contemporary pragmatists are too extensive to be fully acknowledged in the notes. Robert M. Brandom, *Making It Explicit: Reasoning, Representing, and Discursive Commitment* (Cambridge, Mass.: Harvard University Press, 1994) and *Articulating Reasons: An Introduction to Inferentialism* (Cambridge, Mass.: Harvard University Press, 2000). I will refer to these books throughout part 3 as "MIE" and "AR," respectively. Sabina Lovibond, *Realism and Imagination in Ethics* (Minneapolis: University of Minnesota Press, 1983) and *Ethical Formation* (Cambridge, Mass.: Harvard University Press, 2002). Cheryl Misak, *Truth, Politics, Morality: Pragmatism and Deliberation* (London: Routledge, 2000). Nancy Fraser, *Unruly Practices: Power, Discourse, and Gender in Contemporary Social Theory* (Minneapolis: University of Minnesota Press, 1989). Rebecca S. Chopp, *The Power to Speak: Feminism, Language, God* (New York: Crossroad, 1989). Cornel West, *The American Evasion of Philosophy* (Madison: University of Wisconsin Press, 1989).

2. See Bernard Williams, *Moral Luck* (Cambridge: Cambridge University Press, 1981), 125 ff., 130.

3. The thinkers I have in mind include Avishai Margalit, *The Decent Society* (Cambridge, Mass.: Harvard University Press, 1996); Richard Rorty, *Contingency, Irony, and Solidarity* (Cambridge: Cambridge University Press, 1989); and Judith N. Shklar, *Ordinary Vices* (Cambridge, Mass.: Harvard University Press, 1984).

4. MIE, 235–49. The term "shall" is used in each of these examples (in the manner of Wilfrid Sellars) "to express the significance of the conclusion as the acknowledging of a practical commitment" (MIE, 245).

5. "The humean denies that a mere obligation or commitment could provide a reason for action, unless accompanied by some desire to fulfill it. And the kantian denies that a mere desire (*sinnliche Neigung*) could provide a reason for action, unless accompanied by the acknowledgment of some corresponding obligation or commitment" (AR, 92).

6. According to Thomistic moral theology, the appropriate attitude for such a priest to adopt is not one of guilt and repentance but rather one of velleity and regretful sadness. Velleity can be defined as subjunctive willing. The Thomistic teaching is that the priest's will ought to be such that *if* he were not constrained by an absolutely overriding responsibility, he *would* provide the information. He may also feel saddened that he is thus situated. But there is no reason for guilt, because he has done nothing wrong. The thought that he has done something wrong would, by Thomistic lights, be a prideful misconstrual of his responsibilities, for it would

involve the notion that he, and not God, was responsible to make the overall consequences turn out for the best.

7. See Michael Walzer, *Just and Unjust Wars*, 3d ed. (New York: Basic Books, 2000). See also Walzer's important essay, "Political Action: The Problem of Dirty Hands," *Philosophy and Public Affairs* 2, no. 2 (1973): 160–80.

8. For a concise account of this passage, see Charles Taylor, *Hegel* (Cambridge: Cambridge University Press, 1975), 175. For a detailed commentary, see Terry Pinkard, *Hegel's Phenomenology: The Sociality of Reason* (Cambridge: Cambridge University Press, 1996), chap. 5.

9. This sort of discursive responsibility is one of Brandom's major themes in MIE, part 1.

10. Chapters 2–4 of MIE reinforce this conclusion by giving a precise account of how the semantic content of norms depends on a background of (cognitive and practical) material inferential commitments. If a background of such commitments were not—for the time being—taken for granted, the normative language being employed by the critic of some aspect of received tradition would be meaningless. Whether Hegel is right in charging Kant with the error exposed by this argument is another question.

11. Richard Rorty, "Justice as a Larger Loyalty," in *Cosmopolitics: Thinking and Feeling beyond the Nation*, ed. Pheng Cheah and Bruce Robbins (Minneapolis: University of Minnesota Press, 1998), 52.

12. I will not attempt a full specification of what "democratically" means here, but a few words are in order. I mainly have in mind what is sometimes called the requirement of equal voice in contemporary representative democracies. This entails the progressive elimination of certain restrictions on who may participate in the exchange (relating, for example, to class, gender, race, religion, and ideology) and the relaxation of feudal and ecclesiastical expectations concerning who must defer to whom while the exchange is carried out. When Machiavelli raises the problem of dirty hands in *The Prince*, he is not offering advice to leaders like ours but to princes. The problem has a different social significance in a setting where, as Whitman put it in the 1855 preface of *Leaves of Grass*, the president takes off his hat to the people, "not they to him."

13. Similarly, my language has the expressive resources to allow me to speculate about what would have been the case if climatic conditions had been different several eons ago and language users had never come to walk the face of the earth. When I say that there were rocks and lava long before human beings existed, I am discussing a distant past that lacked human beings (and thus the concepts they alone employ). But in talking about a preconceptual age, I am still using *my concepts* of "rocks," "lava," and "human beings." There is no paradox in this. By the same token, I am able to use my moral concepts to say of someone who lacks those concepts that he should not have tortured his victims.

14. Statements about what a person *should* do or *ought* to do tend to be ambiguous between attributions of obligations of the sort I am discussing and what Gilbert Harman calls "inner judgments." For discussion of Harman's views and citations of his works, see my *Ethics after Babel*, expanded ed. (Princeton: Princeton University Press, 2001), 87–90. If all "ought-to-do" statements express inner judgments in Harman's sense, then what I am calling unconditional obligations will have to

be rephrased as judgments about what ought to be the case. For example: "It ought not to have been the case that the monk tortured the heretic." In Harman's view, this would not imply that the reason against torturing people is a reason the monk himself accepts.

15. MIE, 193–98, 259–62, 270, 596–97.

16. The concept of an absolutely overriding obligation can be explained in Brandom's technical language as follows. "To endorse a practical inference as entitlement-preserving is to take the [cognitive] premises as providing reasons for the practical conclusion." A norm that made such an endorsement explicit would express commitment to a prima facie reason for action—perhaps role-specific, perhaps not. To treat the obligation in question as absolutely overriding is to take the relevant practical inference as "not only entitlement-preserving but also *commitment*-preserving," that is, to take it "that anyone committed to the [cognitive] premises is thereby committed to the practical conclusion" (MIE, 252; emphasis in original).

17. It also reflects a commitment to a theologically motivated division of moral labor that strictly limits any human being's responsibility for the unintended consequences of an act required by justice. This commitment turns out to be extremely important, of course, in Thomistic responses to the problem of dirty hands.

18. "[W]e can retain the idea of language as expression—of linguistic institutions as embodying the objective spirit of a community—without making fanciful claims about the degree of internal cohesion or harmony which can be attributed to our own form of life" (Lovibond, *Realism and Imagination in Ethics*, 127).

19. "It happens not infrequently that because of the incompleteness of intellectual authority within the moral language-game . . . people may disagree about the instantiation of moral concepts (about what is permissible, or obligatory, or in bad taste, etc.) without it being possible to refer the dispute to any kind of arbitration which will command general assent" (Ibid., 179).

20. I do not go so far as to define anyone as religious who takes something to be most important—William A. Christian's variation on Paul Tillich's theme of religion as ultimate concern. See Christian, *Meaning and Truth in Religion* (Princeton: Princeton University Press, 1964). But I do think that religious commitments often take the form of commitments about what is most important. I also think that many of our most recalcitrant moral disagreements are, at bottom, differences over the relative importance of various very important things that we care about. These moral debates are connected with religious differences.

21. Someone might object that I have here reverted to a description of the problem as a matter of conflicting desires. But, as Harry Frankfurt has argued, what one cares about has more to do with one's will than with one's desires or preferences. See the title essay in Frankfurt, *The Importance of What We Care About* (Cambridge: Cambridge University Press, 1988); and *Necessity, Volition, and Love* (Cambridge: Cambridge University Press, 1999), esp. 110, 155–58. My argument in this section is influenced by Frankfurt's claim in the latter volume that caring about something can involve a sort of "volitional necessity" that "renders certain actions *unthinkable*" (111; emphasis in original). This is the bridge I use to get from Shklar's idea that cruelty is the worst thing we do to my commitments on the problem of dirty hands.

22. To put the point in Frankfurt's terms, I recognize that not all of my fellow citizens care about individual human beings in a way that renders targeting innocent

civilians unthinkable even in supreme emergencies. What, if anything, one should care about in this way is among the hardest questions anyone can try to think about. It is so hard, in fact, that it would be foolish to require a religiously plural society to agree on such matters before proceeding with political deliberation.

23. This commitment is what is at stake, for example, in the debate raging among Catholics since the 1960s between what Elizabeth Anscombe called "the method of casuistry" and what her opponents have called "proportionalism." For my own attempt to show that traditional just-war reasoning of Anscombe's type is not best viewed as a process of "weighing" prima facie responsibilities, see Stout, "Justice and Resort to War: A Sampling of Christian Ethical Thinking," in James Turner Johnson and John Kelsay, eds., *Cross, Crescent, and Sword: The Justification and Limitation of War in Western and Islamic Tradition* (New York: Greenwood Press, 1990), 3–33. Citations of Anscombe can be found there.

CHAPTER 9
THE EMERGENCE OF MODERN DEMOCRATIC CULTURE

1. For a detailed account of early-modern political thought that plays up the important contributions of the conciliar movement in Catholicism, see Quentin Skinner, *The Foundations of Modern Political Thought*, 2 vols. (Cambridge: Cambridge University Press, 1978).

2. For an account of the relationship between world-formative Protestantism and the low degree of ascriptivism in modern democratic cultures, see Nicholas Wolterstorff, *Until Justice and Peace Embrace* (Grand Rapids: Eerdmans, 1983), 3–22.

3. Thomas Paine, *The Rights of Man* (London: Penguin, 1984), 168.

4. Walt Whitman, *Whitman: Complete Poetry and Collected Prose*, ed. Justin Kaplan (New York: Library of America), 955.

5. Nicholas Wolterstorff, *Until Justice and Peace Embrace* (Grand Rapids: Eerdmans, 1983), 84.

6. Annette C. Baier, *Moral Prejudices* (Cambridge, Mass.: Harvard University Press, 1994), 225–26.

7. AV, 68–70.

8. Whitman, *Whitman: Poetry and Prose*, 6.

9. For an explication of the notion that facts are true claims, see MIE, 327–29.

10. Brandom usually refers to the former as "doxastic" commitments, but I prefer the less forbidding term, "cognitive," which he uses in AR, 83.

11. With this caveat: that the ordinary notions of "belief" and "intention" are ambiguous, whereas the technical notions of cognitive and practical commitment are designed to be univocal. See MIE, 195, 256–59.

12. The issue of Heidegger's relation to pragmatism is a complicated one, which I cannot pursue here, aside from noting that his later work does attempt to rehabilitate a kind of serious questioning. On the pragmatic themes in Heidegger's early work, see Robert Brandom, "Heidegger's Categories in *Being and Time*," *Monist*, 66, no. 3 (1983): 387–409; and Mark Okrent, *Heidegger's Pragmatism* (Ithaca: Cornell University Press, 1988). See also James C. Edwards, *The Plain Sense of Things* (University Park: Pennsylvania State University Press, 1997).

13. See, for example, Edmund Burke, *Reflections on the Revolution in France*, ed. J.G.A. Pocock (Indianapolis: Hackett, 1987), 26–27, 34–35, 41–42, and 72–73.

14. Thomas Paine, *Common Sense*, ed. Karl Heinz Schönfelder (Halle: Niemeyer, 1956), 67, 73–80, and 92.

15. It will take feminists like Mary Wollstonecraft to argue that these normative statuses should be attributed to women as well. And it will take abolitionists like Sojourner Truth to argue that these statuses should be attributed to slaves.

16. Sellars and Brandom both emphasize the first way, because their accounts of ethical uses of language focus mainly on "ought" judgments. As far as I know, Sellars neglects to mention the second way, and Brandom discusses it only in contexts (MIE, 123–30; AR, 69–76) where his primary concern is to correct Michael Dummett's account of the relationship that ought to obtain between the circumstances and consequences of application of a concept. I am simply taking over what Brandom says in those contexts about "highly charged words" like "Boche" and "nigger," extending it to equally evaluative terms like "courage" and "cruel," and then making explicit the role such terms can have in noninferential observation reports.

17. For an analysis of the role played by the emotions in scientific revolutions and religious conversions, see Bas C. van Fraassen, *The Empirical Stance* (New Haven and London: Yale University Press, 2002), 64–110. For a discussion of the role of imagination in ethics, see Sabina Lovibond, *Realism and Imagination in Ethics* (Minneapolis: University of Minnesota Press, 1983).

18. Edmund Burke, *Reflections*, 17, 67, 142.

CHAPTER 10
THE IDEAL OF A COMMON MORALITY

1. David Lewis, *Counterfactuals* (Cambridge, Mass.: Harvard University Press, 1973), 91.

2. See especially Michael Walzer, *Interpretation and Social Criticism* (Cambridge, Mass.: Harvard University Press, 1987), 41–43.

3. Ignazio Silone, *Bread and Wine*, trans. Eric Mosbacher (New York: Signet, 1986).

4. Robert Brandom, echoing Sellars, remarks that " 'Justification' has the 'ing/ ed' ambiguity . . . : justifying, a practical activity, or being justified, a normative status." The remark appears in his "Study Guide" in Wilfrid Sellars, *Empiricism and the Philosophy of Mind* (Cambridge, Mass.: Harvard University Press, 1997), 157.

5. See Nicholas Wolterstorff, "Can Belief in God Be Rational If It Has No Foundations?" in *Faith and Rationality: Reason and Belief in God*, ed. Alvin Plantinga and Nicholas Wolterstorff (Notre Dame: University of Notre Dame Press, 1983), 135–86.

6. For a pragmatic account of explanations as answers to why-questions, see Bas C. van Fraassen, *The Scientific Image* (Oxford: Oxford University Press, 1980), chap. 5. If van Fraassen is right, explanations are answers to questions of the form, Why P? I am suggesting analogously that (epistemic) justifications are answers to questions of the form, Why believe that P?

7. Compare van Fraassen: "An explanation is not the same as a proposition, or an argument, or list of propositions; it is an *answer*. (Analogously, a son is not the

same as a man, even if all sons are men, and every man is a son.) An explanation is an answer to a why-question. So, a theory of explanation must be a theory of why-questions" (134; emphasis in original).

> The discussion of explanation went wrong at the very beginning when explanation was conceived of as a relationship like description: a relation between theory and fact. Really it is a three-term relation, between theory, fact, and context. No wonder that no single relation between theory and fact ever managed to fit more than a few examples! Being an explanation is essentially relative, for an explanation is an *answer*. (In just that sense, being a daughter is something relative: every woman is a daughter, and every daughter is a woman, yet being a daughter is not the same as being a woman.) Since an explanation is an answer, it is evaluated vis-à-vis a question, which is a request for information. But exactly what is requested, by means of the question "Why is it the case that *P*?", differs from context to context. In addition, the background theory plus data relative to which the question is evaluated, as arising or not arising, depends on context. And even what part of that background information is to be used to evaluate how good the answer is, qua answer to that question, is a contextually determined factor. So to say that a given theory can be used to explain a certain fact, is always elliptic. (*Scientific Image*, 156; emphasis in original).

8. Thus Alasdair MacIntyre is right to claim that in ethics, as in science, "what we have to aspire to is not a perfect theory, one necessarily to be assented to by any rational being, because invulnerable or almost invulnerable to objections, but rather the best theory to emerge so far in the history of this class of theories." He continues: "The possibility has always to be left open that in any particular field . . . some new challenge to the established best theory so far will appear and will displace it" (AV, 270).

9. I qualify and expand upon this conclusion in Stout, *Ethics after Babel*, expanded ed. (Princeton: Princeton University Press, 2001), chaps. chaps. 1–4.

10. This God is omniscient by definition, which means that he knows every truth there is, including the moral ones. If he knows all of the moral truths, he must be justified in believing them. On my account of being justified in believing something, this means (roughly) that God is epistemically without fault in believing the moral claims he believes. It does not mean that God is able to justify his beliefs to himself. This is a good thing, for what would count as an omniscient being's relevant reasons for doubting? Of course, this does not prevent God from justifying a belief to someone else if he pleases, for an omniscient being would know what everybody else's relevant reasons for doubting are and also every possible way of eliminating them by presenting justificatory arguments. Compare van Fraassen, *Scientific Image*, 130.

11. Mark Johnston, "Objectivity Refigured: Pragmatism without Verificationism," in *Reality, Representation, and Projection*, ed. John Haldane and Crispin Wright (Oxford: Oxford University Press, 1993), 112.

12. Translated by Elizabeth Wyckoff, as quoted in Lloyd L. Weinreb, *Natural Law and Justice* (Cambridge, Mass.: Harvard University Press, 1987), 22.

13. Martin Luther King, Jr., "Letter from Birmingham City Jail," in *A Testament of Hope: The Essential Writings of Martin Luther King, Jr.*, ed. James Melvin Washington (San Francisco: Harper & Row, 1986), 293.

14. Quoted in Lewis, *Counterfactuals*, 73. See F. P. Ramsey, *Foundations of Mathematics* (London: Routledge & Kegan Paul, 1931), 242.

15. For present purposes, the distinction between moral and nonmoral sentences can be drawn in virtually any way you please. Because of my holistic inclinations in the philosophy of language, I would not in any event want to place too much weight on the distinction or to draw it in terms of the use of particular words that are sometimes thought to be distinctively action-guiding. For a discussion of the vagaries of the concept of a moral language, see *Ethics after Babel*, chap. 3.

16. In the next chapter, I will discuss a version of divine-command theory that does not mystify in this way. Whether the version of natural-law theory advocated by John Finnis and Germain Grisez avoids this problem is an interesting question. What makes the theory prone to ideological abuse is its highly questionable conception of inviolable, self-evident, basic human goods. Scott Davis, a secular Aristotelian, argues that the Finnis-Grisez position, especially when applied to questions in sexual ethics, "is just one more way of smuggling" a medieval Christian understanding of deviancy "into the discussion without paying the price of putting its theological commitments on the line." Davis, "Doing What Comes Naturally: Recent Work on Thomas Aquinas and the New Natural Law Theory," *Religion* 31 (2001): 407–33; quotation from 429. Russell Hittinger argues to a similar conclusion from a theological point of view in *A Critique of the New Natural Law Theory* (Notre Dame: University of Notre Dame Press, 1987). I do not see how Finnis and Grisez can escape the resulting crossfire without abandoning their position. For the most influential statement of the "new" natural-law theory, see John Finnis, *Natural Law and Natural Rights* (Oxford: Oxford University Press, 1980). For an application of the theory to sexual issues, see Robert P. George, *In Defense of Natural Law* (Oxford: Oxford University Press, 1999). The new natural lawyers are at their least ideological, it seems to me, in John Finnis, Joseph Boyle, and Germain Grisez, *Nuclear Deterrence, Morality, and Realism* (Oxford: Oxford University Press, 1987), a work for which I have the utmost respect. One might wish that Finnis's followers were as rigorous in dissociating themselves from politicians who disagree with them on capital punishment and nuclear deterrence as from those who disagree with them on abortion and same-sex coupling.

17. For this reason, there is no point in *defining* moral truth as what we would believe about moral topics at the end of ethical inquiry. See Richard Rorty, "Life at the End of Inquiry," *London Review of Books* (2 August–6 September 1984): 6; and Mark Johnston, "Verificationism as Philosophical Narcissism," *Philosophical Perspectives* 7 (1993): 307–30, esp. 319–27.

CHAPTER 11
ETHICS WITHOUT METAPHYSICS

1. Here my phrasing is influenced by the following remarks by Mark Johnston:

Let us say that metaphysics in the pejorative sense is a confused conception of what legitimates our practices; confused because metaphysics in this sense is a series of pictures of the world as containing various independent demands for our practices, when the only real legitimation of those practices consists in showing their worthiness to survive on the testing ground of everyday life. . . . So defined, metaphysics is the proper object of that practical criticism which asks whether the apparently legitimating stories which help sustain our practices really do legitimate, and whether the real explanations of our practices allow us to justify them. There then ought to be a critical philosophy which not only corrals the developed manifestations of metaphysics within philosophy but also serves the ends of practical criticism. Such a critical philosophy would be the content of anything that deserved the name of a progressive Pragmatism. ("Objectivity Refigured: Pragmatism without Verificationism," in *Reality, Representation, and Projection*, ed. John Haldane and Crispin Wright [Oxford: Oxford University Press, 1993], 85).

2. Victor Anderson raises this question in his book, *Pragmatic Theology* (Albany: State University of New York Press, 1998), chap. 1; see especially 18. Anderson is puzzled as to how I propose to accept Dewey's claim that truth is warranted assertibility while also insisting that truth is a nonrelative concept. But I do not say that truth is warranted assertibility. What I say is that the concepts of truth and warranted assertibility behave similarly in some first-person, present-tense contexts. The similarities lend credence to the notion that our interest in truth ought always to be an interest in accessible truth. I emphasize, however, that the two concepts do not behave similarly in various other contexts. Anderson breaks off his quotation from *Ethics after Babel* immediately before the line in which I explain that "it would be better to avoid [Dewey's] dictum altogether."

3. Anderson holds that I have defined truth: "Because Stout defines truth in terms of traditional philosophy, simplicity, a high grade of certainty, and universality, his characterization of truth is hard to square with his rejections of metaphysical ontology and theology" (*Pragmatic Theology*, 19). I would maintain that because I have not offered a definition of truth, it follows that I have not defined it in terms of certainty, universality, or simplicity. I have never said or implied that the truth of a belief, claim, or proposition entails its certainty, and have on various occasions expressed suspicion of the Cartesian quest for certainty as a guarantor of truth. The term "universality" has at least two senses—one of which pertains to a proposition's logical form, another of which pertains to whether everybody accepts a proposition. In neither of these senses would I be inclined to identify universality with truth. The logical form of a proposition and the number of people who accept it are two distinct matters, and both are distinct from its truth-value. A proposition that is universal in scope, logically speaking, and a proposition that is universally accepted could both turn out to be false.

As for "simplicity," I assume that what Anderson means by this is the familiar notion that truth is one. This notion is simply an implication of the familiar logical principle that a proposition and its negation cannot both be true. This is indeed a traditional philosophical notion, and there have been some interesting arguments against it in recent years by philosophers associated with pragmatism, but it is not implicated, as Anderson implies, in the metaphysical realism of traditional philosophical theories of truth. You can deny the so-called metaphysical realism of a correspondence theory of truth and still accept the standard logical notion that no set of true propositions, including the infinitely large set that includes all true propositions, includes a contradiction.

4. "After all, the only concept Plato succeeded in defining was mud (dirt and water)" (Donald Davidson, *Subjective, Intersubjective, Objective* [Oxford: Oxford University Press, 2001], 155–56). For a critical discussion of atomic, contextual, and

implicit definitions of truth, see Paul Horwich, *Truth*, 2d ed. (Oxford: Oxford University Press, 1998), 33–36.

5. "What is not clear in Stout's position," Anderson writes, "is what one is to make of truth, since it apparently is connected with justified beliefs but not identified with them" (*Pragmatic Theology*, 18).

6. Richard Rorty, "Pragmatism, Davidson, and Truth," in *Truth and Interpretation*, ed. Ernest LePore (Oxford: Basil Blackwell, 1986), 333–55. Rorty discusses the second and third uses, but under different names. In this paper, he distances himself nicely from both realism and antirealism. Unfortunately, he is more famous for other writings that appear to commit him to antirealism, thus muddying the water.

7. Hilary Putnam, *Reason, Truth and History* (Cambridge: Cambridge University Press, 1981), chap. 3. See also Sumner Twiss, "On Truth and Justification in 'Ethics after Babel,' " in *The Annual of the Society of Christian Ethics* (1990): 37–53. Twiss confesses puzzlement about how I propose to conceive of truth "beyond noting features of ordinary usage," and he charitably resolves the puzzle by taking me to be committed to Putnam's position. The trouble is that I do not accept Putnam's position.

8. See Horwich, *Truth*, chap. 4, and Michael Williams, *Unnatural Doubts: Epistemological Realism and the Basis of Scepticism* (Princeton: Princeton University Press, 1996), chap. 6.

9. Mark Johnston, "Verificationism as Philosophical Narcissism," *Philosophical Perspectives*, 7 (1993): 307–30, 307 (emphasis in original). For his criticisms of Putnam, see 319–27 of the same article as well as Johnston, "Objectivity Refigured: Pragmatism without Verificationism," in *Reality, Representation, and Projection*, ed. John Haldane and Crispin Wright (Oxford: Oxford University Press, 1993), 87–99.

10. Arthur Fine, *The Shaky Game* (Chicago: University of Chicago Press, 1986), chaps. 7 and 8.

11. Mark Johnston, "Reasons and Reductionism," *The Philosophical Review* 101, no. 3 (July 1992): 590.

12. Johnston, "Objectivity Refigured," 85.

13. Scott Soames, *Understanding Truth* (Oxford: Oxford University Press, 1999), 229.

14. I discuss Donald Davidson's antidefinitional view, Brandom's deflationism, and Rorty's wavering between antirealism and minimalism in "Radical Interpretation and Pragmatism: Davidson, Rorty, and Brandom on Truth," in *Radical Interpretation in Religion*, ed. Nancy Frankenberry (Cambridge: Cambridge University Press, forthcoming). More important than the details of Brandom's theory of truth, I argue, is his attempt to resituate the topic of truth within the overall structure of his philosophy of language in a way that dramatically lowers the philosophical stakes associated with truth theory. He does this by reversing the relationship of semantics and pragmatics, as understood in the representationalist tradition. He calls his own approach "inferentialism."

15. Horwich, *Truth*, 62. I should emphasize that a minimalist approach to truth, as I understand it, need not entail that the value of having true beliefs is a trivial matter. For an insightful treatment of this value, see Bernard Williams, *Truth and Truthfulness* (Princeton: Princeton University Press, 2002). I agree with Williams's

criticisms of the view that "since truth does not . . . [according to minimalism] come to much, so the value of truth cannot come to much" (65).

16. Horwich, *Truth*, 104–5. See also Grady Scott Davis, "Tradition and Truth in Christian Ethics: John Yoder and the Bases of Biblical Realism," in *The Wisdom of the Cross: Essays in Honor of John Howard Yoder*, ed. Chris K. Huebner and Harry J. Huebner (Grand Rapids: Eerdmans, 1999), 282.

17. In "Radical Interpretation and Pragmatism," I respond to Rorty's qualms about speaking in this way.

18. "Stout writes about the significance in moral judgment of the logical space between what a competent judge holds and what actually obtains. Without this distinction, the nature of moral agreement and the criteria of competence are radically altered. Thus the judgement [sic] 'slavery is evil' does not reduce to a series of statements about what ideal observers would agree on" (David Fergusson, *Community, Liberalism, and Christian Ethics* [Cambridge: Cambridge University Press, 1998], 101). Fergusson refers to me as a "moral realist" on 192 n. 53.

19. See Davis, "Tradition and Truth in Christian Ethics," 278–305.

20. For example, starting from the equivalence use, one can account for the acceptance use as follows. If p is true if and only if p, as the equivalence use implies, then this explains why "believing that a theory is true is a trivial step beyond believing the theory" (Horwich, *Truth*, 57). Other forms of minimalism take the acceptance use as primary, and proceed to explain other uses on that basis.

21. Horwich takes the concept to be useful because it enables "explicit formulation of schematic generalizations" (*Truth*, 37). Brandom, in contrast, takes it to be useful mainly as a pro-sentence forming operator (MIE, chap. 5). It was fatal to redundancy theories that they accounted for the use of the term in a way that made it appear virtually useless.

22. Horwich, *Truth*, 2.

23. In fact, there are many things that we assess as true or false: a carpenter's level, a singer's notes, one's friends, and so on. Nicholas Wolterstorff tells me that he is studying the full range of such usages. But here our interest is confined to beliefs, claims, and the propositions they have as their content.

24. As Brandom puts this point: "What must not be lost is an appreciation of the way in which our discursive practice is empirically and practically *constrained*. It is not up to us which claims are true (that is, what the facts are). It is in a sense up to us which noises and marks express which claims, and hence, in a more attenuated sense, which express true claims. But empirical and practical constraint on our arbitrary whim is a pervasive feature of our discursive practice" (MIE, 331; emphasis in original).

25. To take only three vastly different but concise examples, consider Jean-Luc Marion, "Metaphysics and Phenomenology: A Summary for Theologians," in *The Postmodern God: A Theological Reader*, ed. Graham Ward (Oxford: Blackwell, 1997), 279–96; Bas C. van Fraassen, "Against Analytic Metaphysics," in *The Empirical Stance* (New Haven and London: Yale University Press, 2002), 1–30; and Cornel West, "Dispensing with Metaphysics in Religious Thought," in *Prophetic Fragments* (Grand Rapids: Eerdmans, 1988), 267–72.

26. Thus minimalism is not to be confused with such metaphysical views as *physicalism, materialism,* or *naturalism.*

27. Timothy P. Jackson, *Love Disconsoled: Meditations on Christian Charity* (Cambridge: Cambridge University Press, 1999), 136.

28. Timothy P. Jackson, "The Theory and Practice of Discomfort: Richard Rorty and Pragmatism," *Thomist* 51, no. 2 (April 1987): 294. "It seems a psychological, if not a theological, truth that in the absence of standards and interests 'not just our own,' we tend to be incapable of any standards at all, even prudence" (295).

29. Jackson, *Love Disconsoled*, 139.

30. At one point Jackson acknowledges the possibility of a position that is neither realist nor antirealist with respect to truth, but then dismisses it abruptly: "I do not see how such an a-alethiological stance can be sustained psychologically, however, given that I cannot conceive of how one can live without concern for truth" (*Love Disconsoled*, 137n). But this remark wrongly assumes that concern for truth psychologically involves commitment to a metaphysical theory of truth. As Williams makes clear, moreover, a minimalist account of truth need not entail that concern for truth is a trivial matter.

31. Twiss, "On Truth and Justification."

32. As Iris Murdoch argues in *The Sovereignty of Good* (New York: Schocken Books, 1971).

33. Robert Merrihew Adams, *Finite and Infinite Goods: A Framework for Ethics* (Oxford: Oxford University Press, 1999). As a philosophical account of ethics from a theistic point of view, this book is unequalled in our period, and my remarks on it here will hardly do it justice. I believe its accounts of moral horror, the sacred, devotion, idolatry, martyrdom, and vocation contribute much to our understanding of ethics and religion.

34. It is not necessarily the same question as what water is, however. It might be that Adams's way of talking about water conflates constitution with identity or essence. See Mark Johnston, "Constitution Is Not Identity," *Mind*, 101, no. 401 (1992): 89–105. The final four pages offer minimalist arguments against the metaphysical temptations of scientism in this area of philosophy.

35. Similarly, chapter 14's treatment of politics could easily serve as a model for theists who wish to avoid the pitfalls of the new traditionalism and maintain a proper respect for the significance of democracy.

36. There is a brief reference to the cautionary uses of "good" and "true" in Richard Rorty, "Response to Haack," in *Rorty and Pragmatism: The Philosopher Responds to His Critics*, ed. Herman J. Saatkamp, Jr. (Nashville: Vanderbilt University Press, 1995), 150.

37. For both of these authors, intrinsic worth can also be sacred worth, in the sense that violation of it is abominable or horrible. See Jackson, *Love Disconsoled*, chap. 4; Adams, *Finite and Infinite Goods*, chap. 4. I now hold that this notion, or something like it, is indeed indispensable, and have found their criticisms of my earlier views on abomination instructive.

38. I am alluding to Mark Johnston, "Dispositional Theories of Value," *Proceedings of the Aristotelian Society*, supplemental vol. 63: 139–74; and Johnston, "Objectivity Refigured," 111–119. But I am not endorsing what he calls a "response-dependent" account of values.

39. The quoted phrase appears in Johnston, "Objectivity Refigured," 105 and elsewhere.

40. "The most important basis for a response to this objection," according to Adams (*Finite and Infinite Goods*, 31), "is still the point that the imaging of God by creatures is a matter of distant and fragmentary resemblance." The trouble is that the more distant and fragmentary the resemblance is, the weaker and vaguer the explanation of excellence is. In many cases, the resemblance relation between the finite thing and the transcendent God appears to evaporate into something too indeterminate to do the explaining it is meant to do. The property being explained is much better understood and more determinate than the relation being invoked to explain it. So why bother with the explanation? This problem brings out a worry close to the heart of Pascal and Barth. The metaphysical urge to explain things theologically has a tendency to shrink God. To perform the function of an *explanans*, the posited divinity must not itself be a mystery.

41. Adams discusses the sort of issue I am raising in *Finite and Infinite Goods*, 46f. He ultimately says he is inclined to reject the supposition that "God could have failed to exist or to be a good candidate for the role of the Good" (47). Thus, there is no *possible* world in which God does not exist, in which case my thought-experiment cannot get off the ground. Adams admits that he knows of "no conclusive proof" of God's necessary existence. So for now, at any rate, my thought-experiment stands.

42. For explanations of Barth's distinction between *analogia entis* and *analogia fidei*, see George Hunsinger, *How to Read Karl Barth: The Shape of His Theology* (Oxford: Oxford University Press, 1991), esp. 283 n. 2; and Bruce L. McCormack, *Karl Barth's Critically Realistic Dialectical Theology: Genesis and Development 1909–1936* (Oxford: Clarendon, 1995), esp. 17. Hunsinger discusses "speculation," the term Barthians use when referring to metaphysics in the pejorative sense, on 51f.

43. Jackson's book is extremely interesting in this connection. He affirms the existence of a perfectly loving God, as we have seen, but he rejects *faith* in immortality as wishful self-consolation. In this life, it is permissible to hope for immortality, but not believe in it. Hence the title, *Love Disconsoled*.

44. Timothy Jackson urged the inclusion of this point.

45. Adams carefully avoids concluding that if there is no God, there is no ethical objectivity either. "If there is no God, or if God is in fact not a suitable candidate for the role of the Good, then my theory is false, but there may be some other salient, suitable candidate, and so some other theory of the good may be true" (*Finite and Infinite Goods*, 46). But his critical discussion of alternative theories leaves a strong impression that he finds them unpromising, so ethical objectivity does seem to hang in the balance after all. I am asking whether love of wisdom in this dimension of life actually involves searching for "a suitable candidate for the role of *the* Good." The metaphysician's script has put undue pressure on the casting director to find something godlike to play the part.

46. I allude to both 2 Corinthians 4:7 and James Gustafson, *Treasure in Earthen Vessels: The Church as a Human Community* (New York: Harper, 1961).

47. Ralph Waldo Emerson, "Experience," in *Emerson: Essays and Lectures*, ed. Joel Porte (New York: Library of America, 1983), 471.

48. The assertion could still be wrong, of course. The realization that the view from this stair is not truly excellent might dawn on me as I ascend further. Most adults look back on something they once considered excellent—a favorite book,

movie, or song—as mediocre or poor. Acquaintance with better things transforms their understanding of excellence in a way that requires rejection of evaluative beliefs they once held.

CHAPTER 12
ETHICS AS A SOCIAL PRACTICE

1. The social-perspectival dimension of scorekeeping turns out to be essential to Brandom's account of propositional contents themselves. See MIE, chap. 8.

2. MacIntyre discusses the way in which "human powers to achieve excellence, and human conceptions of the ends and goods involved, are systematically extended" in AV, 187ff.

3. Of course, there are senses in which only scientific discourse would qualify as objective, but they are irrelevant for our purposes. See van Fraassen, *The Empirical Stance* (New Haven and London: Yale University Press, 2002), 153–96, for an account of the uniquely objectifying dimensions of science. The purposes of ethical discourse would obviously be defeated if it aspired to the kinds of objectification scientists aspire to in their strictly empirical investigations.

4. Sabina Lovibond, *Realism and Imagination in Ethics* (Minneapolis: University of Minnesota Press, 1983), 148; emphasis in original.

5. This would be analogous to siding with Stephen Douglas against Lincoln regarding how the issue of slavery was to be resolved. Douglas had said, in effect, that we are in a democracy, so whatever the majority in a given state or territory says on the slavery question *ought* to hold *there*. Lincoln responded that commitment to democracy involves striving to determine whether it is *true* that democratic principles and the institution of slavery are compatible, which is not a matter able to be decided by a majority vote.

6. Whitman refers to "the leveler, the unyielding principle of the average," but argues that this is "offset" by "another principle, equally unyielding," that is "join'd" to it—that of "individuality." See Walt Whitman, *Democratic Vistas*, in *Whitman: Complete Poetry and Collected Prose*, ed. Justin Kaplan (New York: Library of America, 1982), par. 59.

7. For an account of expressive freedom worked out along something like these lines, see Robert Brandom, "Freedom and Constraint by Norms," in *Hermeneutics and Praxis*, ed. Robert Hollinger (University of Notre Dame Press, 1985), 171–91.

8. Brandom briefly discusses the Hegelian version of this idea, and mentions its influence on Karl Marx and T. H. Green in "Freedom and Constraint," 188–89. The Hegelian version emphasizes the state's supervisory role in cultivating established forms of expressive freedom and integrating them into a harmonious social whole. The Emersonian version tends to play down that role, suspecting that the state is necessarily too clumsy and ignorant to perform it properly. The state's proper role is in large part to protect the marginalized and unpopular from harm—a more daunting task now, no doubt, than in Emerson's day. Emersonians expect the expressive freedom actively cultivated by poets and artists to place constant pressure on the conservative, integrative tendencies of established institutions. Small pockets of intense individuality and spiritual aspiration proliferate constantly in a democratic culture. They may take the form of consciousness-raising groups,

sects, political uprisings, or avant-garde artistic communities, but they are always in danger of provoking retaliation from a society anxious to maintain the silence and docility—as well as the virtue—of its members.

9. Robert Merrihew Adams advocated the sort of divine-command theory being discussed here in his "A Modified Divine Command Theory of Ethical Wrongness," in *Religion and Morality: A Collection of Essays*, ed. Gene Outka and John P. Reeder, Jr. (Garden City, N.Y.: Doubleday Anchor, 1973), 318–47. I assessed the limitations of such a theory, making roughly the same points I have just made, in my "Metaethics and the Death of Meaning," *Journal of Religious Ethics* 6 (1978): 1–18. Adams revised his theory, eschewing his previous focus on meaning in favor of claims about the nature of ethical wrongness, in "Divine Command Metaethics Modified Again," *Journal of Religious Ethics* 7 (1979): 66–79, and in *Finite and Infinite Goods: A Framework for Ethics* (Oxford: Oxford University Press, 1999). I discuss the latter in the previous chapter.

10. David Little and Sumner B. Twiss, *Comparative Religious Ethics: A New Method* (San Francisco: Harper and Row, 1978), 103.

11. Little and Twiss, *Comparative Religious Ethics*, 102.

12. David Little, "The Present State of the Comparative Study of Religious Ethics," *Journal of Religious Ethics* 9 (Fall 1981): 210–27.

13. In short, I reject what Brandom calls "regulism" (MIE, 18–26). For influential arguments against regulism, see Ludwig Wittgenstein's discussion of following a rule in *Philosophical Investigations*, trans. G.E.M. Anscombe (Oxford: Basil Blackwell, 1953) and Sellars, SPR, 321.

Conclusion

Bill Holm, *The Music of Failure* (Marshall, Minn.: Plains Press, 1985), 12. Holm writes wonderfully affectionate essays about the people of Minneota, Minnesota, complains eloquently about American greed and foolishness, and often quotes Whitman admiringly and with understanding.

1. George Kateb, *Hannah Arendt: Politics, Conscience, Evil* (Totowa, N.J.: Rowman and Allenheld, 1984), 172.

2. The phrase enclosed by quotation marks is Michael Walzer's. He is characterizing Foucault's view in "The Politics of Foucault," in *Foucault: A Critical Reader*, ed. David Couzens Hoy (Oxford: Blackwell, 1986), 62.

3. George Orwell, "Inside the Whale," in *An Age Like This*, vol. 1 of *The Collected Essays, Journalism and Letters of George Orwell*, ed. Sonia Orwell and Ian Angus (New York and London: Harcourt Brace Jovanovich, 1968), 507.

4. George Orwell, "The Lion and the Unicorn," in *My Country Right or Left*, vol. 2 of *The Collected Essays*, 107.

5. Ralph Waldo Emerson, "Fate," in *Emerson: Essays and Lectures*, ed. Joel Porte (New York: Library of America, 1983), 943.

6. David Hollinger, *Postethnic America: Beyond Multiculturalism* (New York: Basic Books, 1995), 15f.

7. I have learned much about this topic from George Kateb. See his *The Inner Ocean* (Ithaca: Cornell University Press, 1992).

8. Individuality and community are linked here in a way for which neither side of the liberal-communitarian debate adequately accounted. Each of these notions needs to be construed in a way that makes the linkage possible—namely, by being set within an account of social practices. On the one hand, as I have just been stressing, it is shared practices that make the virtues of individuality possible. On the other hand, and equally important, practices held in common are the substance of the relevant kind of community. Neither shared ethnic roots nor shared doctrines of ultimate ends are required. Notice also that *identification with* community is the key concept being employed here, not *loyalty to* or *pride in* community, the concepts Richard Rorty favors in "Justice as a Larger Loyalty," in *Cosmopolitics: Thinking and Feeling beyond the Nation*, ed. Pheng Cheng and Bruce Robbins (Minneapolis: University of Minnesota Press, 1998), 45–58, and in *Achieving Our Country* (Cambridge, Mass.: Harvard University Press, 1998).

9. Stanley Hauerwas and William H. Willimon, *Resident Aliens: Life in the Christian Colony* (Nashville: Abingdon, 1989).

10. I take the quotation from the back cover of Hauerwas's *With the Grain of the Universe: The Church's Witness and Natural Theology* (Grand Rapids: Brazos Press, 2001).

11. A better way of characterizing my position in relation to contemporary political theory would be to classify it as a pragmatic version of *deliberative democracy*. Like other proponents of deliberative democracy, I emphasize the discursive dimension of democratic culture. But my pragmatic expressivist model of democratic deliberation differs significantly from the social-contract model favored, for example, by Amy Gutmann and Dennis Thompson in *Democracy and Disagreement* (Cambridge, Mass.: Harvard University Press, 1996). In many respects, Gutmann and Thompson are much closer to Rawlsian liberalism than I am.

12. I am here responding to the challenge issued to me by Hauerwas in *After Christendom? How the Church Is To Behave If Freedom, Justice, and a Christian Nation Are Bad Ideas* (Nashville: Abingdon, 1991), 33. An excellent account of the distinction between nations and nation-states by a Christian author is given in Nicholas Wolterstorff, *Until Justice and Peace Embrace* (Grand Rapids: Eerdmans, 1983), chap. 5. See also John Dewey, *The Public and Its Problems* (Athens, Ohio: Swallow Press, 1927), 143–44. Hauerwas credits the line about the telephone company to MacIntyre in *Resident Aliens*, 35.

13. For more on this definition, see Bernard Yack, *The Problems of a Political Animal* (Berkeley and Los Angeles: University of California Press, 1993), 1–87.

14. Robert Mangabeira Unger and Cornel West, *The Future of American Progressivism* (Boston: Beacon Press, 1999).

15. This is part of what Hegel appears to mean when he declares that the rational is actual. Hegel was too quick to identify the social form taken by rationality in the modern era with a kind of nation-state. Left-wing Hegelians and their pragmatist cousins see the state as a particular set of institutional arrangements that might or might not be in conformity at any given moment with what rationality demands. The actual locus of rationality, as they see it, is not the state, but the nation, people, or public, conceived as a discursive community committed to actualizing an evolving set of norms and ideals. What Hegel calls rationality, Dewey calls critical intelligence. It is crucial to understand that these are normative notions.

16. Ben H. Bagdikian, *The Media Monoply*, 6th ed. (Boston: Beacon Press, 2000), x.

17. Edward S. Herman and Robert W. McChesney, *The Global Media* (London and Washington: Cassell, 1997), 1.

18. Jeffrey C. Isaac, *Democracy in Dark Times* (Ithaca: Cornell University Press, 1998), 113. "At the level of the nation-state the 'rule of the people' must always be more or less metaphorical, channeled, diluted, and corrupted by mass political organizations and bureaucratic structures. But partial alternatives to such a politics . . . are not only conceivable. Such oases are a part of our political landscape, though an often ignored part" (120). Among the examples of such oases that Isaac mentions are "the Green movements in Europe" and "the many local chapters of Planned Parenthood," as well as "battered women's and rape-crisis shelters" and "the religious and social action committees of synagogues and churches." The list, he adds, "could be easily expanded."

19. See David Bromwich, "Literary Radicalism in America," in *A Choice of Inheritance: Self and Community from Edmund Burke to Robert Frost* (Cambridge, Mass.: Harvard University Press, 1989), 145–59. "A change for the better usually happens like this. A small number of writers get together, agree that their culture has lost its vitality, and decide to blame everything on its habitual arrangements, which they hold in contempt. If their analysis succeeds in fostering a literature that is powerful, the analysis and the literature stand doubly vindicated. But the important moment for a literary radical comes earlier, when he discovers that his analysis is widely shared; and the effect of such moments is to give fresh life to other radicals, who seek political remedies. There is a sense—better understood by historians than by critics—in which an Emerson makes room for a William Lloyd Garrison. What began as a program of literary revisionism thus works its way into all the channels of reform" (149–50).

20. I once heard Michael Walzer argue along these lines.

21. Walt Whitman, *Whitman: Complete Poetry and Collected Prose*, ed. Justin Kaplan (New York: Library of America, 1982), 485.

22. Meridel Le Sueur, *North Star Country* (Minneapolis: University of Minnesota Press, 1984), 321.

INDEX

NEW FORUM BOOKS

New Forum Books makes available to general readers outstanding original interdisciplinary scholarship with a special focus on the juncture of culture, law, and politics. New Forum Books is guided by the conviction that law and politics not only reflect culture but help to shape it. Authors include leading political scientists, sociologists, legal scholars, philosophers, theologians, historians, and economists writing for nonspecialist readers and scholars across a range of fields. Looking at questions such as political equality, the concept of rights, the problem of virtue in liberal politics, crime and punishment, population, poverty, economic development, and the international legal and political order, New Forum Books seeks to explain—not explain away—the difficult issues we face today.

Paul Edward Gottfried, *After Liberalism:*
Mass Democracy in the Managerial State

Peter Berkowitz, *Virtue and the Making*
of Modern Liberalism

John E. Coons and Patrick M. Brennan, *By Nature*
Equal: The Anatomy of a Western Insight

David Novak, *Covenantal Rights: A Study in Jewish*
Political Theory

Charles L. Glenn, *The Ambiguous Embrace:*
Government and Faith-Based Schools
and Social Agencies

Peter Bauer, *From Subsistence to Exchange*
and Other Essays

Robert P. George, ed., *Great Cases*
in Constitutional Law

Amitai Etzioni, *The Monochrome Society*

Daniel N. Robinson, *Praise and Blame*

Timothy P. Jackson, *The Priority of Love: Christian*
Charity and Social Justice

Jeffrey Stout, *Democracy and Tradition*